PRESENTED BY

Dr. Myer Mendelson
and
Margaret Mendelson

2/13/75

The Rise and Fall of Venice

By the same author

THE ART OF VICTORY (1965)
THE UNENDING VIGIL (1967)
THE COSSACKS (1969)
THE THREE EMPRESSES (1972)

Philip Longworth

The Rise and Fall of Venice

Constable London

First published in Great Britain 1974 by
Constable & Company Ltd
10 Orange Street London WC2H 7EG
Copyright © 1974 Philip Longworth

ISBN 0 09459980 7

Set in Monotype Bembo
Printed in Great Britain by The Anchor Press Ltd,
and bound by Wm. Brendon & Son Ltd,
both of Tiptree, Essex

To Ruth

Contents

	Introduction	xiii
I	Beginnings	1
II	The Emergence of a City State	20
III	The Age of the Crusades	40
IV	The Challenge of Empire	61
V	Marco Polo's Venice	78
VI	Venice in the Age of Petrarch	95
VII	Venice Victorious	116
VIII	The Golden Age	138
IX	The Fight for Empire	159
X	The Tide Begins to Turn	181
XI	Retrenchment	202
XII	The Final Years of Glory	219
XIII	Piracy and the Economic Crisis	235
XIV	The Age of Adjustment	254
XV	Luxurious Decline	270
	Epilogue	294
	Bibliographical Note	304
	Index	312

Illustrations

The Polo brothers leaving Venice: English miniature
c. 1400 (*The Bodleian Library, Oxford*)   frontispiece

An early Venetian settlement (*Marciana Library, Venice*)
Torcello (*Anderson, Rome*)   facing page 50

The apparition of St. Mark, St. Mark's Cathedral
(*The Mansell Collection*)   51

Venetian tradesmen. Carvings from façade of St. Mark's
(*The Mansell Collection*)   82

Two flagellants. Italian School, 15th century (*Musée
Condé, Chantilly. Photo: Giraudon*)   83

Tomb of Doge Tomasso Mocenigo (*The Mansell
Collection*)   83

Doge Francesco Foscari (*Civic Museum, Venice*)   146

Doge Cicogna by Veronese (*The Mansell Collection,
Photo: Anderson, Rome*)   147

Venetian oar-maker and naval architect (*Gravembroch,
Naval Museum, Venice*)   178

Faustino's design for a galleass, 1570 (*Naval Museum,
Venice*)   178

A Doge and his allies net the Turkish fleet: representation
of the Battle of Lepanto, 1572 (*Naval Museum, Venice*)   179

Scenes from Venetian life from *Habiti d'Huomeni et Donne
Venetia* by Giacomo Franco, Venice 1609   242

Scenes from Venetian life from *Habiti d'Huomeni et
Donne Venetia* by Giacomo Franco, Venice 1609   243

Scene in the grounds of a Venetian palace (*Victoria &
Albert Museum*) (*The Mansell Collection*)   274

At the gaming house in masks by Pietro Longhi (*The
Mansell Collection, Photo: Alinari, Florence*)   275

MAPS

1   The lagoon and its hinterland   4
2   Venice and the Venetian world   25
3   Venetian trade routes   97
4   Venice and the terraferma   161
5   Venice the city   249

Acknowledgements

I am grateful to Ben Glazebrook who encouraged me to switch my attentions from Russia to Venice; to the St. Catharine's Foundation, Windsor, and also to St. Deiniol's Library, Hawarden, for providing me with facilities when I was without a place to work; to friends, both Venetian and British, for their kindness to me when I was in Venice; to Mark Hamilton, and also to Eileen Crouch who coped so efficiently in typing the manuscript. I am obliged to the British Museum in London and to the Museo Correr, the Biblioteca Marciana, the Museo Storico Navale and the historical section of the Giorgio Cini Foundation in Venice for their co-operation and permission to reproduce illustrations. My debt to scholars who have laboured in the fields of Venetian history is considerable the interpretations, errors and omissions of this book, however, are my own.

Introduction

The beauty of Venice is legendary. It is magnificent, unique. Yet the purpose of this book is not to describe the magic spell the city casts, its countless works of art, nor its multitude of curiosities. Works on its art and architecture abound; the guide-books are legion; so are the volumes in which authors proclaim their devotion to this pearl among cities. This book, by contrast, will be a history, concerned with explaining the origins and development of the Venetian Republic and of Venetian society, and picturing Venetian life and activity through time.

In tracing the emergence of Venice from shadowy beginnings, through its years of blazing glory, to the faded splendour of decline, the chief concern will be to work a coherent tapestry out of the complex interweave of social, economic and political trends; to describe the conditions, the values and the manners of the people; to trace the constant adaptations of Venetian institutions in response to difficulty and change. It will also show how the city came to be built and why it takes the form it does – but only incidentally.

The Venetian Republic lasted for more than a thousand years. During that time Venetians did more than build a city of oriental splendour: they built the most powerful navy in the Mediterranean, a dominant position in world trade, and an empire which stretched from Cyprus to the Alps.

Venetians evolved gorgeous ceremonials to commemorate their success, yet the paradoxes of their history are more intriguing even than the pageantry. The Venetians were cosmopolitans – the descendants of Germans, Slavs, Levantines and Greeks as well as of Italians – and their heritage owed as much to Byzantium as to the western world. Poised precariously between land and sea, Venice was also placed on an uneasy borderland between conflicting political systems and contrasting ways of life. The result was a society and a civilization *sui generis*, unlike any other.

As a result, Venetian history defies crude attempts to classify in terms of periods and types. Venetians were democrats before the 'age of Democracy' and capitalists before the age of capitalism. They were devout Catholics, yet they repeatedly defied the Pope; they maintained a republic in the midst of feudal Europe; and their aristocracy derived not from war leadership or seigneurial tradition but from trade. The Venetian nobles who came to govern the city and its colonies were primarily businessmen – aggressive merchants and financiers dedicated above all things to the pursuit of profit.

Theirs was a powerful, acquisitive society. For centuries the Venetian galley ruled the Mediterranean and the Venetian ducat was the dollar of its day. Yet Venetians were also extraordinarily precocious in the art of government. They evolved the most complex constitution of its time and the most elaborate electoral system – examples which were to influence both the English and the American revolutions – they pioneered the diplomatic system, created an organ of state security as feared in its day as the KGB or CIA and, for all their capitalist spirit, restricted free enterprise, controlled food prices and developed a rudimentary form of welfare state.

Venice sired warriors like Doge Enrico Dandolo and adventurers like Marco Polo. She played host to Popes and Emperors, to Petrarch, Goethe and John Evelyn. She boasted Titian and Tintoretto among her painters, the playwright Goldoni and Vivaldi the composer. Such men will figure in the pages which follow. But so, too, will others with less famous names, and the nameless also – the ordinary Venetian fishermen, the shipbuilders and stevedores, the women sail-makers and courtesans, the bowmen of the galleys, the *bravi* and the buskers, the printers, priests and paupers, who formed the kaleidoscope of Venetian life through centuries of triumph and decline.

Chapter I

Beginnings

In the year 400 Venice did not exist, and the lagoon itself was
virtually deserted. Wild-fowl came in their seasons to nest among
the waving reeds, and migrant people also came, for the fishing
was rich and there was salt to gather. But men were loath to
settle on the lagoon. The winters were too cold and bleak, the
channels and the tides uncertain, and the humps of land which
showed above the waterline were treacherously prone to flood.

The rule of Rome under the later Emperors hardly touched the
area; the world and its traffic passed it by. The roads linking the
main towns of the region – Aquileia to the north, Ravenna to the
south and ancient Padua in the west – ran on firm ground skirting
the lagoon, and though people from the hinterland came to set
up landing-stages on the northern sandbanks to off-load the
scanty cargoes of ships that passed occasionally, the lagoon itself
remained uncharted, unfamiliar. It was shallow, dangerous; a
remote and secret place.

The precise origins of the settlements from which Venice was
eventually to emerge are shrouded in mystery – a mystery which
Venetian chroniclers were only to compound by ascribing im-
aginary origins to their city. There is no evidence, for example,
to support the claim that the Venetians were descended from the
Trojans, nor that Venice was founded at noon on 25th March 421,
though this dubious anniversary is still celebrated in a desultory
way by brass bands ambling through the streets.

Of all the legends the chroniclers retailed, only one has the ring of truth about it: Girolamo Bardi's description of the first inhabitant of the Rialto mudbank on which Venice stands today as 'a poor man' called Giovanni Bono (John the Good) who lived with his family 'in a simple shack by catching fish.' Mythical or not, Giovanni Bono can be regarded as the prototype of the earliest Venetians, those unusually self-reliant souls who built precarious dwellings for themselves on the sandbanks and the marshy islands, and settled down for good.

The early settlers took care to study the peculiarities of their environment – the movement of the earth and waters, the habits of the birds and fish – in order to survive and eke out a meagre living for themselves. No doubt they also exchanged their surpluses of fish and salt occasionally for corn and tools to be had in the towns along the coast or inland along the banks of the several rivers which flowed into the lagoon; and, in time, they began to clear the scrub and scratch the earth to grow a little food. But theirs was a hard life and a lonely one, which tempted few people from the hinterland.

The invasion of northern Italy by the barbarian Huns in the fifth century, however, provoked inhabitants of the coastal plain to seek shelter on the lagoon. Medieval chroniclers describe whole communities arriving, guided to particular islands by supernatural voices and apocalyptic visions which showed them the appropriate spots on which to found new settlements and churches. But this immigration was not permanent. The incursions of the Huns were brief, and most of the refugees probably returned to their former homes once the enemy had disappeared. Nevertheless the population did increase, and as the settlers grew in number a distinctive social and political order began to emerge.

To what extent this was influenced by the cultural traditions of ancient Rome (which had for so long ruled the Adriatic and its hinterland) and to what extent autochthonous, it is impossible to tell with any certainty. What is certain is that the people of the lagoon regulated their own affairs by means of a primitive democracy. They grouped themselves in units of twelve, rather than in tens and hundreds as the Romans did – a more convenient number, perhaps, for the efficient operation of their co-operative fishing enterprises – and, on a broader scale, each settlement had its own informal, popular assembly, the *arrengo*, at which communal affairs were settled and where local tribunes were elected and, not infrequently, overthrown. These tribunes acted both as leaders and as representatives to higher authorities outside – the governors of the mainland towns, and, from the middle of the sixth century, the Emperor Justinian's Exarch at Ravenna. But outside authority received only perfunctory acknowledgement, and imperial control, stemming ultimately from Constantinople, was laxly exercised.

Similarly with the church. The people erected temples on the lagoon spontaneously, long before any ecclesiastical hierarchy came into existence. They built them to meet their own spiritual needs, to come to a satisfactory accommodation with life's mysteries through the proper practice of the new religion, Christianity, and in hopes of obtaining better control of their dangerous environment through prayer. But the early churches also served as community centres and as defensive points, with high bell-towers to give warning of approaching enemies. The church of the primordial Venetians was a purely local institution and run by laymen many of whom were most probably illiterate.

The only contemporary written source from which historians can try to reconstruct what life on the lagoon was like in these early times is a secular, not an ecclesiastical document. It was written in the sixth century by an official called Cassiodorus who served the Emperor's agent in Italy at that time, Theodoric the Goth. Cassiodorus's message to the 'maritime tribunes' of the lagoon area asking them to fetch the imperial tribute of olive oil from Istria conveys something of the feel of life there at the time and in a style that verges on the poetic.

The inhabitants, he wrote, seemed 'equally at home on sea and land.' They lived in huts 'like sea-birds' nests, perched half on sea and half on shore,' and kept boats hitched like horses at their doors. Their settlements were scattered, and were protected 'from the onset of the sea by defences of twisted willow boughs.' Theirs was an environment already in process of being mastered by man, but then as now men were dominated by the constant struggle to

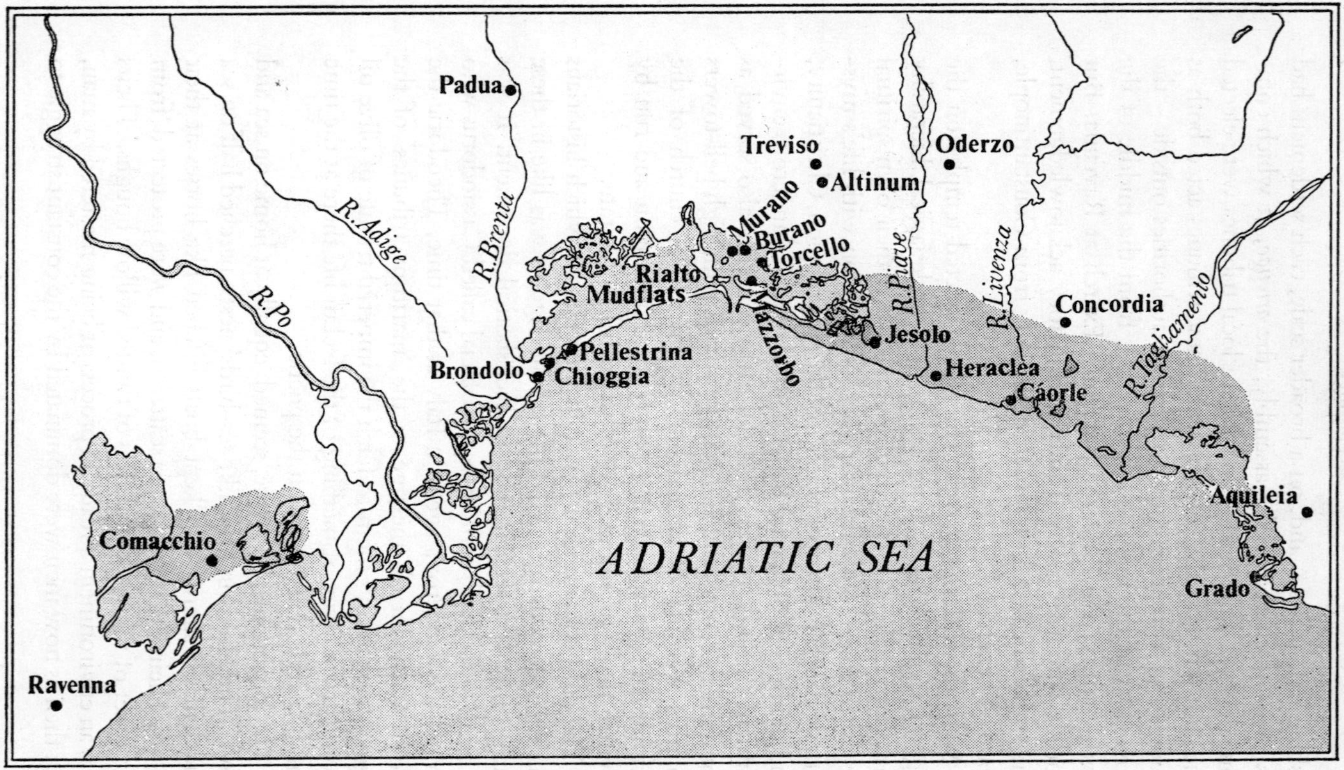

The lagoon and its hinterland

Aquileia

Grado

R. Tagliamento

Concordia

Caorle

R. Livenza

Oderzo

Heraclea

Jesolo

R. Piave

Altinum

Treviso

Torcello

Burano

Murano

Mazzorbo

Rialto

Mudflats

Pellestrina

Chioggia

Padua

R. Brenta

Brondolo

R. Adige

R. Po

ADRIATIC SEA

Comacchio

Ravenna

keep the sea at bay. Moreover, since these early settlers had only a primitive technology and no resources it was a struggle which encouraged the co-operative spirit just as the fishing did, and it seems to have fostered a distinctly egalitarian outlook.

Whereas the towns of the hinterland were dominated by patricians whose life-style contrasted with that of the commoners among whom they lived, on the lagoon, as Cassiodorus put it, everybody lived 'on equal terms.' The same kind of food and the same sort of housing did for everyone, and this despite the fact that some were growing a little more prosperous than their fellows through petty trading and as carriers along the coast. In consequence, 'envy, the vice which rules the world, is unknown to them.'

Such rivalry as Cassiodorus noticed among them, was confined to 'the exploitation of their saltworks,' their chief source of profit through exchange and a valuable one, for, as he rightly noted, 'all the world needs salt.' But although salt provided the inhabitants of the lagoon with their first trading capital, and with it their first source of competition and of differences in income, everyone lived in much the same way.

This would not be so for long, however. In 568 another invading horde, the Lombards, burst in through Istria to occupy most of northern Italy, and once again people fled from the plains to seek refuge on the coast and the lagoon. Patricians fled with their household slaves and bishops with their treasure; Roman farmer-warriors of the plains regrouped there; refugees of every social order gathered up their few possessions and joined the flight towards the sea. A counter-offensive in 590 regained most of the Po valley for the Emperor and many of the refugees presumably drifted back to their homes in the plains as their forefathers had done in the wake of the Huns over a century before. But thereafter the Empire's strength in northern Italy began to fail. Diverted by troubles in Constantinople itself and in its Asian territories – by an army revolt in 602, the murder of an Emperor, the Persians' threat and finally the blazing Arab advance which was to overtake Syria, Mesopotamia and Egypt by 646 – the imperial structure in the Venetian hinterland began its final collapse. By 603 the enemy had occupied Mantua and Padua, by 615 Concordia, and by 640 Oderzo and Altinum too. Everything except the narrow coastal strip was lost to the Lombards. Refugees moved into the lagoon yet again – and this time their settlement was permanent.

According to Venice's first chronicler, John the Deacon, the population of the hinterland fled there *en masse*, prompted, so legend tells us, by portents sent by God. When Altinum was threatened, the birds of the city, divinely inspired, seized their young in their beaks and flew off to the east, at which the people gathered up their young and followed. When they reached the lagoon two strong beams of sunlight striking through a cloud revealed the spot, on the island of Torcello, on which to build a church, and there, obediently, they settled. Elsewhere, according to the legends, the voice of the Virgin herself gave the command; there were glorious visions in the skies; clouds took the form of multitudinous crowds of people, of flocks and herds; the voices of Peter, of John the Baptist, of St. Justina were heard, all urging the foundation of churches and of communities.

Even allowing for exaggeration, the impact of this new immigration must have been considerable, quickening the development of the lagoon and transforming its social character. Henceforth the drainage of marshes, the cultivation of land outcrops, the building of dwellings proceeded at a faster rate. Hamlets grew into modest little townships – Murano, Mazzorbo, Malamocco and others – and churches were enlarged and rebuilt more permanently and more grandly than before. Often they were built of brick and even stone, so as to establish a community's prestige in relation to those of rival settlements, and the seventh-century remains of one such church, built on the island settlement of Torcello, are still to be seen and wondered at.

The influx of newcomers must also have swamped the original population of fishermen, boatmen and saltworkers, and so accelerated the process of social change. The immigrants brought hierarchical values with them, and erstwhile landowners, uprooted from the hinterland, tried to recreate their former existences, carving out estates for themselves on such land as was available, using the slaves and workers they brought with them and anyone else, presumably, whom they could press into their service. All this served to disrupt the homogeneity of the communities of fisherfolk and to change the egalitarian social structure.

People were soon being referred to as 'maiores,' 'mediocres' and 'minores' – the big men, the middling and the small – terms defining their status to an extent previously unknown on the lagoon. Even so, the mainland aristocracy does not seem to have gained an exclusive political dominance, as Venetian writers of the sixteenth century, anxious to bolster up the legitimacy of the ruling nobility of their own time, were later to suggest. Tribunes were still elected by the larger settlements in and around the lagoon, and they were certainly 'maiores terrae,' the big men of the area, some of them very possibly men of property uprooted from the Roman cities of the hinterland. But classification as a 'big man' or a 'little man' does not seem to have implied membership of any exclusive caste; tribunes were frequently overthrown, and no single family seems to have gained a monopoly of power in any settlement.

The Lombard invasions had far-reaching cultural as well as social implications for the development of 'the second Venetia,' as the emigrants from the old Roman province of Venetia called their new habitat upon the coast. The Emperors who had once controlled all Italy from their capital Constantinople, now only had a foothold along the coastal fringe from Istria, through coastal Venetia, to Ravenna, and some territories in the south of Italy. These few fragments of Roman Italy were now its most westerly possessions. By now, theirs had become a predominantly Greek rather than Latin civilization, and, acknowledging the new reality, they dropped the appellation Roman. Henceforth the Empire of the Caesars was called the Byzantine Empire, and from this point we shall refer to Constantinople as Byzantium.

The cultural tensions to which these developments gave rise had a profound influence on the character of the city state which was to emerge on the lagoon. Heirs to the Roman culture of north-east Italy, the people were now surrounded by the barbarian Lombards and yet owed allegiance to the imperial Exarchate at

Ravenna and thus fell within the Greek sphere of influence. Moreover, the upheavals in the region gave rise to another cultural conflict almost as significant: a struggle between rival bishops of differing allegiance.

One party, led by the Metropolitan of Aquileia, was based nearby on the Lombard-controlled mainland, and oriented towards Rome. The other, more orthodox, was aligned with the Byzantine church. Its leader, the Metropolitan of Grado, was the dominant influence on church affairs on the lagoon, but rivalry between the two patriarchal sees, between individual bishops of the area, and between them and the secular authorities, was to last for generations. Seen in retrospect, this was the embryonic stage of the great confrontations between Venice and Rome over ecclesiastical matters which were to arise centuries later.

The marginal position of the lagoon, its delicate perch between the competing political powers of Lombardy and Byzantium, between two rival church hierarchies and two cultural influences, the Latin and the Greek – as well as the tensions generated between the original fishermen and the immigrants – all this was to lead the lagoon communities along quite different lines of development from those of the hinterland. More immediately, the situation was conducive to internal instability and a certain spirit of independence born of the need for self-reliance.

Clashes between rival groups and rival settlements led frequently to bloodshed, which the representatives of imperial authority, whose prestige had slumped in the aftermath of the withdrawal, could not effectively hold in check. Indeed, according to a legend retold by John the Deacon, in 584 the people of the lagoon refused outright to acknowledge the imperial authority. They were willing enough to help against the Lombards, they had told the Exarch Longinus, but 'God, who is our help and our protector has saved us in order that we may dwell upon these watery marshes. This second Venetia which we have raised in the lagoons is a mighty habitation for us. No power of Emperor or Prince can reach us except across the waters, and so we have no fear of them.'

But even if the account was true – and the chroniclers were anxious enough to show that God had destined Venice to be in-

dependent from the start – Byzantium soon reasserted its authority.
An inscription dating from 639 testifies to the fact, boldly stating
the names of the imperial administrators of the area in that year:
Isaac, Exarch of Ravenna and the *magister militum* (chief of soldiers),
Maurice, evidently the local military governor. Moreover, when,
in the same year, Oderzo, the last centre of Byzantine rule in the
hinterland, fell to the Lombards and fugitives from the place
established a new settlement in the lagoon they called their 'new
city' Heraclea in honour of the Emperor Heraclius.

Heraclea, in fact, became the political and administrative centre
of the area, for it was there that the chief of soldiers, responsible
to the Exarch of Ravenna for the defence of the sector against the
Lombards, made his base. Yet there were many other populous
centres at this time – fortified villages, clusters of close-built
dwellings huddling round churches or monasteries (many of
them financed by the imported wealth of immigrant churchmen)
and townships centred on little castles and surrounded by vineyards, gardens and orchards. But though settlement was thicken-
ing round the perimeter of the lagoon and on a number of the
islands, the site on which Venice itself stands – the complex of
mudbanks, called Rialto, Olivolo, Dorsoduro and Spinalunga –
remained comparatively undeveloped.

On the other hand, although the area was probably still largely
self-supporting, a new form of economy was in process of
formation. The lagoon communities had their own craftsmen
now, direct trading contacts by sea with Byzantium as well as
with Ravenna and Istria, and also with the Lombard hinterland,
whose dependence on salt from the local pans, balancing the
Venetians' need for corn, required some continuance of the old
exchanges regardless of the political border – which in any case
was ill-defined.

The geo-political unity of the lagoon area from Grado in the
north to Chioggia in the south was furthered, some time after
690, when the Byzantine authorities established a new administration for the area, distinct from Istria and Ravenna and headed by a
Dux, or Duke – a term ultimately transformed by Venetians into
the title 'Doge.' But the first *Dux* to take up the post at Heraclea

was not the first Doge of an independent Venice as was subsequently to be assumed. He was a Byzantine governor, appointed by the Emperor.

Paulicius Anafestus, the first *Dux* of the lagoon, and his chief of soldiers and successor, Marcellus Tegallianus, set out to define the boundary between the imperial lands and the Lombard territories beyond, placing marker-stones which were later recognized by the Lombard King Aistulf, and generally to take a more effective grip of affairs in the lagoon. But this new, efficient imperial administration was resented by large sections of the population, and in 727 they joined in a general revolt raised in those parts of Italy still under the Emperor's control.

The immediate issue seems to have been Byzantium's new iconoclastic policy. The Italians, in their polytheistic way, insisted on worshipping a multitude of different saints and cult figures, and the papacy, which recognized the strength of local feeling, condoned this predilection. When the imperial fiat ordering the destruction of these venerated religious pictures and statues was issued, the people rose up in arms against it. On the lagoon, the revolt was staged by the locally recruited garrisons of part-time militia-men, under their leader Orso. With the support of the neighbouring Lombards the rebellion succeeded. In 727 the Exarch of Ravenna was killed and the link with Byzantium was temporarily severed. Orso took up the reins of government as the lagoon area's third *Dux*.

But although Orso subsequently received imperial recognition, this period of independence proved brief. The revolt was quelled, Orso was killed and the people of the lagoon returned to their former obedience. In 741 they dutifully supported the Exarch when the Lombards drove him out of Ravenna, and, by way of reward (prompted, no doubt, by the realization that privileges not granted would eventually be seized) they were accorded the right to choose their own *Dux* in future. Byzantium was still sovereign in the lagoon, but its hold was weakening, and, as it weakened, local factionalism grew, heralding a long period of intermittent anarchy and inter-island strife.

When the tribunes had called for election of a new leader after

Beginnings 11

Orso's death, the people are said to have replied, 'We don't want to elect a lord. . . . Why should our ancestors have come to these islands if not to live in freedom? If they had wanted to be slaves there were many better places.' Instead they chose a 'chief of soldiers' on an annual basis. But while this suggests a continuance of a democratic tradition and a certain social cohesion within the various communities, relations between the communities themselves were anything but friendly. The men of Jesolo and Heraclea had fought in 737 and five years later the Malamoccans had risen up against the Heracleans, defeated the Chief of Soldiers and put his eyes out. A new *Dux* emerged who based himself on Malamocco and he was subsequently recognized by Byzantium.

Scholars still argue as to whether this change marked a return to Byzantine authority, or the beginning of a *de facto* independence, and the bloody 'battle of the pinewoods' which took place about this time has been interpreted variously as a struggle between 'democrats' and 'aristocrats', freedom-fighters and elements loyal to Byzantine authority, between centralists and islanders who wanted their autonomy, as a faction fight between communities, and as a clan war between the families which dominated them – the Obelerii of Malamocco, the Barbaromani of Heraclea.

What is certain is that while the people of the lagoon were squabbling, the men of Comacchio, to the south beyond the River Po, were prospering. In 715 King Liutprand of Lombardy had granted them special privileges by way of toll exemptions encouraging them to trade at various centres along the River Po as far upstream as Piacenza. The merchants of Comacchio dealt mainly in salt, bringing back corn and other cargoes in exchange. But salt and salted fish were not their only exports. They also re-exported olive oil and pepper brought from the east in Byzantine ships – a trade which had developed gradually over the course of a century and more and which was to survive changes in the political control of the coastline, including the reoccupation of Ravenna by the Emperor and its subsequent transfer to the Pope.

Aspiring, outward-looking men of the Venetian lagoon to the north regarded Comacchio with envy and did their best to emulate its example – in particular, the traders of Torcello, which was beginning to establish itself as the emporium of the lagoon. The Venetian lagoon, after all, was no less rich in fish and salt than Comacchio was; it also had contact with Byzantium and, though the route was not quite so convenient, access to the north Italian plain.

But Venetians lacked the taxation privileges their rivals had obtained, and the continuing in-fighting among the lagoon settlers inhibited commerical development. One *Dux* was deposed and blinded in 735. His successor was exiled within a year, and the *Dux* who followed him was deposed and blinded too. Early Venetians made a practice of disposing of their leaders in prompt and ugly ways. It was a symptom of their primitive democracy.

In 764 with the election of Maurizio Galbaio a greater degree of political stability was obtained – though only for a time and at a cost. A new, dynastic tendency was developing. Wanting to keep the dukedom in his family, in classical feudal fashion Galbaio made his son, Giovanni, co-ruler with him; and when Galbaio died in 757 Giovanni promptly took his own son Maurizio into partnership. Moreover, there was a commercial cost to pay as well.

The Galbaios had probably established their authority with the help of the imperial government at Byzantium, and they certainly maintained it with Byzantine aid. In return, they helped to defend Byzantine Istria against the Lombards and then against the Lombards' new overlords the Franks, who invaded northern Italy in the 780s. But their staunch support of Byzantine interests led the angry Franks to impose a trade embargo on the lagoon, and their ruthless support of Greek Byzantine culture led to ecclesiastical warfare, which soon triggered off another civil war in the lagoon. The period of fragile authoritarian stability was drawing to a sudden end.

The population of Malamocco had been growing fast as that of Jesolo and Heraclea had declined. Of late it had been overspilling onto Olivolo – now the site of Venice's Castello district – and Olivolo had become populous enough to need a bishop of its own. In 797 *Dux* Giovanni Galbaio appointed one (a sixteen-year-old

Greek boy), but the Patriarch of Grado refused to consecrate him. Olivolo presented a threat to his own see and, besides, the Patriarch's sympathies lay with the Franks rather than with the Byzantine Greeks whose influence the bishop-designate represented. Giovanni reacted promptly by sending armed men to Grado to fling the Patriarch from his palace tower, and in 803 a new Patriarch, Fortunatus, was forced to flee to the protection of the Franks, to the court of Charlemagne. There he was joined by other dissident elements led by Obelerius, tribune of Malamocco, and his brother Beatus. Together they plotted their revenge. The inter-island, inter-family quarrels of the lagoon were being merged into a struggle between pro-Byzantine and pro-Frankish parties.

In 804 Obelerius, who had married a Frankish woman, was elected Doge in exile at Treviso. He and his followers then advanced on the lagoon. The Galbaios fled; so did the young Bishop of Olivolo. Fortunatus returned to Grado; Obelerius proclaimed his brother Beatus co-regnant – and went off to do homage to Charlemagne.

This settled matters with the new Emperor in the west but enraged the Byzantine Emperor who in 806 sent a fleet to the lagoon to reassert his authority. With the Franks prepared to come to terms with Byzantium, Obelerius submitted to a compromise. He was confirmed in office; and Beatus was taken off to Byzantium as a hostage for his good behaviour. The stage seemed to be set for the peaceful development of the lagoon community. But the peace was not to last.

In 808 a Byzantine fleet anchored in the lagoon. Next year it attacked Frankish-held Comacchio and was repulsed. Then the Franks retaliated. King Pepin commandeered Comacchio's ships and bore down on the lagoon. Obelerius at once submitted to him; indeed, he may well have invited Pepin in, for he was an old friend of the Franks and had become so dangerously unpopular with his own subjects that he could barely keep them in order. The people, however, resisted Pepin at all points.

By all accounts, the destruction that ensued was terrible. Brondola and Chioggia were burned; Malamocco suffered much from seige; Heraclea and Jesolo were virtually destroyed. Resistance nevertheless continued. The rebels set up a base among the intricate channels and mudbanks of the Rialto, blocked up all possible approaches, removed the channel markers, and called on Byzantium for help.

The last-ditch defence on the Rialto was to receive epic treatment by the chroniclers. They gloried in the islanders' defiance of Pepin's threats to beat and starve them out, and legend tells (improbably) of how a frustrated Pepin eventually built pontoon bridges to carry his troops across the lagoon towards them, and of how the invaders' horses took fright, ran off into the water and drowned their riders with them. It was all very like the Hebrew myth according to which Pharaoh's cavalry, pursuing the escaping Israelites, were swallowed up in the Red Sea. Yet Pepin certainly withdrew in 810, though not before the Venetians had promised to pay him an annual tribute; and Obelerius was certainly deposed – and subsequently executed when he tried to regain power.

But the most permanent result of Pepin's invasion was the wholesale settlement of the Rialto mudbanks. Some parts of it, notably Olivolo, had been inhabited for some time, but the invasion brought a new influx of refugees from less defensible centres and Pepin's devastation of the older lagoon settlements induced many of their inhabitants to resettle on Rialto. The centre of government moved there too. It was the forerunner of the city of Venice which we know today.

The new Doge, Agnello Partecipazio, presided over this rebuilding of the shattered communities. There was a new mood of optimism, and *rapprochement* between the rival powers of east and west was already in the offing. In 810 a new Byzantine emissary arrived, sent to negotiate an agreement with the Franks, and in 811 at Charlemagne's capital of Aachen an agreement was duly reached.

As ratified in 814, it guaranteed the new Venice against external aggression and recognized its rights over the surrounding territory, while confirming that, along with Istria and Dalmatia, it belonged to the Byzantine sphere. In addition, Venice was to pay the

Frankish Emperor thirty-six pounds of silver a year in return for trading rights within his territories.

This peace established Venice as a bridge of communications between the two great Empires. Her Byzantine connection gave her entry into eastern ports and the arrangement with the Frankish Emperor allowed her to trade relatively freely on the mainland. Able to make the best of both their worlds, the way was open for an expansion in trade that was to lay the foundation of her economic and commercial strength.

Yet, despite the continual political instability, the original primitive economy, by which the people supplied most of their own wants, had already been transformed. The stone churches in existence by 800, however small, bear witness to the fact, and though some of the capital used in their building may well have been imported by rich refugees from the hinterland, some, too, was newly made. Salt was still the major income-earning industry, but there is also evidence that the people of the lagoon were profiting from trade in other commodities besides salt, and in areas quite far afield.

About the middle of the 700s a priest called Zacharias, later to become a Pope and ultimately a saint, noticed Venetians at Rome buying slaves to carry off to the north African coast. These they traded for olive oil, which they could sell in the Venetian hinterland. Nor was this the only route they plied. They would take salt to Dalmatia to exchange for timber and slaves which they would sell in Byzantium along with corn bought from the north Italian plain. In Byzantium they would buy expensive fabrics and the exotic spices carried from the east.

Such traffic must have been extremely small and most of it was doubtless carried in Byzantine ships, but some men from the lagoon had become competent enough as seamen to sail as far as the Levant and Africa, and the economy of the lagoon was already strong enough to provide a surplus for building seagoing ships. A foundation had been laid, and henceforth Venetians were able to exploit their favourable position between east and west, to supply the small but increasing demands in Byzantium and western Europe for each other's products.

Venetian traders were learning fast what goods were in demand and where; how to appraise the different qualities of spices, camlet, serge and taffeta. Along with their rivals, the merchants of Comacchio, they were becoming increasingly involved in international trade, sailing now as far as Egypt, while nearer home they were travelling further up the River Po to Ferrara, Cremona, Piacenza, and, above all, to Pavia.

The annual fair there was soon the main established meeting point of the merchants from both east and west. Venetians took the silks and cloth of gold, the spices, perfumes, drugs and ornaments they imported from the east to Pavia where they traded them for timber, iron, slaves and silver. The Monk of St. Gall in his life of Charlemagne tells of the Emperor's retainers buying their finery from Venetians at Pavia – peacock or flamingo feathers, purple cloth from Tyre, embroidered silks, otter skins and ermine, though the biggest items of Venetian trade about this time seems to have been salt and slaves.

Coins minted by Charlemagne which were found on Torcello in the 1960s provide evidence of a certain accumulation of wealth through trade of this kind. So do the wills of Giustiniano, son and successor of Doge Agnello Partecipazio, and of his kinsman Orso, Bishop of Olivolo from 827. Not only did they leave cash, and real estate on the islands, round the edge of the lagoon, and as far distant as Treviso; they left stocks of pepper and of other spices too, which indicated that they had invested quite heavily and profitably in overseas trade. Not only Comacchians but the Greek and Jewish merchants of Byzantium, who had so long dominated Mediterranean trade routes, were learning to fear Venetian competition.

Nor was commerce the only sector of the developing Venetian economy. Thanks to the Byzantine connection Greek artisans visited Venice and some of them settled there, while Venetians also went to Byzantium to learn skills of the civilized east: enamel and metalworking, ivory-carving and even organ-building. A Venetian called Giorgio is reported to have built the organ for Aachen Cathedral in 826, and recent excavations at Torcello have uncovered not only mosaics, bronze and amber ornaments and terracotta lamps but a glass furnace dating from before 800, the first evidence of a Venetian industry that continues to this day.

More important, however, was the development of shipbuilding. Ships of ever larger size were being constructed, for commerce was growing fast and brought the greatest profits. Such profits were not earned without risk and difficulty, however. Pirates operating from the Dalmatian coast preyed on shipping passing down the Adriatic; there was always the risk of foundering in storms or breaking up on rocks or shallows; and in order to preserve their vital link with Byzantium Venetians had to interrupt their trading operations from time to time and divert their ships to help the Emperor. They did so in 827, for example, when the Doge sent a fleet out in a vain attempt to stop the Saracens overrunning Byzantine Sicily.

Byzantine orders could inhibit Venetian trading operations in other ways as well. In 814, for instance, the Emperor forbade his subjects from trading with Saracen-controlled Syria and Egypt, though in this case Venetians contrived to break the embargo. Competition was growing. Merchants from Amalfi on the western shore of Italy were active now, as well as the Comacchians and the Mediterranean Jews and Greeks. The merchants of the lagoon were simply not prepared to leave the field open to their rivals, whatever the authorities might say, and so despite these constraints the boom continued.

The profits it produced helped to finance the building of a great new settlement on the Rialto flats. Doge Agnello Partecipazio built his home there, next door to a little church dedicated to the local patron saint, St. Theodore, on the site where the Doge's Palace stands in majesty today. But a general building programme was initiated too, and it was thoroughly organized, reflecting some continuity of the old co-operative spirit. According to the chroniclers, three commissioners were appointed – one to supervise the draining of the Rialto flats and marshes, the cutting of canals and the building up of banks; the second to regulate the building work itself, and the third to organize the construction of the dykes on the lido in order to limit the force of the periodic floods which swept through the lagoon.

The Rialto, so recently a dreary, almost deserted place, was transformed into a building site. Men and women dotted the landscape, reclaiming land, clearing scrub, erecting simple dwellings for themselves and building primitive defences against attack. Though only a primitive forerunner of the glorious city it was eventually to become, Venice was in the making.

So was the city state. The Doge might still be a Byzantine official, but he was elected locally; and although he bore ringing imperial titles such as *protoedrus* and *protospatharius*, and received a salary from the Byzantine treasury, he was now called the 'Duke of the Venetians,' not merely 'Duke of the Province of Venetia.' Venice was not yet an independent city state, but already she enjoyed a *de facto* independence so far as most decisions were concerned.

In church affairs, however, the situation was rather less clear-cut. A synod meeting at Mantua in 827 decided to abolish the patriarchal authority of Grado and subject Venetians to a new Patriarch of Aquileia on the Frankish-controlled mainland. This challenged Byzantine authority over the lagoons and threatened the Byzantine culture of the area. As such the step was fiercely resisted. Venice's leaders wanted autonomy in church affairs as well as politics, and they adopted a curious device to get it.

In order to make the new Venice an autonomous religious centre a great prestigious boost was needed. This could most surely be gained by the acquisition of the body of some great saint, but though the Byzantine Emperor had already presented her with the body of St. Zacharias, a more potent saint was needed – one like Zacharias's son John the Baptist, or better still of an apostle like St. Mark.

Mark was reputed, quite wrongly, to have stayed at Aquileia prior to his departure for Rome and his martyrdom at Alexandria. The possession of his remains would be a potent argument, given the beliefs and sentiments of the time, for Venice's spiritual independence, and present the greatest imaginable snub to the see of Aquileia of which St. Mark was reputedly the first incumbent. The difficulty was that St. Mark's remains lay in a church at

Alexandria. But this proved no bar to a group of audacious Venetian merchants who in 827 sailed in ten ships to Alexandria in defiance of the Emperor's ban on trade with Egypt and almost certainly with the Doge's knowledge and probably at his instigation.

Two of these merchants – Buono of Malamocco and Rustico of Torcello – according to the legend, set out for the church where St. Mark lay, and prised the lid off his sarcophagus. Lifting the mummy it contained out onto the floor, they cut the shroud down the back, slipped the corpse out of it, substituted the remains of St. Claudian from a neighbouring tomb, bundled their trophy into a barrel, and, covering it up with cabbages and pork to distract the attentions of Muslim customs men and the city's Christians, smuggled their contraband to their ship, and so to sea.

Thus, in the words of John the Deacon, on 31st January 828, Doge Giustiniano Partecipazio 'was thought worthy to receive the body of the most holy Mark the Evangelist, brought by the Venetians from Alexandria.' And when St. Mark arrived (if it really was St. Mark and not some nameless Egyptian mummy) the people of the lagoon came out to greet it singing and dancing. They had reason to rejoice. God had allowed them to acquire the saint; He must therefore favour their city's welfare. It all seemed greater than a miracle. St. Theodore, their patron saint till now, was immediately forgotten. 'San Marco!' was the cry henceforth, and the population rejoiced in their new allegiance.

But the postscript to the story has more significance than the tale itself. Until some more suitable resting place could be devised, St. Mark was placed not in a church, as might have been expected, but in a corner of the Doge's house. St. Mark was intended to serve not only as a symbol of ecclesiastical independence, not merely as the rallying point of a growing civic consciousness of the lagoon people. His presence was meant to give charisma to the secular power of the Venetian Doge.

B

The Emergence of a City State

From the beginning of the ninth century the pace of life on the lagoon began to quicken. While in distant England King Alfred fought to keep the alien Danes at bay, Venetians found themselves to be at the centre of the known world. More and more foreigners, chiefly merchants and seamen, visited the lagoon, and as Venetians had more frequent dealings with people of differing cultures – Greek and Frankish, Lombard and Dalmatian, Slav and Muslim – they became more outward-looking and more aggressive in seizing commercial opportunities.

The nature of their conflicts changed accordingly. The relative scarcity of a valued resource is always the primary cause of conflict between men. At one time salt had been the only source of wealth occasioning disputes between Venetians, but opportunities for profit were more diverse now and demanded a greater degree of co-operation in order to exploit them. Aggression therefore tended to be directed outward, against competitors abroad, and particularly against the people of Comacchio fifty or so miles to the south at the outlet to northern Italy's chief trading highway, the River Po.

But political power, so essential for men of property who want to protect that property, was another scarce resource – so the wealthier Venetians struggled ferociously with each other for the Dogeship, and when they gained it they fought ruthlessly to cling on to power and, if possible, to keep it in their families.

Survival was a major preoccupation of any Doge, and in order to survive he was well advised to ensure that the basis of the community's prosperity was maintained. This basis was threatened by Byzantium's abrogation of its general *détente* with the West, but Doge Pietro Tradonico, who ruled from 837 until 864 proved equal to the challenge. He succeeded in re-establishing the trading arrangements which underpinnned Venice's economic growth and in setting Venice's relations with the Western Empire on a more permanent basis than before.

Between 840 and 845 agreements concluded with the inheritors of Charlemagne's Holy Roman Empire confirmed the line of Venice's old territorial boundary with the mainland and laid down the procedure for settling disputes. The westerners promised not to aid Venice's enemies, and to help her against the Slavs based across the Adriatic – who in 842 had ravaged Cáorle, at which Venetians had rushed to build two great ships called *falandrie* to block up the most vulnerable entrances to the lagoon. By the same agreement, Venice promised not to harbour runaways from the mainland or sell Christians into slavery – though Venetians continued to deal in slaves regardless, bringing them from the Dalmatian coast when they could not snatch peasants from the hinterland. Nor did they hesitate to sell Christians to Muslim territories where fine prices were to be had for them.

But most important of all the treaty recognized Venice's right to control the outlets from the Po, and allowed her people to trade with the Carolingian territories inland, paying a modest tax of only two and a half per cent of the value of the goods they carried at each landing place – this in return for reciprocal rights and a modest annual tribute. All in all, it was a fine march stolen over their rivals from Comacchio. Doge Pietro Tradonico might have been illiterate, but he had a shrewd eye for a bargain.

This treaty with the Franks, made initially for five years, remained in force with the successor states on the break-up of the Empire. It was renewed repeatedly over the next 150 years, providing a stable framework within which Venetians were encouraged to invest in trade and transport and so profit from the growth of European commerce which centred on the north Italian hinterland.

Yet this friendly compact with the west did not imply any deterioration of relations with Byzantium. Locked in a fierce struggle with the Saracens and threatened by enemies nearer home, the Eastern Emperor was content for his little underling in the west to fend for itself. It saved a further drain on his exchequer while preserving Venice's goodwill. And the Venetians responded by providing naval help for the Emperor on demand. In 840 they sent out sixty small ships to help the imperial forces against the Saracens at Taranto, though the enemy prevailed and captured most of the Venetian vessels. In 842 Venetian ships were routed again by the Saracens off the island of Sansego near the southern tip of Istria. Yet despite these reverses Venice was soon widely recognized as the strongest naval power in Italy.

She was building more and more ships of every kind – ships for long voyages equipped with oars and sails and smaller craft to ply the rivers of the hinterland; ships fit for use in war as well as ships for trade. The Saracens and Slavs did not succeed in driving them from the seas; merchants from the rival ports of Ancona and Amalfi could not prevent the volume of their trade increasing, nor the growth of Venice as a market. Even in the harsh winter of 860, when the outlets to the rivers froze, the wide expanse of the lagoon was dotted with the forms of merchants carrying their wares across the ice in wagons.

This growth in trade encouraged immigration and produced a corresponding spurt of urban development. Even so, the new city still had a rustic atmosphere. Most of the dry land was covered with scrub and meadow rather than with buildings, and though local brick was used in the construction of churches, houses were usually built of timber and reed thatch. Most of them had garden plots; even the Doge's residence had its orchard.

Yet despite this idyllic, almost rural aspect, the widening vista of commercial opportunity, and the spirit of co-operation which this encouraged, the Venetian community was racked by factional jealousies and plots. The Barozzi intrigued against the Barbolani, the Iscoli against the Selvi, the Selvi against the Giustiani, and the Giustiani against the Polani clan. Even the position of so successful a Doge as Tradonico, who had himself ousted his predecessor and seized power, was constantly threatened by conspiracy. His reign was punctuated by violent outbreaks fomented by rivals and enemies, and in the end he was murdered – cut down in the church of San Zaccaria on Easter Monday 864 by members of the Barbolani family.

The retainers of the fallen Doge barricaded the palace and fought off the insurgents for almost a week. Then neutral forces intervened. Leading members of the rival groups were forced into exile on some of the less comfortable marshy islands of the lagoon, and the resultant power vacuum was filled by Orso Partecipazio, who was elected Doge with the help of his personal retinue of strong men.

Orso lasted seventeen years, and not the least of his achievements, apart from merely surviving for so long, was making better provision for law as well as order. The population of the lagoon had been expanding fast – the creation of five new bishoprics bears witness to this. It had become far too large for one man to settle every grievance and dispute, yet to allow the island tribunes to dispense justice would have served to increase their power and prestige at the expense of the central authority. So special judges were appointed and, in addition to their judicial functions, they acted as aides to the Doge, keeping him in touch with popular opinion, informing him about the strength of factions and advising him generally on the conduct of affairs.

Orso was successful in war too, defeating the Dalmatian Slavs and helping Byzantine forces to drive back the Saracens who had been mounting raids right up the Adriatic. Grado was saved from Saracen attack, Venetians helped to crush the Infidels off Taranto in 867 and to capture Bari four years later.

In return for service to the Byzantine Emperor (which coincided happily with their own defence interests) Venetians trading at Byzantium were given preference over all other western merchants. On the other hand, though Byzantium banned the export of strategic commodities like timber and iron to the Saracens Venetians continued to export them – just as they persisted in smuggling slaves through to eager customers abroad, despite Doge Orso's alleged suppression of the trade in obedience to Byzantium's continuing demands. It fell to Orso's son and successor, Giovanni II, however, to achieve the most important commercial *coup* of the age for Venice – the crushing of Comacchio in 881.

The process which led up to it involved elements of communal economic interest and private dynastic ambition which, like so many aspects of Venetian life of that age, are impossible to disentangle. Shortly after his accession, Doge Giovanni persuaded the Pope to invest his brother with the lordship of Comacchio. The Marquis of Este, however, claimed Comacchio for himself, intercepted Giovanni's brother and forced him to return to Venice, inflicting a wound on him from which he subsequently died. In retaliation the Doge delivered a crippling attack on Comacchio. The town survived, but it was never to recover its former prosperity. Nor did it ever again present a serious threat to Venice's dominance in the business of supplying goods from overseas to the trading centres along the River Po – though, just to make sure, fifty years later the Venetians were to burn it down.

A new period of political instability, however, prevented the merchants of Venice from exploiting these newly-gained advantages to the full. With the Doge's health failing and the absence of an heir, latent unrest threatened to boil over into anarchy again. In 887 Doge Giovanni renounced his office, calling in Pietro Candiano to succeed him, but though Candiano was an able and a pious man, falling to his knees at dawn and sunset and whenever else the bells of Venice rang out their signals of worship, within five months he had been killed in another battle against the Slavs, and the ailing Giovanni Partecipazio took up the reins again until such time as a more vigorous leader should emerge. Such a man was found in 888. His name was Pietro Tribuno.

Tribuno ruled the lagoon like a despot from his little palace on the Rialto. He dealt ruthlessly with rivals and stripped the tribunes of the separate settlements of most of their remaining authority. But an iron grip was easier to exercise at a time when danger threatened from outside, and the Hungarians, fierce mustachioed horsemen from the eastern plains, were sweeping towards Venice.

They had come through Friuli in the year 900 and ravaged their

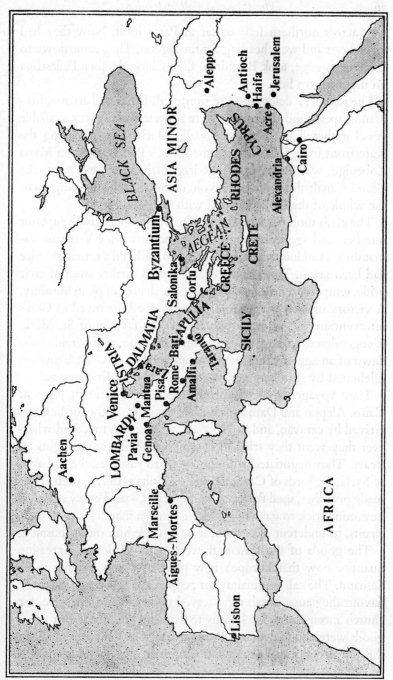

Venice and the Venetian world

way across northern Italy as far as Pavia itself. Now they had
turned east and were heading for the lagoon. They came down to
the water's edge, took Brondolo, then Chioggia, then Pellestrina
on the southern lido.

The islanders' defences were mustered. Bows and arrows, fire-
brands, spears and slingstones were collected, and every available
vessel gathered in. The great wall, which stretched along the
waterfront from Castello, past the Doge's Palace, to Santa Maria
Zobenigo, was fortified; a huge iron chain was slung across the
Grand Canal; the castle of Olivolo crammed with fighting men;
the whole of the Rialto bristled with defences.

The clash took place on the water, where the enemy's superior
numbers and aggressive spirit proved no match for Venetian seamanship. The Hungarians' leader, Arpad, ordered a retreat. Venice
had been saved. This victory called forth a further swell of civic
pride, tempered a little by an appropriate degree of pious humility.
A victory of such proportions must, after all, be owed to God's
intervention and more particularly to the favours of St. Mark.
It engendered a resurgence of confidence, too, and heralded the
dawn of an age of almost uninterrupted peace – which Venetians
celebrated by searching yet more boldly for profit overseas.

They voyaged more frequently now to the distant ports of
Cairo, Aleppo and Damascus, where goods from the furthest east
arrived by caravan, and to Sicily and to Kairwan too. And wher-
ever they went they tried to consolidate their trading rights by
treaty. They negotiated with the Egyptian Fatmites, the Abbasids
of Syria, the lords of Cordova, and the Sultans of Maghreb. They
made promises, used flattery, offered bribes – used every so-called
Levantine trick to gain a privilege or steal a march on rival merchants, to undercut a competitor or squeeze him out of business.

The goods of the Orient flowed in to Venice in increasing
quantity now that Europe's new prosperity was creating more
demand. The call was mainly for pepper, cinnamon and ginger to
flavour the nauseous salt meat served up in lordly halls, spices for
church incense and for lotions to embalm the dead. But other
goods were also in demand. From Byzantium Venetians obtained
the purple silks and ornaments so much in demand by Italian

priests and prostitutes; ermine and sable skins came in from Russia and exotic carpets woven on the looms of Turkestan. Local traffic up the Po, the Brenta and Piave increased apace, and caravans were formed to take the goods over the dangerous Alps to Germany. But the chief commercial centre of tenth-century Europe was still Pavia.

Venetians were regular visitors at the fair there, pitching their tents at the outskirts of the city, paying out dues to the local customs men – and bribing them with ivory combs and mirrors for their wives. This done, they would set about the problematic work of trading. Should they sell their silks and spices and articles of luxury for coin, or barter them for the local products or the goods brought in from northern Europe? Was there a market for rough cloth in the east? What price would swords and shields and spears of northern manufacture fetch in Egypt? What price should they put on amber brought from Germany, on horses and on greyhounds? Were the slaves from the north offered for sale fit enough to stand the journey to Africa or to the East? And how much would it cost to feed them on the way?

The tenth century has been called the heroic age of trade, and though its volume was trivial by any modern standard the profits were heroic by the standards of the day. A successful voyage or two could make a man wealthy beyond a peasant's wildest dream – but it could also bring him death or slavery. Many Venetians were reduced to ruin on their ventures, robbed by bandits, or drowned at sea.

The trade in oriental luxuries was by no means the only and probably not yet the main pillar of Venice's prosperity, however. The less venturesome could make decent profits dealing in bulkier products nearer home – oil from Aquileia, corn from Lombardy, salt from the local pans, and timber from Dalmatia. Again, the quantities were not vast. But Venetians were gaining a lion's share of what inter-regional trade there was. And both the cake and their share of it increased now as the years went by.

Merchants and seamen must have formed a minority of the working population. Fishing and salt extraction, the latter an occupation for women mainly, were still important; so, too, was shipbuilding. But the economy was growing ever more complex and more variegated. By now Venice had dyers to colour cloth with the traditional blue local dye, and iron-founders able to cast bells of a quality fit to ring out in Byzantium. There were glass-makers and saddlers, jewellers, smiths and masons, butchers and water-carriers, boxmakers to produce those heavy chests in which merchants carried the more costly of their wares, customs men to collect the landing dues on goods brought in and to take their cut on every load of salt moved out for export. There were stevedores and ferrymen to carry off arriving cargoes, and still farmers and shepherds who watched their flocks on the marshy coastal strip and on some of the remoter islands.

The life people led was simple and regular, almost as rural as it was aquatic. People ate frugal meals, except on feast days, and wore simple smocks or gowns. Even the affluent, though housed more solidly, adorned by jewels and attended by retainers, lived quite plainly. Everyone rose at latest when the birds sang their dawn chorus, and when curfew rang all traffic ceased. The pace of life was governed by the seasons as interpreted by the calendar of the church; and the church was the major cultural hub round which life on the lagoon revolved. Rich men flaunted their affluence by embellishing churches and endowing them; poor men sought the church's consolations; and not a few earned their living through the church.

One such was Doge Tribuno's son, who, perhaps in reaction to his worldly father, took holy orders, becoming Bishop of Olivolo in 929. Hence when his father died the Dogeship went to Orso II, another Partecipazio. But this Orso lacked his predecessor's firm-ness, and it was left to the more aggressive Pietro Candiano II, son of a former Doge, to suppress the vendetta which had burst into ugly flower again and to impose Venice's will on the opposite shore of the upper Adriatic.

Istria, long a useful source of slaves, was forced to trade on Venetian terms, but the Slavic tribes in the Istrian hinterland and in Dalmatia remained troublesome, threatening the coastal towns with which Venetians traded, making pirate expeditions into Venetian sea-roads and even daring to mount small-scale raids into the lagoon itself. Once, according to legend, a group of Slavic raiders carried off a dozen Venetian brides as they waited, clad in white and clutching their dowries, to receive their Bishop's blessing. Fortunately the pursuing grooms overtook them at Cáorle, slaughtered the pirates, and rescued the brides – a feat thought worthy of commemoration by an annual re-enactment on the day of the Purification of the Virgin by twelve poor and virtuous long-haired maidens at a quaint ceremony at the church of Santa Maria Formosa. But not all such incursions ended so happily for the Venetians.

Slavic pirates continued to prey on Venetian shipping during the reign of the next Doge, the unfortunate Pietro Candiano III. Even his own son Pietro IV, whom he took into government with him, intrigued against him, and though the son was exiled after a great fight on the Rialto between their respective retainers in 959, he succeeded in replacing his father. Nor did Pietro IV's opportunism cease there. He proceeded to send his wife to a nunnery, banish his own son to a monastery and to marry Gualdrada, a lady with powerful connections and a considerable fortune.

Gualdrada was the niece of the Western Emperor Otto whose client Pietro became. She brought him considerable estates in the regions of Friuli and Treviso, and castles near Ferrara. Individual Venetians and religious houses had acquired farms and mills by feudal tenure in the hinterland before, but never on a scale like this. Pietro Candiano IV was a man on the make in the feudal style; with more interest in becoming a mainland potentate, apparently, than being Doge of Venice. It even seemed that he might merge Venice with his possessions in the hinterland.

The ducal couple's alien style of life made them unpopular. They lived in unwonted splendour, surrounded by slaves, guards and retainers who kept the people at a distance; their social circle centred on the feudal lords of Padua and Vicenza; the Doge insisted on being addressed as 'My Lord,' a term borrowed from the feudal mainland, and his wife seemed as much puffed up with pride as he was. This feudal pride of lordship conflicted with the Venetian instinct, as a later chronicler was to put it, 'to keep on terms of equality one with another.' But there were more solid grounds for discontent as well.

Venetians resented the presence of troops raised on the Dog-aressa's estates, and of being sent to fight in the Doge's interest on the mainland. Some feared that he would turn himself into the personal possessor of Venice; others that he would sacrifice the Byzantine connection in favour of the west.

The Doge did trim his sails. In 971 when the Byzantine Emperor made the most 'terrible threats' to Venetians for selling arms and timber to his enemies the Saracens, Pietro called a council of eighty-one people representing all sections of the community: clergy, great men, middling and the poor – only eighteen of whom could sign their names – to confirm the ban. Sensing the swelling tide of resentment and dissent the Doge was searching for a concensus. But neither this step nor the augmentation of his personal bodyguard with a contingent of Croatian slaves could save him in the end.

In August 976 a mob stormed the palace and overpowered the guards. A fire broke out, and the flames spread from the palace to engulf the surrounding district, gutting three churches and a hundred times as many houses. For a moment the Doge, his wife and their small son were lost sight of in the confusion, but the mob caught up with them in the vestibule of St. Mark's. The Doge fell to his knees begging forgiveness. They cut him down all the same, and his son with him.

For the next fifteen years the Venetian community was racked by internal strife. Gualdrada escaped to take sanctuary with the Dowager Empress Otto's widow, vowing revenge. But though she was quietened by an offer to return all her property – her land, her houses, her gold and silver plate, her slaves, her beds, her iron pots and lead utensils – a powerful group of exiles gathered round her stepson Vitale Candiano, Patriarch of Grado (whom the new régime had dispossessed). Backed by the Emperor Otto II, they were soon baying for the blood of the man who had led the rising and was now Doge of Venice, Pietro Orseolo.

Doge Pietro meanwhile had set about restoring the chapel of St. Mark, which had been gutted in the recent fire, engaging

Greek artisans to embellish it with enamel, jewels and gold. But the body of San Marco had been lost among the ashes in the fire, and a bad omen this turned out to be. For two years the Doge struggled to retain a grip on Venice. Then, on the night of 1st September 978, he fled. According to tradition he entered a monastery, lived on for another nineteen years and was subsequently canonized.

His place as Doge was assumed by a representative of the rival Candiano clan, under whom relations with Byzantium again deteriorated. Even the practice of dating documents according to the year of the Byzantine Emperor's reign was dropped. But this Doge only lasted fourteen months and in 979 it was the turn of Tribuno Memmo to cope with the two great feuding factions.

Shortly after Memmo became Doge, Domenico Morosini was stabbed by Stefano Caloprini as he was leaving the church of San Pietro di Castello. It was a blood feud now between the rival clans, but it was a vendetta involving more than family feeling and lust for revenge.

The Caloprini favoured the pro-western Candiano interest, while the Morosini supported the newly-exiled Orseoli and the Byzantine connection. Tribuno Memmo, who had married the daughter of Pietro Candiano IV, backed the Caloprini, restored Vitale Candiano's property to him and proposed submission to the Western Emperor on humiliating terms. But with the death of the Emperor Otto II in 983 the Morosini emerged as the stronger side, and with the exiled Orseoli gaining strength from day to day the Doge at last switched sides.

He now cracked down upon the Caloprini, who fled to Verona, and called up Byzantine support to help restore internal peace. After a time the situation seemed calm enough to allow the exiles back – but the vendetta soon blazed up again more fiercely than before. In 991 the Morosini dispatched three Caloprini brothers in one day. The Doge was helpless. He had alienated both sides, and had no alternative but to take the cowl.

His successor, Pietro Orseolo II, was described by a contemporary as 'no degenerate son of his sainted father so far as virtuous actions were concerned and yet excelling almost all the ancient doges in knowledge of mankind.' This compliment (which suggests an interesting dichotomy between the two contemporary ideals of virtue and knowledge of men) was penned by the chronicler John the Deacon, Pietro's chaplain and his friend, but it seems nonetheless deserved. The new Doge ended the vendetta by marrying his son Domenico to the granddaughter of Pietro Candiano III: he restored political stability, and he reduced the tensions generated between the rival partisans of the two domin-ant outside powers and cultures by re-establishing good relations with both East and West.

An agreement with the Western Empire concluded in 992 re-moved the fear of intervention from the mainland, and in 996 when Otto III was crowned Emperor in Rome he allowed Venice to open three permanent trading posts in the hinterland to the north of the lagoon, which could serve as bases for the develop-ment of trade across the eastern Alps to southern Germany. Later the Doge was to welcome the Emperor to Venice, when their conversations are said to have embraced metaphysics as well as politics. The Doge presented his visitor with a silver bowl and a chair of carved ivory, and the Emperor responded by waiving the fifty pounds of silver Venetians paid annually for their commercial privileges.

Relations with the East were not neglected either. The Doge named his younger son Ottone, in honour of the Western Em-peror, but he followed ancient tradition in sending the elder son, Giovanni, to complete his education at the Byzantine Court, and then married him to a great niece of the Emperor Basil II. More-over, in 992 he persuaded Byzantium to grant Venetians a privi-leged trading position throughout the Eastern Empire without making any explicit reference to Venice's allegiance. Though Venice continued to provide shipping for Byzantine troops in the struggle against the advancing Saracens, she was now free to treat independently and trade openly with the Saracens, as well as with Byzantium, where Venetians now had a permanent trading base of resident merchants. This concord gave Venice an immediate advantage over the merchants of Apulia, and particularly the

Amalfitans, her strongest competitors in the Mediterranean trade these days.

Doge Pietro was a builder and a warrior as well as a diplomatist. The renovations to St. Mark's which his father had begun were completed in his reign, he built himself palaces at Grado and at Heraclea – and in May 1000 he set out from Grado with six ships crammed with fighting men. 'Ploughing the waves of the sea,' as John the Deacon pictured it, he sailed across the Adriatic to crush the Slavs who continued to prey on both Venetian shipping and on Dalmatian settlements with which Venice had valuable trading connections.

Soothsayers had prophesied that the world would return to chaos in the year 1000, and there were many in Venice who never expected to see their Doge alive again. But he returned in triumph, bringing forty hostages in train as proof that he had smashed the pirates. He had freed the people of Zara and of other settlements along the coast from paying tribute to the Slavs – making them pay tribute to Venice instead for the privilege of her protection. In commemoration of this feat, the words *Dux Dalmatiae* were added to the Doge's title, and the triumph was henceforth to be commemorated every year upon Ascension Day, when the Doge would sail out beyond the lido to celebrate Venice's 'Marriage with the sea.' This evolved as the greatest feast-day in the calendar – but it was more than a simple celebration of victory in war: it was a purification of Venetian sins, a symbolic warning to the Slavs, an act of thanksgiving, a magic act to propitiate the angry sea.

Struggle with the sea was the dominant factor of Venetian development in this new expansive age. It could be seen in the bulwarks built to protect their frail settlements against high tides which swept into the lagoon, in distant trading voyages and in maritime battles especially against the Saracens at Bari and off Sicily. As one contemporary remarked, Venice was not only 'rich in money and rich in men' but none could be 'more valorous in naval warfare, or more skilful in guiding ships upon the ocean.'

When Doge Pietro Orseolo II died full of achievement, leaving a third of his estate for the *festa* of the 'Brides' to furnish dowries for

poor young virgins, and his second son, the sixteen-year-old
Ottone, succeeded him (his brother Giovanni having died two
years before) Venice was poised to take full advantage of a huge
upsurge in the European economy. Between 1000 and 1200 productivity is reckoned to have increased tenfold. Agricultural surpluses became more frequent, inter-regional exchange expanded
and the demand for eastern luxuries grew enormously. The
Amalfitans met much of this demand and Pisa and Genoa were
also beginning to venture strongly into shipping and into trade,
but Venice was more strongly established and the best placed of
all to reap the biggest profits.

She had formal trading arrangements now with virtually every
major state in Europe, the Levant and northern Africa. Most of
the traffic between Europe and Byzantium was carried now on
Venetian ships and Egypt depended on her as much for Dalmatian
timber as most states in northern Europe did to bring them
spices and silk from overseas. Venetian merchants were resident
in Byzantium, Egypt, Lombardy and Dalmatia, where they
acted as commercial agents, and they were soon to be found on
the Black Sea, Syria, Marseilles, Aiguemortes, and Toulouse.
This was the beginning of the great Venetian network in the
Mediterranean; the basis of the city's capitalist power.

Rich Venetians continued to invest in the safe field of landed
property, but trading profits were becoming so alluring that more
of them were offering their property as security for trading loans
on which they were willing to pay as much as twenty per cent
interest. The economic picture had changed almost beyond recognition from the time when Venetians had hauled their meagre
loads up river a few miles in hope of finding a little surplus corn.

The appearance of Venice was changing fast as well. The
population increased steadily as peasants fled in from oppressive
rule in Lombardy and Dalmatians arrived hoping for opportunity
and a safer life. The urban centre was more concentrated than
ever, and though most buildings were still made out of timber,
daub and reeds, far more incorporated bricks and even stone
shipped in from subject Istria. The Rialto settlement had been
extended and was drained by new canals; the Doge's palace had

been completed, though is was infinitely less grand than the palace as it stands today; the church of St. Mark's next door was in process of rebuilding, and a tiny hospital had been built nearby. Yet despite this new sophistication the community's disputes were still settled under an open sky in the courtyard of the ducal palace, where crowds would gather in times of rejoicing and emergency, to brag of victory or overturn a Doge.

The crowd and the faction were still forces in Venetian life. Doge Ottone Orseolo might emulate his father in mounting another expedition to fight off the Slavs and to extract new pledges of tribute from the settlements along the Dalmatian coast, but he eventually fell victim to enemies at home. They seized him, shaved off his beard and hair to prepare him for the monastery, and shipped him off to Byzantium. And with Ottone gone anarchy returned.

For the next six years Orseoli and Centranigi struggled for the leadership of Venice until in 1032 a new man took up the reins of government – Domenico Flabianco, a merchant specializing in salt. This proved to be the end of the dynastic tendency in Venetian politics. Never again was the ducal chair to be the monopoly of a single family, as the Orseoli had so nearly contrived to make it; never again were Doges to be allowed to associate their sons with them in office.

The change was a product of the development of trade. A new and large clan of merchants, of which Flabianco was the representative, had become dominant in Venetian society. These men were more professionally entrepreneurial than their predecessors had been, not men of property dabbling in trade. It was they who gave the most employment; and they now had the greatest patronage at their command.

Henceforth consultation with leading citizens seems to have played a larger part in the governmental process, but the common people were also given a bigger say in public affairs than they had had for decades, and the *arengo* meant something again as a popular assembly, particularly in the election of new Doges. An alliance between the merchant interest and the ordinary artisan had come to replace the power of the clans and their retainers.

On the death of Flabianco's successor, Domenico Contarini, in 1071, the people assembled in their boats near San Pietro di Castello and yelled for the man they wanted. Domenico Selvo received the overwhelming majority of shouts and he was carried down to the boats upon their shoulders. They rowed him to the Piazza and there, in token of his humility, the Doge elect took off his shoes and stockings and went barefoot into St. Mark's to receive the regalia of office.

Doge Selvo continued his predecessors' work of embellishing St. Mark's, whose endowments had become so rich that a Procurator had to be appointed to keep account of its wealth and to supervise the building. Craftsmen had been brought in from Byzantium and Lombardy to work on it, and Selvo himself sent 'to all parts to seek out marbles and precious stones, and master masons fit to carry out his large and marvellous designs.' The church was taking on the form we know today with its five great domes, its pinnacles and its mosaics, its stiff madonnas and emaciated saints. But St. Mark's above all reflected the Byzantine influence, a connection reinforced by Selvo's marriage to the Emperor Michael's sister Theodora.

Chroniclers present an awesome picture of her: decked out like an idol, lazy and luxurious. According to the monk Peter Damiani 'she scorned to wash in ordinary water,' sending her servants out 'to gather the dew of heaven for her bath' instead. Nor would she take her food with her hand like an ordinary mortal, but had her eunuchs cut it in small pieces for her, and used a golden fork to transfer it to her mouth. Her rooms were always scented with the costliest perfumes. The very thought of such rich living was an affront to the monastic spirit; and she was reputed to have met an appropriately grisly end – struck down by a loathsome malady which gradually ate away her body in a great stench of putrefying wounds, a sickness so terrible that no one could be found to nurse her, so that she expired alone in horrible agony.

Such at least were the cautionary tales of luxury put about by monks. Other accounts indicate that the people mourned her when she died; and she seems to have had no adverse effect on Selvo's popularity. But Selvo had difficulties enough. Pope

Gregory VIII, who as Hildebrand the monk had defended the Doge's authority against his opponents in the church, now took a different attitude, because of Venice's alignment with his enemy the Western Emperor. And Selvo also had to take account of the sudden descent of the Normans on the Mediterranean.

These rough warriors, careless of shedding blood and greedy for lands to exploit, had already grabbed northern France and, under William the Conqueror, were imposing their hated rule on England. Now they were establishing themselves in southern Italy and in Sicily. By 1073 they had occupied Amalfi and were threatening Byzantine outposts and, more particularly, Venice's holdings in the Adriatic and her trade routes to the east.

The Byzantine Emperor was in no position to cope with this new threat. The Seljuk Turks had routed his army at Manziket in 1071 and were already threatening the Bosphorus itself. Venice had to look to her own defences. She prepared for an onslaught against her holdings in Dalmatia, but when the Normans attacked in 1082 they struck farther to the east, at the Emperor's domain.

The attack was led by Robert Guiscard, the Norman King of Apulia, and his son Bohemund. They raided Epirus, Durazzo and Corfu. Beset by barbarians in the Balkans and by the Turks in Asia, the Emperor Alexius pleaded desperately for Venetian aid, and Doge Selvo responded. Byzantium, after all, was the greatest city in the world. It had a population of a million people, it was the largest manufacturing centre, the busiest port, the gathering point for silk brought in from central Asia, for Bulgarian slaves, for Russian wax and honey and for Crimean wheat – in sum, the key point in the Venetian commercial network. Hundreds of Venetians used the city as a base for voyages to ports in Asia Minor, Greece, Syria and Egypt. Venice had to help – but she exacted a high price for her services.

In return for aid the Emperor had to promise to exempt Venetians from all customs duties, give them preference over all her commercial rivals, notably the Genoese and Pisans, freedom to trade throughout the Eastern Empire except with Crete and Cyprus and some Black Sea ports, and the outright ownership of shops, warehouses and landing-stages at Byzantium itself. In addition the Emperor offered to pay twenty pounds of gold every year for the benefit of San Marco – a tribute from an erstwhile lord to an erstwhile subject city.

Only then, in the summer of 1082, did Doge Selvo lead out his fleet to rescue the Byzantine forces beseiged by the Normans at Durazzo. A lusty fight ensued at the approaches to the harbour. Venetians had made a floating fortress, lashing their larger ships together and hauling the little boats full of men armed with missiles up into the masts. When Norman ships under Bohemund engaged, the Venetians flung their iron-tipped spears and nail-encrusted cudgels down upon them, and eventually succeeded in holing Bohemund's own ship. As it sank the others turned in flight, and the Venetians pursued the enemy as far as Robert Guiscard's camp, collecting much booty as they went. The Byzantine general made a sally, but though the allies won this victory the Normans remained outside Durazzo, and eventually took it in 1083.

When Robert was called away to help the Pope against the Western Emperor the pressure on Byzantium was relaxed – but not for long. In October 1084 Robert returned to attack Epirus and take Corfu and Cephalonia. The fighting swung one way and then the other. At first the Normans got the worst of it, but then, off Corfu, the Venetians were surprised and routed. Doge Selvo led the battered remnants of his fleet back home.

He was immediately turned out of office. But the new Doge, who was said to have 'induced the people to depose his predecessor by promises and gifts,' continued Selvo's policy. By 1095 a new fleet had been fitted out; and it sailed out to successs against Robert. The old Norman warrior was defeated and died soon afterwards.

There was great rejoicing over this in both Byzantium and Venice, especially among the merchants who were now able to exploit the vast privileges the war had brought them. And there was a suitable setting for their celebrations, for the embellishment of St. Mark's on which Doge Selvo had lavished so much wealth was now complete. The glorious occasion was marred by only one thing – the loss of St. Mark's body in the great fire more than a century before.

So, for three days, the Doge, the Patriarch of Grado, and all the bishops fasted and prayed, imploring the heavens for their patron to be restored to them – and, suddenly, their prayers were answered. The earth trembled; a marble pillar near an altar shook. A piece of plaster fell away and in the cavity a bronze sarcophagus was seen, with a human hand projecting from it. Joy was complete.

Venetians already commemorated St. Mark's arrival in Venice on January 31st, his Passion on April 25th, and his reinterment and dedication on October 8th. Henceforth they had another feast to celebrate, the Apparition of St. Mark. The cult of the saint could not have been entrenched more deeply. The banner of the saint was borne aloft, waved about and tossed into the air on every conceivable occasion for civic rejoicing. But the saint's motto, 'Peace,' was less appropriate than the winged lion, symbol of Venetian ferocity in trade and war – and the banner with that dominating symbol would be flaunted with even greater menace in the coming age of the Crusades.

Chapter III

The Age of the Crusades

In 1095 Pope Urban II called on Christendom to deliver the Holy Land from Muslim occupation. Two years later a great armada set out from Constantinople to accomplish this mission. The first Crusade had been launched.

It provided a welcome fillip to the Pope's prestige; a splendid opportunity for land-hungry Norman knights to carve out little empires for themselves in the Levant; and it allowed certain Mediterranean towns to profit from a sudden boom in shipping. Genoa and Pisa were active from the start, yet Venetians stood aloof. Only in 1099, when the Crusaders took Jerusalem and Genoa and Pisa shared in the spoils, did they appreciate the opportunity they had missed – the profits to be made supplying the Christians in the Holy Land and shipping pilgrims to a Christian-held Jerusalem. An expedition was prepared at once.

Though the Doge, Vitale Michiel I, was reputed to be a man of pious spirit, the Venetian Crusaders were led by his son and by Enrico Contarini, Bishop of Olivolo. They arrived at Jaffa in June 1100, in time to take part in the seige of Haifa. When it fell that October they gained a prearranged share of the spoil – a church and a market site, exemption from local taxes and the right of wreck throughout the kingdom of Jerusalem.

But their outward voyage had not been without its profits either. At Rhodes they had ambushed the Pisan fleet returning from the battle-grounds and relieved them of their plunder; at Myra in Lycia they had stolen the bones of St. Nicholas, having tortured their custodian into revealing where they lay, and they had snatched the remains of St. Theodore as well. They returned home to a rapturous welcome in December 1100, laden with plunder, relics and good news.

Venice had come late upon the scene, but had lost no time in extracting huge commercial privileges from the new Christian princes of the Levant and now, by undercutting her rivals Genoa and Pisa, she gained a major share in the carriage of recruits and supplies to Palestine – and in the carriage of pilgrims too: an achievement owed partly to the shorter sea-route from Venice to the east, and partly to the religious relics the city continued to accumulate.

In 1105 a prior of San Giorgio in Venice, sent to govern its subject church at Byzantium, abstracted the corpse of St. Stephen the Martyr. The same year a fragment of the true Cross and remains of St. Plautius and St. James arrived. They were welcomed by the Doge in person at the head of a great crowd, for such relics touched the spirit, conferred prestige and brought in business. Devout Christians seeking merit made pilgrimages to the churches which contained their shrines, and so spent their money in Venice rather than at other points of embarkation which boasted fewer saints.

Venice took no more active part in the Crusades for several years, and with Pisa and Genoa preoccupied against the Saracens in north Africa she was able to concentrate on more peaceful pursuits and on developing the city. The vast area to the south and west of the Grand Canal, virtually uninhabited the century before, was being built up fast as the population swelled, and in 1099 the Rialto market which had overtaken the old commercial centres like Torcello was enlarged to cope with the ever-increasing flow of business. Much rebuilding, however, was also occasioned by natural disaster.

The lagoon was always subject to inundations and earthquakes. In 1102 the island of Malamocco gradually subsided beneath the water, and its population had to re-establish itself at Chioggia. Moreover, since most buildings were of wood and thatch fires were frequent and extensive too. One great conflagration gutted large sections of the eastern half of Venice, and a second engulfed much of the south side, damaging part of the Doge's palace and St. Mark's; there were other appalling conflagrations in 1115, 1120 and 1149, and, despite precautions, including a ban on burning lights after the first hour of the night, in 1174 alone as many as 3,000 dwellings were to be destroyed by fire. Venetians were constantly building and rebuilding. But of all the developments of the age the most significant was the construction of the great dockyard called the Arsenal.

The first state-run industrial enterprise in early modern Europe, the Arsenal was started in 1104 on a pair of marshy islands to the east of the city centre. The work, which took fifty years to complete, involved draining the site with water mills and cuttings, building docks and digging trenches to hold the boiling pitch. It was a large investment for so small a state, but it paid handsome dividends. The Arsenal became the foundation of Venice's future strength at sea. Here shipwrights would construct the galleys and carve the masts and oars; here the sails would be made, the ships caulked, repaired and equipped with catapults, mangonels, tubes for 'Greek fire' and other armaments.

The undertaking of so vast an enterprise was dictated by the need to maintain parity at sea with rival Genoa and Pisa, to provide sufficient ships to ply the routes to Latin Syria where much of the trans-Asian trade was now arriving and, generally, with affairs in the Mediterranean in such a state of flux, to build a war fleet of a size beyond the resources of the private shipyards.

The early 1100s found Venice engaged in war on many fronts. In 1108 Venetians took part in the Crusaders' attack on Sidon, then helped to defend Byzantium against the Norman Prince of Antioch, and after Zara's rebellion in 1111 spent five years of military and diplomatic effort to recover it. Control of the Dalmatian coastline was essential not only because of its timber and the need to keep down pirates, but to provide staging harbours for her ships, which usually sailed only by day, seeking the shelter of a Dalmatian port at night. Dalmatia, and Zara in particular, was essential then to Venetian interests further afield.

The year Zara rebelled the Emperor allowed the Pisans an establishment at Byzantium and cut their customs rate to four per cent. Venice's privileges there were no longer exclusive, and with Genoa as well as Pisa accumulating important bases in Palestine – Genoa already had quarters in Acre, Antioch and Jerusalem – Doge Domenico Michele set out to make up the deficit.

In 1122 he led out a fleet of twenty-eight great galleys equipped with rams, forty smaller ones, four large transports and about thirty other ships to help the hard-pressed Crusaders against the Saracens. Success attended him. In 1123 the Venetians beat the Egyptian fleet at Askelon, took four merchantmen at El Arish, and eventually settled down to beseige the port of Tyre. Here the Doge ran out of cash to pay his followers, but rather than turn back he persuaded them to accept scraps of leather instead, pledging to redeem them in Venice afterwards.

Tyre fell within five months, and the victory brought the Venetians a third of the port and a third of Askelon as well. These were to be self-contained colonies complete with bakeries, mills, warehouses and baths in which Venetians would run their own affairs, using their own weights and measures, operating their own courts under their own *bailo*, and appointing their own *vicecomes* to direct their share of the defences. In addition, King Baldwin of Jerusalem exempted them from all duties in the Christian territories except for a third of the pilgrim tax and enfeoffed them with some property in Acre. Along with Genoa and Pisa, Venice was now one of the largest property-owners in the Holy Land.

At this point the Byzantine Emperor, egged on by Venice's competitors, tried to reduce Venetian privileges in his Empire, holding the Venetian residents at Byzantium hostage to this purpose. But the Doge was not to be blackmailed. Interrupting his homeward voyage, he raided Byzantine Chios, Rhodes and the isle of Cos, carrying off the relics of Saints Donatus and Isidore in triumph home to Venice, and within two years Byzantium's dependence on Venetian sea power – and her inability to stand the losses in trade contingent on the breach with Venice – forced her to give her former underling what she asked.

For all her interests overseas, Venice was much concerned about her hinterland. The city's growth and the tendency to use such plots of cultivable land that stood out from the grey moor of the

Dogano surrounding the lagoon as orchards and vineyards, made Venice increasingly dependent on mainland corn. This need had led to the establishment of trading posts at Ferrara and Fano in the early 1100s, and in 1141 to the first of a series of commercial treaties with the Marche aimed at guaranteeing the city adequate supplies of corn, oil and wine, sometimes in the form of tribute. Relations with neighbouring Padua, however, concerned different, but equally important issues.

A dispute with them over boundaries had been settled in 1111 through the mediation of the Emperor Henry V. But the friction persisted, and escalated strongly when, early in the 1140s, the Paduans cut a channel to divert the River Brenta which ran through their city and had been overflowing its banks. As a result some channels of the lagoon silted up. For centuries Venetians had struggled to control their watery environment and now the delicate balance they had achieved was being threatened. At once they declared war, trounced the Paduans in a short campaign and forced them to concede.

Inexperienced in land warfare, Venice had employed mercenaries for the campaign. But she continued to fight her own battles overseas. In 1146 when the Normans under King Roger of Sicily invaded Greece the Byzantine government cried out for Venetian help, offering a bigger quarter at Constantinople and a larger annual payment to St. Mark as inducements. The terms were accepted and a fleet set out to defeat the Normans at Cape Malea, but then the allies fell into dispute among themselves. The Venetians took a Byzantine ship, decked it out like the Emperor's own galley and paraded a black slave on it dressed in imperial robes. This apparently trivial exercise in mockery reflected a growing hatred between the two, which was exacerbated further when Venice made a separate peace with the Normans, who promised to stop their piracy in the northern Adriatic; and the Emperor drew closer to Genoa, and became increasingly hostile towards Venetians at Byzantium.

By the middle of the twelfth century Venetian affairs both at home and overseas had become too complex for the Doge, aided only by a couple of advisers, to cope. In consequence a number of governmental bodies gradually emerged: the Council of Sages, a group of prominent men who advised the Doge, and helped supervise the executive; an elected Great Council – a product apparently of the old rumbustious, democratic assembly – and a more exclusive Lesser Council. These bodies emerged in *ad hoc* response to particular circumstances, but in time they became entrenched. Many of their original forms and functions were to change, and powerful organs of government were yet to emerge, but even so, the foundation of that delicately-balanced Venetian constitution so much to be admired in later centuries was being laid.

The almost monarchical powers of the Doge, and the intermittently exercised influence of the mob were being perceptibly eroded. A system for the selection of leaders based on city districts and electoral colleges was in process of formation and policy was coming to be determined by a more or less exclusive group deriving from about thirty families – men with interests in common, usually wealthy merchants, who were also experienced in political administration and naval affairs. Doges were still to be confirmed in office by the acclamations of the crowd, but they were always found from among the dominant group, a group which however narrowly based constituted another manifestation of the old collective spirit. Yet although the group was not exclusive, an attitude seems to have been taking root among them – an attitude summed up by a Venetian writer of the sixteenth century, when he wrote that 'artisans . . . hired labourers and servants, while essential to the functioning of a city, cannot truly be termed citizens.'

The majority of Venetians soon lost any real share in the conduct of affairs, but they continued to share in the sense of community, acclaiming each new Venetian victory and the arrival of each stolen saint. Civic festivals had a similar function. The dozen pigs and the boar which the Patriarch of Aquileia sent as tribute to the Doge each year were turned over to the people, who, calling them the Patriarch and his canons, chased them with patriotic gusto through the streets before finally slaughtering them and scrambling for the meat.

Another, more exalted, example was the annual Feast of the

'Brides,' which had been transformed into a very elaborate occasion by the 1140s. Young men sounding drums and trumpets would proceed from the Doge's palace to the church of Santa Maria Formosa led by gold-coped priests. There they would be welcomed by the twelve elected Brides, each from a different parish, to whom they would offer sweets and wine. The afternoon would be spent feasting at the Brides' houses, and the celebrations would continue to a climax some days later when the Brides, escorted by a boat-load of clergy and armed men, would sail to Castello for the Bishop's blessing and then on to the Piazzetta where the Doge, in his state barge, called the *Maestra*, would join them for a grand procession along the Grand Canal. The proceedings would conclude with a splendid banquet in the Doge's palace.

Such ceremonial provided spectacle, entertainment, and, since all sections of society from the Doge downwards had parts to play, it fortified the sense of community. The extent to which newcomers were accepted by this community is doubtful, however. Venice, always a polyglot city, was more polyglot now than ever. Crowds of pilgrims arrived, and contingents of the old and sick, seeking cure and grace at the city's many shrines. Immigrants poured in from every part of the Mediterranean world – imported slaves, aspiring runaways, peasants starving after harvest failure, rootless vagrants. Some settled down for good, others moved on, but there was always a sizeable proportion of temporary residents among the city's population.

Like any prosperous urban centre, Venice acted like a magnet for the discontented and distressed. Destitute women sold their favours; children were prostituted; sturdy paupers lived by robbery, and those too sick or old to rob abased themselves for charity. They had, after all, to live somehow.

Men of any substance took care to go about the city armed, and the authorities dealt sternly with such offenders as they could catch – flogging, branding, imprisoning, executing.

Penalties were equally draconian for personal offences. An adulteress could suffer life imprisonment; raping a minor might be punished by the loss of a hand, or even hanging; infanticide by being burned alive. Yet mercy was also shown, and sometimes in the most curious of forms. Doge Vitale Michiele's daughter, a nun, was allowed to renounce her vows and marry a monk, the last surviving Giustiniani, for fear that otherwise his family would become extinct – and they did not resume their service to God until they had produced twelve children. Family counted no less than order and piety in Venice.

Yet the dominant theme for most was work. As Venice's spectacular economic growth continued her own craft industries were encouraged to ever greater output. The rough, opaque glass and the products of the dyeworks there were in ever greater demand abroad; artisans of all types found employment, not least workers in precious metals who manufactured reliquaries, and armourers, one of whom constructed a cross-bow machine capable of firing fifteen darts at once. But the leading sector of the growing economy was still trade.

Venetians were soon venturing out of the familiar Mediterranean into the Atlantic, putting in at Lisbon, the first Christian port beyond the straits. But though trade retained adventuristic aspects, the element of financial risk was often tempered. Long voyages were frequently mounted by groups of merchants whose members shared the profits and risks; and the perils of shipwreck and piracy often came to be off-loaded onto a financier who stayed at home, though the interest rate for such a sea loan would far exceed the standard twenty per cent.

Loans were made on a small and a large scale, to finance a galley-load of precious pepper, or to tide a poor widow over a difficult few weeks. And all sorts of people lent as well as borrowed – in 1176, for example, Giovanni the Dyer was to lend twenty soldi to Carlotta of the parish of San Zulian on the security of her wooden house. The merchants, too, comprised a wide range in terms of wealth and status. There were entrepreneurs and financiers who operated on a considerable scale and amassed vast fortunes, but most were small men by comparison, and of these Romano Mauro can be taken as the archetype.

Romano was a trader of no mean resource, and his career makes a fascinating story in itself. In 1155, at about the age of twenty-five he moved to Byzantium where as many as 10,000 other Venetians, not to mention Genoese and Pisans, made their homes. From there he made a series of trading voyages to Smyrna, Thessaly, and Macedonia – and, from 1162, farther afield to Acre and even Alexandria. In 1167 he organized his most ambitious venture yet: a voyage to Salonika and Alexandria. This was a complicated operation involving two ships and no fewer than eight contractual loans, and since four of the investors insisted on accompanying him and being paid off at Alexandria he needed yet another to finance the remainder of the voyage.

In 1169 Romano returned at last to Venice, but a settled life in his native city seems to have offered too dull a prospect for this merchant venturer and, having obtained a commission to farm the Patriarch of Grado's revenues at Byzantium in return for an annual fee, he left Venice after only six months' stay. He reached Byzantium in good time for the disaster which overtook all Venetians there in 1171.

Relations between Venice and Byzantium had been cool for decades and had deteriorated steadily. Venetians there resented the increasing rates they had to pay for their shops and warehouses; the Greek Emperor resented Venice's alliance with the Pope against the Western Emperor in 1167 and in particular her dealings with Hungary. The crunch came when the Genoese were granted a quarter in the city. Venetians were infuriated. A few hotbloods attacked some Genoese. The entire Venetian colony was blamed for the attack and on 12th March 1171 they were all rounded up, their goods sequestrated and their ships seized.

Romano Mauro managed to cut his ship loose from its moorings and put to sea. He was one of the few to escape, but his losses had been heavy, and the affair had grievous repercussions for Venice as a whole.

The government raised a forced loan to mount an expedition and in due course one hundred galleys and twenty transports set out to take revenge. But off the Greek coast it was struck by epidemic. Thousands of seamen died and the survivors returned home in disarray, bringing the disease with them.

So great a disaster required a scapegoat, and the scapegoat was the Doge. He tried to seek sanctuary in the monastery of San Zaccaria but the crowd lynched him before he reached it. Six trying months passed before a successor, the great merchant and financier Sebastiano Ziani, finally emerged, but the outlook remained grim. The government was bankrupt; repayments on state loans had to be suspended; military operations dropped; ambassadors sent to the Byzantine Emperor Manuel were badly received, and to cap it all food prices were soaring, and with them popular discontent.

Ziani's administration gradually took control of the situation. A new system of loan-taxation was devised. Citizens were assessed by specially-appointed inquisitors and forced to pay one per cent of their net income to the Loans Office, for which they were to receive four per cent interest repayable half-yearly, the six quarters of the city balloting for their turn to receive repayment of their capital. Mercantile and naval affairs were also better ordered by new laws; more Venetians were encouraged to serve at sea, partly by a promised share in prize money and salvaged cargo. Above all, political tensions were soothed down. 'Leave open a career of honourable office to the more powerful citizens,' ran a precept attributed to Doge Ziani, 'and make sure that the people never suffer famine.' He certainly lived up to this precept by introducing a law to control food prices. Beef was to cost no more than two soldi a pound, fish from two and a half to three and a half, corn a maximum of seventeen a bushel, and the prices of oil, wine, eggs and other produce were limited as well.

While the Doge was reforming the community's affairs, Romano Mauro was picking up the pieces of his career. In 1173 he raised sufficient capital to take ship to Alexandria with a cargo of timber. He returned with a load of pepper and alum, to find a new backer in the Doge's son, Pietro Ziani, a property magnate who owned half the Merceria, Venice's main street. Another voyage to Alexandria, Bougie and Ceuta in 1177 turned out to be a failure, but, nothing daunted, he made another voyage to Syria, Palestine and Egypt in 1179. Five years later he built a new ship, and some while afterwards when Venice, strengthened by an alliance with the Normans, at last forced the Emperor to restore her old privileges and pay an indemnity of 1,500 lbs of gold, he ventured back to Byzantium again.

Mauro did not retire until he was sixty-two. Within nine years his savings seem to have run out – at least in 1201 his cousin lent him fifty lire interest free, 'for love' as he put it. Romano died shortly afterwards, survived by a daughter who had entered a nunnery; his son is thought to have predeceased him, possibly lost at sea together with his ship, which may have accounted for the father's difficulties.

There were many others of Romano's type – merchants and sailors specializing in every kind of good. The Venetian markets of his day dealt in commodities as diverse as tin and mead, iron and emery, brass and alum, glass and vitriol. Sugar and rice changed hands there, prunes and almonds, nutmegs, aloes, cloves and cardomom. Wine, myrrh and indigo, gum arabic and galingale were to be had; oil, ammonia, camphor, and cubebs, gallnuts and mastic wax all found buyers, as did timber, hides and leather of all kinds, linen and wool, silks and cotton, and that universal currency, pepper. Goods from every part of the known world were handled on Venetian wharves, and while Venetian merchants discussed affairs with their colleagues in the market places, or sat over their warehouses busying themselves with contracts and accounts, Venetian agents in a score of ports dealt with merchandise which never touched Venice at all, but still yielded profits for the city.

A proportion of these profits was salted into the fabric of the city – in the campanile of St. Mark's begun in 1148, in the new church at Jesolo, in the rebuilding of San Zaccaria and the enlargement of the Piazza, which Doge Sebastiano Ziani framed with houses graced by collonades and delicately sculptured windows. He built a front towards the canal side of the Palace too, and had the two Grecian columns erected on the Piazzetta, an engineering feat accomplished by the opportunistic Niccolò Barattiari, who claimed the right to erect a public gaming table between them rather than collect a fee.

Industrious, belligerent, rich and proud, Venice was becoming a veritable peacock of a city. Though a place built for man's con-

An early Venetian settlement

Torcello

Ascension of SS. Mark. St. Mark's Cathedral

venience with narrow streets and arcades affording shelter from the rain and sun, the dominant features were those great Byzantine domes and Gothic pinnacles, grandly impressive viewed from the ground, yet even sweeter from above. The medieval Venetian knew what it meant to build things pleasing in the eyes of God.

Venice attained a pinnacle of prestige in the eyes of men when in 1177 it was chosen as the most appropriate venue for the most momentous summit meeting of the age – between Pope Alexander III and the Emperor Frederick Barbarossa who had agreed to settle their long and bitter feud. Venice had first opposed the Emperor and then stood neutral and it was this stance that made her the only state capable of mediating between the mutually suspicious parties when Frederick at last sought peace.

It was a delicate negotiation. In May 1177 the Pope arrived to join the ambassadors of the Lombard League and the Emperor's Chancellor, the Archbishop of Mainz, in talks. But in July, when the Emperor reached Chioggia, the Pope and the Lombard League ambassadors were terrified. The ambassadors fled to Treviso, and only the assurance that four Sicilian galleys stood by to carry him to safety persuaded the Pope to stay.

The Doge promoted truces between the Emperor on the one hand and the League and Sicily on the other; and finally between Emperor and Pope. Frederick repented his disobedience, and Alexander agreed to absolve him. The stage was set for a pompous reconciliation.

Early on Monday July 23rd the clergy, ambassadors and a crowd of other notables assembled outside St. Mark's, where the Pope sat enthroned. At ten o'clock Frederick arrived on the Ducal barge accompanied by the Doge and the Patriarch of Grado. Advancing towards the Pope, he removed his purple cloak and knelt down to kiss the papal foot. The Pope gave him a kiss of peace, and everyone adjourned to hear *Te Deum* in St. Mark's. Next day, while the Pope said Mass and gave a sermon, Frederick served as an acolyte, and having kissed the papal foot again and held the stirrup of the papal mule while Alexander mounted, received the papal blessing and dismissal.

The peace was formally ratified on August 1st and two weeks

C

later the congress closed. Yet the representatives of both sides stayed on in Venice for several weeks, the Emperor until September 18th, the Pope until October 16th. All this time the city teemed with foreigners. The Archbishop of Cologne for one had brought 400 retainers with him, and money poured into the pockets of Venetian shopkeepers.

More permanent benefits accrued, however. Frederick guaranteed Venetians safe passages throughout the Empire, paying only two and a half per cent landing duty on their goods, while the Pope rewarded 'his dearest friend' the Doge by granting indulgences to Christians visiting St. Mark's and other churches – which brought yet more money to the city. And her diplomatic triumph of 1177 gave a tremendous fillip to Venetian prestige. The world remarked not only her continuing economic success, but her new political stability as well, which seemed the more amazing at a time when so many Italian cities were racked by feuds.

While some new Italian communes, resentful of Venice's commercial success, ill-treated visiting Venetian merchants, others particularly subject to internecine fighting began to engage neutral outsiders to judge their disputes, and since Venice seemed so rich in experienced judges and administrators Venetians were soon much in demand for such positions. Matteo Quirini, called in as *praetor* to Treviso in 1186, seems to have been the first Venetian magistrate appointed in a foreign city; but so many others followed that the government had to forbid the practice for fear that Venice itself would run short of able men in time of need.

Doge Sebastiano Ziani, who had served Venice so well, had retired to the Monastery of San Giorgio on 12th April 1178. He died soon afterwards, leaving a huge fortune and a will so complex that an additional procurator had to be appointed to administer it. The bequests included rents to pay for the support of poor prisoners and for an everlasting lamp to be placed over the relics of St. Stephen, a dinner for twelve paupers to be provided every Tuesday, and another of lentils and cheap fish for his own family each St. Stephen's day.

Such was the piety of Doge Ziani, a piety common among Venetians and which often took extreme forms – one Pietro

Acotanto gave all his wealth to the poor and died a beggar in 1187. Sometimes entire families would take the cowl. All Venice, it seems, revered the prim mystic Madonnas and the proliferation of chaste saints depicted in the paintings and mosaics of the time; churches were filled with people prostrating themselves before shrines and icons, praying fervently with outstretched arms as if dragging down blessings from the Lord.

But despite the intensity of religious feeling business was always business. The church might forbid usury in 1179 and deny Christian burial to those who practised it, but leading Venetians, along with others, not least members of the papal curia, continued to demand high rates of interest and were nevertheless buried reverently in consecrated ground. Nor did religious foundations hesitate to milk their peasants almost dry – in 1183 the administrators of Santa Maria della Carità demanded a third of the grain produced by its peasants in the hinterland, or half their harvest if the foundation supplied half their seed corn. Venetians were disinclined to recognize any conflict between commerce and religion.

Yet for all their wealth, rich Venetians usually ate frugal meals – a custom based upon tradition, piety and a saving ethic, but which served another purpose too, in softening resentment against the rich. Such resentments were easily engendered in a city where everyone lived cheek by jowl, but frugal living narrowed the apparent gap between the powerful and the weak, and so helped stave off popular disorders – a purpose also served by the careful maintenance of food supplies and by the staging of civic spectacles, particularly those intended to advertise the city's power, in which both rich and poor alike could take pride.

These spectacles were becoming increasingly magnificent, especially the one on Ascension Day. The Doge would proceed in state from his Palace, shaded by a vast umbrella (said to have been presented by the Pope) to board a barge ornately carved and shimmering with gold. Surrounded by a crowd of Venetian notables, canons of St. Mark's and ambassadors of foreign states, and followed by a host of galleys, barks and gondolas, the Doge would sail out to Santa Elena, where the Bishop of Castello would greet him, and monks would present him with damask roses set in a silver goblet. The flotilla would then move out beyond the lido to the sea, where the Doge, standing high on the poop of his barge, would address the ocean. 'We espouse thee, O sea, in token of our true and perpetual dominion over thee.' So saying, he would cast a ring into the water – a ring blessed by the Pope himself in 1177 and thenceforth by the Patriarch of Grado – and all would return for Mass at St. Mark's, a banquet at the Palace and for the fortnight's rejoicing that marked the annual fair.

Dalmatia, whose subjection this ceremony commemorated, was still restive, however, and in the 1180s, provoked beyond endurance by the increased taxes Venice imposed upon her, the town of Zara rebelled again. In 1187 the Doge set out to recapture it, mounting an expedition financed by the leading citizens in another series of forced loans – though since the four per cent interest payments were guaranteed by the salt tax the poor of the city also paid. And in this case they paid in vain, for in 1188 the Doge called off the seige.

His withdrawal was prompted by a crisis in the Holy Land. In 1187 Saladin had forced Jerusalem to surrender. Acre, in which Venice held a share, was lost as well, and so when Pope Gregory VIII proclaimed a new crusade the Doge responded and called all the city's shipping in from overseas. The third Crusade set out from Venice and from Pisa in 1189. Its first objective was to retake Acre; Acre duly fell into Christian hands again, and Venice regained her quarter of the city.

Soon afterwards, at the beginning of 1193, a new Doge was elected, and by the new method. Representatives of the six quarters of the city and of the outer lagoon settlements met to choose forty electors. They in turn chose four, and these four selected another forty, three-quarters of whom had to agree on who the next Doge should be. The candidate who eventually emerged from this exquisitely intricate procedure was Enrico Dandolo.

He was an old man, an experienced diplomat and man of war, a member of the inner group of powerful families, and possessed of such poor eyesight that many called him blind. He duly took his oath of office or *promissione* (another innovation designed to limit a Doge's power) and was acclaimed by the mob.

The problems he set out to solve had become hardy perennials: how to safeguard navigation up the rivers of the hinterland and security of trading rights in north Italian towns; how to obtain confirmation of Venetian privileges in Byzantium; how to overcome Zara's defiance; and how to raise money for these purposes. The last three presented the greatest difficulty, but they were soon resolved, and through an unexpected agency of change.

In 1198 a keen Crusader became Pope and his missionaries were soon touring Europe, preaching war. The knights of northern France and Flanders responded most strongly to the call, and their leaders, Counts Louis of Blois, Thibaud of Champagne, and Baldwin of Flanders, sent ambassadors to Venice to enquire if the Doge could provide the necessary transport to the Holy Land and if so at what price. Doge Dandolo received them well, for they represented men who claimed to be the greatest uncrowned heads in Europe. Moreover they were prepared to pay hard cash for the Venetians' services. It was good business and a holy cause.

By April 1201 agreement had been reached. Venice would lease sufficient ships to the Crusaders for a year, and supply them with nine months' provisioning. The crusaders, estimated to be over 30,000 men plus horses, would pay 85,000 silver marks for the service, the last instalment of 50,000 two months before departure. Additionally Venice volunteered to provide fifty armed galleys free, in return for a half share of all lands and property that the Crusade won.

From then on everything went wrong from the Pope's if not from Venice's point of view. The Count of Champagne, projected leader of the expedition, died, and Boniface, Marquis of Montferrat, took over. Differences of view emerged as to whether the expedition should land in Syria or in Egypt, with which Venice was negotiating a trading agreement at the time; and only half of the expected numbers of Crusaders arrived – and they such a rough crowd that the Venetians kept them out of harm's way on the lido. Finally, and most seriously of all, the Crusaders could not raise the agreed amount of cash.

The Doge went into conference with his advisers, and presently emerged with a suggestion. Venice would proceed regardless,

waiting for the outstanding 34,000-mark balance until such time
as it could be paid out of captured booty. There was only one
condition. The Crusaders must deal with Zara on the way. The
plan agreed, the Venetians set about melting down the Crusaders'
plate and money into a coinage of their own, the first produced
in Venice – tiny pieces of silver ·965 fine embossed with the
images of Christ enthroned in glory and of the Doge being invested by St. Mark.

In July, however, Cardinal Pietro Capuano arrived – sent by the
Pope to stop the attack on Christian Zara. But though he managed
to clear the Crusaders' camp of prostitutes for a time Capuano was
unable to persuade the Doge to by-pass Zara, and when he demanded to be allowed to accompany the expedition as papal
legate he was told that he would be welcome only as a preacher.
Capuano at last conceded the point about attacking Zara – on
condition that the Venetians went out as Crusaders, too, not
merely as auxiliaries. This deal was accepted. On 25th August
1202 old Dandolo took up the Cross, and in October 1202, six
months behind schedule, the Crusade sailed.

It was an extraordinary spectacle. The Doge led the way on a
galley painted bright red for easy recognition, standing erect
beneath an awning of vermilion silk. Four men sounded silver
trumpets at the prow, priests intoned *Veni Creator*, and the vast
gold and crimson banner of St. Mark stood out proudly from the
masthead. At least 200 other ships followed behind – ships
crammed with mortars, catapults and mangonels, and swarming
with warriors who shouted in anticipated triumph. Rows of
shields hung over the sides and the pennants of thousands of
knights streamed out overhead. Gradually the beating drums, the
clash of cymbals, the shouts, the shrill sounds of a hundred trumpets
faded into the distance; the shapes began to merge, the colours
dim, and at last the great fleet passed beyond the sight of the great
crowd on the waterfront.

The fleet arrived off Zara in November, broke the chain that
barred the entrance to the harbour, and forced the city to surrender.
The Crusaders camped there all that winter, during which time
the Venetians set about tearing down the town's defences and

their shrewd old Doge planned the next step in his strategy.

The situation was as convoluted as some abstract illumination in an early medieval manuscript. For a year now Dandolo had known that the Byzantine Emperor Alexius III was negotiating with the Genoese who stood to gain considerable privileges at Venice's expense. He also knew that in 1201 the son of the ex-Emperor Isaac, whom Alexius III had overturned and blinded, had escaped from Byzantium. This son, also called Alexius, had already been in contact with Boniface of Montferrat, and now word had come that Alexius was ready to pay the colossal sum of 200,000 silver marks in return for the Crusaders' help in seizing the Byzantine throne. Moreover, Alexius promised to provide 10,000 men for the Crusade, maintain 500 knights in Jerusalem once it was captured, and, as if anticipating objections from the Pope, to merge the Eastern with the Western Church. The bribe worked. Dandolo was willing enough to receive 100,000 marks for hiring the fleet for a further year; Boniface was anxious for the extra pickings offered – he had been promised Salonica as an outright gift – and together they agreed that they would head for Byzantium before the Holy Land.

In April 1202 the Crusaders sailed from Zara to Corfu, where young Alexius joined them, confirmed his promises and offered Boniface Crete as an additional inducement. On Midsummer's Day 1203 they arrived at the Bosphorus and sailed round the city of Byzantium showing Alexius to the people as their 'rightful' Emperor. The inhabitants were evidently less impressed with him than the Crusaders were with what they saw.

Dandolo, like many Venetians, knew the city well of old, but 'those who had never seen it before gaped with astonishment,' wrote an eye-witness in retrospect; 'for they had never dreamt that so rich a city existed in the world.' They gasped in wonder at its vast palaces and churches, and as they set eyes on the high walls and mighty towers which had never fallen to attack 'there was not a man among them, however brave, that did not tremble.'

But in July the attack went forward. They stormed the tower of Galata, released the great chain that stretched across the Golden Horn and went on to destroy the imperial galleys in the harbour.

A general assault started on the 17th – the Venetians approaching from the water, the others overland.

While some of Dandolo's men operated the war engines on board the ships, hurling missiles against the sturdy walls, others brought a battering-ram to bear and set scaling-ladders to the ramparts. The enemy stood ready to receive them. Greek fire, arrows and hot oil rained down onto the raw-hide canopies under which they worked. But at last they forced an entry and occupied a bastion.

The knights, meanwhile, in their heavy armour, fought astride sweating horses under the July sun. Against them came the Genoese and Pisans, the Danes and mustachioed English warriors wielding their huge axes. The battlefield was confused. Men thrust lances, bowmen and slingsmen took their aim; there was neighing of horses, blaring of trumpets, shrieks of men – total confusion.

Yet that night Count Baldwin slept in the Emperor's scarlet tent and by next morning the garrison had quit the walls and left the Palace undefended. The Emperor Alexius had escaped; the blind ex-Emperor Isaac was led out from his dungeon and placed upon the throne.

This pleased neither Dandolo nor Boniface. It was their protégé Alexius, not his father Isaac, who was beholden to them, and at their insistence he was duly made co-Emperor with his father. Alexius, however, could not pay his bill. Half the money was found, and in time another 34,000; but that was all.

The Crusaders who had taken Alexius hostage were persuaded to return him and move outside the city walls. But by October 1203 popular opposition to Alexius was growing. Fires were started, fighting broke out in the city, and a desperate Alexius now begged the Crusaders to stay on until the spring of 1204 to help protect him. They agreed, but popular resentment continued to increase.

On 25th January 1204 a huge crowd of Greeks assembled under the vast domes of St. Sophia. A popular movement was in train against both the Crusaders and their clients the Emperors. It was led by Alexius Ducas, son-in-law of Alexius III, and nicknamed 'Murtzuphlus' because his eyebrows met in the middle of his forehead.

The Greeks sent fire-ships in against the fleet, but the Venetians held them clear with iron boat-hooks and made them harmless. Then in February, with the help of the Palace Guard, Murtzuphlus murdered Alexius. His father, Isaac, died a few days later and Murtzuphlus took over.

The Crusaders were furious. Determined to obtain the balance of Alexius's debt, they set out to impose their own will on the city. Thoughts of the Holy Land still haunted some of them, but Dandolo reconciled his Crusading vow with the fantastic argument that God had obviously led him to do His service in Byzantium, while Baldwin justified himself by calling the Greeks 'the filthiest of Gentiles' who had 'provoked the loathing of Christ.' Besides there were Jews and a few Muslims in the city.

The Crusaders attacked early in April 1204 and were forced to retreat. They tried again four days later and succeeded. Lashing their ships together, the Venetians had built superstructures upon them so as to set tower against tower, and leap from them onto the city's battlements. By evening the Crusaders had entrenched themselves inside the walls; Murtzuphlus fled soon afterwards. The invaders had Byzantium at their mercy once again.

This time they spared nothing. An ordered form of plunder had been planned and excommunication threatened for excess. But in the event only one knight was hanged for looting; for the rest all restraint went by the board.

Countless atrocities were committed by these shield-bearers of Christ. As the Pope himself was to declare, the Crusaders had 'bathed in Christian blood . . . committed adultery, fornication and incest,' ravishing 'matrons and virgins, even those vowed to God.' They robbed churches and murdered the defenceless. The holy library in St. Sophia was destroyed; soldiers drank from consecrated cups, wrenched gems from altars, tore reliquaries to pieces and squabbled over the remains. They even placed a prostitute on the Patriarchal throne and reeled as she sang them a ribald song.

The sack of Constantinople brought Venice another hoard of

trophies: the head of St. Philip, the arm of St. Stephen, some flesh of St. Paul, one of John the Baptist's teeth, and a dish from the Last Supper. But this was only a fraction of the plunder. The entire Byzantine empire was at the Crusaders' mercy, and they had already decided how to carve it up.

A month before the last assault they had agreed that one of them should be the Emperor. The choice fell upon Baldwin of Flanders – and this being so a Venetian was made Patriarch. Baldwin was to command one fourth of all Byzantine territories; the rest was to be divided equally between Venice and the Latin knights. In this way Venice acquired title to the entire coastline of Ionia, from Epirus to Morea, Adrianople in Thrace, Gallipoli, the great isle of Euboea and many islands of the Archipelago. In addition she bought Montferrat's rights to Crete for a thousand paltry marks.

But title was one thing and possession quite another, and this problem of subduing their new properties drove all remaining thought of a campaign in the Holy Land out of the Crusaders' minds. Dandolo actually applied to be relieved of his Crusader's vow on the grounds of great age and infirmity. The Pope refused at first, but then allowed an indefinite postponement. Yet neither age nor infirmity prevented Dandolo from fighting one last campaign – by Easter 1205 he was at war with the King of Wallachia trying to secure Adrianople. He died that June and was buried in St. Sophia.

The fourth Crusade had solved Venice's age-old problem of securing the Adriatic shipping route and preferential treatment in the markets of Byzantium. It had also turned the wheel of fortune round full circle. A few centuries before, Venice had been a minor outpost of Byzantium; now she was that Empire's conqueror. A Venetian *podesta*, Maria Zeno, strutted round Byzantium wearing the red ankle-boots the Emperors themselves had worn. It was symbolic of the new imperial role that Venetians had suddenly begun to play.

Chapter IV

The Challenge of Empire

Venice's sudden acquisition of a vast Mediterranean empire confronted the new Doge, Pietro Ziani, with a host of unexpected problems. How were these extensive territories to be secured? How should they be governed? And since Venice itself lay at the extreme western edge of all of them where should the centre of administration be?

The Venetians at Constantinople seemed to have pre-empted the position by electing their own *podesta* without reference to Venice, and the new Doge had no alternative but to confirm him in office. As to the occupation of the empire, there were sufficient resources available to secure only a few points reckoned to be of particular strategic value as naval bases and staging posts for merchant ships.

In 1206 a fleet sailed to occupy Methone and Korone at the south-west tip of Morea, which some Latin knights had seized and Venice wanted as a 'special nest for our galleys . . . on their way to the Levant.' A colony was soon established at Chalkis too, though the subjection of the rest of Euboea, which Venetians called Negroponte, was to take decades. For the most part, however, Venice had to resort to feudal methods – ceding territory as fiefs to individual citizens, who were to conquer them at their own expense, exploiting them for the most part as they pleased, but hold them in the name of Venice.

Gallipoli, Corfu, Crete and Lemnos, Skyros and many other

Aegean islands were all colonized in this way, for there was no lack of Venetians ready to accept such challenges. Close contact with Crusaders from feudal Europe had fired many of Dandolo's men with enthusiasm to play the part of lords, and the man who, above all others, exemplified this new pride of lordship was the unscrupulous Marco Sanudo.

He ploughed his fortune into eight galleys and, gathering his friends together, set out to carve out a private empire for himself in the Cyclades, occupying Andros, Melos, Naxos and fourteen other islands great and small. The new Latin Emperor Henry confirmed him in possession of them and Sanudo abandoned his allegiance to the Doge. Other Venetians turned themselves into counts and marquesses; and henceforth the sons of Venice's leading families could choose another road to fortune – wooing, or even kidnapping, an heiress of the islands.

The division of the old Byzantine Empire was a free-for-all in which warriors of all allegiances and none laid hands on what they could. But although the pickings were rich, the risks were heavy. Opposition – from local Greeks, rival Latins and not least the Genoese – was always strong, and as a result many Venetians eventually sold their rights and returned to their former existence as plain merchants.

Venice itself fought desperately to keep an exclusive hold of the few territories it regarded as valuable – particularly out of rival hands – especially Crete, where the rival Genoese already had a colony. Venetians landed there in 1205 but the following year the Genoese Count of Malta, Enrico Pescatore, invaded, roused the local population and soon mastered the island, at which, in 1207, Venice sent in a larger force and drove him out.

The Venetian government installed its own governor, Jacopo Tiepolo, in Crete. But he only had sufficient resources to control the main town, Candia, the coastal strip around it, and another point or two. The rest was parcelled out into fiefs which were offered to Venetians, and also to Veronese gentry, prepared to go out and subdue them. Even so, independent war lords, notably Marco Sanudo, had to be called in to help suppress the Cretans – and he turned out to be so troublesome that it took the arrival of another Venetian army and a *douceur* of thirty knight's fees to get rid of him.

The government of Crete evolved into a curious blend of the imperial, the feudal and the democratic. The governor was elected by the Great Council in Venice, but he held the title Duke; the island divided into six *sestiere*, mirroring the division of Venice itself, and each of these districts had its own democratic council who owed allegiance to the mother city.

The indigenous population, however, had no say in the proceedings, and in 1217 they rebelled. Venice bought off the leaders with a few estates but the majority of Cretans remained resentful. They were unused to feudal lords and arrogant Venetian governors, and became so fiercely and persistently rebellious that Venetians eventually came to believe that Cretans were cursed with a double dose of original sin.

Yet while the Cretans got harsh treatment, elsewhere Venice took care not to alienate the local people. In 1207, for example, when the government portioned out Corfu between ten Venetian lords, who were to maintain its defences and pay an annual fee, it charged them not to tax the islanders more than the Byzantine authorities had done; and in 1209, when Ravano, Prince of Euboea, became a Venetian vassal, he was also made to promise not to treat his people worse than his Byzantine predecessors.

In all, there was no standard system, but a patchwork of contrasting systems – direct Venetian control, democratic assemblies of settlers, dependent feudal rule exercised by Venetians, local Greeks and even complete outsiders; independent government by individual Venetians, and Venetian quarters in cities belonging to quite different powers. There were colonial Venetian lords who had no greater voice than any other citizen when they returned to Venice, and 'white' Venetians – Greeks or Syrians who shared certain rights with true Venetians.

Virtually everywhere Venetians were unpopular, not least Tomasso Morosini, the new Patriarch of Byzantium. He went about clean-shaven – a thing unthinkable for a cleric of the Eastern Church – wore fashionable tight sleeves and leather gloves like a warrior rather than a man of God, and fed himself, so the

Greeks alleged, better than a fatted pig. Only gradually would Venice develop a more sympathetic attitude towards the Greek Church in its colonies.

Its concern to keep shipping routes open and to protect its trade, however, remained constant, though this proved to be no easier a task than it had ever been. The seas were full of pirates. No ship dared leave Venice without fighting men on board, and even armed ships were ill-advised to sail overseas alone. This being so, the government began to operate a regular convoy system, to station special squadrons to patrol the Adriatic and Black Seas, and order its governors and feudatories in Greece to look to the safety of Venetian shipping off their coasts.

Then, in the midst of this struggle to control the dangerously fluid situation overseas, on Christmas Day 1223, another great earthquake shook Venice itself. The Monastery of San Giorgio collapsed; two islands between Venice and Burano had to be evacuated, and Venetian morale was so badly shaken that a wholesale emigration to Constantinople was mooted. It took some time for the old confidence to return, and when it did so it was not reflected in great trust of Doges.

The Venetian head of state enjoyed resounding titles. He was not only Doge but Duke of Dalmatia, and now 'Despot of a quarter and a half of a quarter of the Roman Empire' too. His powers, however, were more limited than his titles suggest. In England the barons had forced King John to sign Magna Carta in 1215, and in contemporary Venice the lingering fear of a Doge trying to turn himself into a feudal monarch had been reinforced of late by the obvious taste for feudal lordship so many prominent Venetians had acquired from their experiences in the east, and so from 1229, when Jacopo Tiepolo was narrowly elected, 'correctors' were appointed to define the limits of the Doge's powers.

These limitations were set out in a *promissione*, or oath of office, and reinforced by a procedure whereby inquisitors would review a Doge's career at the end of his reign and take possession of his estate if he was found to have transgressed – a strong sanction for any loving head of family.

Doge Tiepolo's *promissione* bound him to administer justice fairly and to observe the laws himself, to promote the honour and prosperity of his people; to have no dealings with foreign princes without the consent of the Senate, nor grant any public property without the Council's consent. To ensure that he was not bribed, he was forbidden to accept any gifts except rosewater, flowers, fragrant herbs and balm, and this restriction was extended to his wife as well. The oath also incorporated policy directives, obliging the Doge to import a minimum quantity of corn each year, for example, and it defined his income too, Tiepolo's salary being made up in part of two-thirds of the tax on Lombardy apples, one fortieth of the import duty on crabs, and two thirds of the sum levied on cherries from Treviso. From now on the finances of the Doge's household and the state were kept distinct, and he was expected to pay his due of any forced loan like any other citizen.

Restrictions on the Doge's power increased over the years. When Tiepolo retired in 1249 the electors themselves – forty-one this time, to prevent the chance of an evenly split vote – had to promise to choose impartially, without heed to canvassers or bribes, and additional promises were extracted from the man they elected. He was to refuse all offices outside the city, obey the Great Council, and let no one pay him homage; nor was he allowed to engage in trade – all of which suggests that his predecessor may have done such things to the detriment of the community.

This practice of clipping the Doge's wings was accompanied by a growth in the importance of the Senate and the Council and also by a spate of legislation. In 1242 the law was codified in five great tomes. Their pages revealed the degree of complexity which Venetian life had reached, and also the priorities of Venetian society, no fewer than three of the five volumes and a good part of a fourth being devoted to property, commerce, dowries, contracts, wills, securities, mortages and other things involving wealth.

By 1255 the maritime code had been revised as well. Shipping laws forbidding overloading and the like had existed for a long time, but now they attained a new degree of fineness and exactitude. A ship of 240 tons, for instance, had to carry a crew of fifty men, all over eighteen years of age. Loading between decks was limited except for ships carrying wine and foodstuffs; ships bound for the Levant had to leave all space between decks clear for stores, arms and passengers; decks were not to be encumbered by bales of merchandise which might impede the handling of a ship in bad weather or in combat, and new ships were to be built to specific standards so that they would handle in the same way when in convoy.

Provisions for the training, pay and living conditions of the sailors were also laid down: seamen had to be Venetians or Greeks, they were to receive sufficient food and adequate quarters between decks, be allowed to carry a small quantity of goods free of duty as an extra inducement for them to serve, and be fairly paid – and by 1268, at least, they were getting a silver mark for every twenty-five days spent at sea.

The new host of officials who supervised load-lines and the like and fined offenders must have aroused resentment. Yet hardly a rumour has come down to us of any great outcry against all these regulations, despite the restrictions they placed on men of enterprise. But then the framers of these laws had commercial and shipping interests and they were united in their fear of dangers shared at sea.

Despite the unprecedented range of career opportunities now available for members of the leading families – as fief-holders overseas, as naval commanders, administrators, governors – commerce, shipping and lending capital remained their major preoccupations. From their wharves on the Golden Horn to their pony caravans which wound their way across the Alps with goods for northern Europe, merchants anticipated market trends in every sort of commodity and considered carefully the modes of carriage. Most merchandise was moved in small ships – none of them carrying more than 500 tons, and most of them much less. Yet these little ships were still the sinews of Venetian prosperity. They loaded any cargo – furs or hides, soap or spices, timber or fabric, fatstock for slaughter, or captives to sell into slavery; and pilgrims too, of course – Muslim or Christian – a Venetian carrier did not discriminate, provided passengers paid a silver mark apiece for a place abaft the mainmast.

Venice was well placed, of course, to catch this traffic. By going that way pilgrims could venerate the heads of Saints Abdon and Sennon now, the arm-bones of St. Sergius, and the feet of St. George, as well as see the Holy Land. But rival ports had rival saints, and the business was subject to some ruthless undercutting. By 1268 both Ravenna and Ancona had been forced out of the business. Marseilles tried to capture the market by reducing the first-class fare to sixty soldi and by charging as little as twenty-five for passengers prepared to sleep with horses.

Competition was particularly fierce for large contracts. In 1216, for instance, Venice had offered to carry King Andrew of Hungary and his troops to Palestine for the modest fee of 550 silver marks per ship, plus a renunciation of his claim to Zara and permission to trade free in Hungary. During the century the rate seems to have gone up. Charges quoted to take the army of Louis IX of France to north Africa amounted to 1,400 silver marks per ship – but then Louis went via Genoa instead. So, though contracts were occasionally lost, Venice generally seems to have held her own.

But Venetian men of substance, especially those too old to lead an active life as travelling merchants and shipmen, were branching out more and more into lending for a profit – financing entrepreneurs and keeping kings in funds. In the latter case, particularly, they were careful to take good security. When the Capellos made a loan to the Latin Emperor Baldwin II they took his son, Philip, his palace roofs and the Crown of Thorns as guarantees. But lending mostly involved smaller deals, often within the family circle. In 1213, for instance, a member of the prominent Gradenigo family guaranteed his widowed mother ten per cent for the use of her money, a modest rate when commercial investments commonly brought in returns of fifty per cent, though he later offered her seventy-five per cent of the profits that her money earned provided she took her share of the sea risks too.

In the 1230s a new flare-up between Emperor and Pope posed

a delicate problem for Venice. The Emperor, Frederick II, was master of Sicily and the most powerful ruler in the north; the Pope commanded central Italy. Venice wanted good relations with them both. But neutrality itself eventually became dangerous, and so the wise men of Venice made their calculations – and came out for the Pope.

As the Emperor's soldiers crossed the Alps all north Italy took to arms, and wooden forts rose up in the lagoon. Verona was attacked, Vicenza burned, a dangerous conflict raged round Este and through the Marche to the south. Venice herself escaped attack, but the war involved her nonetheless. The Emperor forbade the export of corn and cattle to her, and his Admiral, the Genoese renegade Nicolino Spinola, prevented Venetian ships from putting in at Tunis. Worse still, Ferrara, which was already attracting some business away from Venice through the Comacchio lagoon, was encouraged to set up as a serious competitor and drive away Venetian ships blockading the Po delta.

Venice hit back. After a thorough-going four months' seige, her troops captured Ferrara and imposed restrictive commercial terms upon the city. This success provided ample compensation for the considerable costs of the war. But no sooner did matters in the hinterland turn out well than trouble broke out overseas.

In 1242 Zara rebelled again. The town was reoccupied, but several rebel ships escaped to sea and began to plunder Venetian merchantmen in the upper Adriatic. At this, Venice confiscated the rebels' lands and sent reliable colonists out to take possession of them – but then trouble broke out with the Genoese.

Venice and Genoa had been allies with the Pope in the war against the Emperor; they had even flown each others' flags at sea. But their rivalry smouldered on and flared up at last in distant Palestine. A Venetian murdered a Genoese at Acre, whereupon his compatriots attacked the Venetian quarter of the city; six years afterwards a Venetian fleet burned Genoese ships in Acre harbour, and though there were instances of co-operation between individuals of the rival cities – during the 1250s a Venetian and a Genoese combined to monopolize alum production in Anatolia and raise its price – the enmity between these two leading Mediterranean powers increased steadily to culminate eventually in a struggle to the death.

At home, meanwhile, the government had become concerned about the quality of goods and the protection of her nascent industries. The introduction of the draw-loom and the spinning-wheel was encouraging the development of textile manufacture in Italy, and Venice set out to gain advantage from it. From 1244 she had begun to legislate accordingly. Cloth imported from the hinterland was taxed; the export of wool and other raw materials to areas with rival industries was banned, and, since craftsmen tended to move about from one city to another, from 1281 Venetian woollen workers were forbidden to emigrate to Padua or Treviso for fear that their expertise would make competition more intense.

The government also began to interfere in other fields besides industry and trade. After 1281, for example, the medical profession was closely supervised, surgeons being forbidden to practise until they had been sworn in before the justices. Fines were imposed on people riding horseback in the city centre, and in 1293 all games other than chess and backgammon were forbidden.

This indicates a concern for public order and morals, as well as prosperity and health, and it was enforced by an improved policing system. From 1262 the number of Signori di Notti, who were responsible for keeping order during hours of darkness – and who also judged murderers and thieves, extracting confessions with machines of torture in the upper story of the Doge's Palace – was increased from two to six. Parish elders were charged to assist them on demand, a militia of 500 reliable men was organized in each *sestiere* to deal with public riot and disorder, while the effectiveness of law-enforcement was strengthened by the practice of holding an entire family responsible for the misdeeds of an individual.

Martino da Canal writing in the late 1200s might have exaggerated when he boasted that no heretic, usurer, murderer or thief dare live in Venice – usury certainly continued despite state legislation dating from 1254 – but Venice does seem to have been more orderly than most other towns in Italy.

As for lighter sides to life, there were fêtes in the city and in the hinterland where Venetians could enjoy themselves. In 1214 they had flocked out to Treviso where a mock battle was fought between two armies of children, armed with scent and flowers, for possession of a 'Castle of Love' – though the occasion was marred when a fight broke out in earnest between adult Paduan and Venetian spectators. The arrival in Venice of Rainiero Zeno, the Doge-elect, in 1253 was celebrated more peacefully by a tournament in the Piazza, contested by knights from the hinterland and Venetians.

The idea of chivalry was catching on. Even common artisans would act out the parts of knights. When Doge Lorenzo Tiepolo made a second marriage and the tradesmen of Venice paraded through the streets to offer their congratulations, bearing the banners of their crafts and wearing all their finery, two barbers posed as knights errant. They rode on chargers and led four 'foreign' damsels whom they claimed to have won in war. Acting out their chosen parts they challenged any knight present to prove his valour by winning the damsels from them – at which the Doge replied gravely that no one at his Court would wish to contest the issue with them. And so the procession proceeded on its way.

Shows like this imitated the pomp and dignity of the official ceremonials which punctuated the yearly round, occasions which no one missed. 'As long as I have lived in beautiful Venice,' wrote Martino da Canal, 'I have watched the processions which my Lord the Doge makes upon high festivals.' On Easter Day, the Doge 'comes down from his palace preceded by eight men bearing . . . silken banners emblazoned with the insignia of St. Mark and surmounted by imperial eagles. Behind . . . come two boys who carry the Doge's fadstool and his cushion; then six trumpeters sounding silver trumpets, and two men with cymbals, also made of silver. A cleric comes next holding a great orb all beautiful with silver, gold and precious stones; another cleric carries the Gospels, and a third the silver censer, and all three are dressed in cloth of gold. There follow the twenty-two canons of St. Mark's in their robes, chanting, and behind them walks my Lord the Doge,' shaded by his cloth-of-gold umbrella.

'Next to the Doge's side is the *primiciero* of St. Mark's wearing a bishop's mitre, and at his other side the priest who will perform the Mass. . . . Hard by the Doge walks a gentleman who bears a sword of exquisite workmanship; then follow the gentlemen of Venice.

'In this order my Lord the Doge enters the Piazza of St. Mark . . . walks as far as the church of San Gimigniano and returns in the same order, bearing a white wax candle in his hands. They halt in the middle of the Piazza, and three of the ducal chaplains advance before the Doge and chant beautiful verses and responses to him. Then all enter the church of St. Mark.' At this three chaplains would move forward to the altar rails and proclaim in a loud voice: 'Let Christ be victorious, let Christ rule, let Christ reign; may our Lord Renier Zeno by the grace of God illustrious Doge of Venice, Dalmatia and Croatia, conqueror of a quarter and a half of a quarter of all the Roman Empire have salvation, honour, life and victory. Let Christ be victorious; let Christ rule; let Christ reign.'

Martino da Canal almost burst with patriotic pride, describing the ceremonial and its setting. For him the Piazza was 'the loveliest square in all the world,' St. Mark's 'the loveliest church in all the world,' and the Doge's Palace 'grand and marvellous,' even though its ground floor was still used as a stable, and elder bushes sprouted thickly where now the Merceria clock-tower stands.

But by this time, providing stark contrasts to all the brightness, pomp and beauty Martino delighted in, friars and the flagellants had begun to invade Venice. Followers of St. Francis had first arrived soon after the saint's death in 1226. They went begging from door to door in the service of the sick and poor and had soon raised enough to begin their austere but immense conventual church dedicated to Santa Maria Gloriosa and known as the Frari. But their works of charity were considerable too. They pioneered the idea of cheap credit for the poor and helped found the Tertiary order to provide for a secure if ascetic life of good works for spinsters lacking the necessary dowries to enter an ordinary nunnery. It was a friar, Lorenzo, who founded a hospital for women in 1272, and others of his order inspired laymen to charitable works as well. In 1262 Leone Paulino had established an isolation hospital for lepers on the island of San Lazzaro and, faced with such examples, Doges and Dogaressas dared not lag behind – when Doge Zeno's wife died, she left all her cash, dresses, furs, robes, beds, mattresses, quilts and featherbeds to provide comforts for the poor patients of the hospital of St. Mark's.

But if the barefoot friars went about their work of alleviating misery with an air of cheerfulness, the arrival of the flagellants cast a gloom over the city. They would parade through the narrow streets in heavy veils, shrieking and moaning, as they lashed each others' backs with whips and iron chains. The government disliked them and the mystic trend they represented. It eventually forbade members of the clergy from joining the governing bodies of these brotherhoods. But the movement grew nevertheless. Flagellation appealed especially to the poor, the maimed, to those who had no stake in government or trade, and to those miserable women who bore life's trials with utter meekness and found insufficient outlet even in church where they would weep and supplicate with outstretched arms, pleading histrionically, arguing their luck with God.

Some of the rich were attracted too, for membership of a 'fraternity of the discipline' and participation in the ritual whippings at set times of the day served as expiation of their own sins as well as those of the world, and offered the hope that their souls might pass swiftly through to Heaven when they died, while others languished long in Purgatory. But in social rather than personal terms these devotional brotherhoods of flagellants were significant in that they gave rise to an important new social institution, the Scuola.

The Scuola of San Giovanni Evangelista founded in March 1261, the Scuola di Santa Maria della Carità which preceded it, and the Valverde della Misericordia and Scuola di San Marco which followed, all seem to have originated in this way, as more and less well-to-do brotherhoods devoted to the cult of the Virgin Mary, to penance and good deeds. But by 1300 their original functions had begun subtly to change. Members still vowed to hear Mass every day, dress plainly, fast frequently, abjure public amusements, fighting, swearing, gambling and the like; not to marry, and if married already to forswear sexual relations. But less emphasis was placed on public displays of self-chastisement and more on charity – especially alms to needy members of the brotherhoods themselves.

Other groups also engaged in mutual social insurance. Sailors on board Venetian ships, for example, would 'invite St. Phocas to dinner' every night, setting aside the value of his food for distribution among old and disabled seamen at the voyage's end. But the *arti,* or trade associations, which were developing at this time were more important in this regard. Members of a given *arte*, each of which was centred on a particular church or monastery with a shrine dedicated to the patron saint of their trade, would help out their own poor and sick on a co-operative basis, and have Masses said for their own dead, meeting the costs out of subscription income and from such devices as selling off the leavings of their communal feasts.

Their functions ranged far wider, too, for each *arte* set standards for its craft, both in the behaviour of their members, and the quality of the products they produced, and since the state stepped in to supervise them, they frequently came to operate as governmental agents in regulating anything from the payment of apprentices and working conditions to professional qualifications and the settlement of disputes.

This was particularly important in the vital shipbuilding industry. Carpenters, caulkers and sawyers – each group had its own *arte* and its own *gastaldo*, 'deacons' and 'judges' to represent the membership in any corporate dispute, collect membership dues and enforce the association's state-approved statutes, which not only defined their entitlement to employment at the Arsenal but obliged them to work on the Doge's barge for nothing. But in time the state was to regulate other trades as well – not only the surgeons but the physicians, who took care to maintain professional standards, refusing to bleed patients except when bleeding would be good for them, that is when the moon was in its second quarter; the glass-makers, whose by-laws were laid down in 1271;

and the painters, whose regulations of the same year show them to have produced dining-tables, chests and altar pieces as well as wall paintings, banners, and figures of saints sketched on bits of parchment which were hawked round to pilgrims and to members of particular groups on the feast days of their patron saints.

But while social organization in Venice was becoming more complex and sophisticated, the vista of an extensive empire overseas which had opened up so dramatically at the beginning of the century was fading fast. In 1261 the Greeks under Michael Paleologus recaptured Constantinople from the Latins, and the Emperor Baldwin, the Patriarch and the Venetian *podesta* escaped hurriedly by sea.

The Genoese who had helped Paleologus now superseded Venice as the most favoured nation at this still vital trading centre. But though many Venetians there were ruined, a foothold was retained; and though Venice's trading position in Egypt was carefully consolidated, Constantinople remained central for Venetian merchants, bankers and shippers operating in the east.

It could have turned out much worse. Moreover, Methone, Korone, Negroponte and most of the Aegean islands were still Venetian and so was Crete. Crete was by now an important source of agricultural produce as well as a strategic staging point to Egypt, Syria and Palestine. As Doge Zeno remarked, 'the whole strength of the Empire lies in Crete.' But if Crete was still Venice's key holding it was extremely difficult, subject as it was to Greek attack and to internal revolt. In 1268 Venetian settlers there tried to cut their ties with the mother city, making a unilateral declaration of independence. They were crushed by the Venetian authorities with the help of an influential Cretan Alexios Kallerges, but in 1283 Kallerges himself rebelled. Sixteen chaotic years were to pass before order was restored, and then only at the cost of mounting expensive expeditions and conceding Venetian citizenship and knightly status to Kallerges. In the interim, one Venetian governor was lured into the mountains and done to death; another was besieged in Candia, the capital, and the Genoese seized the chance to burn Canea in western Crete.

Venice and Genoa were almost constantly at war in the last four decades of the century. They fought in the Black Sea, in the Adriatic, off the coasts of Sicily and Greece, in almost every patch of ocean crossed by the trading convoys of either city. Such sea fights spurred the pen of Martino da Canal, whose descriptions of them were predictably heroic. He describes Giberto Dandolo with thirty-one galleys suddenly confronted with a Genoese force of almost fifty ships in eastern waters shortly after they had routed the Venetians at Constantinople. Faced with these odds, Dandolo 'did not quail at all,' Martino assures us, but 'like a lion, proud and confident, he cleared his decks for action.' His men, too, were soon 'on flame, full of great prowess and daring' and, crying 'God be with us, and St. Mark of Venice,' they attacked. The enemy was routed, 'and so the Venetians . . . avenged the ruin of their compatriots in Constantinople.'

But Venetians did not always win the day; indeed the rival fleets of galleys often failed to find each other in the wide seas. Venetian warships scoured every likely hide-away and harbour where Genoese might lie in wait; yet whenever a convoy ventured into apparently quiet waters without an escort the enemy always seemed to pounce. At last, early in the 1270s, a truce was arranged. It was to last only for five years, but Venice was thankful for the respite.

The effort against Genoa had involved a huge expense on armaments. The outgoings proved so heavy that as early as 1262 the government was unable to repay the temporary forced loans still outstanding and had to convert them into a permanent national debt – the 'Monte Vecchio' as it came to be called – yielding a modest interest of five per cent. From this point on the debt grew steadily, new levies always seeming to exceed repayments. But indirect taxation provided the bulk of state income, and this was raised to dangerous heights to finance the war with Genoa. When the tax on grinding corn was doubled there was a riot. Doge Rainier Zeno appeared to treat it gently, then, when tempers had cooled, arrested the ringleaders and had them executed. Even so the tax had to be reduced for fear of further disturbances, whereupon the main burden fell on the colonies and trade.

Venetian commerce seemed well able to bear the strain. As Martino da Canal remarked, 'merchandise rushes through this noble city like water gushing from a spring.' Corn poured in from Apulia and Crete, vermilion-dyed clothes from distant Ypres, and the bulk of oriental luxuries bound for western Europe still came through Venice. True, when heavier dues were placed on imported goods bound for the hinterland ships tended to unload at other Adriatic ports, and in the 1270s Venice tried to stop this by force of arms, going to war with Bologna and Ancona. She failed, but her foreign trade continued to expand to such a degree that, increasingly, Venetian merchants had to combine together in order to satisfy their customers.

Such private arrangements were made compulsory in 1283 when the government actually required cartels to be formed to buy pepper at Alexandria and cotton at Acre. In order to prevent any Venetian wildcat outbidding his colleagues for scarce goods, deals were to be struck whenever two-thirds of the merchants thought the moment right; and in order to give the smaller man a chance against the 'heavies,' anyone with a hundred ducats to invest was legally entitled to a share of the market. These consortia with which Venetians fronted foreign competitors were a new expression of the co-operative spirit, though the same monopolistic tendencies were stepped on heavily at home, as when a butchers' cartel was smashed in 1297 for fear the public might be roused to fury at the cost of meat.

Thanks partly to restriction on land purchases and the usury laws which barred lending at a decent profit, most ready cash in Venice still went into trade and often in a co-operative form, through *colleganza* deals. Old men and widows gained an income in this way; so did religious institutions; but the bulk of such investment came from the really big men – people like Doge Raniero Zeno himself, who died in 1268 leaving 132 *colleganza* contracts worth 22,935 lire still outstanding, sixty per cent of his entire estate.

When Zeno died the office of Doge was so strongly contested that in order to prevent open conflict within the inner power group it was agreed to inject a much larger element of chance into the electoral process. The thirty initial electors were chosen by ballots drawn by a boy picked at random from the congregation at St. Mark's; there followed a complex ritual, punctuated by the ringing of bells, whereby the initial thirty spawned a succession of electoral groups, either by lot or by election, until a final group of forty-one emerged who actually chose the Doge.

The Doge-elect, Lorenzo Tiepolo, was taken to the Palace and thence to St. Mark's to be shown to the crowd. This was a purely formal presentation, calculated to ensure his confirmation. It was the last vestige of what once had been a truly democratic process. The small group who provided the electors and from whose ranks the Doge was always chosen were coming to believe that Venice belonged to them, that ordinary folk, many of whom were certainly immigrants or recently descended from immigrants, were outsiders – useful, necessary even, but with no fundamental stake in Venetian society.

Members of the oligarchy still rubbed shoulders with ordinary people in the streets, but the differences between rich and poor, literate and illiterate, between people with famous names like Zeno, Morosini, Contarini, Tiepolo, and people without them, were gaining more and more significance. A myth was developing that only the ruling few were fit to govern; and the hideously complex electoral system, which must have seemed impenetrably mysterious to most Venetians, gave some credence to the myth.

Nevertheless, although the new system kept the electoral process in the hands of the few (and even made it possible for a Doge to be elected with minority support among the ruling group), by giving formal recognition of that prime factor in the affairs of man – sheer luck – it served to avoid the factionalism prevalent in so many other Italian cities riven by dissent. Well might Martino da Canal beg 'Sir God . . . and His Lady Mother,' to 'pardon us and maintain Venice without any discord.' The blend of oligarchy and chance was to prove a partial answer to his prayer.

Chapter V

Marco Polo's Venice

Marco Polo was born about 1254 at a time when even leading Venetians still tended to devote most of their energies to trade. His father Nicoló was a specialist in precious stones and in commerce with the Orient, though his influence on the child was small, for in 1260 he and his brother Matteo set out on a business venture which was to keep them abroad for almost a decade.

The Polos took ship to Soldaia in the Crimea where a relative, Andrea, had set up as a trading agent; but once there they realized that the Greek advance towards Constantinople might prevent their returning through the Dardanelles and so, being men of 'remarkable wisdom and foresight,' as Marco later described them, they invested in jewels and set out to do business with the Khan of the Bulgars at Sarai on the Volga. From there they proceeded to Bukhara in Central Asia, and three years later arrived in China at the court of Kubla Khan. Only then did they begin their circuitous way home.

Venetians had traded in Kiev as early as 1247; a friar had already reached Mongolia, and in 1253 two other friars had visited the Great Khan Baty's court at Karakorum on a mission from the Pope. But the Polo brothers had ventured farther than any other known westerner. Theirs was a long and perilous journey – but at last they heard the familiar sound of bells, and seeing the banners floating over the walls of Acre realized that they were in Christian territory once more.

Nicoló Polo returned home to find that his wife had died, so

when, two years later, he and Matteo set out for China once
again they took young Marco with them. Marco was barely
seventeen at the time and probably illiterate – though he could
doubtless add, calculate rates of interest, handle a bow and arrow,
and understand the merchant venturer's style of talk. With this
equipment he set out for China – a journey to excel all journeys
even in an age of intrepid travellers.

At every stage along the way young Marco took extensive
mental notes, with a view to telling all the wonders he had seen
on his return, for tales of travel were a major entertainment of the
age and provided a vital source of commercial information too.
He set out to describe the 'peoples, animals and birds' he came
across, where 'gold, and silver, precious stones and pearls' were
to be found, the nature of the merchandise and all the other things
he saw – always more about goods and prices than other objects
of experience, but then young Marco was Venetian.

They went first to Acre and Jerusalem, and from there to Ajas
in Lesser Armenia, a busy place, as Marco observed, 'for you must
know that all the spices and cloths from the interior are brought
to this town and all other merchandise of great value; and
merchants of Venice and Genoa and everywhere else come here
to buy them.' But after Ajas the Polos vanished into limbo.
Years passed by with no word of them, and at last their associates
in Venice must have given them up for dead.

During their absence, in 1284, the first gold ducats were minted
in Venice, the port of Pisa, once a powerful rival, was ruined by
the Genoese, and the lagoon itself was shaken by another destructive earthquake which caused so much distress that the government had to sell grain off at a loss to help relieve the victims. But
the city soon returned to normal, and while the forgotten Polos
continued their venture into the unknown, their fellow-Venetians
continued to amuse themselves as well as work.

Dice, knuckle-bone, hazard and various other betting games
were highly popular, though gaming was not allowed in the
portico of St. Mark's or around the Doge's Palace, and professional gambling forbidden altogether. The twelve pigs were beheaded annually in the Piazza amid great rejoicing, there was bull-

baiting, street fights between the young bloods of one parish and
the next, while young hooligans among the rich amused themselves by chasing mastiffs through the streets and scattering the
people. More wholesome were the mummers who appeared in
masks at wedding feasts to act out scenes designed to remind the
newly-weds of the prowess of their ancestors; there were hot
baths available for those with a taste for oriental relaxation, and
for the more prominent citizens, of course, there was the ever-
fascinating game of politics.

Who should sit on the Great Council was the great issue of the
moment, and the view that membership should be hereditary was
gaining ground. A proposal to this effect was put forward in 1286
and defeated, but in 1289 Doge Giovanni Dandolo, who had led
the opposition to it, died and the election of Pietro Gradenigo
indicated that the change would come about.

'Pierazzo' Gradenigo was thirty-eight and extremely unpopular,
as ruthless men of commerce usually are. The announcement of
his election was met with stony silence by the mob. They wanted
Jacopo Tiepolo, the grandson of a Doge; they had shouted for
Jacopo at Dandolo's funeral; but it was Gradenigo who took up
the reins of power, and Tiepolo ultimately retired to his estate in
the hinterland to nurse his injured pride, and in time to plot
rebellion. For the moment, however, rivalries in Venice were
overshadowed by troubles overseas.

Crete was in revolt still, there was constant feuding with the
Genoese, despite repeated truces, and in 1291 the Saracens took
Acre, the last Christian outpost in the Holy Land. At once the
trading routes were thrown into confusion. The Knights Templar
and Hospitaller, ousted from Acre along with the Venetian colonists, retired to Cyprus and used their galleys to stop Christians
trading with the Saracens; Venetian relations with Egypt were in
any case bad after the recent fighting and the caravan routes
through Syria were disrupted. Venice's commercial channels in
the east were now virtually restricted to Ajas in Lower Armenia
and, what was worse, the Genoese dominated the Egyptian and
the Black Sea trading centres. Desperate to enlarge her dwindling
hold in the markets of the Orient, Venice, allied to the Pisans,

decided to grab the ports of Galata and Keffa from the rival Genoese. The truce was over. Both sides mustered their strength for battle.

In the summer of 1294 the parish chiefs of Venice drew up lists of all male residents between the ages of seventeen and sixty and an inventory of all their arms. Venetians needed for the coming fight were enlisted in the traditional groups of twelve; seamen were issued with helmets which were reckoned safer than the chainmail hoods they used to wear; the call went out to the richest families to prepare and man up to three galleys apiece, according to their wealth; and the fleets sailed out to fight another bitter war.

It was at this critical juncture that the Polos arrived back in Venice after an absence of a quarter of a century. According to legend they looked so much like Tatars with their drooping mustachios and were so badly dressed that no one recognized them. But then at a banquet they suddenly ripped open the seams of their clothes and a shower of jewels spilled out onto the table. From that time on Venetians dubbed Marco Ser Marco *Il Milione*, Sir Marcus the Millionaire – a patronizing title, for in fact he proved to be by no means wealthy although he had enough to live on comfortably.

From Marco's story it appeared that they had trekked through Armenia and Georgia to Tabriz; from there across Persia, through Turkestan and on via Kangchow, Liongchow, eventually to reach Peking – an adventurous journey that had taken up to four years to accomplish. At Peking Marco had been presented to the Great Khan himself, who took him into the imperial service. In the years that followed Marco's duties had taken him right through China, and as far afield as Indonesia, Malaya, India – the lands where the camphor, the aloes, the brazil wood and the pepper which Venetians dealt in came from, but which no known Venetian had ever seen before. The Polos had eventually left China bearing the Khan's safe-conducts and the Princess Cocachin whom they were to deliver as a bride to the Khan of the Levant.

This time, they travelled by sea, visiting Singapore, the Ceylon straits and western India, seeing many wonderful sights and undergoing many dangers. But having delivered the Princess they at last reached Trebizond, their first contact with the Christian world (where they were robbed), and finally the city of their birth.

Most Venetians, even if they believed Marco's stories, were probably bored by his telling of them. The fabled Kubla Khan was presented mundanely as a man 'of good stature, that is to say well proportioned, neither short nor tall, but of medium height'; and Marco's interminable down-to-earth descriptions of places and products seemed at once far-fetched and dull when set beside those exciting and convincing accounts of astrology, geomancy, necromancy and other sciences, the tales of wondrous Prester John and of the Old Man of the Mountains which were current at the time.

Some while after his return, Marco Polo married. His bride was Donata Loredano Badoer, a predictably practical choice – for she was a lady of excellent family who proved extremely money-minded, which was perhaps understandable since she was to bear Marco several daughters who would all need dowries. But with the war with Genoa still raging Marco's domestic interlude was brief and he soon left Venice to help his city in the fight at sea.

The fortunes of war had swung furiously from one side to the other. The Venetians attacked the Genoese in Cyprus, destroying their tower at Limassol and razing their quarters at Larnica and Famagusta; the Genoese sank Venetian ships in harbour at Methone and then, at Ajas, disposed of twenty-five Venetian galleys at one blow. This encouraged the Greek Emperor Andronicus, who had long favoured the Genoese, to seize the Venetian *bailo* at Constantinople, sack the Venetian quarter and hand its inhabitants over to the Genoese who butchered many of them. In retaliation Rogiero Morosini led a fleet up the Bosphorus, setting fire to every Genoese vessel and Greek ship he met, includ-cluding ships at anchor in the Golden Horn below the very palace of the Emperor. This bloody raid forced the Greeks to come to terms, and Morosini returned home taking care to deal with the Genoese alum works near Smyrna on the way.

Venetian tradesmen. Carvings from façade of St. Mark's

Two flagellants. Italian School, 15th century

Tomb of Doge Tommaso Mocenigo

In Venice people were sunk in gloom one moment and crowing at news of victory the next. Venetians succeeded in taking the Crimean port of Keffa from the Genoese and held their own in the fighting off the coasts of Sicily and Cyprus. But in 1298, near Curzola off the Dalmatian coast, they were routed in the greatest battle of the war so far and lost at least sixty-five out of some ninety galleys. Their commander, Andrea Dandolo, humiliated at being taken prisoner, dived to his death from the mast-head of a Genoese ship.

Marco Polo was also taken prisoner, though whether in the battle of Curzola or in the earlier defeat at Ajas remains a matter of some doubt. At any rate he survived and committed his story to posterity by dictating it to a fellow-prisoner, Rustichello of Pisa, in his Genoese dungeon.

While Marco sat captive in his prison a Genoese squadron penetrated the lagoon, and a Venetian force created havoc in Genoese home waters. Another great armada of a hundred ships was fitted out and a force of crossbowmen hired from Catalonia. They were not to be needed, however. A treaty negotiated with Sultan Nasser Muhammed gave Venice exclusive trading privileges in Egypt which made her far less concerned about Genoa's grip on the Black Sea routes. In return for selling timber, arms and slaves to Egypt (which the Pope had forbidden Christian powers to do) Venetians were allowed to buy all the oriental goods they needed there and export them free of tax. The Sultan had also granted them safe conduct in the Holy Land, allowing them to resume the pilgrim shipping business too. There was no point now in persevering in such a costly war and so in May 1299 a truce was mediated with Genoa. Keffa was surrendered and prisoners were repatriated – among them Marco Polo.

In his absence early in 1297 Doge 'Pieruzzo' Gradenigo and his friends had at last succeeded in establishing heredity as the sole qualification for membership of the Great Council. The inner group of forty was to confirm each Venetian's right to membership, ensuring that only men who had sat on the Great Council during the last four years or who at least could prove that a paternal ancestor had sat on it at some time since 1176 should be

D

admitted. The immediate effect was an increase in membership from less than 400 in 1295 to over 1,000 by 1311. But from that time on most Venetians were rendered permanently ineligible to take any part in government. The process was furthered by the institution in 1315 of a Golden Book of the Nobility in which members' names were registered and by purges of members thought to be of doubtful ancestry carried out in 1316 and 1319. By 1323 membership became completely hereditary. Political power had become the monopoly of a self-perpetuating caste.

This closure of the Great Council to outsiders was to be justified in the sixteenth century by Donato Gianotti as a means of vesting power in 'the flower of the city . . . lest the race of the Venetians should be mixed up with alien races and its nobility contaminated.' Yet the Venetians had never known 'racial purity'. Nor had they ever had a 'nobility' which was definable in any but the vaguest terms, usually of commercial standing. But they had one now.

The new system was only the culmination of a very gradual process by which power had become concentrated in the hands of the wealthy – that class of people whose houses were like town fortresses to keep out thieves and street mobs. It also broadened the power-base of that class by including many new rich as well as the old rich families; and it may have promoted a rather greater diffusion of power among the leading group as well. But henceforth ordinary citizens who became wealthy were to find it virtually impossible to attain political or social standing, which were the exclusive preserves of the Council members, while the labouring class were left with no say in the conduct of affairs at all.

There had been violent opposition to the move. In 1300 a rich Venetian, Marino Bocconio, who had himself been denied membership of the Great Council, raised a revolt – but the government was no less violent in its response. When Bocconio and his followers stormed up to the door of the Council chamber clamouring for admission, so the legend goes, they were let in one by one and promptly done to death inside. Certainly several corpses were soon on display hanging head down between the columns in the Piazzetta, and the end of the episode was such that, as the chronicler

Sanudo wrote afterwards, 'no one dared open his mouth again in such a fashion' – at least for a time.

On a lighter note, in 1299 a law was passed to limit luxury and ostentation at weddings and in women's dress. Wedding presents other than goblets for the bride, the groom and the officiant were forbidden, and no more than forty adults were allowed to attend a wedding feast. No woman, other than a bride, was to wear pearls in her hair nor ornaments about her head or neck, nor have more than four dresses and two fur cloaks, while the trains of women's dresses and their under-garments were restricted to a given size, only the Doge's relatives being exempted from the rule.

This law, however, was neither universally popular nor universally observed, and in 1306 most of it was repealed. Nevertheless the attempt reflected a serious and continuing concern. Perhaps it was feared that too much expenditure on luxury might waste merchant capital and impoverish the city; perhaps it was aimed at reducing the more obvious differences between rich and poor, so as to reduce social tensions in the city; perhaps it reflected a current feeling that females had a particularly unhealthy proclivity to conspicuous consumption, a view which was certainly widespread at the time.

In the words of Fra Paolino, writing in 1304, a wife 'interferes with the study of wisdom. . . . While the husband takes pains to provide her with everything in fashion, such as expensive clothes, gold and jewels, servants and household goods, she is forever complaining saying "That woman is better dressed than I am; that one gets more attention than I do, while everyone looks down on me, poor wretch – So what have you brought me from the Rialto?".' A husband, thought Paolino, ought to dress his wife as he thought fit, and extravagance should be banned by law.

This passion for ostentation reflected a growth in wealth which was to increase to unprecedented heights over the following half century. As the wills of the period show, Venetians invested fortunes in property – houses in the city, vineyards, salt pans, and estates in the hinterland. Venetian artisans were also thriving. The city's goldsmiths were becoming world renowned, and Venetian earthenware and glass products – from fine stained glass to ordinary tableware, each piece incorporating a distinctive blue band according to government decree – were much sought after. But commerce was still the mainstay of Venetian economic growth.

Venetian merchants were remarkably well-travelled. Marino Sanudo, known as 'Torsello,' spent many years in Greece, voyaged to Cyprus, Armenia, Alexandria and Rhodes, frequented Acre and Alexandria, and later visited Bruges and Avignon, settling down in Venice only as an old man. Tramp shippers also ranged far afield. In June 1312 Giovanni Placoni sailed from Venice with a cargo of stores for the Venetian commandant at Zara. From there he carried timber to Sicily, where he loaded grain for the Balearics, and from the Balearics he proceeded to Sardinia where he loaded salt for the voyage home. Men like Placoni and 'Torsello' were comparatively small-time operators, but they and men like them were linch-pins of the Venetian economy.

Another basis of the economy was shipbuilding, an industry of which the state-run Arsenal, celebrated by Dante in Chapter XXI of *Hell*, was by far the biggest sector. In 1303 the place was extended and the Tana rope factory was founded on an adjacent site – a long narrow building, constructed to ensure that ships' ropes would be of the highest quality and that Venetians should be provided with bow-strings which would not snap in battle. And in 1325 the Arsenal itself was enlarged again to four times its former size. This vast enterprise soon teemed with workers – with caulkers, who boiled glutinous pitch and smeared it over ropes and timbers, with carpenters, oarmakers and sailmakers, who spent their days hammering, shaping, stitching, plugging. The workers were fed on the premises and their operations were supervised by three *padroni* who lived nearby in houses nicknamed according to their amenities: 'Paradise,' 'Purgatory' and 'Hell.'

Large-scale private yards were active too, most of them owned by merchants, though a few craftsmen also seem to have been developing into capitalists in this field. Ever more ships were being built – galleons, brigantines and frigates; twelve-oared gondolas with iron beaks, great round sailing ships used by shippers of bulky cargoes like Placoni, but most significantly the

great galleys – those large, long, narrow ships, which were increasingly used for the great state-organized trading convoys.

Such convoys ran regularly to Syria and Egypt, despite the
fulminations of the Pope, and from 1319 to northern Europe too.
For the first voyage north, state-owned galleys were offered free
to private operators as an inducement for them to carry spices,
silks and Cretan wine to Flanders and bring back cargoes of
French cloth. But the voyage proved so profitable that no subsidy
was subsequently required. The galleys soon added Southampton
to their ports of call, though relations with the English did not get
off to a good start for a fight broke out between the townsmen
and the crews after which the English ports were avoided for a
time. Nevertheless fortunes were made out of the run, not least
by Dardi Bembo, who brought large quantities of sugar to
London, loaded wool at Boston in Lincolnshire, took it to
Flanders, which was the chief centre of the weaving industry, and
sold it there for finished cloths which he subsequently exported
to the Levant.

With the help of its diplomatists Venice soon had excellent
trade relations with Brabant and Limburg, the Duke of Lorraine,
the Count of Flanders and the echevins of Bruges. The echevins of
Antwerp were soon begging the Doge to allow Venetians to
frequent their city too, so important were Venetian commercial
services to an aspiring northern city. Neither Genoese pirates, nor
the imprecations of the Pope, who excommunicated Doge
Gradenigo and the city for disobedience in 1309, could stem the
gushing flow of commerce for long, and pilgrims still assembled
in Venice every spring waiting for the galleys to put to sea on
Corpus Christi Day.

As to the men who strained at the galley oars and lashed the
flapping sails in time of storm, we know that they were a hetero-
geneous crowd, deriving from Zara and Istria as well as Venice,
and from the shipping project worked out by 'Torsello' in about
1320 the American scholar Frederick Lane has calculated an ap-
proximation of their living standards. An oarsman, he reckons,
received just over eleven pounds of biscuit a week, twelve ounces
of salt pork (half of it used in a bean broth and most of the rest

served up on Sundays), one and a half pounds of beans, nine ounces of cheese, and a gallon of wine. These rations provided an average of 4,000 calories a day at a cost of almost thirteen *piccoli*, a ducat being equivalent to about 750 *piccoli*. The men also received pay of at least forty-two *piccoli* a day, while bowmen earned sixty-four, leading oarsmen who set the stroke got eighty-three, and a galley master almost 200. Even an ordinary seaman, then, earned enough to supplement his diet with purchases of fresh food on touching port – a frequent occurrence on a normal Mediterranean run and on a pilgrim voyage almost a nightly one.

In addition to their pay and rations seamen were entitled to a share of any booty and a small amount of duty-free freight, so that, all in all, an ordinary seaman could maintain a wife and even a family – but only so long as he was regularly employed and, bearing in mind that his working life with all the heavy labour it entailed was likely to be short, a man was probably as well off as an unskilled labourer at home in Venice where he could earn anything from forty-eight to sixty *piccoli* for a day's work.

A skilled craftsman, of course, was much better off. A master stonemason earned twice as much as a common labourer, and an artist might demand up to ten times as much, for artists were esteemed in Venice as were skilled foreign artisans, especially if their skills were rare or novel. After 1310 thirty-two silk manufacturers driven out of Lucca were welcomed to Venice because of the know-how they brought with them. They were soon employing 300 workers, thus justifying their welcome. By then German mirror-makers were established on Murano, and references are found to many other foreigners as well – Filippo, a glover from Pisa, Giovanni, a jerkin-maker from Verona, Messer Roberto, a physician from Bologna, Frederigo of Passau, a cutler, two other Germans, Philip and Conrad, who were dyers, and Messer Rabacino, the reader in grammar from Florence. Such immigrants could claim citizenship after as little as two years, if they brought their families and paid their taxes, otherwise this might take twenty-five.

Citizenship was defined by the state, whose involvement now extended from collecting taxes and customs dues, maintaining a permanent war fleet and running the Arsenal to the enforcement of a whole host of regulations about ship-ratings and components, load-lines, convoys, and ships' armaments – rules which required the services of a host of bureaucrats and petty functionaries to enforce. New regulations were regularly added. In 1303 the Senate had ordered each galley to carry thirty bowmen, who should also be able to row, though on the inside posts so as to be able to get into action quickly. And to ensure that enough good bowmen should be available butts were erected and citizens organized in groups of twelve for compulsory practice exercises. These exercises were given a festive atmosphere, however. Competitions took place on the lido on the first Sunday in March, on May 3rd and at Christmas, and the government furnished prizes for them – a length of scarlet cloth for the best shot; a smaller piece and a crossbow and quiver for the runners-up. But encouraging a people to bear arms brought dangers along with benefits, and in 1310 the government was faced with a rebellion far more serious than Bocconio's ten years before.

All sorts of issues were involved in the affair – a schism within the nobility itself and in particular the hatred of the Tiepolos and their friends for Doge Gradenigo and his supporters; resentment about the new arrangements for membership of the Great Council; and, not least, Venice's excommunication by the Pope.

The excommunication had followed Venice's occupation of Ferrara, and resistance to papal troops who intervened against them. As a result, in 1309, Venetians were denied the sacraments and even Christian burial, the clergy being ordered to leave the city, while abroad the Pope offered indulgences to anyone attacking Venetians or their property. In consequence Venetians were robbed as far away as England, France and the Levant as well as throughout Italy. The despair of the religious, the anger of men who suffered financial loss and injury, combined with the resentment of the disenfranchised, led to serious political instability and to the rise of an opposition movement which eventually solidified under the leadership of the related Tiepolo and Querini clans.

The first symptom of trouble was a marked increase in the number of violent brawls in the city. Realizing that matters were getting out of hand, the Doge forbade men going armed about the streets with their retainers. But one evening, when Marco Morosini, a 'Lord of the Night,' stopped Pietro Querini to search him for arms, Pietro promptly knocked him down. As the mood of the city became increasingly tense the Doge began to curry popularity by instituting an annual banquet for the poor and ploughing huge sums into civic ceremonials to compensate the people for their loss of the Church's rites – and Marco Querini and his kinsman Baiamonte Tiepolo plotted to take over power.

Tiepolo was the grandson of a Doge, rich and popular, very well connected with members of the older leading families, including some who had been excluded from the Great Council, and he had the support of many of the poorer gentry too. Condemned for peculation in 1300, he had nevertheless been elected to judicial office in 1302, but had then left Venice for his villa near Mestre in a huff at being passed over for the post of Ducal Counsellor in favour of a Dalmatian, Count Doimo of Veglia. Baiamonte Tiepolo was popular, capable, and an experienced warrior – a very real danger, in fact.

The conspirators planned to assemble with their men at Marco Querini's house on the night of Saturday 13th June 1310 and to set out at dawn on the Sunday in two groups, led respectively by Marco and by Baiamonte, which were to converge on the Piazza from separate points. And just to ensure that enough men would be available to overthrow Gradenigo's government Badoer was to bring in a third force raised in Padua.

Saturday came and the activity at Querini's house was noticed. Investigators sent by the authorities were stopped by men with drawn swords at every approach from the Rialto bridge, and then one of the conpirators, Donato, turned informer. This gave the Doge time to prepare. Promptly he ordered the men of Chioggia and the islands to deal with Badoer, ordered the Signore di Notte to call out all armed men considered loyal to his régime, mustered all his allies and their retainers – and waited.

The fateful Sunday dawned. A storm had blown up which delayed Badoer's arrival, but the other rebels set out according to plan. Tiepolo was delayed when a rabble of poor Venetian followers induced him to pause along the way while they sacked the magistrate's offices and the corn exchange, and he stopped again across the Rialto to regroup his following. As a result the operation got out of phase.

Badoer ran aground in the lagoon and was captured by the *podesta* of Chioggia; Querini's men burst into the Piazza long before Tiepolo arrived and were overwhelmed by the Doge's supporters, Marco Querini and his son being among those killed. Then Tiepolo's men were forced to turn tail. They fled up the Merceria and, turning left, tried to rally in the Campo San Luca but were driven back across the Rialto bridge. The remnants eventually barricaded themselves in Querini's house.

In order to avoid more bloodshed, the Doge offered terms: Tiepolo and his chief lieutenants must leave Venice never to return; the small fry would be pardoned. Tiepolo accepted; but he did not give up the struggle, continuing to plot from exile in Padua and Treviso. But the government now looked very carefully to its safety. In July 1310 a new body, formed by a typically complex electoral system, was given responsibility for state security and for keeping track of Tiepolo in particular. This temporary body was to become a permanent committee of public safety and it worked in absolute secrecy. This was the Venetian equivalent of the KGB; it was known as the Council of Ten. The agents of the Ten shadowed Tiepolo for some twenty years, just as Stalin's agents were to hound Trotsky. But Tiepolo kept on running and eventually died before they reached him.

Meanwhile fifteen more families had been admitted to the Great Council as rewards for their loyalty during the rebellion, but when Doge Gradenigo died in 1311 the city still lay under interdict. Not until 1313, after papal troops had stormed the castle of Ferrara and massacred every Venetian defender they could find, did Venice make its peace with the papacy – and at a cost of 100,000 ducats. The new Doge, Giovanni Soranzo, also suppressed another rebellion at Zara, but a domestic problem proved more intractable. When Soranzo's daughter, wife of the exiled Nicolò Querini, returned to Venice after her father's election in 1314 the Council of Ten ordered her to be kept under house arrest in a remote suburb, and even after her husband died her régime was only slightly relaxed. Not even a Doge, it seems, could countermand the Ten.

With a rash of dictators appearing elsewhere in Italy – military men who gained power on a swell of populism and then kept power in their families – men like Visconti of Milan, della Scala of Verona and da Carrara of Padua – Venice was going her own way, free of autocracy and feudalism. The Doge's powers were severely circumscribed, even though as an experienced political manipulator he carried more weight than any other man, and power was diffused – between the Senate, which regulated foreign affairs, the *Savii*, who prepared detailed public business, the sinister Council of Ten, and a plethora of committees all stemming from the electoral Great Council.

The middle and the lower orders of society were excluded from political activity, along with slaves and women, and even the craft and trade associations – the *arte* – were stringently controlled. But the government remained sensitive to the needs of the people, and there was the Church and the Scuole to provide scope for non-nobles to gain power and prestige among their fellow men. The Scuole were in many ways the most democratic institutions in Venice. At least one, the Misericordia, allowed noblemen to join, exempting them from the rule of self-chastisement in return for an annual subscription of twenty soldi; and, up to 1327, another, San Giovanni Evangelista, accepted women. All of them accepted the poor as well.

The Scuole's main purpose still was the promotion of the pious life, and thanks to the overwhelming sense of sin which they promoted, they helped to distract non-noble Venetians from their political disabilities. 'Man,' ran one statement of a Scuola's purpose, 'is oppressed with care, overwhelmed by toil, and imprisoned in bondage to the Devil.' Only prayer, penance and good works provided an escape, and then not in this world – only as a passport 'to return to our heavenly country.'

All was not prayer and gloom, however. Members of a Scuola would meet every fourth Sunday in Lent for a 'love-feast' of fish cooked in herbs (the greatest delicacy permitted during Lent), and since a meal was also prepared for a similar number of paupers charity was involved as well, though most of this was channelled among needy members.

Marco Polo was a member of more than one Scuola, and otherwise lived on quietly, surrounded by his wife and daughters, his accumulated stocks of cloth and jewellery and the relics of his adventurous past. He had a Tatar slave to run his messages and do his chores, took pleasure from his book, which received ecclesiastical sanction, did his duty by his Scuole, and steered clear of dangerous political involvements. He took only a limited interest in commercial matters too, but he was nevertheless anxious to employ his capital profitably.

In 1311 he sued his agent Paolo Girardo for six pounds of musk, and he was ruthless in exacting interest due to him on loans whether from family or outsiders. As he himself admitted, he was 'exceptionally careful and prudent,' and thanks to his prudence his daughters married to his satisfaction – one to a Bragadin, another to a Querini, which may have had awkward political implications – but then the youngest ultimately entered the Gradenigo family, which was certainly a *coup*.

As he approached old age Marco saw Venice extending. With land so scarce, official reclamation works were in progress at Santa Elena, and elsewhere individuals eager to find ballast for private reclamation works were undermining canal banks – in which the government had to intervene. Marco heard teams of navvies chanting as they hammered heavy piles into the water off the Giudecca, saw men framing them with timbers and packing the resultant boxes with clay and rubble to form platforms on which building could begin. He had seen the new Arsenal in the building, the road from San Marco to Castello paved, the great church of the Frari rising and, as an old man, the beginning of the Servi church. And he had also watched the Doge's rebuilt barge, the *Bucintoro*, towed by on innumerable occasions rich with carvings, ornaments and hangings.

Marco had survived shipwreck, piracy, battles and wild beasts, and he had seen his city survive many crises too – fierce wars, two attempted *coup d'états*, excommunication by the Pope, and a lonely refusal to swear allegiance to the Emperor: this on the ground that Venice was 'a quintessence and will belong neither to the Church nor to the Emperor, neither to the sea nor to the land.'

Venice owed allegiance to no one, and that son of Venice, Marco Polo, was his own man too. But while his city was on its way to greater glory Marco's days were drawing to an end. He spent them immersed in parish gossip and family affairs, surrounded by trophies of his former glories – the silver belt marking his status as Mongol knight, a Buddhist rosary and the 'golden tablet of command' which the Great Khan himself had given him. In January 1323/1324 Marco drew up his will. He freed his Tatar slave, left his wife an income of about 100 ducats a year, and most of the remainder to his daughters. But he did not forget the Church – there would be a tithe for the Bishop of Castello, bequests to the church of San Lorenzo, to various monasteries and to every Scuola of which he was a member. He died soon afterwards. By then other Europeans were following where he had led, finding their way to India and China. The Genoese were prominent among them. Venice's great commercial rival still thundered at her heels.

Chapter VI

Venice in the Age of Petrarch

When Francesco Petrarch, poet, administrator, and shining herald of the dawning Renaissance, was only a young man, Venice, whose upper crust later clasped him to their bosom, was still as practical as ever she had been. Though dutiful towards the church, and even philanthropic, Venetians did not exercise their minds about poetry and ideals. Except perhaps for the study of law, learning counted for but little, and the attentions of most Venetians were concentrated on ways by which they and their city could increase their prosperity and power.

The outlook seemed favourable. Comacchio, Amalfi, Pisa, the rivals of ages past, were spent now as commercial powers; only Genoa remained as a serious competitor. But though Venice's trading machine chugged ever faster thanks to the continuing economic expansion of Europe as a whole the struggle to maintain her leadership became fiercer too. Not only did she have to protect her shipping against predators and hold bases overseas against attack, she had to maintain a series of often incompatible trading arrangements with the Muslim and the Christian worlds, extend her holdings in the hinterland to ensure the city's food supplies and secure her trading routes across the Alps. All this required more intervention on the part of government.

There was hardly a Mediterranean port which was not familiar with the banner of St. Mark, but while some ships sailed alone others went in convoy; and while some convoys were state-run others were organized privately. There was no pattern to it all, and the fitful interventions by the state and continual changes of arrangements made it impossible for Venetian merchants to know when important consignments would arrive or leave. The result was a certain unwillingness to invest, and so in 1321 five *Savii ai Ordini* were elected to bring order to the situation and in particular to ensure that convoys departed and arrived at regular times, so as to achieve faster turnover and avoid the worst of the winter weather. Periods were fixed during which ships were to be loaded, and regulations were drawn up for the chartering of state-owned ships by means of auctions.

The Black Sea voyage, among the most dangerous, was strictly regulated from 1328. The ships had to load in the second half of April and return by the end of October; the Flanders galleys, on the other hand, which now included Margate, Sandwich and Boston among their ports of call, had to leave in March so as to be back by the end of the year, and loading dates were also fixed for voyages to Constantinople, Armenia and Cyprus. Such rules applied not only to the fast safe galleys carrying the costly goods, but to round sailing ships which carried certain bulkier cargoes such as cotton – though ships carrying grain, salt and other heavy goods for which there was an all-year market remained free to sail as they pleased, at least in peace-time.

This trading system was supported by commercial agents resident at important foreign commercial centres, by ambassadors who negotiated commercial treaties, and by the commanders of the galley convoys. All these functions were fulfilled by the same class of men who moved readily from trade to state service and back to trade again. Dardi Bembo, for example, a big investor in the Flanders galleys, became ambassador to France, and in 1327 commanded the Black Sea convoy. Diplomacy then, like state policy in general, was largely carried out by members of the merchant nobility whose interests it served.

Venetian diplomatists paid 2,000 florins to the King of France to exempt Venetian traders from arbitrary imposts; they negotiated a deal with Abu Said of Persia, which clarified the tax concessions to which Venetians were entitled – namely their rights to protection from brigands and to pitch camp, and the rights of

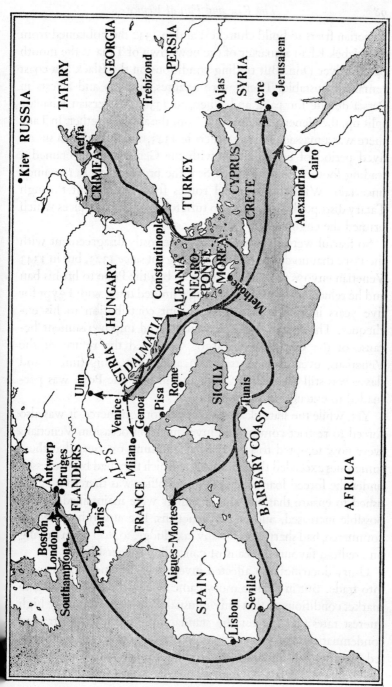

Venetian trade routes

Venetian friars to build churches; and in 1332 they obtained from the Uzbek Khan a quarter of the new town of Tana at the mouth of the River Don. But trading conditions on the Black Sea coast remained unstable. There were seizures, imposts and arrests in Persia despite the pact, and when, in 1336, the Persian Khanate split up, the Venetians withdrew from the area altogether. In Tana there was a massacre of westerners in 1343, and though in a short-lived period of co-operation with the Genoese they retained a trading foothold on the Black Sea, the prospects there remained uncertain. With the overland routes from the Orient through Tatary disrupted, Venice had to turn to Egypt for the spices which primed the engines of her trade.

So fearful were Venetians of another costly disagreement with the Pope that no convoy had visited Egypt since 1323, but in 1343 Venetian envoys went to Avignon to beg the Pope to lift his ban and he reluctantly agreed, allowing a limited trade with Egypt for five years in return for an exorbitant contribution to his exchequer. The Sultan, whose country faced impoverishment because of the Christian embargo, welcomed the return of the Venetians, even though traffic in arms, iron, ship-timber and slaves was still officially blacked. But in time the Pope was persuaded to extend his concessions.

Yet, while the state cleared the roads for commerce, it was also forced to restrict commercial investment on occasion. Venetians were now tempted to invest such large sums overseas that these sometimes exceeded the amounts for which they had been assessed under the forced loan scheme. A new office was therefore established to ensure that assessment ratings were maintained, where possible increased, and, since Venetians, like any other men of commerce, had sharp eyes for any tax-dodge, to stop them buying on credit, a favoured means of concealing ownership.

Usury doctrines also affected investment, forcing more capital into trade. But in Venice usury came to be defined according to market conditions so that only unusual security or unusually high interest rates (much over the standard eight per cent) attracted condemnation, and prosecutions do not seem to have been directed against one businessman lending to another. Venice was already developing into a banking centre and a money market; Venetian money-changers had begun to accept deposits and Can Grande of Verona himself deposited 26,000 ducats there to provide for his illegitimate children when he died.

Can Grande (Big Dog) della Scala was a notable jouster, a huntsman keen enough to keep 300 hawks, and an ambitious climber, living up to his family name, della Scala – the ladder. As such he soon proved dangerous to Venice. Hungry for territory, he added Vicenza to his dominions, then Belluno and Treviso on Venice's own doorstep. And finally he began to cast covetous eyes on the city with which the wandering Petrarch was to be associated above all others – Padua.

Padua was only twenty miles away from Venice, the centre of a wheat-producing area, on whose produce Venice was largely dependent, and it had long come within the Venetian sphere of influence. Its ruler, Jacopo da Carrara, had married Doge Gradenigo's daughter and been entered in the Golden Book of Venice's nobility. But his successor, Marsilio, was forced to switch allegiance to Can Grande, who became lord of Padua in 1329.

Can Grande died that year, at the age of thirty-eight, but his nephew and successor, Mastino (Little Dog), proved no less dangerous. He had married da Carrara's cousin, and now he took the city over as its direct ruler, and when he imposed new duties on Venetian goods and erected a toll-house on the River Po, Venice was forced to retaliate. She imposed prohibitive duties on Paduan goods and tried to starve Mastino's territories of salt. But Mastino got salt from Germany – and proceeded to add Parma and Lucca to his empire. Soon it was feared that the 'Little Dog' of Verona would snap up all north Italy. But Doge Francesco Dandolo was not called 'il Cane' for nothing – and this Venetian dog soon bared his teeth.

In 1336 Venice raised a large army and, in alliance with Florence and the dispossessed lords of Parma, went to war. The lido became an encampment once again as soldiers of fortune poured in from as far afield as France and Germany, for the rates of pay the allies offered were high – nine golden ducats a year for every fully-equipped man-at-arms with a war-horse and a hack, permission to keep any booty, plus a reward of three ducats for every ordinary enemy soldier handed over. The army included enlisted men as well, and it soon marched.

Treviso was taken, but the allies' successes were only partly due to force of arms. When Mastino sent Marsilio da Carrara to negotiate a settlement the Venetians promptly offered to restore him to the lordship of Padua if he would open the city gates to them. He agreed. In August 1337 the Venetians duly entered Padua and took Mastino's brother prisoner. Visconti of Milan captured Bergamo and Brescia, and with his enemies pressing in all round him Mastino was forced to submit. By the terms of the peace, Venice gained all the territories between the Alps and the lagoon, free navigation up the River Po and a useful war indemnity. A great celebratory tourney was held in the Piazza.

Venice had become an important *terraferma* power, but her new territories needed managing, and rather than assume direct control of all of them she handed over Castelbaldo, Cittadella and Bassano as well as Padua to da Carrara. The government Venice imposed on Conegliano and Treviso, however, set the pattern for her future imperial system on the mainland. A Venetian *podesta* (civil governor) and a *capitano* (military commander) were installed in each major town and a single administrator in minor ones to control defence and policing functions and collect state taxes, but municipal councils and local lords were otherwise allowed a wide degree of autonomy.

The system gave young Venetian nobles broader opportunities to gain experience of affairs in minor office, but to ordinary Venetians the accretion of empire meant little enough. The shipyard workers laboured on as usual, fashioning keels out of oak trees, carving oars from Croatian beech-wood, capstans out of elm, rudders out of walnut logs and planking the ships and decking them with fir and larch trunks brought from the Alps and Apenines. The stevedores, supervised by chiefs in their various *sestiere*, worked on day and night sometimes to load and unload the cargoes of the world, stumbling down the gang-planks with precious bags of drugs and spices, wrenching out the close-packed bales of cotton from between the decks, manhandling the grain and sugar sacks, the casks of oil and the great blocks of stone used for building – for a new hall large enough to seat all the members of the Great Council was being built, so was the southern façade of the Doge's Palace, not to mention the huge public granary rising on reclaimed land near St. Mark's.

Every canal seemed crowded with barges; the Rialto hummed with activity, and the wharves and warehouses were crammed with merchandise. Venice's population in the 1330s was in the region of 110,000 – according to some sources, approaching the 200,000 mark – yet even this seemed inadequate to meet the great demand for labour, and the shortage of sailors was especially acute.

At last, the government was forced to re-define the seaman's terms of service. Stricter penalties were imposed on men jumping ship, paymasters were rewarded for recruiting men to the galleys, and prisoners were pressed into the service. Many of these were in fact good sailors gaoled for debt, but the tendency to use the bonded man increased – as did the pressure on the colonies to furnish men to keep the fleets in service – ultimately to the service's detriment.

The state galleys were comparatively small ships, rarely displacing more than 500 tons and crewed by as few as sixty oarsmen, though the larger Flanders galleys needed up to 180 men apiece. The average size of east-bound convoys was also small – four galleys perhaps except in times of boom, and sometimes as few as two. In 1335 only twenty-six merchant galleys left Venice altogether carrying barely 3,900 metric tons. It was little enough by modern standards, even though the goods they carried, especially the spices, were very light in proportion to their value.

But Venetian shipping, of course, was not confined to galleys and organized convoys. General shippers using the round high-castled sailing ship manned by crews of almost any nationality carried a large proportion of the total tonnage, and there was considerable coastal and river traffic too. Similarly, although the traditional commodities – spices, slaves, cloths, timber and the rest – retained importance, new ones like cotton and sugar were increasingly sought after, and while traditional routes retained popularity there were always men prepared to pioneer.

In 1338 Giovanni Loredano heard that the new Moghul Sultan would welcome foreign merchants, and persuaded his brother Paolo and four other noblemen to mount a joint trading venture to India. During their journey from the Crimea, however, Giovanni died, at which Paolo took over his brother's share of the joint 'pile.' They received a warm welcome from the Sultan, who made them a cash gift equivalent to 7,500 Venetian lire and allowed them to buy pearls before setting out for home. But two more partners died on the way back, and when they finally arrived customs men relieved them of a tenth of the Sultan's gift. Even though there were only three not six to share the proceeds of the venture, their profits do not seem to have been excessive bearing in mind the risks involved.

Yet even familiar routes could be dangerous. Turkish pirates were now a force to be reckoned with in Grecian waters, and in 1332 Venice, the Greek Emperor and the Knights of St. John planned a 'crusade' to meet the Turkish threat. This came to nothing, however, thanks to more trouble in Crete. When the Cretans again rebelled resources had to be diverted to cope with it and the proposed 'crusade' was first postponed and then abandoned.

The crude method of bundling troublemakers into sacks and tossing them into the sea did not succeed in bringing the Cretans speedily to heel. Venice's vassals on the island were slow to turn out with their retainers (and not surprisingly, since many of the poorer knights could not afford to equip themselves properly for military action); others supposed to pay fees in lieu were unable to pay; many were half inclined to see Venetian control go anyway. As a result the entire island apart from Candia and a few castles was soon overrun.

Yet Crete was vital, both for its wheat and, increasingly, as a stepping-stone to Egypt now that the old silk routes through Central Asia were disrupted by the Mongols. Venice had to win it back. Eventually she did so; but Crete continued to give trouble; so did Zara, which rebelled again in 1345. It was fortunate that Venice's other colonies in Greece – Negroponte, Korone and Methone, where Jewish silk-workers set up shop – proved more tractable. Relations between Venetian expatriates and local Greeks became so relaxed, indeed, that the former were ordered to go about clean-shaven so as to be distinguishable on sight from the indigenous population.

While Venetians sometimes merged with local populations overseas, foreigners were still merging into the life of Venice, encouraged to settle there permanently if they had useful expertise by the offer of up to two years' tax exemption. The newcomers included many Germans, among them a number of shoemakers, one of whom left a bequest in 1340 to help infirm and needy cobblers.

Like looked after like in Venice – Germans for Germans, Armenians for Armenians, seamen for seamen, Jews for Jews. Even the little hospitals and almshouses those devotional confraternities, the Scuole, were founding were designed primarily to benefit their own members in much the same way as the Freemasons' hospitals do today. In 1330 the Scuola di San Giovanni Evangelista decided to establish a four-bed hospital for poor, sick and destitute brothers, and the Misericordia subsequently established a 'house of poor,' the bulk of the funds needed for the project coming from subscriptions in return for flagellation exemptions and entrance fees as high as twenty-five gold ducats. In addition the Scuole would admit doctors free provided they treated sick brothers without fees.

It was left to the friars and individual philanthropists to stretch the net of charity much beyond the group. Friar Pietro became a well-known figure about 1343 as he tramped barefoot about the city gathering up foundlings and knocking on doors, begging loudly and tearfully for alms with which to keep them. Bartolommeo Verde, a private philanthropist, built a hospital for fallen women in 1357 and, when pilgrimages to the Holy Land became impossible, the San Giobbe hospice was to be converted into a 'Home of God' for fifty respectable widows. This last act was undertaken by the Procurators of St. Mark, the administrators of large public bequests, who were soon supervising several almshouses and hospitals.

The Procurators, who ranked in precedence second only to

the Doge, were public officials, and other aspects of charity were also supervised by government. The Scuole, no doubt because of their nature as semi-secret societies, were watched carefully by the Council of Ten who feared that the Church might become too influential in their affairs, and the state also interested itself in the trade guilds, whose statutes they overruled from time to time, in the conduct of hospitals and of the medical profession. From 1321 no physician was allowed to practise in Venice without a doctor's degree, while, contrary to Church proscription, Jews were allowed to do so from 1331. From 1326 physicians and surgeons were obliged to attend anatomy courses at least once a year, and from 1368 to meet once a month to discuss cases, so as to keep up to date. The merchants of Venice set high store on their medical care.

The state also tried to control consumer spending through a revival of sumptuary laws, proclaimed twice a year at the Rialto and in St. Mark's Square. In 1334 it barred women, apart from the Doge's relations, from wearing cloth of gold and males over the age of ten from wearing silk, velvet, cloth of gold or any ornaments apart from fastenings and buttons. Nor were any corpses to be dressed in secular clothes, except those of scholars, knights and physicians. To this extent sumptuary laws were concerned with precedence as well as with conspicuous consumption – and some were concerned with public order too. In 1336, for instance, the Senate decreed that no man was to ask a lady to supper except a near relative between Michaelmas and Easter on pain of being fined, since there had been so many 'follies' committed at wedding feasts and similar celebrations.

Despite the reputation for gravity and refined behaviour, which Venice's nobility was to acquire, many younger noblemen of the 1300s were simply hooligans. They would prowl in disguises about the streets at night threatening passers-by, and sometimes indulged in far more outrageous activities. In 1343 a youth of good family called Paolo Steno broke into the house of another nobleman, Pietro Faliero, and raped his daughter while two of her own servants held her down; on another occasion Marco Grimani tried to rape a girl in the atrium of a church. These were not isolated cases, but still the vast majority of those who came before the magistrates were commoners, and then chiefly for crimes against property.

Though their ostentation was restricted, albeit not always effectively, the Venetian rich these days lived very well. Bernardo Morosini's household, consisting of four bachelor brothers and four female servants or dependants, spent twenty-eight ducats on wine alone during the winter of 1343-4 – enough to buy 3,500 litres of the ordinary quality. In addition they spent thirty-three and a half ducats on meat, fish and eggs – at a time when a ducat bought over seventy pounds of beef, twenty-four geese or four gross of eggs in season – and only a fifth of their food budget on wheaten bread, whereas on a galley five times as much went on the men's biscuit as their meat.

The Morosini household spent several times as much on food alone as a master caulker earned in a year. A household servant earned three ducats a year plus keep, a teacher as little as three quarters of a ducat a year per pupil; a clockmaker might comand as much as 800 ducats for a particularly fine clock, for which, however, he had laboured half his life, while a successful doctor could get as much as a ducat a day for treating a rich patient. There was thus a huge disparity of incomes reflecting the social priorities of Venetian society. True, bread was comparatively cheap and so was wine, but oil was more expensive, and wool cloth cost over half a ducat a yard. So, while a craftsman could live decently enough on forty ducats a year and employment was rising, there was never any lack of paupers in the city.

Even the very poor had their distractions, of course – the profusion of great public ceremonials in which, as guildsmen or as *arsenalotti*, they often participated; the informal entertainment provided by itinerant buffoons, church services and self-made entertainments such as singing. Lovers serenaded loves, navvies chanted as they laboured; there were songs for fishermen and cobblers, ribald and uncouth songs – all sung in the soft, distinctive Venetian dialect.

The delights of learning, however, were only for the few, and though tutors were cheap enough many noblemen remained illiterate. Nevertheless, perceptibly more importance was being attached to learning, and in 1343 a learned man was actually elected Doge. Andrea Dandolo had been Professor of Law at Padua as well as holding several government posts. He was still in his thirties, extraordinarily young for the job, a close friend of Petrarch, the most celebrated poet of the age, and was to earn rather more fame as a chronicler than as Doge.

In his chronicle Dandolo dwelt on Venice's moral decline, which was not surprising in an age when calamities were seen as God's punishment for sins, for his reign had its full measure of disasters: first a great earthquake in January 1348, and then bubonic plague. The 'Eastern Tempest,' as Petrarch called the disease which was to carry off his beloved Laura, hit all Europe, but it struck Venice first and the impact was terrible. People fell dead within hours of the dreaded buboes appearing on their bodies and they perished in their thousands.

The state promptly engaged three noted physicians as consultants and appointed three commissioners to enforce special sanitary regulations. Quarantine was imposed; separate burial of the plague dead ordered, and barges were sent through the city every day to collect the corpses. But advanced as these provisions were at a time when physicians thought that leprosy was transferred through coitus or through the vapours of the air they hardly held the plague at bay. Day after day, month in and month out, while Friar Pietro of the Pietà went about the city wailing for his orphans, the grim steersmen of the death barges sailed through the canals with their cry of 'corpi morti!' and always gathered in a heavy crop.

The plague carried off as many as 100,000 souls, perhaps half the population. Fifty noble families were totally wiped out, and the terror was so great that sometimes only twenty or thirty noblemen out of a possible thousand attended Council sessions. Worse still, the plague depopulated the hinterland as well as Venice. Harvests declined – so did disposable incomes, and a serious economic depression set in which lasted for decades.

And as the plague receded Venice became involved in a plague of wars. In September 1348 Capo d'Istria revolted and that winter

Count Albert of Görz invaded the Veneto from the north-west of Trieste. Somehow both challenges were beaten off, but in 1353 the King of Hungary demanded the surrender of Dalmatia, three years later the Count of Görz and the Patriarch of Aquileia teamed up with him, and then trouble flared with the Genoese again. There had been intermittent clashes in the 1340s, but from the outset of the fifties the two plague-impoverished cities sprang at each other's throats in earnest.

Fourteen armed Genoese merchantmen were routed off Greece; twenty-three Venetian ships were lost at Negroponte. In 1351 Nicolò Pisani's galleys defeated Genoese ships at Pera harbour and forced a reluctant Greek Emperor into an alliance. But the Genoese were soon back at Pera and while twenty-five sages in Venice pored over their secret war plan and the people grumbled at the increased taxes on salt, oil, wine and meat, Pisani sailed again for Constantinople. This time his attack failed and he retired to Methone for the winter. Early the next year, in company with a flotilla sent by Venice's new ally, the King of Aragon, and a force of half-hearted Greeks, he engaged the enemy again – and again got the worst of the encounter, although in the following year Venetians did have the satisfaction of taking thirty-two Genoese galleys off Sardinia.

It was at this point that Petrarch himself arrived in Venice bringing peace overtures from Genoa's new protector, Visconti of Milan. Venice rejected them, the war continued, and from then on Petrarch, who made a practice of sending letters to his friends on both sides offering condolences at defeat, had more frequent cause to commiserate with Dandolo. The Genoese under Doria ravaged their way up the Adriatic towards the lido. The port of San Nicolò was hastily blocked up and the Genoese sheered off, but later in 1354 the Venetians were crushingly defeated off Methone. Five thousand of them were taken prisoner; so was their admiral Pisani. That autumn, before this news arrived, Doge Andrea Dandolo, already overcome with cares, had died.

Thanks to the war, the public debt which had been gradually reduced since early in the century rose sharply once again; compulsory loan contributions were increased from about two to

forty per cent of assessed wealth, and trade, which had been re-
covering from the plague, became riskier than ever. Dandolo's
successor seemed well qualified to cope, however. Marino Faliero
was vigorous, though in his seventies, and had unrivalled experience of affairs. He (or a kinsman of the same name) had sat on
commissions to enlarge the Merceria and to define usury, been a
member of the Ten, served as governor of various colonies overseas and as *podesta* of several *terraferma* towns. Marino (or his
namesake) had naval experience in command of the Black Sea
galleys, military experience at the siege of Zara and against the
Hungarians in 1346; and diplomatic experience too, on embassies
to Austria, Genoa, the Emperor, and most recently to the Pope.
He held the golden pennon of knighthood and a fief in the
hinterland, was Lord of Tenedos under the Greek Emperor – and
he had all the arrogance to match his titles: indeed, he had once
struck the Bishop of Treviso in his own Cathedral for keeping
him waiting one Corpus Christi Day.

Marino Faliero, however, came to a grisly end within nine
months and at the hands of his own people. Venetian chroniclers
said he was executed for his dynastic ambitions, yet he had no
sons to succeed him; they hinted that he was jealous of the twenty-
three-year-old Michele Steno's relationship with his much younger second wife – yet the Dogaressa, though only in her forties,
was twice young Steno's age; they said he wanted to destroy the
nobility, yet many of them must have been his friends. The story
can only be explained by reference to the general situation in
Venice in 1354–5.

Venice had still not recovered from the earthquake and the
terrible plague six years before. The wars with her northern
neighbours and with Genoa had been expensive in money and
in men; taxation was higher than it had ever been before, and
within weeks of Faliero's election came news of the Venetian
fleet's débâcle off Methone. Feeling ran high against the government and against the nobility in general – the arrogant officers of
state, the strutting commanders who proved so incompetent in
battle, the rowdy young nobles who seemed to think the streets
of Venice belonged to them.

A nervous government stamped viciously at every squeak of opposition. Men were imprisoned, had their tongues ripped out or were strappadoed for mere talk 'against the state and honour of the government.' Yet when Faliero arranged for three experienced non-noble seamen to command a flying squadron, many aristocrats were displeased.

The situation in Venice was extremely tense, and one aspect of this tension was highlighted when Michele Steno was sentenced to ten days' imprisonment for scrawling offensive graffiti on the Palace walls, having been turfed out for insulting members of the Dogaressa's retinue. The Doge was said to be enraged at the leniency the judges had shown. Insolent young toughs like Steno needed discipline. But so, too, did some older nobles who were alienating Venetians with their arrogance – men like Marco Barbaro, who assaulted Stefano Gisello, chief of the Arsenal workers, and Giovanni Dandolo, who slashed ship-master Bertuccio Ixarello's face open with his ring. Complaints reached the Doge; counter-allegations were made. From then on the situation becomes confused.

According to the chroniclers Doge Faliero now hatched a plot to seize absolute power. His nephew Bertuccio and the Arsenal foreman Gisello and Ixarello were all involved along with many merchants, artisans and seamen. But their plans misfired. The Council was warned that a *coup* had been planned and was able to prepare. Reliable men were brought in from Chioggia, guards suddenly appeared everywhere, and thousands of men were mustered under Marco Cornaro in the Piazza. Arrests multiplied, the torturers got busy, and at last Doge Faliero himself was arraigned before the Ten – some say for plotting against the 'people,' others for bribing the people to rebel with promises of loot and rape. At his trial a paper was said to have dropped from Faliero's clothes conveniently proving his guilt, and he was duly condemned.

Yet the proceedings were kept secret, and such accounts as exist seem to stem from propaganda put about by the successful party in the affair. None of them convinces, and other interpretations seem infinitely more probable. Perhaps the Doge, fearing a bloody revolution, threw his hand in with the people in order to control them. Perhaps there was a popular rising in the name of the Doge, as inarticulate proletariats the world over have rebelled in the name of a 'just' king or Emperor, and Faliero was held responsible by his class. Perhaps the Doge was made a scapegoat for popular discontent by a terrified nobility. Perhaps there was a straightforward *coup d'état* by Marco Cornaro, who held the city in his power for several weeks, and Giovanni ('the Nose') Gradenigo, who was eventually made Doge in Faliero's place.

Whatever the truth, as Petrarch wrote, Faliero 'fell down dead a headless corpse.' His body was put on display and ten years later his portrait in the Palace was painted out. The government tried to pretend that Faliero had never existed, but for centuries to come chroniclers would decorate the margins of their manuscripts with crude ink drawings of rebel corpses drooping from the gallows and red blood gushing from the Doge's head.

The new régime ended the war with Genoa within the year. This helped to contain the internal situation, but the war against King Louis of Hungary and his allies, including the treacherous da Carrara of Padua, went from bad to worse. By the end of 1357 Venice had lost Serravalle and Asolo, Traù, Spalato and Zara; the Bishop of Ceneda had rebelled; Venetians were thrown out of Ragusa – and then the city was struck by plague again. With the enemy advancing to the very edge of the lagoon, Venice sued for peace. The terms were harsh: all claims to Dalmatia and Croatia, Aquileia and Padua had to be renounced. Venice's enemies were powerful indeed, but the greatest enemy of all was the plague. It struck again in 1359 and in 1361. Indeed, for the next century and a half hardly a decade would pass without a serious outbreak.

With Faliero's execution, however, a dangerous political crisis had been surmounted, the city was at peace and the government set about reforming the morals of the city. Once again it was forbidden to hold feasts late at night in winter; people under the age of twenty-five forbidden to wear ermine, and prostitutes were barred from common lodging-houses and forbidden to solicit in the streets – except on Saturdays in the 'red light' Castelletto district at Rialto. Not for nothing did Petrarch deprecate the 'foul language and excessive licence' of Venetians. Nevertheless, although a Paduan, he chose to settle there.

In 1362, when Lorenzo Celsi was Doge, Petrarch applied for suitable lodgings in Venice, offering to leave his library for the benefit of noble and lettered Venetians in return. The government welcomed him for he was the most celebrated scholar, raconteur and poet of his age – and besides he had many friends among its members. From the towers of his new residence, the Palazzo Molin on the Riva degli Schiavoni, Petrarch commanded a view right across the lagoon. He saw innumerable ships 'as large as my house,' ships 'like mountains floating upon water.' They crowded the harbour even in 'the gloom of winter and the roughest storms of spring,' and he watched them sail out to sea bound in all directions, some 'turning their prows eastwards, some to the north, others southwards to the sands of Libya.'

Spurred on by the same lusting after gold that had driven Jason to seek the Golden Fleece, they visited 'all parts of the world,' and faced 'a thousand dangers,' carrying wine to the English, timber to Egypt, and honey to the Scythians. 'And where the sea stops, their sailors quit their ships and travel on to trade with India and China, crossing the Caucasus and the Ganges to reach the Eastern Ocean.'

As was proper for an immigrant, Petrarch lauded Venetian enterprise and the wisdom of its government. For him Venice was 'strong in power, but even stronger in virtue,' the 'true refuge of the human race, the only home of liberty, justice, and of peace.' He was for ever pressing his advice upon Venice too. They should attack Persia and the Arabs, invade Thrace and Dalmatia – but before any such plans of conquest could mature yet another great rebellion broke out in Crete.

Venice had insisted that the expatriate Venetian knights pay for the maintenance of Cretan harbours, although their income derived from the land not trade, and yet refused them representation on the Great Council. When the Cretan knights asked to send twenty sages to represent them in Venice, Venetians retorted we were not aware there were twenty sages in Candia.' But in 1363 the Cretan crews of three Venetian galleys mutinied; and then the local knights rebelled. The Duke of Candia was put in irons, Greek Orthodoxy was accepted in order to win over the indigenous population, and the banner of St. Titus was run up in place of the banner of St. Mark.

News of the uprising created consternation in Venice. The government rushed to engage the Veronese *condottiere*, Luchino dal Verme, raise an army of 3,000 men and ship them out in a fleet of over thirty galleys. Petrarch watched them go.

Some weeks later he saw the galleys arriving back again, their masts garlanded with flowers, their crews waving banners in sign of victory. They had taken Candia within three days, and killed the expatriate Venetian knights who had led the revolution. All Venice rejoiced, and so did Petrarch. Right had been vindicated in his view and he was at the Doge's right hand at the great public thanksgiving.

'The crowd was immense,' he wrote, 'the front of St. Mark's, the bell-tower, roofs, porticoes and windows seemed like a living wall of people.' Yet 'there was no confusion, tumult, or ill-humour' as they watched the games in the Piazza facing the Doge and his entourage – an entourgae which included visiting relatives of the King of England who 'were astonished at the sight of so much magnificance.'

Only the celebrations were a little premature. Venice held Crete's major strongpoints, but rebels continued a guerilla war which took two years and ferocious methods to suppress. Venice had little to learn from later imperialist powers. 'Thanks to God's grace,' Paolo Loredano, who had charge of operations, proudly reported, 'I have ended a cruel war, and made . . . [the Cretans] incapable of further revolt. The rebels are now without leaders of whom I have made a terrible example. I have destroyed all forts . . . which it seemed undesirable to keep, deported their inhabi-tants, laid waste to the surrounding districts and forbidden people on pain of death ever to return. All locally made laws . . . have been abolished; every native has been removed from office . . .' Petrarch, who considered the Cretans 'crafty' and 'deceitful,' thought they thoroughly deserved their fate.

Two years later Petrarch left Venice and in 1369 retired to the

Eugaean hills near Padua. He died there five years later, leaving his library for the greater glory of St. Mark – a gift, however, which the Government was content to leave in crates, gathering dust for many years. Meanwhile a new campanile was rising in the Piazza, Pisanello was among the painters decorating the grand new hall for the Great Council and the city generally was showing the wealth it had accumulated in the golden age before the plague. But commerce was also picking up now – strongly enough for the bigger merchant nobles to be less concerned about trying to squeeze the small trading operators out of business by pressing for restrictionist policies. 'Nothing is more conducive to increasing and enriching . . . our city,' ran a law of 1363 making trade freer for all citizens, 'than to offer every freedom and opportunity for merchandise to be brought and procured here rather than elsewhere.' Yet even privately owned ships were subject to rules about load-lines and the minimum crews that they should carry, and the state continued to limit the operation of all Venetian ships.

Certain private voyages were banned altogether and others subjected to a licence; but the more valuable cargoes and the more dangerous voyages were much more rigorously controlled, the ships used for these purposes being owned, run and officered by the state, or at least auctioned off to private individuals bound to observe the convoy rules.

As to trading policy as a whole, maintenance of the link with Egypt had priority. But this ran counter to the interests of the King of Cyprus, who feared for Cypriot trade in oriental goods shipped through Armenia. With the Pope's support, Cyprus was still fighting a 'crusade' against the Sultan, and in 1366, with the octogenarian Marco Cornaro installed as Doge, Venice again sent ambassadors to the Pope at Avignon begging him to sanction a resumption of trade with Alexandria. Any delay, they urged, would bring 'serious damage to our country,' which the papacy 'could not wish to happen to us, the most devoted servants of the Holy Church.' Next year Venice sent five galleys to escort the Pope in triumph back to Rome, and eventually succeeded in wresting from him limited dispensations to trade with the Sultan.

Although Cyprus had been strongly opposed to such a development, Venice itself had considerable business interests in Cyprus. The man most concerned there was Frederigo Cornaro, merchant, moneylender and perhaps the richest Venetian of his time. He shipped spices and other goods from the Levant as well as from Cyprus, where his brother Fantin represented a family partnership which was completed by another brother, Marco, and one Vito Leone. In 1365 their partnership was worth 83,275 ducats and a single cargo they shipped from Cyprus and Rhodes the same year was valued at a phenomenal 67,800 ducats.

Frederigo entertained King Peter I of Cyprus at his palace on the Grand Canal in 1361 when the King came to Europe seeking help against the Turks, and subsequently lent the King large sums of money in return for which he received the magnificent estate of Episkopi in Cyprus. This he exploited in a vigorously capitalistic way, driving his workers, most of them serfs or runaways, and using the water from the river that passed through his land so lavishly that he ran his neighbours' estates dry.

His main crop was sugar, which he had refined in immense copper kettles, but he had big interests in Cyprus salt and cotton too, and held estates in Crete where he grew food for his plantation workers. The cartel in the export of sugar, salt and cotton which he formed raised a storm of protest in Venice, and a commission was set up to draft legislation to stop it. A law was passed in fact, but it lacked teeth. Cornaro was too powerful.

By the late 1370s he had become a financier of international standing. A personal friend of the King of Cyprus and the Count of Savoy (to whom he also advanced loans), a knight, a feudal lord, and with fingers in a dozen tasty trading and financial pies, he was assessed the richest man in Venice. Here was a prince outstanding even among the many merchant princes of the city, and by comparison with him the Jewish money-lenders who settled in Venice in 1366 looked the smallest of small fry.

The wealth of Frederigo Cornaro and his peers paid for the towers and cupolas, the patterned stonework and ogival windows of a city which grew more splendid with each year; it enabled Venice to find 75,000 ducats with which to buy off Leopold of

Austria and reduce Trieste into submission in 1369; and it enabled the city to engage the services of mercenaries to deal with the Carraras of Padua who were cutting their own route to the sea to by-pass Venice. At last, by the peace of 1373, Carrara had to pay Venice an indemnity, pull down the forts he had erected on the border and hand over others in Feltre and Belluno besides. Carrara's elder son, Francesco, arrived in Venice, and with him Petrarch, who delivered an eloquent oration on the subject of peace.

The swan-song of the poet did not herald complete peace, however. Venice was still at war with the Duke of Austria in the Treviso region where the Venetians employed cannon: the first time they were used in Italy. And when peace with the Austrians came at last in November 1376 it was to provide Venice with only a brief respite. A struggle was looming that would make all these little wars pale into insignificance. Venice was soon to be fighting Genoa again, and this time to the finish.

Chapter VII

Venice Victorious

The trouble started in Cyprus at the coronation of Peter II in 1372. As the King set out from Famagusta Cathedral the Venetian consul grabbed the right rein of the King's horse, leaving the left rein to Paganino Doria, the Genoese. This calculated bid for precedence provoked a riot. The Venetians and the Genoese were eventually separated, but at the coronation banquet Doria and his colleagues began bombarding the Venetain guests with bread pellets. At this, with Cypriot help, the Genoese were hurled out from the windows, and at this they took to arms. The streets of Famagusta were soon filled with fighting men, and by the time they were cleared the Genoese quarter had been sacked and strewn with corpses.

When the news reached Genoa two war fleets set out to take revenge. In 1374 they captured Famagusta and forced King Peter to become their tributary. Venice's favoured position in Cyprus had been lost, but worse was still to come.

Genoese influence had become predominant at Constantinople too, and, fearing their passage to the Black Sea would be blocked, in 1375 the Venetians seized Tenedos at the southern approaches to the Dardanelles. The Emperor Andronicus promptly arrested Venetians at Constantinople and called on Genoa for help. But in 1377 when a Genoese ambassador demanded the surrender of Tenedos the Venetians gave him a dusty answer. The Genoese then attacked the island and were repulsed; and the dispute escalated into total war.

Ranged with the Genoese were Padua, Aquileia, Ancona, Hungary, Naples and the Duke of Austria. With Venice stood Genoa's powerful neighbour the Duke of Milan. Venetians between the ages of eighteen and fifty were mobilized, taxes increased, and forced loans ultimately raised five million gold ducats for the war effort. *Condottieri*, bowmen and extra galleys were hired, and the Captain-General Vettor Pisani led the main fleet out to battle.

In the spring of 1379, however, he was crushingly defeated by the Genoese at Pola and limped back to harbour with only six remaining ships. He was promptly imprisoned and frantic messages were sent out to fetch back a raiding squadron under the command of Carlo Zeno which had been sent out into Genoese waters. Until they arrived Venice had virtually no naval defences – and the enemy was already at the gates. That July forty-seven enemy galleys under Pietro Doria burned Grado and Càorle, seized Tommasso Mocenigo's cog arriving fully laden from the east, and at last anchored off the very entrance to the lagoon. The bells of Venice pealed out their warning.

The convent at San Niccolò had been hastily fortified; the entrance was blocked by iron-pronged beams laid below the waterline and by three cogs chained together on the surface. Seeing these defences the Genoese sheered off; they were repulsed from Malamocco too, but in August they seized Chioggia, which Doria made his base. The enemy was now established inside the lagoon itself.

In Venice a committee of seven leading officers of state, relieved every eight days, stayed in session night and day directing the defences. Every parish liable to direct attack held its contingent at the ready; *provveditori* were appointed to prepare Murano, Torcello and Mazzorbo against attack; the populations of more exposed settlements were evacuated. Crack cross-bowmen and troops armed with grenades and slings took up station in Venice and the lido; primitive cannon were deployed; armed boats patrolled the lagoon, and 4,000 mercenary men-at-arms took up post to guard the overland approach from Padua.

Disaster piled upon disaster. A joint Genoese-Paduan force

struck at the lido and burned Pellestrina; enemy guns bombarded Mestre, and Malamocco, only five miles away from Venice itself, soon had to be abandoned, while, further afield, Castelfranco, Treviso, Trieste, Pola and Capodistria were all lost.

By dint of a tremendous effort, Venice fitted out thirty-four galleys, and in response to popular demand entrusted their command to a rehabilitated Vettor Pisani. On the longest night of winter the ships put silently to sea to block the channels round the Genoese positions, and then, on New Year's Day 1380, Zeno's fleet hove into sight. The tide was beginning to turn at last, but the struggle was still tense.

The Genoese tried to dig a new canal between the lagoon and the sea as a means of getting its forces into Venice now that the lagoon approaches had been blocked; but meanwhile the defenders edged their way along the lido, pushing back the enemy. A fortunate shot which struck the bell-tower of Brondolo Cathedral killed the Genoese commander; and in February the Venetians forced his successor, Napoleone Grimaldi, back into Chioggia and cut his supply lines from Padua. Two Genoese attempts to break out failed, and Venetians who had so recently faced starvation watched the enemy starve instead. In June 1380 the Genoese at Chioggia surrendered.

Within weeks Vettor Pisani sailed out to reoccupy Capodistria and defeat a Genoese force on land near Manfredonia. But the immensity of the effort had exhausted Venice as well as Genoa, and in August 1381 a general peace was signed. By this, Venice ceded Dalmatia to Hungary, Treviso to the Carraras and Tenedos to Savoy, who had acted as mediator. Almost all Venice's possessions on the *terraferma* had been lost – but her ancient rival Genoa was finished as a mercantile power. This only became clear in retrospect, however. At the time Venetians merely sighed with relief, mourned their dead, and set about recouping their diminished fortunes.

They had lost much, particularly those nobles and citizens subject to forced loans. Thirty citizens, including a provision merchant called Vendramin, were made nobles in recognition of their contributions, but a corn factor called Leonardo dell'Agnello who had offered to finance 150 mercenaries for a month was not among them, and died, it was said, of a broken heart.

The contributions had been made in the form of interest-bearing loans, but many of the lenders were forced to sell their bonds immediately for as little as seventy-five per cent of their par value. Moreover, because of the suspension of interest repayments holders of the old loan bonds found they had slumped from ninety-nine and a half points before the war to a mere eighteen by March 1381. Nor had forced loans been the only impositions. There had been heavy war taxes and levies too – and those without the ready cash to pay had had their property seized and auctioned off.

Frederigo Cornaro, who bore the highest assessment, had to shell out 25,000 in forced loans, besides personally guaranteeing payment to the Duke of Mantua for keeping the city supplied with grain. When Cornaro died in 1382 his executors faced bankruptcy, the King of Cyprus being unable to repay his debts. However, the Cornaro family still held the productive Episkopi estate and then King James I ceded them two salt works worth 9,000 ducats so that by 1417 all Frederigo's creditors had been paid and Frederigo's son was rich enough to spend over 2,000 ducats on his father's tomb.

Many families were less fortunate, but there were others who had profited hugely from the situation – men under-assessed for loans or with fortunes made so recently that they were not assessed at all. Such people were able to buy up government stock at a fifth of its face value and obtain the property of state debtors for a song. The patriotic Morosini, a future Doge, had spent most of the war snapping up real estate at rock-bottom prices, and he was only one such profiteer.

But the overwhelming majority of Venetians were not rich, nor ever had been. For most of them it was merely a matter of a gradual return to normal, but the demand for charity increased markedly. The state did something to increase the number of 'pepper poor,' those retired and disabled sailors who were supported by a brokerage tax on pepper, by diverting more taxes for the purpose, but this was little enough and the Scuole soon had to place limits on their doles to needy members.

Fit men with a trade had no need for such charity. Workers in the building trade were kept particularly busy repairing the shattered areas of the lagoon; so were the shipbuilders. Despite the hugely increased productivity of the shipyards during the war, losses had been considerable and had to be replaced – and every new ship built kept two sawyers, four carpenters, five caulkers and a supporting force of apprentices and stevedores employed for a whole year.

The *élite* of the shipbuilders were the foremen carpenters of the Arsenal. They designed the galleys – and kept the mysteries of how to shape a ship secret, continuing their expertise within their families and never committing their designs to paper. As a result, when Theodore Baxon, a Greek shipwright with the best reputation for ship design in the Arsenal, died the authorities determined to keep some of his galleys so that other shipbuilders could emulate his style.

The great galleys, so important in war, were declining somewhat in popularity, and were used now only as flagships and for the roughest sea voyages. The light galley, just over 120 feet from stem to stern and a mere fifteen in the beam, was the standard man-of-war, while the smaller still narrower *fusta* was used chiefly for patrol work. All these ships used oars, albeit only to manœuvre quickly in battle and move in and out of port, but oared ships were no longer the sole mainstay of the Venetian marine. The high round sailing ships were growing steadily in popularity, for, though vulnerable in battle, they were far more economical in men and had far more stowage for the heavy cargoes which formed an ever-increasing proportion of Venetian commerce.

Venice was building the right sort of ships, and she was thrusting open more doors for trade in all directions too. Early in the 1380s she obtained trading privileges in the ports of southern Italy, consolidated her hold over Negroponte, and in 1386 acquired the island of Corfu, eventually paying the Kingdom of Naples 30,000 ducats in compensation for it. Then, in 1389, with Genoese power fading fast, she was able to re-establish her position as the most favoured outside power in Cyprus. But though the Genoese challenge was weakening, the Ottoman Turks were growing ever more powerful, and Venice took care to secure more bases in eastern waters in order to protect her interests against them.

She acquired Argos and Nauplia from the widow of Pietro Cornaro in 1388, Mykonos and Tenos in 1390 after the Sanudo dynasty had died out, and in 1407 Lepanto from its Albanian lord. Sometimes Venice was actually invited in as a more effective protector than the Greek Emperor. Such was the case with Athens, which became Venetian in 1394. But it was a poor place with only a thousand households, and though its cathedral did boast some attractive relics it hardly seemed worth holding. In 1402 the Turks occupied lower Athens. The Venetians clung on to the Akropolis, but only for a time. They soon accepted an offer to withdraw.

This new surge of colonial expansion was expensive. *Podestas bailos* and *provveditori* had to be appointed at salaries sufficient for them to maintain a suitable number of servants. Castellans earned about seventy ducats a year and other lesser officials also had to be paid, not to mention garrisons and the circuit judges sent out from Venice every year.

These expenses were easily met, however, mainly by taxing the colonies themselves but also thanks to trading profits which were rising again, producing an increase in taxation revenue. By about 1400 the Venetian treasury received over a million ducats annually, having paid about a quarter of that sum in collection costs. Pilgrimages and the spice trade both contributed heavily to the boom.

The pilgrim ships took five weeks over their summer voyage to Jaffa and allowed pilgrims fifteen days to tour holy places before embarking on the 800-mile journey home. The spice trade, however, operated on a far longer and more complex cycle. A convoy left every August for Alexandria arriving back the following January. The spices would then be decanted into the merchants' houses and traded in the little piazza of San Giacomo di Rialto, where Venetians, Jews and Germans struck their deals, tiny credit slips changed hands and coins of every currency were carefully weighed. In the spring an export caravan would set out overland for Germany, and by July the remainder of the spices would be loaded for the voyage to London and Flanders. These ships returned to Venice ten months later, in time for their next convoy which left in August.

Cogs left for Syria in February and in midsummer when the Black Sea and Beirut convoys also sailed; galleys bound for Tripoli and Tunis left in March, and ships for the Barbary coast and southern France in spring time. Winter was therefore the busiest period, for by then the ships bringing corn and spices from the east, merchandise from Spain and slaves and metals from the Black Sea had all arrived in Venice. But the summer months were also busy, especially for the cotton specialists. By buying in early summer and selling for coin or cloth to be exported in midsummer in exchange for more cotton which arrived in time to sell off ready for the spring sailings, they could turn their money over twice a year – much quicker than the spice men.

The economic recovery also enabled the state to start reducing the public debt by buying bonds in at market prices. This helped to raise their value. By 1403 they had climbed from their low point of eighteen during the war to sixty-six. Bonds were still a popular form of investment – along with merchandise, property and lending. Canon law might restrict personal lending for investment purposes, but Venetians knew how to side-step laws they found obstructive. Only small-scale loans to the poor were avoided, these being left largely to the Jews who in 1385 were allowed to set up three loan banks in Venice in return for an annual contribution of 4,000 ducats to the exchequer. But as soon as the rate of interest they were allowed to charge rose from four per cent to twelve per cent non-Jewish Venetians eagerly entered into partnerships with them.

By 1400, however, the unfortunate Jews were restricted to appearances at set times to bid for unredeemed pledges at the Rialto and were then barred from the city altogether – though in 1419 Master Solomon the physician was allowed to practise in Venice, and other exceptions were made for 'useful' Jews.

Venetian Jews still had to wear the yellow star, but no such impediment was attached to other strangers. Indeed, the merchants from southern Germany were allowed their own hostel-warehouse, the celebrated Fondaco dei Tedeschi near the Rialto. It contained a kitchen, a room for salting fish, first floor dormitories, a fine courtyard in which to stack their goods, and a stout gate, firmly barred each night, to keep out thieves.

Fed an ever richer diet of trade, the Rialto had become too cramped to cope and had to be enlarged. The Piazza was raised and repaired following another flood in 1382; the Campanile was re-erected after the fire of 1400, and by 1409 Doge Michele Steno had decided that his personal apartments in the palace were too pokey, and they had to be extended too.

Along with this went a further attempt to clean up the city. From 1409 the monks of San Antonio were no longer allowed to let their pigs wander about the streets to be fed free by the people, and anyone found lurking about the city in possession of a sharp knife could expect a twenty-lire fine or fifteen days in prison. Yet order and spaciousness were not typical of the city.

Venice was a hive of crowded tenements and squalid booths and workshops. A few Venetians dwelt in palaces, but their slaves were housed in tiny attics, and though the more affluent visitors lodged comfortably at the 'White Lion' or the 'Moon,' the horde of poorer pilgrims dossed down where they could. While merchants in expensive gowns counted money at the exchange, ragged porters humped their goods about and labourers touted for odd jobs. Only the church embraced both poles of society, reflecting the grandeur of its benefactors, providing consolations for the distressed, and administering the sacraments to all – though in this more curious age some friars and priests eager to explore mysteries beyond those officially santioned by the church treated human bones with consecrated oil and practised other rites of sorcery.

But while the chief Venetian preoccupation was still with money, Venice was not now the philistine city it had once been. Family pride and the urge to demonstrate devotion to religion and the state provided artists with good employment, and though bullfights and tournaments held in the Campo Corner gave excitements to the mob more refined entertainments were appreciated too. The city which had clasped Petrarch to its bosom was producing poets of its own, and scholastic pursuits gained ground as well, albeit more slowly than other Italian towns – not only theology, jurisprudence and medicine, but natural philosophy as well, for which purpose Venice's first public school was founded in 1408.

More noticeable, however, were changes in dress. Until quite late into the 1300s men and women had dressed much alike in long gowns decorated as richly as the wearer's pocket and the law would allow. But by 1400 tailors had arrived from France. From then on greater differences between the sexes became apparent, and fashions changed much faster. The government reacted immediately, bringing prosecutions under the sumptuary laws, and forbidding wide-sleeved dresses, collars reaching above the chin, and various trimmings 'displeasing to God and damnable to the individual and his family.' It was like trying to hold back the tide. Tailors were prepared to risk a month in gaol, their customers glad to pay a heavy fine, in order to keep up with fashion – and the government was never as stern in enforcing these laws as it was in countering religious movements which it thought subversive.

It took particular exception to the 'Bianchi,' so called because the men and women who followed the spiritual leader of the movement, the Florentine Dominican Giovanni Domenchini, wore white gowns as they walked through the streets chanting litanies and orisons. When the 'Bianchi' attempted to form such a procession at SS. Giovanni and Paolo in 1399 the Council of Ten's constable snatched the crucifix out of their leader's hands, smashed it to pieces and dispersed his following. Domenchini was expelled, and the nobles who had invited him to Venice were banished too.

The shrewd men who ran Venice kept sharp eyes on the troubled hinterland as well as on their city, and they needed to. By 1382 Carrara had acquired Treviso, Ceneda, Feltre and Belluno, which gave him control of Venice's route north into southern Germany, and then together with Giangalezzo Visconti, the powerful new

Duke of Milan, set out to smash della Scala of Verona, Venice's ally. In 1387 Visconti took Verona, and Antonio, last of the della Scalas, fled to Venice where he died. But Visconti continued his advance, overrunning Padua itself, Carrara appealed for Venetian help, and so did Florence. Visconti, it seemed, was out to conquer all north Italy.

The Signoria, the collective leadership comprising Venice's chief officers of state, calmly offered help – but at a price: the return of the Treviso area. By 1392 Carrara had been reinstalled in Padua and Venice had recovered Treviso, Ceneda and Feltre. Switching her attentions to the south, Venice then decided to help Nicolò d'Este of Ferrara against his rival, Azzo, lending him money on security of the Polesine territory which she proceeded to occupy in 1395. She was not done with the volatile da Carraras yet, however. After Visconti died in 1402 Carrara turned expansionist, himself laying siege to Vicenza. Venice sent word to him that he must lift the siege, and Carrara responded by cutting off the envoy's nose and ears. At this Venice roused herself to capture Padua. Francesco Carrara and his two sons were carried off to Venice where later they were quietly strangled. 'A dead man,' as Venetians said with truth, 'does not make war.'

Within a few years and at remarkably little cost Venice had recovered Treviso and the Istrian coast, occupied the mouths of the Po, and gained Padua, Vicenza and Verona too. Suddenly she had become an important power in the *terraferma* as well as overseas. Luck was with her once again, and in general her new subjects were fortunate as well.

Relations were easy from the start. A club was established in Padua where Venetians and the local nobility could mix, and Zaccaria Trevisan, the new Captain of Padua, seems to have been model governor. 'The particular qualities of a Venetian governor,' he was to tell his successor, 'should be . . . humanity and clemency, to make yourself loved, by contrast to other lords who rule citizens from the remoteness of their castle towers.'

Yet though a Venetian commoner found it virtually impossible to gain noble rank through wealth or state service, as he might,

conceivably, elsewhere in Europe, unlike their foreign counter-
parts Venetian noblemen commonly participated at all levels of
government – and those who eventually reached the top had
received a thorough apprenticeship in administration. The first
rung up the ladder was to be elected a *Savio ai Ordini*, in which
capacity a young noble could attend the sessions of the Collegio,
or Executive Council, and pick up the details of day-to-day
affairs. From there he might progress to membership of the
Quarantia al Criminal, the chief court and initiating legislative
body, become a Signore di Notte, in charge of the nightly police
patrols, or hold one of the other lesser offices. After this he might
hope for election to one of the more exclusive assemblies such as the
Senate, which dealt principally with foreign affairs and also drafted
laws, or for a governorship, an embassy or an important specialized
administrative post at home. Eventually he might progress to
membership of the Council of Ten, the chief organ of security, to
the dignity of Ducal Counsellor and Procurator of St. Mark, and
even become Doge.

However, the government was not professional in tone.
Noblemen would move regularly from office to private life and
back to office again, making the system genuinely democratic for
members of the enfranchised class at least and keeping it adminis-
tratively fresh. Moreover, as the constitution had evolved, office
had proliferated to a point where citizens could also carve out
careers for themselves as bureaucrats in what had by now become
the most complex political organism in all Europe. Many educated
citizens could rise to become a permanent secretary to the Senate,
the College, or the Council of Ten, and even become Gran
Chancellor, a post equivalent to the headship of the civil service
and one that was generally held for life.

A citizen could also grow rich as an advocate, notary or
physician, and trade on equal terms with merchant-aristocrats.
Almost two-fifths of the wealthiest inhabitants assessed for forced
loans in 1379 were non-nobles; so were a fifth of the very richest
people in the city. It was men such as these who most resented
their disenfranchisement, and they were not without sympathizers
among the nobility itself, not least among the three chiefs of the

Quarantia who pressed unsuccessfully for their admission. A Venetian citizen, then, might aspire to riches, to office in a Scuola, nobles being excluded from these by order of the Ten, or to influence as a bureaucrat. But he could hope for little prestige.

A Doge, by contrast, was surrounded by it. When Michele Steno was elected at the dawn of the new century, jousters came from Treviso, the guilds paraded, the Compagnia della Calza – flashy young nobles dressed in gaudy wear – strutted before him, and sumptuous jewels and dresses were displayed to do him honour. The Doge was no longer addressed as 'lord'; 'mister' was the approved form now. Nevertheless, he was the 'Most Serene Prince,' head of the 'Serenissima,' the 'Most Serene Republic,' and he lived up to that title. Doge Steno had as fine a stable as any in Italy, and he resided in one of the finest palaces, surrounded by as much pomp as any potentate in Europe. Yet a Doge was increasingly the prisoner of his pomp. He could not abdicate without permission, and soon he was not even to be allowed to call Council sessions without prior approval.

But if many still remembered Steno as the youthful prankster who scrawled graffiti on Doge Faliero's walls and suffered a few days in prison for it, people who ridiculed their rulers these days could not expect the leniency he had enjoyed. In 1404 Ludovico Contarini lost a hand for publishing caricatures of the Serenissima.

The majority of Venetians were well advised to steer clear of politics other than those of their own corporate institutions. Bakers, tailors and silkspinners, Germans and Armenians were at liberty to debate the running of their hospitals; Scuole members could argue about the administration of their mutual sickness benefits, dowries, pensions and burial expenses. Caulkers and carpenters could ensure an income for older colleagues by forcing their employers to hire one 'veteran' over fifty-five for every six masters they employed and to pay them the same wages as their best workers. But they questioned the actions of the Signoria at their peril.

Yet though the guilds were self-governing they did not enjoy the degree of independence trade unions do today. Though the government co-operated with them in protecting trade secrets, they kept a close eye on their activities – as indeed they did on every organization in Venice, not least the Church. Venetians holding ecclesiastical posts were suspect – and their families too. Churchmen, so prominent as high state functionaries in other countries, were excluded from the Great Council and government office, and from 1411 nobles with a beneficed priest among their relatives were barred from all debates on ecclesiastical matters.

Resentment of papal interference in what Venice considered to be her secular affairs was great and increasing. Priests continued to be elected by the city parishes, and Venetian bishops were elected by the Senate although confirmed by the papacy. From 1378 the schism in the church had presented greater opportunities for taking an independent line. Even when a Venetian, Angelo Cornaro, was elected Pope as Gregory XII in 1406, the Signoria chose not to recognize him, though in 1409 when both the Pope and the Anti-pope were deposed and another Venetian subject, the Cretan Pietro Filargi (Alexander V), was elected, Venice thought it wise to promise her obedience; and in 1420 when Martin V was triumphantly installed in Rome, Venice, while continuing to maintain that a Council of the Church had more authority than any Pope, took care to send four delegates to congratulate him.

Elections of Doges now went more smoothly than those of Popes, and early in 1414, the year before Henry V beat the French at Agincourt, Venice celebrated the election of a new one, Tomasso Mocenigo. The Marquis of Ferrara and Gonzaga Lord of Mantua both attended his installation; the goldsmiths and jewellers appeared in scarlet robes on lace-decked horses, hired at three ducats apiece. The guilds gave feasts and revels and the parades and jousts went on for several weeks disrupting the activities of the hucksters and street traders who normally set out their goods on trestles round the Palace and the Piazzetta.

Under Tomasso Mocenigo Venice attained a new height in prestige. Lesina, Spalatro, Sebenico and Traù were all reoccupied and in 1418 the Friuli was conquered – an achievement hallowed by yet another ceremony, at which the Doge would enter the great hall and knock down toy castles representing the Lords

Friuli. Moreover, although in 1411 Venice had begun paying tribute to the Turks, she was increasingly looked on as the prime defender of Christendom against them.

In May 1416, a Venetian fleet under Pietro Loredano engaged a Turkish fleet off Gallipoli. The battle was vividly described by Loredano himself, who did not omit mention of his own heroic part in the affray.

'I the commander, battling like a man, attacked the first galley, which defended itself with great courage, for the Turks . . . fight like dragons. . . . By God's grace I took her . . . but I had great difficulty in saving the prize, for other galleys bore down on my stern . . . raking me with javelins and arrows. And I felt them, I assure you, for I was wounded in the left cheek, just under the eye, [and] by a dart which . . . passed right through my left hand. These wounds were serious. I was wounded, too, about the body . . . but these were of no consequence compared with the other two. I fought on, however, and drove the attacking galleys back, taking the first of them, and running up my flag. Then I rammed and disabled a galliot [and] cut her crew to pieces. . . . The rest of our fleet fought splendidly, and although the Turks . . . made a brave defence . . . we routed them.' A delighted government immediately announced this brilliant victory to all Europe and by way of thanksgiving the Signoria and clergy paraded through the city carrying all their numerous saintly relics.

But Venice had other enemies hardly less dangerous than the Turks. In 1415 the Emperor Sigismund had severed Venice's overland trade route to the free cities of Augsburg, Ulm and Nuremberg in southern Germany. The dispatch of goods through foreign intermediaries helped partially to pierce the embargo. Beyond this the government sought to overcome the problem by having the Emperor poisoned, and in 1419 the Council of Ten received an offer from a Cretan called Michellotto Mudazzo to carry out the operation in return for a pension of a thousand ducats.

Mudazzo was truly a Renaissance figure in the scope of his knavery. He was a thief-catcher, having earned a reward of 4,000 ducats for bringing in Giorgio Bragadin to be hanged for treason. He had also served four months in gaol for striking an adversary in court and another year and banishment for suborning a witness. But the Ten gave him a safe conduct to Venice, and the search began for an appropriate poison. Slow and rapid poisons, poisons administered with food or drink, poisons said to work by touch or smell, pounded diamonds, poisons from the village of Puegnano by Lake Garda (a celebrated source of noxious recipes), and poisons brewed by learned alchemists in Padua and Vicenza – all were considered. The poison cupboard of the Ten filled up with phials and amphorae, but eventually the project petered out and Mudazzo was dismissed.

While the Council of Ten schemed to uncover plots at home and dispose of enemies abroad his Serenity the Doge fulfilled his ceremonial role in innumerable processions and received important foreigners, including Henry V's uncle the Bishop of Winchester, with the utmost dignity and pomp.

Among the spectators at such grand occasions was an eighteen-year-old nobleman called Andrea Barbarigo, whose career has been regarded as the archetype of others of the time who tried to grow rich through commerce. When the Bishop of Winchester visited Venice, Andrea's family was under a cloud. His father Nicolò had lost a ship, contravening regulations while in command of a spice convoy from Alexandria, and the fine of 10,000 ducats he had to pay for his negligence had reduced the family to ruin.

Andrea's only assets were his ability to read, write, work an abacus, shoot a cross-bow, and 200 ducats which his mother scraped together for him. With these slender resources for a man of his class Andrea had to make his own way in the world. He began by obtaining a free commercial apprenticeship as a 'bowman of the quarterdeck' on a merchant galley bound for Alexandria.

At sea he messed with the officers and merchants, and was therefor able to strike up acquaintance with experienced operators who might be useful to him in the future, learn from their experiences, receive advice as to how best to put his modest capital to use, and to see for himself how trade was conducted in foreign parts. On his return Andrea consolidated this commercial apprenticeship by a study of commercial law, and spent most of his twenties as an official attorney. Fees came relatively easily, since litigants had to retain official attorneys even in cases beyond their competence when expert citizen lawyers had to be engaged as well, but by the time he was thirty-two Andrea abandoned the courts to concentrate on a purely commercial career.

He realized that the free enterprise market of Rialto was not the sole interpreter of supply and demand. Government constructed the framework within which commerce proceeded, taking naval as well as market factors into account in dictating the pattern of galley voyages, the terms on which they were to run, and even freight-rates and priorities on the chief items likely to be loaded. Yet Andrea also knew that there was wide scope for individuals to choose their methods of operation within these bounds. Goods could be shipped in cogs rather than in galleys, for instance, and more cheaply too, albeit at greater risk; and there was a choice of agents overseas as well who usually charged a two per cent commission on the goods they sold and one per cent of those they bought new, rather than share in the profits as once had been the custom.

Living in Venice, Andrea knew its routines. He heard the bells of the Arsenal peal out at sunrise every day to summon in the workers, knew of the constant pilfering that went on there and of the dismissals, floggings or sessions in the stocks which those culprits who were caught received. He saw the salt barges coming in from Chioggia, Istria and Cyprus to keep the city and the hinterland supplied now that the local pans were drying up; he admired the workmanship of the city's many craftsmen, and knew all the large-scale specialists in commerce, for Venice was small enough for him to be on bowing terms with every person of importance.

Thanks to their gossip, Andrea was also aware of conditions in the outside world. He knew that Florence had begun to send trading ships to Egypt, and heard the buzz raised on the Rialto when Florence captured the market in Bologna hemp, which was so essential for the manufacture of ships' ropes. He learned how monopolies were acquired and how they could be broken. In fact Andrea had all the knowledge, the connections and the shrewdness necessary to be a successful merchant – everything, in fact, but capital.

How he must have envied his thousand fellow-nobles with incomes of over 700 a year; how he must have sighed to see rich young men squandering their substance on banquets and bright costumes. While Andrea had to watch the pennies, Procurator Marino Contarini paid stonemasons up to 140 ducats a year plus wine to build himself a palace so flamboyant that by the time it was finished ten years later Venetians had dubbed it the Ca' d'Oro, or the house of gold. Thanks to his father's indiscretion Andrea would have to labour long and hard before accumulating a thousand ducats, a sum Doge Mocenigo spent merely to induce the Senate to allow him, contrary to his oath, to embellish his palace, which needed rebuilding after a fire – and in a style to match the greatness of the state.

The Doge's wish reflected the feelings of all those who bragged that Venice was the best power in all Italy – feelings expressed by Mocenigo himself in a 'state of the nation' address delivered on his death-bed in the spring of 1423. The public debt, he reported, had been reduced from ten millions to six; merchants turned over ten millions a year in trade at a forty per cent profit, and a million golden ducats were being minted every year. Venice had a considerable empire, a fleet of forty-five galleys, 300 other sea-going ships and 3,000 smaller vessels; the city boasted a famous dyeing industry, sugar refineries, soap and candle manufactures, and a weaving industry employing nearly 20,000 hands. The State's income exceeded one and a half millions a year, over half of it coming from the empire. Venice's housing stock was worth seven and a half millions and produced half a million a year in rents. Mocenigo might have exaggerated a little, but he was justifiably proud of the city state's success – and he had grave fears about the future.

Greedy to invest in estates in the hinterland which were producing profits of up to twenty per cent – a tempting return now that the trading outlook in the Levant was uncertain because of the Turkish threat – many nobles were urging an offensive alliance with Florence against Milan. By this means, they thought, Venice might wrest the rich lands of Brescia and Bergamo from Milan, an expansion which would enrich the state and allow them to realize their new dreams of cheap and profitable land investment.

Andrea Barbarigo had too little capital to have much interest in such schemes, but the old Doge was set against risking present affluence by such adventurism. Good relations with Milan were vital, he considered, to Venice's prosperity. Venice was highly dependent on Milanese agricultural produce, and Milan bought a quarter of all Venetian exports. It was a 'fine garden for Venice' and to devastate it would be folly. Moreover, the scheme would require the maintenance of a much larger army which would be a constant drain on the Venetian exchequer. 'War with Milan,' warned the dying Doge, would risk 'our treasure, our honour, our authority. From being lords of the world you will become the servants of the *condottieri* you employ.'

As well as speaking against the policy itself, the Doge attacked its spokesman – Francesco Foscari, Procurator of St. Mark's, the man tipped to succeed him. Mocenigo referred to him disparagingly as the 'youthful' Foscari, although the Procurator was almost fifty years of age, said he was a man who grasped at much but could hold little, that he lacked experience, that if he became Doge money would depreciate by ninety per cent. Mocenigo recommended several other candidates, any of whom he thought preferable to the Procurator. But when the Doge died early in April 1423 Foscari was elected.

It is not known how Andrea Barbarigo voted nor if he joined the other 900 Great Council members in their magnificent new chamber which was inaugurated on the first day of the new reign to hear Foscari's inaugural address. The amateur chroniclers who reported all these happenings, who laboured over lists of Doges past and family genealogies, decorating the margins of their manuscripts with brightly coloured coats of arms, made no mention of Andrea. Their attentions were firmly focussed on their own families and on great happenings of the day – wars, natural disasters, the activities of Doges.

Doge Foscari began his reign by gaining sanction for yet another reconstruction of the Palace, welcoming the Greek Emperor

Manuel Paleologus to Venice, and accepting the submission of Thessalonika, which was threatened by the Turks. But, as Mocenigo had forecast, attention soon turned to the hinterland.

Florence was frightened of the expansionist Visconti, who already dominated Cremona, Crema, Bergamo, Brescia and Genoa, besides Milan, and Venice was also anxious to clip his wings. Yet policy did not change overnight. Visconti was expanding southwards, posing no threat to Venetian interests, and when Florence suggested an alliance in 1424 the Signoria's response was cool. But by 1425 Florence had been seriously defeated by Visconti's forces and Venice now preferred to intervene rather than see her overrun. Florence, that 'other head of freedom in Italy,' urged Doge Foscari, must not perish, and an alliance was duly made.

The Signoria took care to prepare thoroughly for the war. As usual, they set out to hire professional war leaders, and this time they chose Count Francesco Bussone, called Carmagnola, the toughest *condottiere* of them all.

Carmagnola had been born near Turin over forty years before, the son of a swineherd so it was said, and had risen, ironically enough, in Visconti's service. He had captured Genoa, beaten the Swiss near Bellinzona, been promoted supremo of Visconti's army, chief councillor, and governor of Genoa. He had been given estates, promised a Visconti wife, and a palace in Milan. But of late, sensing he was falling out of favour, he had offered his services to Savoy, and failing to obtain a positive response he had turned to Venice.

Carmagnola arrived in February 1425 and the negotiations began. He demanded supreme command, the right to all prisoners and booty, a salary of 6,500 ducats a month and a down-payment of 30,000 in advance. However, he accepted supreme command and 1,000 ducats a month, and now that Visconti had impounded all his property Carmagnola set out to rebuild his fortunes in the service of the Serenissima.

In December 1425 the Venetian Senate approved a ten-year alliance with Florence, and on the 15th of that month the sly-eyed, bull-necked, flabby-faced Carmagnola swore loyalty to Venice at the high altar of St. Mark's and was entrusted with the banner of the saint. War was declared within a month and Carmagnola led the troops out to besiege Brescia. Then, complaining of jaundice and a fall from his horse, he asked for leave to take a cure.

In May 1426 he was made a nobleman of Venice, but though he returned to the siege in October he soon absented himself again and Brescia was taken in his absence. A peace was concluded at the end of 1426, but within a matter of weeks the war flared up again. In the spring of 1427 Visconti took the offensive. Carmagnola allowed him to advance, but then mounted a grand counter-offensive of his own: 22,000 cavalry and 14,000 foot surged into Milanese territory south of Bergamo – but then Carmagnola flagged again. He neither advanced on Milan nor on Pizzeghetone to the south as the Signoria wished. In July, when the Milanese attacked, Carmagnola drove them back on Cremona; but then he retreated. There was another, indecisive clash and once more Europe's best-paid mercenary withdrew.

Throughout the sweltering summer months the Venetian Senate waited uneasily for positive news. It did not come; yet they expressed pain rather than anger when Carmagnola proposed ending the campaign. In the cool of October 1427, however, he at last obliged them, defeating the Milanese under Carlo Malatesta at Maclodio.

At this a joyful Signoria showered him with gifts – a palace in the city, an estate near Brescia worth 500 a year, and promises of more. But Visconti had not yet been crushed. Negotiations proceeded throughout the winter, and concerned Carmagnola's former estates in Milanese territory to no inconsiderable extent. Suspicious of his loyalty, the Signoria was delighted when Carmagnola declared that his allegiance would be exclusively to Venice. The Senate actually thanked him, and when a plague scare and a money shortage dictated the hasty signing of another peace in April 1428 it was in Carmagnola's palace that the Signoria held their celebration. Already, as Mocenigo had forecast, it seemed that the tail was wagging the dog.

Nevertheless, Venice was now the happy possessor of Bergamo and Brescia with its iron and its arms industry. Some feudal lords were dispossessed and their estates transferred to Venetian nobles eager to invest in land. But, as with her other *terraferma* territories, Venice ruled her new provinces very lightly, preferring to mediate between local lords and peasants rather than dispossess the former and rule the peasantry direct. A governor sent to Brescia was instructed to 'talk gently' to the people, so that 'all may be content with our dominion,' to tax them no more heavily than the Milanese had done and to 'ask them if they will accept our rector or if they would prefer to elect their own consuls under the Republic.'

The Signoria dealt lightly with Carmagnola too, despite the fact that, though still Captain-General, he maintained correspondence with Filippo Visconti, was offered his former position by him, and was soon building a family tomb in Milan. The Signoria was suspicious – but when he threatened to resign early in 1429 it hastily offered him a new two-year contract, a fief worth 6,000 a year in addition to his 1,000 a month, and allowed him to keep a personal guard of 500 lances loyal only to him. When the *condottiere* persisted in his dealings with Visconti, the Signoria did at last ask him to stop; but with war looming again they did not take too hard a line. Indeed, they promised him that once victory was won he would be given the outright possession of any enemy city captured, other than Milan, as well as the estates Visconti had confiscated from him.

The war was not universally popular in Venice, however. Taxation was high again and the city's population had been swelled by an influx of refugees from the war areas. The Signoria did try to win the war by methods short of fighting, and when the would-be poisoner Mudazzo appeared again, offering to despatch Visconti, the Council of Ten immediately took up the idea. They proceeded to test on pigs the poisons it had collected for use on the Emperor Sigismund. But the pigs survived, news of their plan reached Visconti, and the idea had to be abandoned. Mudazzo was packed off to Corfu.

The war was to continue; so was the uneasy relationship with the powerful war boss Carmagnola. Yet so far Venice had been splendidly victorious, and for all its attendant inconveniences the war did not put a stop to commerce. Prices were high; Germans ignored the Emperor's continuing embargo and were coming south to buy. War or no war, there were bright commercial prospects – as Andrea Barbarigo realized as he set about recouping his family's shattered fortunes.

Chapter VIII

The Golden Age

By 1431, when the Republic was approaching new pinnacles of power, wealth and prestige, Andrea Barbarigo had accumulated 1,600 ducats and decided to devote all his energies to commerce. His capital was still insufficient to operate on any substantial scale, however, so his first step was to raise more cash. He sold his government loan stock at half its nominal value and his mother's too – her only asset. He sold off a small estate in Crete which he had inherited jointly with his brother Giovanni, let out rooms in the house the family rented, and borrowed money as well. By these means he doubled the amount with which he had to play.

He was often at the Rialto now, watching market trends and trying to memorize significant facts and prices – indeed, in March 1431 he invested thirteen ducats in a memory course given by 'Maestro Piero of the Memory' to help him fix them in his mind. And now he joined the other merchants who bargained, switched investments, schemed for shipping space, exchanged information about the merits of commission agents in foreign ports, and tried to forecast the demand for various commodities in a dozen different countries.

A man with 3,300 ducats to invest, however, was still a small-scale operator. The brothers Luca and Andrea Vendramin could send goods worth 400,000 on a single voyage to Alexandria and give each of their daughters a dowry worth twice Andrea's capital. But little fish could wax fat enough on tit-bits picked up by following the big fish, and Andrea was socially acceptable, intelligent and loyal – just the man great capitalists might employ to handle a small deal or offer a hot tip.

Nevertheless it was a family contact which first helped Andrea. His cousins, who owned large estates in Crete, appointed him their agent in Venice to sell their produce and buy the goods they needed on commission. He was also charged to look after the illegitimate daughter one of them had left in Venice, and both were eventually to make Andrea their heir. Andrea did not form a commercial partnership with his own brother, however, as was common. He was a lone wolf, keeping his profits to himself and taking his own risks.

He had mixed luck from the start. The goods he shipped by cog to northern Europe in 1430 were captured by pirates. On the other hand, the six bags of pepper he sent by galley to Flanders reached Bruges safely, where his agents the Capello brothers sold them on his instructions, and invested the proceeds in more than 1,600 ducats' worth of cloth and English pewter for shipment back to Venice.

By then war with Milan had broken out again. Genoese warships controlled by Milan were on the prowl for Venetian ships taking their customary route from Flanders, and threatening Andrea's venture. Fortunately, however, the Flanders galleys, warned by the Signoria, altered course in time and steered clear of the enemy, so that in April 1431 Andrea's goods arrived.

He disposed of them briskly, selling most of the cloth through his godfather Lorenzo da Vigna's shop, sending the rest off to the hinterland and consigning the pewter to Ferrara, Verona and Apulia. Then Andrea pondered as to where he should invest the proceeds.

The Levant seemed an obvious choice. The Mameluke Soldan of Egypt, Palestine and Syria had monopolized the spice and cotton trade in order to raise prices. Venice had retaliated by restricting trade there to state convoys, whose admirals were instructed to refuse payment of the Soldan's dues. The convoy returning in 1430 carried no spices, but now relations with the Soldan were on the mend, and with Venice short of oriental goods Andrea decided to invest heavily in a shipment to the Levant.

He first had to find shipping space, however. The state galleys were all full, and Andrea was lucky to find space in one of the additional six ships, which, after heated argument between merchant interests and government, were allowed to leave for Syria that September. He chose to consign his goods to a new agent, Alberto Dolceto, who was about to set up business at Acre, and reckoned that because of the lack of competition he would be able to buy cotton there cheaply. Andrea looked forward to a quick turnover and a handsome profit. But he also hedged his bet by sending to Constantinople for a few hundred ducats' worth of gold thread – and it was just as well he did, for while the gold thread arrived safely enough and was sent overland to London in the spring of 1432, he was unlucky with his main investment.

In the autumn of 1431 Venice decided to seize Schio from the Genoese and the ships carrying Andrea's goods had to off-load at Crete and join in the assault. The merchants travelling with the convoy were furious, and thanks partly to their pressure the siege was abandoned in January 1432. But when the ships finally docked at Venice that April, months behind schedule, Andrea's cotton was not on board. The galleys had no room for it. Instead it had been transferred to sailing ships which were now being hunted by the Genoese. They took one ship carrying half Andrea's cotton off the coast of Crete, and Andrea waited apprehensively for news of the rest. When three more ships sailed into harbour his hopes rose – but only two of his bales were on board. The rest, it transpired, was in two other sailing ships which had turned back to Crete.

In the meantime Andrea concentrated on his other investments, handling the wine, the cheese and kermes dye his cousins sent him, and on exploiting his contacts to the maximum. The most important of these were the rich Cappello brothers operating at Bruges, and Francesco Balbi.

Balbi owned several ships, was a considerable merchant, an entrepreneur in local industry, and had just opened a bank. Balbi liked Andrea and helped him, allowing him overdrafts, letting him collect bills of exchange which gave him further credit, and sometimes discounting bills owing to Andrea for cash, allowing him to turn his money over quicker. Andrea also shipped in Balbi's name and joined in many of Balbi's schemes. He was a seagull perching on the great whale's back.

Thanks to Balbi's help Andrea was able to buy modest quantities of Florentine and English cloth, sheepskins, canvas and silver coin for export. But with the war with Milan occasioning losses and delays he was soon looking for investment opportunities nearer home. Realizing that war so often brought a famine in its wake, early in 1432 he decided to invest in wheat, instructing an agent in the Marche to buy a 1,000 bushels on his account. But by the time Andrea entered the market grain prices had risen and he turned instead to buying animal skins to send overland to Bruges, the safest route in those days, and the safest foreign market, thanks to the war.

The war was not going very well for Venice. In the campaign of 1431 her highly paid commander, Carmagnola, had been so sluggish that at times he hardly seemed to move at all. Yet only in October when he had allowed an assault on Cremona to go unsupported with his main force cantonned just three miles away did the Signoria's patience with him begin to fray. In February 1432 they ordered him to have no communication whatsoever with the Milanese, but doubts soon arose as to whether he was obeying them. Carmagnola's actions and inactions suddenly seemed sinister; more and more Venetians were coming to believe that he was deliberately obstructing the war effort; fears grew that he was about to desert to his erstwhile lord, Visconti of Milan.

At the end of March 1432 the Council of Ten decided that Carmagnola must be arrested. But since the Captain-General was always surrounded by a personal bodyguard of men-at-arms, this was more easily contemplated than done. The Ten called on the advice of twenty additional sages and the Senate sat in constant session for two days before it was finally decided to send the Secretary to the Ten to Brescia to 'invite' Carmagnola to Venice to 'consult' over the next campaign.

If the Captain-General refused to come the governors of Brescia were to attempt an arrest. But fortunately Carmagnola suspected nothing. Those in the know kept their mouths tightly shut, and care was taken to keep any fears on Carmagnola's part allayed. All honours were shown him as he rode towards Venice accompanied by his usual entourage of bodyguards, and on arrival he was welcomed by eight distinguished noblemen and an invitation to have dinner with the Doge.

When Carmagnola arrived at the Palace, however, he was told the Doge was ill: could he dine tomorrow? The guest and his escort were then conducted out. But they were not shown out the usual way. When Carmagnola noticed this his guides muttered something about palace alterations. Then suddenly a door clanged shut and the mercenary found himself imprisoned and alone.

His property and papers had already been seized, and the examination of his wife, his mistress and associates was already in progress. Within two days he himself was charged, and his trial, adjourned during Holy Week, produced the predictable result. Innocent or guilty, Carmagnola was too dangerous to live. On 5th May 1432 the Captain-General, clad in a crimson jerkin, scarlet leggings and red velvet cap, was brought out gagged onto the Piazzetta, and his head sent rolling from his bull-like neck.

A few weeks after Carmagnola's execution Andrea Barbarigo received twenty splendid cloths from London through the German shipping firm of Johann Keller of Memmingen. Since English cloths now seemed an excellent investment he decided to buy heavily, reckoning his profits would justify the eight or ten per cent interest on the money he borrowed. He ordered over a thousand ducats' worth from the Cappellos at Bruges sending them goods in payment. But the cloths consigned to him were impounded at Ulm following the instructions of the Emperor. At the beginning of 1433, then, most of the cotton he had bought at Acre was still at sea; another consignment of gold thread from Constantinople was delayed while the galleys carrying it went off to plunder Genoese ships, and his English cloth was blocked at Ulm.

But at last his luck began to turn. Fourteen bales of cotton arrived, and thanks to inflated prices due to the war he sold them that March at a handsome profit. The skins he had sent to Bruges and London fetched good prices too; in February his consignment of gold thread arrived, and in June a consignment of cloth, probably thanks to a Münich merchant whom he had engaged to get his goods through Ulm. Moreover they arrived in time to be sent off with a convoy sailing for the Levant, where prices were even more generous than in Venice.

That April the war ended at last. Freight rates dropped accordingly and there was a rush of investment in the east. With the big merchants in the market again, Andrea looked like being squeezed out, and in fact his next shipment from Acre had to be sold at a slight loss. But he persevered and in the summer of 1433 sent consignments to many agents, couching his instructions to them in terms of the utmost *politesse*. Goods were sent for their 'honour and profit,' as if the agents' interests not his were the point of the transaction, and he made a practice of promising larger orders to encourage them to do their best for him.

His connection with the Cappellos remained excellent, and though he used other agents in the north he took care to keep his fact a secret – especially once a Cappello got command of a Flanders galley, which put him in a position to refuse the cargo of a personal enemy and find room in a crowded ship for the consignment of a friend. But Andrea had known the Cappello family since childhood and relations were otherwise very close. He even bought the grain and wine for their mother's household, and borrowed money from their sister.

On the other hand his relations with Dolceto at Acre deteriorated. In 1434 Dolceto sent him a large quantity of cotton of such poor quality it was almost unsaleable. 'Having bad cotton,' wrote Andrea, 'is like a penalty in hell.' Yet he continued to use him even when he found out that Dolceto had cheated him over the cotton ladings of 1432.

Andrea kept as fluid as possible, was ever alert to anticipated price fluctuations, and ready to turn his attentions from one comodity or area to others. To the extent he specialized it was in the cloth trade between Flanders and the Levant. Yet in 1435-6, with the Cappellos contracting their business at Bruges and trouble brewing with the Soldan, he shifted his main investments to Spain. In this he anticipated a general switch of interest, and was able to profit by getting in ahead of the rush.

Between 1436 and 1439 Andrea invested about 4,000 ducats with Bertuccio Zorzi in Valencia. Zorzi was Francesco Balbi's son-in-law, a connection Andrea did not fail to stress. 'I am sending you funds,' he wrote once, 'chiefly to please . . . your father-in-law, and for your honour and profit.' And Zorzi was to serve him well.

Meanwhile, other Venetian nobles sought profits much farther afield. In 1436 Josafa Barbaro left Venice to set up as a trading agent at Tana. During his sixteen years abroad he searched for hidden treasure on the Russian steppe – though the great burial mounds he and his friends excavated yielded only a few silver pots and ewers besides human remains – raided Circassians, encountered gypsies, saw the wild geese flying, and meanwhile earned his keep buying Russian slaves from Tatar raiders for shipment home to Venice. In later life Barbaro was to visit Poland, Muscovy, exotic Georgia and Azerbaidjan. But others ventured even further. In 1431 three Venetians sailed out into the Atlantic and eventually beached on the bleak shores of the Lofoten Islands; others were soon visiting Madeira, the Canary Islands and Senegal. But many less venturesome Venetian noblemen preferred safer careers in government.

The overseas colonies needed new governors every two years, while Venice's possessions on the mainland were now so extensive that there was often a lack of candidates to fill all posts – or at least of candidates considered suitable, for opportunity for graft in addition to salary made such posts very attractive. Early in the 1430s, in fact, twenty-three nobles were found guilty of conspiring to help each other accumulate offices. But it was the more lucrative and less onerous posts that were chiefly in demand.

The installation of officials was not Venice's only means of trying to digest its conquests. Determined efforts were also made to establish Venetians as landowners on the immense estates of the territories' former rulers, especially in the more sensitive areas like Padua where particular concern was expressed lest the Carrara estates 'pass into the hands of foreigners.' By 1446, in fact, Venetians owned a third of all lands in that province, though they acquired barely a quarter of the Scaligeri estates in the province of Verona when they came up for sale, most of the buyers being local lords.

Increased involvement with the mainland strengthened humanist tendencies in Venice's intellectual life. And this proved to be the dawn of a Golden Age – in architecture, painting and in clothes as well. The Doge's palace might have been unfinished, but the Ca' d'Oro with all its flashy gilding and battlements painted to resemble marble was. Venetian streets might be filthy – which probably induced so many women to go about on high choppines and men to ride on horseback (though this was banned in certain sectors and horses now had to carry warning bells)–but the great churches of the Frari, SS. Giovanni and Paolo and San Stefano all belong to this period, as do the Gritti and Priuli palaces, and a dozen other famous buildings. Much of this building reflected an irrepressible surge of sensuality, but this found expression in other forms as well.

Courtesans were beginning to display yellowed hair and painted bosoms, friars were soon inveighing against wigs and hair-pieces, 'sensuous' books and pictures, and when the government persisted in trying to control extravagance in dress people proceeded to slash their sleeves so as to show off glittering underwear. A new sense of freedom was seen in painting too. The Vivarinis' painting workshop was founded in the 1430s. Jacopo Bellini had a studio, and his more famous sons Gentile and Giovanni were about to follow him. Smiling sensuous faces and scenes of Renaissance pomp were beginning to supplant the formalized religious pictures of the Byzantine and Gothic traditions.

Yet Venice was still a great religious centre. Since 1431 the Pope, Eugenius IV, had been Venetian too, though this fact did not alter the Signoria's attitude to the church. The Doge still pronounced benedictions on great occasions, and still claimed the right to nominate bishops. But in 1434 Venice did ally itself with the Pope against Milan, which had occupied part of his territories, an alliance which a newly independent Genoa soon joined, and from that point on Venice maintained a diplomatic representative in Rome – probably the first permanent resident ambassador to the Holy See. The most delicate diplomatic task on hand, however, was the acquisition of a formal title to her new possessions on the *terraferma*. Legally the Friuli still belonged to the Patriarch of Aquileia, and Vicenza, Verona, Brescia and Bergamo to Visconti. But in August 1437 a Venetian ambassador to Prague took a formal oath of fealty to the Western Emperor, who invested Venice with the titles to them all – in return for a paltry annual tribute of 1,000 ducats' worth of golden cloth. The timing of this recognition was particularly opportune in view of the new flare-up with Milan.

For this war Venice had found a new mercenary to lead her armies: Francesco de Narni, called Gattemalata. Like Carmagnola he was ennobled and given a handsome residence in the city; unlike him, however, Gattemalata's loyalty was never questioned and so far from being slothful he immediately accomplished a remarkable feat of military art. Trapped by the enemy between Lake Garda and the Alps, he managed to extricate the army by marching it through the mountains and emerged to interpose it like a barrier between Visconti's troops and Venice.

Not all Venetians saw the conduct of war as a function of strategy alone, however. Prayer and piety were also thought to count. With Brescia and Bergamo already lost, the government, 'appealed to God, ordered many sermons to be preached, much alms to be given, and devout processions to be held,' and the Bishop of Castello sought God's favour in this hour of crisis by ordaining that from August 1st, 'no woman might wear silk or false hair . . . nor ornament her sleeves with pearls, on pain of excommunication.' This measure, however, ran counter to Venetian tastes, and the Signoria soon prevailed upon the Pope to revoke it.

The government also put on great displays of pomp despite the war, notably in 1438 when the Eastern Emperor, John Paleologus, arrived. He was rowed across the lagoon upon the

Doge Francesco Foscari

Doge Cicogna by Veronese

Bucintoro by *arsenalotti* wearing silken jerkins emblazoned with the Lion of St. Mark and the imperial eagle. The air resounded with the sounds of cheers and trumpets as the Emperor was carried along the Grand Canal, sighing, as Gibbon wrote, to see all the 'spoils and trophies' which had once adorned Constantinople.

Then another outbreak of the plague, the first of any note for almost thirty years, drove festive thoughts from Venetian minds as well, and the air became suffused with odours as aromatic spices were burned in hopes of keeping the pestilence at bay. But early in 1439 the plague began to ebb and news that Brescia had been recaptured provoked demonstrations of frenzied joy – so frenzied, indeed, that they ended with a riot. The city's poor broke open the prisons and into the Mint; a Signore di Notte who intervened was killed, so was a *Savio* dell' Armar; and it took that garrulous old hero Pietro Loredano to calm things down.

Such contretemps as a military reverse, a plague outbreak and rioting proved to be only minor interruptions to a generally expansionary progress, however, and all through these excitements Andrea Barbarigo had been busy with his deals with Spain. He had made a quick 1,000 ducats out of the wool his agent sent him, and he made an even bigger *coup* in February 1439 by marrying the Capellos' sister Cristina who brought him a dowry of 4,000 ducats. Two sons were born of the marriage within four years, and, love apart, it was a marriage much to be desired. From now on Andrea was much less involved with Balbi; he had no need to be, having capital enough now to stand upon his own two feet.

He used every penny of it too, still rented a house rather than buy one, and, though he did spend 147 ducats on three slaves to help his wife, he kept so much of his capital in commerce that he once had to pawn a ring for ten ducats in cash. Thanks to his care, however, he could now deal on equal terms with others and even patronize fledgeling merchants like Andrea da Mosto and his brother Alvise who was to earn fame later discovering the Cape Verde Islands for the Duke of Portugal.

These two acted as his agents in North Africa where state

F

galleys now made regular runs. Andrea invested 1,500 ducats' worth of goods with them between 1443 and 1445, and his deals with Barbary proved profitable. But they were by no means his only ones. In 1442 he had no less than 10,000 ducats in play between England and Egypt – investments in cloth and cotton, dyes, stone, leather, pepper, pewter, grain, cheese, arsenic, ginger, copper wire, kerseys, brazil wood, oil, wool, roasted almonds, Spanish silk, sugar from Palermo, slaves from Tana, and sand ballast from Flanders.

From the records he left Professor Lane has reckoned that between 1431 and 1445 Andrea made an average profit of over fifteen per cent – about three per cent above the market average. At last in a position to relax his stern principles of home economy, he bought land at Montebelluno, at the foot of the Alps, and built a house where his family could spend the summers – and which saved him paying inflated prices for accommodation at Treviso where they fled each time there was a plague scare.

But if Andrea Barbarigo prospered many Venetians felt the pinch of war and were relieved at every short-lived peace. At one stage the value of some state bonds had slumped to twenty points and the collection of forced loans became so difficult that the government was eventually forced to tax incomes. Such was the cost of becoming a major land power – but it was to produce quite handsome dividends.

Some muted discontent at home was matched by unrest in the colonies. Crete was reasonably quiet; so was Corfu; but the serfs of Morea voiced complaints enough to the visiting magistrates – monthly labour service for their masters, demands for straw and forage for the governor's horses, and animals for his hunting parties. But an increasingly common form of protest was a silent one – flight by Christians from Christian government to the protection of the Muslim Turks.

Despite the fulminations of Christian potentates against them, and regular calls by Popes for a Crusade, Muslims commonly treated their subjects with more charity; and while the Pope barred Venice from taking Jewish dead to the Holy Land for burial the Soldan allowed both Jews and Christians to visit it. The

Western Emperor was one who took advantage of this policy, and his call at Venice on the way occasioned another great display of pomp; but it did not match the celebration of Lucrezia Contarini's marriage to Doge Foscari's son Jacopo in 1441.

Jacopo's father did them proud; so did the bride's family. 'We gave her a dowry of 16,000 ducats,' wrote one of her brothers, besides a 'trousseau, on which, seeing she was marrying into the Doge's family, we could not but spend 600 ducats.' Lucrezia held herself so well at the ceremony that her brother believed 'she must have been inspired by God.' There followed cavalcades, tournaments, jousts and balls, banquets in the great hall at which 'nothing but capons, partridges, peacocks, oysters, and sweet-meats' were served and 'all in such quantities that there was plenty to throw away after everyone had eaten his fill.' The Compagnia della Calza paraded in all their finery, and Andrea Barbarigo's business associate Balbi gave a grand feast for the bride and groom; the *Bucintoro* was brought out, and 'everything went off as merry as a marriage bell.'

Within three years, however, Jacopo Foscari was exiled for taking bribes, trying to influence the disposal of state offices and having illicit dealings with the Republic's arch enemy, Visconti of Milan. Nothing that the Doge could do could save him. Yet he continued in office and the grieving Dogaressa still had to carry out her public duties. A few weeks afterwards she received the Marchioness of Ferrara, daughter of the King of Aragon, with such graciousness as she could muster, surrounded as she was by dignitaries who had condemned her son.

The occasion was marred for others too, for the crush barriers gave way and more than seventy people drowned in the canal – but even this was a minor matter to set beside the heavy cost of the struggle with Milan, which still continued despite periodic intermissions. When the fighting flared up for the sixth time in 1447, however, it went Venice's way. Her troops took Crema, and in August Filippo Maria, Duke of Milan, suddenly died, at which the people of the city rose and proclaimed a republic. Despite the urgings of such humanists as Francesco Barbaro, who wanted Venice to form an alliance with the new republic and 'unite the energies of northern Italy . . . on a basis of equality,' the Venetian army proceeded to seize Lodi and Piacenza.

The Count Sforza's mercenaries crushed the infant republic, took control of Milan and drove the Venetian army out of Piacenza. Everything was thrown into the melting-pot again. Not until 1453 was peace to come at last; but when it came Venice added Crema and Treviglio to her possessions.

The Republic was now the strongest power in all of Italy, and commercially she led the world. While a miserable and backward England, ravaged by the Wars of the Roses, could not even dream of empire, a triumphant, glittering Venice ruled extensive territories both on land and overseas. Her prestige and pride stood high, and although this age, like any other, brought disappointments and reverses, and more glories were yet to come, these were to stand out in retrospect as Venice's most golden years.

The Signoria's persistence, pragmatism and greed over the years had been fully justified; abstract notions of the common good promoted by humanists had gone by the board and most Venetians continued to concentrate on money rather than ideals. This was the principle by which Andrea Barbarigo lived, and he had increased his fortune from 200 to 15,000 ducats by the time he died in 1449.

Nevertheless, material success bred a desire to excel in other fields and the accumulation of wealth bought the leisure necessary for scholarship. The new learning not only acquired some followers among the Venetian nobility, it attracted a degree of sponsorship from the state. Free lectures were given by distinguished scholars at a new school of liberal arts, to which a Venetian Pope, Paul II, was to grant university status in 1470. In the private sphere, conversations held at Barbaro's house were to influence many noblemen, not least a future Patriarch, Leonardo Giustiniani, while in the outside world humanists were coming to regard Venice as the only state in Italy whose government was both stable and legitimate.

Stable it may have been, but thanks only to the comparative solidarity of the ruling group and the effectiveness of its political policy. And despite attempts made by historians to categorize it

Venetian society was rich in contradictions. Its government was in many respects 'enlightened,' as, for example, in barring the employment of children in dangerous trades or in its condemnation as 'unjust and inhuman' of evictions of peasants from estates – yet it spied upon its own subjects, encouraged people to drop 'secret denunciations' of their fellow-citizens into the mouths of marble lions embedded in walls about the city, and was barbarian in the punishments it meted out, displaying criminals, for example, in cages slung half-way up the Campanile of St. Mark's. Similarly, while Venetians were all accounted equal before the law they had no appeal from the executive decisions of the Ten, and the system by which magistrates received a percentage of the fines they imposed or of the values at issue in a case encouraged partiality and graft.

The Venetian Republican system, with its complex system of checks and balances, was widely admired, but it was susceptible to corruption and abuse, if not noticeably more so than most democracies today. Great Council members often tried to cheat the system. In 1454 two noblemen lost their right hands for putting more than one ballot ball in the voting urn. Ludovico Foscarini, *podesta* of Verona from 1451-2, might claim with justice that he tried 'to reconcile quarrels,' that he racked his brains to improve the city's amenities, that he favoured the poor, was careful to do justice and 'ready to hear and give judgment to anyone who comes to me,' but many other administrators, especially those overseas, were blackly corrupt. And while humanists discussed the qualities of just government, the common good and a peaceful commonwealth, sections of the ruling group behaved as ruthlessly as the worst of the Renaissance princes.

One night early in November 1450 the acting head of the Council of Ten who had stopped on his way home to relieve himself in a doorway on the Campo Santa Maria Formosa was assaulted and stabbed in the back. He died of his wounds, and two months later Jacopo Foscari, whose father's pleas that he be allowed to return to Venice had at last been granted, was denounced as the murderer. The Doge's son was arrested, imprisoned, tortured and condemned – even though he had not confessed, a fact attributed to the 'various incantations and magic words he uttered under torture.' Nevertheless he was only exiled again – this time to Canea in Crete, an exposed outpost of the Empire.

The Signoria was becoming increasingly concerned about its interests in the eastern Mediterranean. For some years now the Turks had been advancing out of Asia Minor, despite desperate attempts by the puny remnant of the Byzantine Empire to fight them off. All this while Venice had been snapping up possessions in Greece and taking over island bases from the failing hands of their feudal owners to serve as additional bases to guard their shipping routes. But as a war with Turkey seemed increasingly a long-term possibility a much more powerful navy was needed too.

Already Venice had what was probably the largest fleet in the Mediterranean, but it consisted for the most part of round ships which, though larger and more manœuvrable than they had been, were still virtually useless in battle. So in 1442 the Signoria had decided to complete fifty new galleys immediately and to lay down the keels of another twenty-five.

The supervision of the work fell to a new chief foreman of the Arsenal, Giorgio the Greek. He and his men worked furiously to complete the ships on time and to keep the existing fleet repaired. But there were many days when work in the Arsenal's great open yards became impossible – days which were too hot even for men supplied with periodic gulps of wine, and days in winter when the rain teemed down. In 1449, therefore, the Senate ordered sheds to be built around the yards with wooden roofs which would allow work to continue the year round.

Nevertheless, while Venice made long-term preparations for war against the Turks, in the short term she was fully committed in northern Italy, and so, in December 1452, with the war with Milan still raging, Venice came to an accommodation with the Turks. By now it was inevitable that the Turks must overrun Constantinople and the Republic decided to guarantee its position in the east as best it could. So when Byzantium was besieged by the Turks in 1453 Venice sent only a token force of five galleys to her aid, pleading heavy military involvement on the mainland, and by the time they arrived Byzantium had already fallen. The city which had successively mothered Venice, been its mistress and been raped by her in 1204, had been allowed to fall to the Muslims by tacit consent.

While all Christendom showed consternation, and exiles from the stricken city flowed into Venice, the Signoria grabbed the islands of Skyros, Skiathos and Skopelos in the northern Sporades and set out to acquire more relics brought out of Constantinople. The bodies of St. Spiridon and St. Athanasius arrived, and, ultimately, St. George's head and the body of St. Rocco too, though an offer of 10,000 ducats for the Coat without a Seam did not succeed in obtaining it for Venice.

The peace with Milan, concluded in 1453, did not bring any immediate change in the Signoria's policy. In April 1454 the Venetian-Turkish agreement reached at the end of 1452 was confirmed, giving Venetians free access to the Black Sea, and limiting the duties they had to pay in Turkish ports to two per cent, the terms being reciprocal. There was a non-aggression pact as well, and Venice further agreed to pay tribute to the Turks in respect of her possession of Lepanto and of Scutari and Allessio in Albania. Bartolomeo Marcello, who had negotiated the deal, took up post as *bailo* at Constantinople. It was to be business as before.

The Pope was incensed, but Venetians merely shrugged their shoulders. '*Siamo Veneziani, poi Christiani,*' they would say – 'We are Venetians first, and Christians only afterwards.' Their position in the eastern Mediterranean was exposed; Crete was restive. Nevertheless few expected the Turkish advance to halt for long, and Venice continued to prepare to meet it when it came. No sooner had the treaty been made with the Turks than another fifty galleys were laid down. Moreover, from 1453 the government also began to tighten up the nautical laws, drawing up stringent rules for minimum crews, and stopping the practice by which boys, pilgrims, soldiers or servants were countable as sailors.

The costs of the enlarged fleet were met more easily now that the war with Milan was over and a new rating valuation had been made, for building had been booming and rents had soared. The old monoply on salt still yielded over a tenth of all revenue, but the new territories on the *terraferma* were already bearing dividends, both for the state and for the increasing numbers of poor nobles seeking salaried office.

So far as the professions were concerned, law and medicine paid the best. Law professors received the largest salaries, while doctors attending the rich charged considerable fees for their prescriptions – musk or galangal to serve as tonics, borax for glandular disorders, spikenard for the stone, sandalwood as an astringent, rhubarb to stimulate the bowels. The poor who fell sick, on the other hand, could count themselves fortunate to be attended by a good physician. A skilled craftsman might save a little for sickness or old age; a guild or a Scuola might help in emergency, and the church dispensed its alms. No one expected more; after all, the poor were treated no better in most other European cities, and employment was high in Venice.

The traditional crafts thrived (except for the long-established woollen industry, whose expansion was hampered by a lack of water power to turn a mill) and the state still tried to attract new ones to the city. Emigrants from Florence and Lucca had introduced terracotta and silk manufacture, and in the 1460s, attracted by the cheapness and the quality of paper in Venice, the brothers Johann and Windelin of Speyer and the Frenchman Nicholas Jensen set up as printers. Henceforth presses in the city multiplied, and were soon to become the most famous in the world.

Trade guilds were allowed to black employers who failed to pay the approved rate, and when a temporary recession in shipbuilding led shipowners to drive wages so low that caulkers could barely make a living the state was to fix a wage scale while the caulkers agreed to distribute such work as was available among themselves.

Still shipbuilding remained the largest employer, and it was nurtured like a loving mother by the state. It was a care that led to another excursion into the field of state enterprise. Because of the Florentine monopoly on Bologna hemp, the basic raw material for ropes, in 1455 the Signoria decided to promote a new hemp-growing project of its own. Marshes at Montagnana near Padua were drained, ponds were formed in which the hemp could soak and the local peasants were given the appropriate technical training, ordered to grow hemp as a crop, and offered a bounty for all hemp delivered to the Tana factory.

The sage governors of Venice looked to future needs, as did men of substance who were investing more in property and erecting buildings in the new style. Curved-topped arches were soon replacing those of the pointed Gothic type; architects and sculptors working in the new styles found increasing opportunities, while the birth in about 1455 of a child named Vettor to a family of fishermen and boat-builders called Carpaccio was to herald a new, adventurous trend in painting.

The prime Venetian art of Carpaccio's childhood, however, was ceremonial. The Venetian calendar was punctuated a dozen times a year by one of those occasions of ordered splendour in which the Doge and the grandees of the Republic would commemorate victories abroad and the unmasking of conspiracies at home. And this Venetian flair for ceremonial extended to ordinary craftsmen too. The caulkers hired trumpeters and pipers to accompany their corporate masses; Scuole members would mount evening processions carrying flickering tapers in their hands; polyphonic music accompanied occasions for group mourning and rejoicing, and even the public hangings were carried out ceremoniously at night between the columns of the Piazzetta to the light of flaring torches.

The Doge was the central actor, the idol, the personification of the city's greatness, round which the chief processionals revolved. Yet the ageing Doge Foscari, under whom Venice had scaled such dizzy heights of success as possessor of a great Italian empire, was not a happy man. In 1456 fresh evidence was produced to show that his son Jacopo had asked the Turks to rescue him from exile. At once Jacopo was fetched to Venice to face the Ten again, and this time a confession was wrung out of him. He was taken back to Canea and by the following January he was dead. Then, in October 1456, the Chiefs of the Ten decided that their 'Illustrious Prince,' Doge Foscari, was 'decrepit,' had been ineffective for some time, and must therefore resign.

They offered him a modest pension for this service, but poor old Foscari, who had started on his long reign with such authority and success, obstinately refused to answer them. In the end, however, he was forced to. He was to be the central figure in one final ceremony, but this time his role was a humiliating one. Having made a rambling farewell speech and handed over his insignia of office, he had the horn and gold fringe stripped from his ducal bonnet and his ducal ring broken, just as if he had already died. Leaning on his wife's arm, he left the palace for his house at San Pantaleone, talked of spending his retirement 'going in boats at our leisure to visit monasteries,' but was dead within six days.

His wife objected to a sumptuous state funeral but they dragged his corpse away from her by force. So the bells tolled, the priests chanted and the customary hired mourners wept and wailed. Foscari's successor, Pasquale Malipiero, attended the obsequies, but it was the Council of Ten which wielded decisive power in Venice now. It could even overthrow a Doge.

This was more than the people could. The state might care for the basic welfare of the city, doling out free corn to the poor in time of famine, maintaining an isolation hospital to keep disease at bay and a public health system supervised by three *provveditori*, but the 'people' was a term no longer used in justifying a new law, and even the word 'commune' was falling out of use. 'Signoria' and 'Dominium' were now the official designations of the government.

The common people had no say in state affairs, but they did enjoy satire directed, however obliquely, at the governing class. The foolish figures of 'Magnifico' or 'Pantaloon' presented by mountebanks on their rickety stages in the Piazza owed their popularity to the fact that they ridiculed the rich and powerful. And, gradually, a large section of the Venetian nobility was coming to resemble pantaloon a little.

The rough, tough, merchant-venturer type was beginning to disappear as more members of the mercantile class came to invest a greater proportion of their wealth in property instead of trade. Andrea Barbarigo's son Nicolò, for example, increased his fortune from 15,000 ducats in 1462 to 27,000 by the time he died in 1500, and discounting his wife's dowry the major part of the increase came from the rise in property values – a wheat farm near Verona, the Treviso estate, and the house on the Grand Canal which his mother had had the sense to buy. Nicolò also held a stake in government bonds, but he only ever made one voyage and that to sell the family estate in Crete and settle the proceeds on his illegitimate second cousin, Marcolina – and though he dabbled in spices, cotton and Barbary gold, he and his descendents gradually withdrew from trade almost completely.

This discernible turn by the nobility to property, government bonds and salaried office was not a universal one, however. Fortunes were still made in trade. Andrea Vendramin had accumulated 160,000 gold ducats mainly from trade by 1476 when he was elected Doge, and Andrea Barbarigo's old helper Francesco Balbi stayed successfully in business up to his death in 1470 at the age of eighty-four.

The improved profitability of land was only one reason for the trend away from trade. Another was the uncertain outlook in the east and particularly fear of the Turks. The fears were soon justified. In 1461 Venice joined the Pope in a 'crusade' against the infidel and set out to occupy Morea. In the fighting which followed, Lemnos and Argos changed hands three times; the area of Methone, among others, was pillaged; the Venetians rebuilt the great wall across the Corinth isthmus; the Turks knocked it to the ground again – and by 1464 Venice could count herself successful chiefly in holding Lepanto against fierce Turkish attack and the occupation of the rocky fort of Monemvasia, centre of a wine producing area that produced the celebrated brew the English knew as Malmsey.

The league with Pius II against the Turks had not lasted long, and in 1463 Venetian relations with the papacy had deteriorated sharply because of a dispute over the territory of Cervia in Italy which the Signoria had negotiated to buy from the church's vassal Malatesta. Pius reacted to this by a flood of unrestrained invective. The Venetians, he remarked, had acted 'with the good faith characteristic of barbarians'; they weighed 'everything according to its usefulness, like traders, paying no regard to honour.' The Venetians were creatures of the sea, 'not so much the companions of men as of fish,' and what did fish care about law? Were not aquatic creatures the least intelligent of all brute beasts? Venetians were, moreover, hypocrites. 'They wish to appear Christians before the world but in reality they never think of God, and except for the state . . . count nothing sacred.'

The Venetians saw themselves quite differently, of course. Power breeds arrogance, and, as the Pope's ambassador remarked, they were always boasting they were 'the successors of the Romans, and that the sovereignty of the world belongs to them.' Their very pride enraged the choleric Pius. 'Your cause is one with thieves and robbers,' he screamed at the Venetian ambassador. 'You think your republic will last for ever but it will not last long. Your populace . . . will! soon be scattered abroad. The scum of fishermen will be exterminated. A mad state cannot long stand.' But the Republic survived. In 1464 it was the Pope who died.

Chapter IX

The Fight for Empire

The Republic had reached the very zenith of her power. The problem now was how to keep it. The struggle against the Turks in Greece put heavy pressure on the exchequer. By the middle 1460s revenue had fallen to barely seventy per cent of the 1420s level, and the bulk of this came from Venice itself – not least from a new incomes tax, revenues from the Empire, particularly the Empire overseas, having slumped disastrously.

Nevertheless, in 1466 another fleet was sent out against the Turks and fierce fighting was soon in progress for possession of Morea. The Turks got rather the better of it. Before long they held fifty castles there, forty more were in ruins, while Venice clung on to only twenty-six. And then, in the summer of 1470, the Sultan Mohammed II sailed towards Venetian Negroponte with a fleet so large that to one Venetian galley captain it looked like a 'forest on the sea.'

'If Negroponte is lost,' he wrote, 'the whole of the Levant as far as Istria will be lost.' And the Signoria thought so too. Negroponte's defenders – Venetians, Greeks, Dalmatians, Cretans – resisted sturdily, waiting for the return of Admiral Antonio Canale who had left to fetch reinforcements; but when he returned, he reckoned his seventy-one ships too few to risk engagement with such powerful enemy artillery ranged against them. The Turks stormed Negroponte for the third time, broke in and captured it; Canale was brought back home in irons, made to repay his salary, and banished.

The Signoria set their teeth and ordered greater efforts. They were already ploughing 100,000 ducats a year into the Arsenal; but in 1473 they ordered it to be almost doubled in size. Work on the 'Newest Arsenal' proceeded apace, though the walls and towers were not begun until 1476 and it would take years for the covered docks to be completed. The cost was enormous. Yet while the Arsenal was busier than ever private shipbuilding was experiencing a slump.

It had begun in 1463, and by 1482 virtually no ships were being built in private yards. Smaller vessels were more cheaply constructed in the hinterland; the yards of Istria and Dalmatia provided competition that Venice could not meet, and despite various protectionist measures even Venetians were beginning to buy or have ships built overseas.

The Turkish war, however, presented a series of more immediate and much graver difficulties. The loss of Negroponte was followed by an influx into Venice of destitute refugees from Greece and from Albania, for whom the government had to provide bread and soup. The old governmental loan stock, the Monte Vecchio, fell to an all-time low of thirteen points in 1474; and fear of the Turks produced an anti-Jewish frenzy. Lies about Jews murdering Christian children for their Passover rituals swept like wildfire through the hinterland and the government was hard put to it to prevent large-scale pogroms. Yet despite the atmosphere of panic a Turkish offer of peace in 1476 was curtly refused.

Then, in 1477, the enemy mounted a great raid through Friuli. Threatened close to home as well as overseas, stretched to the limit of her resources and then struck by plague, Venice was eventually forced to cut her losses. In 1479 she conceded the loss of Negroponte, Argos, Scutari and various possessions in Morea; agreed to pay an indemnity of 100,000 ducats, a tribute of 10,000 a year, and twice the former duty rates in return for continued trading rights at Constantinople.

It was a necessary peace, yet Venice's enemies in the west took it as further proof of her perfidy. Such vilifications did little immediate harm, however. The Signoria's grasp of *Realpolitik*

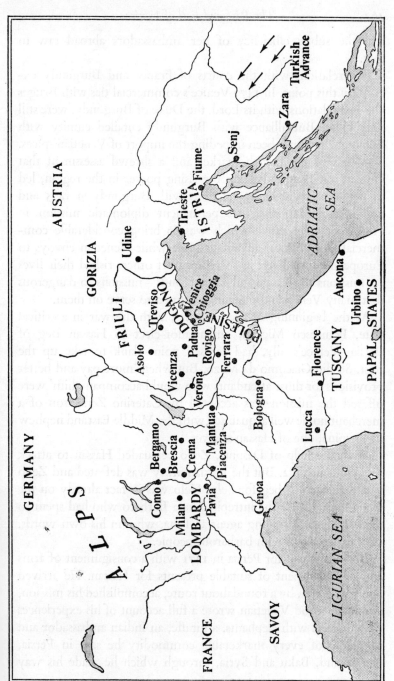

Venice and the terraferma

and the subtle efficiency of her ambassadors abroad saw to
that.

Her relations with the courts of France and Burgundy ex-
emplify this point. In 1470 Venice's commercial ties with Bruges
and her relations with its Lord, the Duke of Burgundy, were still
very close. But alliance with Burgundy entailed enmity with
France, which had been impeding the import of Venetian spices.
This loss of the French market and a shrewd assessment that
France, not Burgundy, was the rising power in the region, led
to the Signoria severing relations with Burgundy in 1475 and
then establishing the first permanent diplomatic mission in
France – a risky move which was to bring considerable commercial and political advantage. But while Venetian envoys to
European courts lived in some comfort others risked their lives
on missions to strange and distant lands – missions so dangerous
that many Venetian diplomatists refused to serve on them.

At the beginning of the seventies, with the war in a critical
state, Francesco Michiel, ambassador-elect to Hassan Beg of
Persia, Venice's ally, had refused point-blank to take up the
post. So did Giacomo da Mezo. But when 'more pay and better
provisions for those attendants who would accompany him' were
offered the mission was accepted by Caterino Zeno, son of a
merchant noble well acquainted with the Middle East and nephew
of Despina, one of Hassan's wives.

With the help of Despina, Zeno persuaded Hassan to attack
the Turks in 1472. But the Persian army was defeated and Zeno
was sent back to beg for help. Help was in fact already on the
way – brought by the intrepid Josafa Barbaro who had spent so
many years as a trading agent at Tana, who, in his own words,
was 'experienced with barbarous people.'

He had set out for Persia in 1471 with a consignment of arms
and an assortment of suitable presents for Hassan. He arrived
safely in Persia, by a roundabout route, accomplished his mission,
and like a good Venetian wrote a full account of his experiences
– encounters with elephants, a giraffe, an Indian ambassador and
the price of every marketable commodity he saw in Persia,
Samarkand, Baku and Syria, through which he made his way

back home. And Josafa dedicated his journal with a typical blend
of piety, patriotism and sense of cultural superiority 'to our Lord
Jesu Christ . . . unto whom we Christians, especially those born
in our most excellent city of Venice, are so much more bound than
are these barbarous people, who are ignorant of all good manners
and full of evil customs.'

Ambrogio Contarini, who left Venice on yet another mission
to Persia soon afterwards, was another of the breed, and the
account he left illustrates how the Signoria contrived to be so
much better informed about conditions in distant lands than any
other government and what risks its envoys faced.

Ambrogio set out with a priest to act as his chaplain and secretary, Dmitri, an interpreter, and two servants. All five dressed
'in thick clothes' for they were bound over the mountains into
Germany – a journey perilous enough for them to take the
sacrament as close to home as Conegliano. They arrived safely
at Nuremberg, and made their way to Poznan, and thence into
mysterious 'lower Russia,' where their sojourn was 'not without
peril on account of the celebration of a couple of weddings;
nearly all the population being drunk, and on that account very
dangerous.' But worse was yet to come.

Passing south across the wild steppe-lands to Keffa, they
reached Kutaisi in Georgia. Here Ambrogio had to suffer the
hospitality of the local governor. 'A skin spread before us served
as a table-cloth, and on it was a layer of grease. . . . I was offered
bread, turnips and a little meat . . . as well as several other un-
savoury things,' and 'they did all they could to make me as drunk
as they were. Since I would not drink, however, they held me
in much contempt, and I left them with great difficulty.'

He went on to meet the King of Georgia and then, in cold
and fear of robbers, he passed through the terrible mountains of
that 'accursed country' into Persia. At Isfahan he met his colleague
Josafa Barbaro, and discussed the alliance against the Turks with
Hassan. He found the Persians gentlemanly by comparison with
the other strange peoples he had encountered and he did not look
forward to the journey home. This took him through Georgia
again, to Astrakhan where he was threatened by Tatars, and

thence, short of food, across the dangerous steppe once more. Ambrogio eventually reached Venice after an absence of three years, and promptly offered up his thanks 'to our Lord God and to his devoted Mother who saved me from so many perils and hardships and brought me safely back . . . which was more than I ever expected.'

While men like Contarini, Barbaro and Zeno risked life, limb and inconvenience abroad, their peers at home enjoyed many pleasures free of such discomforts. Venetian nobles banqueted with customary richness, and the septuagenarian Pietro Mocenigo, Doge from 1474 to 1476, kept ten lovely Turkish slaves as concubines. Despite the pressures of the Turkish war, there was a strange normality about the pleasures of ordinary Venetians too. Blind men still chased and killed their pig each Sunday of the Carnival, and the glittering ceremonials continued as before.

One such sumptuous occasion which took place in April 1472 marked the beginning of a curious story which illustrates some of the less orthodox methods the Signoria used to promote its imperial interests. It concerned the adoption of the eighteen-year-old Caterina Cornaro as 'a child of the Republic,' prior to her departure that September, with a dowry of 100,000 ducats and handfuls of jewellery furnished by her father, for Cyprus as bride for its King, James II Lusignan.

Caterina's adoption proved a shrewd move, for it established a prospect, however faint, of adding Cyprus to the empire. In fact Caterina soon became pregnant, but King James died, some said of poison, before the child was born and the Signoria proceeded to take over. A Venetian fleet arrived at Famagusta, and Andrea Cornaro, the new Queen's uncle, took a seat on Cyprus's governing council. As soon as the fleet left, three other councillors and the Archbishop of Nicosia seized the palace. Caterina's doctor, her uncle and her cousin were slaughtered and her infant son carried away. The Venetian fleet was ordered back again, but by the time it arrived the conspirators had fallen out among themselves and a rebellion had raised against them, so that the Venetian order was restored with little difficulty.

A *provveditore* and two councillors were now appointed to

govern Cyprus in Caterina's name, and in August 1474, when her baby died, the Signoria took further steps towards securing the kingdom for itself. Caterina, guarded by Venetian troops and ships, reigned unchallenged now – yet she was only a Venetian puppet obeying Venetian advice. Venice appointed Cyprus's governors, captains, treasurers and *provveditori*, and Caterina herself was soon protesting that her correspondence was being interferred with and that *provveditore* Soranzo behaved as if he were 'lord and governor of this our kingdom.' But only in 1479 when the Turkish war was ended did Venice relax her tough line. Cyprus had served as a splendid base for operations against the Turks, and now peace had come it provided safe harbours for the Venetian galleys sailing to the Levant.

This was the last great hey-day of the galley, and Fra Felix Fabri who sailed to Palestine in one about this time left a splendid account of it and of what life was like on board. His ship was built 'of the stoutest timbers and fastened together with many bolts, chains and irons.' 'The prow is sharp,' he wrote, with 'a powerful iron beak somewhat like a dragon's head with its mouth open so that it can ram any [hostile] ship it meets.' On the broader, downward-curving stern stood the high castle, containing a latticed chamber for the steersman, another for the captain, and a third for lady passengers and the valuables.

In Fabri's eyes the galley was a floating township, fort, monastery and farmyard all combined. 'On deck beside the mast there is an open space wherein men assemble to talk as in a market place'; there were various machines of war, including 'a movable iron swivel' from which 'stones were shot'; the galley was 'like a monastery' with a 'place of prayer' beside the mast and a 'refectory' in the centre of the poop; while beside the open kitchen was a 'stable . . . wherein sheep, goats, calves, oxen, cows and pigs stand all together,' waiting to be slaughtered to feed the passengers and crew.

Pilgrims like Fabri bedded down in the sand-covered hold, a place unpleasantly close to the bilges from which 'a most loathsome smell arises.' Conditions for a merchant on a normal trading run were more comfortable, but there were still points to watch, as Benedetto Sanudo solicitously warned his brother Andrea when Andrea set out on his first voyage.

'Keep yourself from the perils which occur only too frequently on a galley,' he warned, 'and be ever careful of your health.' More specifically, Andrea was to show 'reverence' to 'the magnificent captain,' 'proper civility' to the eight other noblemen going on the voyage (while not becoming 'over-familiar with them, especially as they are older than you'), and to be kind to the servant, Pietro, accompanying him on the trip, tipping him appropriately, 'having seen what the other nobles give their servants,' but not trusting him with the key to his chest or writing case.

'As you value your honour,' warned Benedetto, 'never play cards or draughts with anyone.' Instead, Andrea was to 'read one of the books that you have with you,' or write – though if the tedium of the voyage should become totally unbearable he might play draughts with the ship's chaplain. Andrea was also warned 'not to wander too far from the landing stage' when the ship reached port, lest he miss the sound of the drum calling everyone on board and be left stranded, not to eat too much if he felt ill, not to lose any of his effects overboard when he opened his locker, and to avoid the 'sirens' of Corfu and Crete.

'On arriving at Alexandria,' he was to call on the consul Piero Bembo, 'do him reverence and touch his hand.' He could sleep at Bembo's house or, 'since the air of Alexandria is said to be unwholesome,' on board the galley as he pleased, but was to 'take care to take someone with you, for there are Moors about who are wont to be insolent.' It might seem strange that a lad in need of such meticulous advice should have been entrusted with goods worth over 3,500 ducats to trade on behalf of Benedetto's company.

Andrea was instructed to spend the proceeds on pepper or sugar or even nutmeg if pepper was scarce or of poor quality. 'Your return will probably be in the depth of winter,' concluded Benedetto, 'so be careful to dress up warm . . . and, above all, to protect and cover up your mouth.'

Pepper-buying expeditions to Alexandria could be risky even

in times of peace like this. In 1480, for instance, the Sultan imprisoned visiting Venetians when they refused to pay over twice the market price as he demanded, and would not let them go until they had paid a premium of at least forty per cent. Yet pepper was still the most important commodity in Venetian trade with the Levant and in her dealings with the Germans, who constituted her most important market outside Italy. The once profitable voyages to Flanders had to be subsidized by as much as 5,000 ducats these days and the Aiguesmortes and Barbary runs were unprofitable too.

Meanwhile the accompanying slump in private shipbuilding deepened, and workers who had once regarded service in the Arsenal as a burden now clamoured for employment there. They also tried desperately to prevent their trade becoming overcrowded by limiting apprenticeships, and the State eventually helped by engaging workless carpenters and caulkers as bowmen for the galleys. But times were changing and wise fathers thought of setting children to new trades – as armourers, perhaps, now that the Arsenal manufactured cannon, armaments and gunpowder on a massive scale, or else as printers.

A printer could earn a very comfortable living – Jensen was worth 4,000 ducats when he died in 1480 – and before long there were as many as 150 presses in Venice, almost as many as the rest of Italy combined. They produced and sold editions of the classics, the Bible, primers, breviaries and missals, treatises on canon law and even histories of Venice retelling ancient legends in ponderously heavy Latin. Copies of Dante complete with commentaries fetched a ducat apiece, but the best sellers were cheap poetry books, tales of chivalry, and romances.

New types of investment were beginning to overtake the old ones in popularity among the moneyed classes too. By 1496 Andrea Barbarigo's son Nicolò was advising his sons to hold on to the family estates at all costs and prize government bonds too, 'since commercial activity does not succeed as it once did.' True, as Domenico Malipiero noted, many Venetians prized real estate much less highly, arguing that it involved 'expenditure without income, for one has to spend to maintain them, while taxation eats up the rents.' Nevertheless, a discernible shift to property investment was already under way – a movement encouraged not only by the less certain commercial outlook, but by the decline of confidence in government stocks.

In 1480 the state was twenty-one years behind in its payments on the Monte Vecchio – and that after having cut the rate of interest. The peace with Turkey offered a chance for the State to set its financial house in order, but by 1482 Venice was at war again – both at sea and on the mainland – and everyone was made to feel the pinch. A new issue of loan stock was raised, tantamount to a renewal of the old forced loans abandoned thirty years before; each of the Scuole Grandi were ordered to provide a hundred men to serve as seamen, while indirect taxes were extorted with even greater vigour.

Things began well enough. Venetian forces defeated Alonso of Calabria and his Turkish bodyguard in southern Italy, and wrested the Ionian Islands from the Catalans. But the war over Ferrara by which Venice hoped to occupy the mouth of the River Po turned out less well and in June 1483 provoked the Pope to place Venice under interdict.

The Venetian emissary in Rome refused to forward the Bull to Venice, and the Venetian Patriarch feigned illness in order to avoid carrying its instructions into force. This gave the Council of Ten time to prepare. The clergy was dragooned into carrying on as usual; government inspectors sent out to the provinces were told to show particular 'humanity and a smiling face' so as to avoid any unnecessary trouble; tempting pensions were offered for denouncers of spies and traitors; and a recent law barring members of the government from discussing state affairs with foreigners was stringently enforced. Yet Venice suffered from the interdict nonetheless. In August 1484, for example, the Flanders galleys were attacked off Portugal by privateers (who included Christopher Columbus) flying the French flag and lost over 400 men killed or wounded and a considerable quantity of merchandise.

Eventually Venice was forced to surrender all the towns she had recently acquired in southern Italy and Cephalonia as well, though she held on to Rovigo and the Polesine nearer home. And to add to the strains of war and excommunications Venice suffered another severe outbreak of the plague.

As a result of this latest epidemic in 1485 the Board of Health was placed upon a new footing with a permanent staff who were to see to it that water supplies were maintained, that vagabonds and prostitutes were kept under control, that burials were properly regulated, and the streets kept clean – though eight years passed before barges were provided to carry out regular rubbish collections.

The government itself had some unsalubrious aspects, however. Agostino Barbarigo, who succeeded his brother Marco as Doge in 1486 and reigned until the end of the century, was not only imperious and obstinate but eager to accept bribes too. According to the diarist Priuli, 'he did whatever he liked . . . gave offices to all his friends and servants,' and after his death was found to have been involved with his brother Carlo in a large-scale wine-smuggling ring to cheat the public exchequer – an affair some nobles wanted hushed up for fear that public knowledge of it would 'bring the state into disrepute.' The lessons of the Watergate are not altogether new.

Yet Doge Agostino was eloquent, shrewd and able as well as corrupt, and under him Venice revealed something of her underlying strength in effecting a quick recovery from her recent troubles. By 1490 exchequer revenues had risen by almost 200,000 ducats over the 1469 level, and the prestige of Venice and of its Doge, not to mention their arrogance, reached an all-time peak. Venice was widely regarded as the 'jewel-box of the world,' and Charles VIII of France went so far as to call Agostino the 'new Augustus.'

These reputations were not altogether undeserved. The Republic was still immensely rich; it was experiencing a new flowering of arts and letters and energetically extending its Empire in the east again. Naxos and several other islands off the coast of Greece were seized for the Republic, and it was in Agostino's reign that Cyprus was finally annexed.

Towards the end of 1488 emissaries were sent out to procure

Caterina's abdication; the flag of the Lusignans was duly replaced by the banner of St. Mark and in March 1489 Caterina sailed for Venice. The new government of Cyprus followed what was by now a customary pattern in the Venetian colonies overseas. It was headed by a Lieutenant who was elected in Venice by secret ballot for a two-year term and paid a generous salary of 3,500 ducats, half of which the state retained as caution money. He was assisted by two Counsellors, each earning 2,400 ducats a year, who maintained half the number of servants and horses as the Lieutenant, namely four of each apiece; three 'rectors' to exercise judicial and financial functions, and a *capitano* based at Famagusta, who was paid the same as the Lieutenant. There was also a 'Great Council' formed of Cypriot nobles and Venetian residents – including non-nobles, so long as they were not artisans – to provide a measure of home rule.

Individual Venetians were already well entrenched there, of course – especially the Cornaros with their great estate and sugar refinery at Episkopi, though they were fast extending into the more profitable field of cotton. But though Venetians and the polyglot local nobility of Cypriots, French and Catalans held the bulk of the islands' riches, ordinary Cypriots were to benefit to the extent that the serfs were gradually liberated and townsmen given opportunities to become nobles.

As for ex-Queen Caterina, she was given a heroine's welcome when she arrived in Venice, still dressed in widow's black, in the summer of 1489. A gold and crimson awning was ready to shade her from the sun, and the Doge came in person to conduct her to her lodgings. There followed three long days of banqueting and ceremonial, and then a second solemn abdication ceremony at St. Mark's. This done, Caterina went to Asolo where she had been assigned a sizeable estate on which she built a splendid residence. It was a pleasant enough retirement. Caterina was attended by a considerable entourage and a miscellany of parrots, apes and peacocks. She enjoyed the cool gardens, the fêtes and allegorical pageants staged there, and the company of guests.

Among these was young Pietro Bembo, who wrote a number of insipid poems about love and patience and praising Caterina's 'whitest chest' – and was to end his life a Cardinal. Disputes about 'vile luxury' and the 'right' and 'wrong' kinds of love; disquisitions on poetry, and the composition of songs to the accompaniment of lutes were the stuff of cultural intercourse at Caterina's Court, as they were, too, in fashionable circles in Venetia as a whole.

Yet heady though these pastimes were, cultural life had its heavier aspects too. Venice boasted an oriental scholar in Hieronimo Ramusio, who translated Avicenna from the Arabic, and from the 1490s a Greek immigrant called Aldo Manuzio, who was a classicist, grammarian, critic and historian, founded Venice's most celebrated printing press and formed a small circle of humanist scholars which crossed class barriers – even the noble Pietro Bembo was proud to be a member of Aldo's circle.

Ermolao Barbaro, another humanist, had an additional dimension, however. Born in 1454, he not only wrote a treatise on marriage (which he reckoned a useful institution), lectured on Aristotle at Padua, and exchanged epigrams and belles lettres with the literary set, but practised what he preached in terms of the active life and civic responsibility, becoming a Senator from 1483 and subsequently serving on various diplomatic missions culminating in the post of emissary to Rome.

While there he penned some advice to a friend about to enter the diplomatic service. The purpose of an ambassador, he wrote, was to win and keep the friendship of princes, and 'to do, say, advise and think whatever may best serve the preservation and aggrandizement of his own state.' An envoy should never stoop to bribery or assassination, nor should he be long-winded or include rumour, inventions or forecasts in his reports. Nevertheless Barbaro's principles did not prevent his allowing the Pope to appoint him Patriarch of Aquileia. His own government objected strongly, however, and Barbaro had to remain in Rome, where he died in 1493 having just been made a Cardinal.

Barbaro exemplified only one type of Renaissance man. Another, no less admired, was the shipwright Leonardo Bressan, foreman at the Arsenal from 1498. A round ship armed with cannon which he built in 1492 had made his reputation, and another ship of his, launched in 1497, was described by a contemporary as 'one of the most beautiful things' to sail upon the sea.

Bressan's prestige reflected a shift in naval architecture which corresponded to the revolution in shipping. The trend was away from slim-lined galleys to much larger ships propelled by sails alone, for the low-slung galleys were almost defenceless against the fire which large pirate ships could rain down on them from their towering castles. Between 1488 and 1498 the State built at least five such ships to strengthen the war fleet, hunt pirates, and carry bulky cargoes – this at a time when ship building had reached a nadir of its depression due to high building costs, a shortage of local oak, the increasing unwillingness of Venetians to invest in long voyages, and a gradually changing pattern of international trade now that the supply of northern European textiles had dried up.

Most of Venice's ships were now built in the Arsenal, 'truly one of the finest things in the world,' thought one Venetian nobleman. And with its many docks, its vast rope factory and sail-making rooms, its timber yards, powder plant and gun-foundries, it was certainly the greatest industrial complex in Europe.

Here was the practical symbol of Venetian might at a time when the city was approaching the triumphant zenith of her splendour – an interweave of alleys, piazzas and canals with richness crammed into almost every corner between the cupolas and soaring towers. There were façades of inlaid marble, sculptures and bronzes by Verocchio and Donatello, paintings by Gentile Bellini and a dozen other brilliant artists. And the seeds of future patronage were to be observed in almost every quarter of the city.

Despite a tendency on the part of many noblemen to invest less in trade, a major part of the world's business was still conducted in and around the Piazza San Giacometto di Rialto where the money-changers and the goldsmiths had their shops. Barges jostled for moorings along the Grand Canal and merchant store-houses swarmed with stevedores. The inns between Rialto and St. Mark's were often full, and urban Venice was abundantly supplied not only with luxuries from virtually every country in the globe but with a profusion of herbs, vegetables and fruits. The fish market was also a sight to see, and slaves could still be bought, if not quite so easily as fish, at anything from sixteen to 100 ducats a head; indeed, by 1500 there were reckoned to be about 3,000 negro slaves alone in Venice; almost three per cent of the entire population.

Yet all the outward signs of wealth could not compare with the sumptuous interiors of many palaces. Pietro Casola, a Milanese priest who visited Venice in 1494 on his way to the Holy Land, was rendered speechless with admiration at the sight of a noble-woman's apartments. 'The Queen of France herself,' he wrote, 'could not display such pomp.' The bedroom decorations alone must have cost 11,000 ducats and he was no less impressed with the lady's attendant damsels clad in low-fronted gowns.

Church and government might frown on women overdressing but little regard was paid to that. Ordinances governing the length of trains, the height of pattens, the circumference of sleeves, were honoured mainly in the breach. The rich gladly paid the fines imposed for wearing such fashionable clothes, and some even applied for papal dispensations – Christina Correr, for example, claimed her family's position and her personal beauty obliged her to dress accordingly and was granted her dispensation for just over four ducats.

Women dyed their hair and bought hair-pieces which, despite the urgings of puritanical friars, were still displayed on poles in the Piazza. Those unable to afford real jewellery hired it or bought glass imitations, so that whether they could afford it or not they all contrived, as Casola remarked, to be 'magnificent in their dresses, wearing large and costly jewels . . . ornaments of pearl about their heads and necks, and many rings upon their fingers.'

Venetian noblemen dressed more soberly in plain long robes, though their behaviour was not always so restrained as their apparel. Fornication was commonplace – Marino Sanuto, who sired two illegitimate daughters, was nevertheless considered an upright man – although eyebrows were raised when two noblemen raped a nun, and when the inmates of another convent were found to have had intercourse with various visitors, including a doctor and a priest. The Scuole still tried to raise the moral tone, staging flagellation processions, with faces hooded and shoulders bared. But the spirit of the times affected even these devotional institutions. As the governors of the Carità noticed in 1490, people were joining not from devotion but simply to receive the charity doled out to needy members.

The fact that so many people were prepared to flagellate themselves for alms reflected a certain rise in unemployment and inadequate state aid to maintain the poor. Not that the government failed to recognize the Christian merit of charity. The Great Council had resolved that 'the chief and most salutary means of obtaining divine favour for a state and republic, as for private persons, is the maintenance of the poor,' but the state's new foundation of Gesù Christo di Sant'Antonio catered only for some thirty paupers, most of them ex-servicemen 'who have deserved well of our state.' Beyond this, some hungry folk could expect the occasional free dinner, such as the Doge gave for a hundred poor in March 1492 to celebrate the completion of the enlarged ducal apartments, or else beg mercy from corporate or private charity or the church.

Poverty had begun to touch noblemen as well as commoners. In 1499 Andrea Contarini forced his way into a meeting of the Collegio shouting that, though he came of a famous family and knew no other trade than governmental service, he had held no office for sixteen years, and yet had to support nine children, repay sixty ducats' worth of debts and find accommodation for his family on an income of only sixteen ducats a year. And poverty drove another Contarini to burglary.

Pity for their less fortunate brethren eventually persuaded wealthier nobles to build almshouses for them. Yet in 1492, when Francesco Faliero and Gabriele Bon, a Chief of the Quarantia, proposed paying 70,000 ducats out of the public purse to relieve poor nobles, they were told to keep their mouths shut, and when they persisted the Ten banished them to Cyprus on the grounds that they were trying to curry popularity and obtain the votes of the nobles they hoped to benefit.

The state was content to restrict its involvement in the social sphere to maintaining food supplies, keeping the city free from epidemic and safe from crime. Quarantine regulations were enforced, lepers controlled and hostelries inspected to make sure they were salubrious. Constables stood ready to lay into any rabble of slaves and other low people given to brawling, and the Signori di Notte patrolled the streets at night. Thanks partly to measures such as these, Venice presented an ideal of civic order. In Florence Savonarola introduced a Great Council based almost precisely on the Venetian pattern, while Philippe de Commynnes considered Venice to be the only city in Italy which 'does not know civil discord.'

Yet the case of Gabriele Bon and the discontent of the poor nobility ran counter to this image. And despite the apparent concord among Venice's ruling class the Hall of the Great Council was the scene of fisticuffs as well as elevated debates. At one session Domenico Calbo gave Bernadetto Minotto a black eye and a bloody nose, and there were other more general brawls as well. Moreover, corruption was too deeply entrenched in the administration for the system to justify all the plaudits of its admirers.

In 1497 a special inspection of the financial administration of the overseas colonies revealed that colonial governors had misappropriated public funds, oppressed the poor and associated with the very pirates they were supposed to hunt down. Arrests were made, but the clean-up did not touch central government, presided over by that most ancient and corrupt of Doges, Agostino Barbarigo.

Only the friars dared speak out and only then in general terms. In 1497 Fra Timofeo of Lucca, giving the Christmas sermon in St. Mark's with the Doge and various ambassadors present, condemned 'the selling of justice everywhere in favour of the rich.' And on the same occasion the following year another friar condemned various injustices including the failure to pay sailors their due wages. The words do not seem to have touched the Doge or his cronies, but then he had other more pressing concerns just at that moment.

Early in 1494 a new 'Holy League' had been formed between Venice, Maximilian, King of the Romans, suzerain of many fiefs in Italy, and Ferdinand and Isabella, rulers of Sicily and Sardinia as well as Spain. The Holy League, however, belied its name, for although it had the blessing of the Pope as well as backing from the Emperor the Turkish ambassador who watched the signing ceremony from behind an arras had been assured that no harm was intended against the Sultan. The League in fact was directed against France.

Venice raised a large army in Italy and overseas; sent ambassadors and then residents to her allies in Spain and Germany, and in November 1496, the year Gentile Bellini painted his famous picture of the procession in St. Mark's Square, the first resident Venetian embassy arrived in England. Heavily embroiled in war with Naples and against Florence, the Republic established a training school for gunners at the Arsenal that year, and since some gesture to raise public morale seemed called for the clock tower of the Merceria was begun, 'to show,' as Malipiero wrote, 'that the city was not without money.' But by the time it was finished, in February 1499, the city was struck by a whole series of crises.

They were all recorded by Marino Sanuto, a twenty-nine-year-old nobleman of modest means who on 1st January 1496 began a diary which he was to keep until September 1533, filling fifty-eight thick volumes. The Republic's luck had begun to turn for the worse in 1498 when Sanuto was Signore di Notte for the district of Santa Croce. In the first place there was another outbreak of the plague; then the Secretary to the Senate was found to have leaked state secrets; another war with Turkey was looming and there was a terrible financial crash.

In January 1499 Andrea Garzoni, owner of the largest of the four Venetian banks, warned the government that he was about to fail. The Council of Ten decided to support him, but the secret was ill kept. Marino Sanuto, for one, who was daily about the Broglio and Rialto and did not miss much, heard what was in the wind and quickly warned his brother to withdraw their mother's 500 ducats which was held on account there. He was only just in time. On 1st February 1499 Garzoni's went bankrupt.

Venetian banks had failed before but the Garzoni failure proved far more serious for it created a run on the other banks. There was panic on the Rialto as investors large and small, nobles and citizens alike, rushed to get their savings out; and crowds of anxious depositors were soon milling round nervous cashiers and scriveners at their booths in the market-place shouting for their money.

Alvise Pisani held out by sheer force of personality, convincing his creditors in an impassioned speech that he was really solvent. But he too was soon forced to liquidate, though he did eventually pay out in full. The banker Girolamo Lippomani, on the other hand, could not, and the outcry against him – accusations that he had squandered the savings of lifetimes, the dowries of young maidens, and the funds of hospitals and monasteries – be·· came particularly vehement once it became clear that he himself and his business associates were the bank's largest debtors.

Yet the crash, which only Matteo Agostini's bank survived, was not simply due to mismanagement or faulty book-keeping. Copies of Luca Paciolo's treatise on arithmetic, which explained accouting methods including double-entry book-keeping, had been available at his shop in the Borgo San Sepolcro for the past five years. The basic cause was public nervousness at the prospect of Venice fighting wars on two fronts – in Lombardy and against the Turks. The Monte Vecchio dropped accordingly – to a miserable five and a quarter points in 1499 – so did the Monte Nuovo. Money was tight; no one wanted to invest; in short there was a lack of confidence.

An imbalance in the relation of silver currency to gold had also played a part in the crisis, though the ducat itself and some other coins like the 'marcello' were sound enough. Indeed, they were imitated by Ferdinand and Isabella in Spain, by the Turkish and Egyptian Sultans, and by some enterprising Venetians too. In 1499 a clandestine mint was discovered in the house of Francesco de Usnagi. According to evidence given by the daughter of Francesco's mistress, his rooms were filled with 'alchemy' equipment and Francesco had spent his nights experimenting with various metals and engraving methods until he eventually produced a satisfactory coin. The outlook seemed bleak for Francesco the forger – but so it did for the Republic. A sudden reversal of policy involving alliance with France made Venice more enemies than friends and in the east matters went from bad to worse.

Before the second Turkish war broke out Venice had been busy consolidating her position – picking up small Latin principalities before the Turks could occupy them, fending off pirates, building up garrisons and reforming government. In 1494, when Venetian forces occupied Naxos, they had been welcomed as saviours, as well they might be, after the rapacious rule of the Dukes and raids by corsairs like Paolo da Campo and Black Hassan. Cyprus was held firmly; Crete was calm; the fort of Korone, centre of a rich oil-producing area, was well-maintained; so was Methone with its pig-breeders who furnished Venice with 5,000 carcasses a year. The corrupt administration of Lepanto had been reformed, and Monemvasia, Mykonos, Tenos and the Ionian islands were all garrisoned.

Yet when the war broke out Venice was caught with only thirteen war galleys at sea. Merchant galleys were promptly ordered into service, and eventually ninety-five ships were mustered to face the Turkish fleet. But Venetian organization was bad, many of the captains were inexperienced, and the new admiral, Antonio Grimani, was chiefly famed for having made an immense fortune in a very short time. 'Mud and dirt turned to gold as soon as he touched it,' wrote Girolamo Priuli, and most Venetian businessmen looked to Grimani for a lead. 'If he sold, they sold, and if he held, they held too.' But Grimani's Midas touch did not work in war. He failed to despatch the Turkish fleet near Navarino and the enemy penetrated the Gulf of Corinth to seize Lepanto.

When this dread news arrived in Venice everyone blamed Grimani. 'Once almost everybody worshipped him,' wrote Priuli, 'and now everyone shouts "Crucify him!"' While the street children took up a new chant, 'Antonio Grimani, the ruin of the Christians,' the admiral was tried for cowardice and banished in disgrace. This scapegoat did not appease the gods' disfavour,

Venetian oar-maker and naval architect

Faustino's design for a galleass, 1570

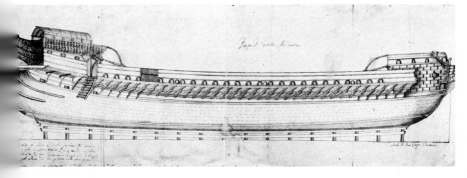

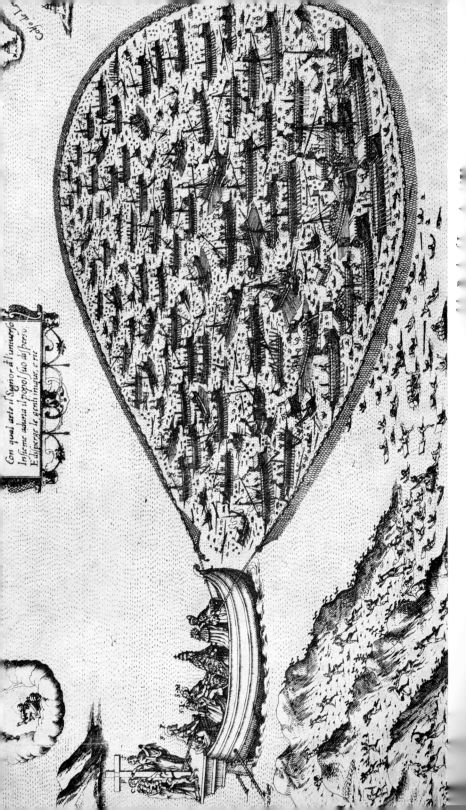

Con qual arte il Signor d'ammasso
Insieme aduna il popol suo di presso.
E disperge le genti insù, e in là.

however. Nor did the specially commissioned horoscopes and prophecies which were read out in secret sessions of the Collegio. Fever broke out in the fleet; the Turks attacked Zara, and in June 1500 raided Friuli again. The Signoria appealed for help – but though the Pope proclaimed a Holy War the Emperor and the King of Hungary did virtually nothing, while Naples and Milan had no interest at all in saving Venetian skins. Apart from a token contingent from Spain and a few ships sent by France, the Republic stood alone.

Venice had been cheered when in April 1500 her ally France conquered Milan allowing the Republic to seize Cremona as its reward, but four months later Methone, that lovely harbour at the south-west tip of Greece, half way, as a contemporary traveller put it 'to every land and sea' was lost. The Council of Ten burst into tears when they were told. And Methone was not the only treasure lost. Navarino and Korone soon fell too. Perhaps King Louis was right when he remarked, after Grimani's débâcle, that Venetians were wise and rich – but too afraid of death to succeed in war.

That September a new and urgent call was issued to every King in Christendom warning that the Turks now threatened all of Europe, and the need for another forced loan was debated in the Senate. Affairs were critical – yet though Doge Agostino willingly appealed to others to contribute he was taken aback when asked to set a personal example. He made a long, rambling speech – to the effect that he had already spent 80,000 ducats of his own money, that everybody wanted presents, and that, anyway, he had no money left. However, if the need was felt to be absolutely essential he was prepared to pledge his plate – and with this grudging gesture he shuffled from the chamber.

Yet matters could have turned out much worse. By the end of the year Cephalonia was occupied with Spanish help. Crete held firm; Venice was still as rich as she was beautiful, still the strongest power in northern Italy and her voice still carried influence in the affairs of Europe. But the Turkish menace was keenly felt, and a much graver threat of quite a different kind was creeping up almost unregarded.

G

Attempts had long been made to find a sea route to the Orient. In the 1450s Fra Mauro of San Michele monastery had even constructed a globe showing the southern tip of Africa with a ship headed prophetically towards the east. Yet when Diaz rounded the Cape in 1486 Venetians had shown little interest, and they had little time either for Cabot's scheme of finding a westward route to China, for which project Sebastian Cabot had to look to England for finance. In August 1499, however, a report arrived from Cairo which caused an eye or two to blink in Venice.

Three Portuguese ships had put in at Aden and at Calicut, inquiring about the Spice Islands. This was the first Venetians heard about Vasco da Gama's discovery of the sea route to India. 'If this news . . . is true,' wrote Priuli, 'it seems to me of great importance; but I do not believe it is authentic.'

By the time Priuli wrote those words the discoverers had already returned to Lisbon, yet when the news was confirmed Venice was so preoccupied with the war that it made little impact. The Signoria remained far more concerned to persuade Portugal to help against the Turks than with the departure from Lisbon in March 1500 of thirteen ships under Pedro Alvarez Cabral, bound for Calicut and spices.

If this mission succeeded, Venice's dominance in the spice trade would be challenged and the economic consequences of that could be disastrous. But Venetians reckoned that most of the Portuguese caravelles would probably sink on the long and dangerous voyage to India; and even if they survived, the spice suppliers would probably prefer to sell to Arab traders, whom they knew, rather than to strangers. There would be time enough to worry if ever Cabral's ships returned.

Chapter X

The Tide Begins to Turn

The discovery of America, the emergence of France and England as united, outward-looking nation states, the looming power of Spain, and the growing dominance of the Turks over the eastern Mediterranean were combining to change the whole balance of world power – and the change was not to favour the Republic. The threat to Venetian wealth posed by the revolution in trade routes, however, was much more immediate in its impact. Venice's strength, built up over the course of centuries, had been based on her unique position as the vital trading link between Europe and the Orient, and now that foundation had been knocked away.

In June 1501 seven of Cabral's ships nosed their way into Lisbon loaded with spices. The news created consternation in Venice. 'The wisest heads,' wrote Girolamo Priuli, 'take it to be the worst piece of information we could possibly have,' graver even than the Turkish war. Not only would foreign buyers find spices cheaper in Lisbon than in Venice, which had to pay Egyptian dues, but a continuation of the voyages would curtail supplies coming by the old route to the Levant. 'Venetian merchants will be like a baby without its milk,' wrote Priuli, 'and in this I . . . see the ruin of the city.'

That September Leonardo Loredano succeeded Doge Agostino Barbarigo, and under him Venice braced its every sinew to strengthen its alliances against the Turks and overcome the threat to commerce. Ironically enough, Portugal was now an ally

against the Turks. King Manuel even sent a force out to Corfu to
co-operate with the Venetian fleet – though thanks to Manuel's
secret orders the Portuguese lost time engaging the King's
enemies near Oran and then in capturing some Genoese ships,
and so arrived too late to be of any use.

Venice was hardly less duplicit, however, in her relations with
the Portuguese. Her new ambassador to Lisbon might praise
King Manuel's honesty, piety, magnanimity, glory and even his
achievement in finding the sea route to the Indies. But in December 1502 the Signoria sent an envoy to persuade the Egyptian
Soldan to pressurize the Samarin of Calicut into cutting off
Portuguese supplies and 'find quick and secret remedies' to dis-
courage them from ever coming back to India. In effect, Venice
was inciting Muslims to attack Christians, an idea inexpressible
in Europe at the time. Moreover Venetian agents in Lisbon were
trying to convince visiting Indians that the Portuguese were
primarily men of war and that the Venetians were preferable to
deal with. Yet when the Portuguese did experience difficulties
in building forts at Calicut they merely moved farther down the
coast to Goa.

Towards the end of 1502, the Monte Nuovo, that most sensitive barometer of Venetian sentiment, which had plummeted to
fifty-two in 1500, recovered twenty-three points on hopes of
peace with Turkey, and the hopes were not disappointed. By the
settlement, formally proclaimed in Venice in May 1503, the
Turks retained most of their conquests, but Venice clung on to
Nauplia, Monemvasia and Cephalonia, and was now free to
devote greater priority to the spice war.

It was not a moment too soon. That January Venice learned
that the Germans were about to open a trading station at Lisbon;
rumour soon had it that a whole fleet of spice ships had arrived
there, and that the Portuguese were trying to blockade the Red
Sea in order to cut off spice supplies to Egypt, a move which,
if successful, would force the Venetians themselves to buy in
Lisbon. Priuli's gloomy forecast was being realized.

The Signoria, however, did not give up the fight. While continuing to maintain the diplomatic courtesies it stepped up its

espionage and sabotage programme against the Portuguese. In March 1504 an agent was dispatched to Lisbon, posing as an Italian merchant, to collect intelligence. Imprisoned on suspicion as soon as he arrived, he contrived to talk his way out of goal and spent the next two years sending reports back to Venice about the morale of Portugal's seamen and her plans to blockade the Arab ports.

In May 1504 the Signoria sent another agent to Cairo, to warn the Soldan of the increasing volume of spices arriving at Lisbon and to assure him that the Republic still preferred to buy from Egypt rather than at Lisbon, if the terms were right. And an attempt was made at blackmail, too, arrangements being made to inform the Pope that unless the Portuguese abandoned their voyages to India, the Soldan would destroy the Christian holy places in Palestine – though Portugal immediately countered this by promising to mount a Crusade if the Soldan fulfilled his threat.

In 1504 a desperate Council of Ten even contemplated the digging of a Suez Canal to shorten the sea route between India and the Mediterranean and bring the spices flooding back to Venice once again. As it was, the galleys were bringing in less than a third of the spices that they had shipped before the Turkish war, and despite all the pressure placed upon him the Soldan was no more tractable on prices – in 1505 the galleys had had to beat a hasty retreat out of Alexandria under fire after a dispute about duties. The Germans were going to Lisbon to buy; the convoys to Syria and Alexandria were a fraction of their former size; Venetian ships no longer passed the Dardanelles and rarely touched at Constantinople; the Flanders run was soon abandoned altogether – in short the whole of commerce was in complete disorder when in 1506 the Signoria set up new board of five trade commissioners to find ways of reviving it.

With the bulk of Venice's overseas trade now restricted to the Adriatic and the Aegean, the Venetian colonies took on a new importance and Venetian policy towards them changed accordingly. Inspections became much more stringent, much greater emphasis was laid on crop development and, where necessary, repopulation. On Corfu, the administrative centre for all the Ionian islands, 'good' citizens were given a share in government, a tolerant religious policy encouraged an influx of Jews expelled from Spain, and serfs enjoyed some chance of self-enfranchisement, although flight and even peasant rebellions remained frequent. Ithaka was repopulated, thanks to land grants free of tax for the first five years of occupation, and a programme for growing grapes for currants eventually succeeded in converting Cephalonia and especially Zante from drags upon the exchequer into handsome revenue-producers.

Cyprus, whose well-paid governors went about their business shaded by official red umbrellas, paid handsomely as well, and even Nauplia, where plebians demanded and eventually gained the right to elect at least one out of the three inspectors, produced a surplus despite having to make considerable payments of bakhshish to the Turkish Aga of Morea. The effective exploitation of the colonies, however, still demanded a healthy shipping industry, and by the end of the Turkish war Venetian shipping was in a parlous state. With freight rates low and state dues and regulations so restrictive virtually no private operator thought it worthwhile to build ships. So in 1502 the government took appropriate action, raising many restrictions, reducing dues, laying down minimum rates for freight and offering to subsidize the builders of new ships. The result was a great revival in round-ship building – to carry corn, oil, wine, cotton and all the other bulky cargoes which were the staples now of Mediterranean exchange.

Nevertheless the revolution in commerce and the effort expended in the war against the Turks had left their marks. As Sanuto wrote on New Year's Day 1507, there were 'great warehouses with few bales of merchandise, many ships but few departures; many banks, but little money.' Hopes were to be raised in 1509 when Egypt and Calicut finally combined to challenge the Portuguese at sea, but it was the Portuguese who won, and they continued to develop Goa, mount trading expeditions as far east as China, and develop an empire in the distant Orient and south America of an extent and richness few Venetians had even dreamed of. The merchants of Venice shook their heads as they sat in their office mezzanines above their empty store-rooms, and racked their brains to find new ways of making money.

The general sense of crisis was reinforced by other panics, great and small. The plague had come again in 1502, syphilis had become endemic, and there were epidemics, too, of teenage gangs who roamed the city smashing gondolas and of harlotry among Venetian nuns. Some noblemen at least were said to maintain nuns as mistresses, and according to Priuli the inmates of some convents 'were fed with every delicacy, and indulged in every refinement of perfumes, music and song.' A dispensation obtained from the Pope for a few ducats enabled them to leave their convents for months at a time and do what they liked – 'a shameful thing, scandalous, full of all ribaldry.'

Gambling also seems to have increased, and complaints of workers' slackness mounted. Craftsmen at the Arsenal were accused of shoddy workmanship, spinning out time and knocking off early. And Venice's hectic, nervous mood was reflected in the government's expulsion of preachers, its order that sermons should deal with sins and not politics, in the frantic changes in women's fashion (trains were in, then out, then in again), and the equally frantic efforts to hold them in check.

In October 1504 the Senate condemned the 'useless expenditure by women . . . in order to show off.' The constant changes in fashion, it warned, could do 'considerable harm to the fortunes of our gentlemen and citizens,' since dresses which had been cut short would be thrown away, necessitating the purchase of new ones. Women were therefore ordered 'to be content' with what they once considered fashionable, and the order went out that 'no female dress shall be worn . . . of any fashion other than that in use at present.'

Almost exactly a year later the Senate thundered yet again, condemning 'certain new fashions,' even 'uglier, and more dishonest' than former ones. Slashed robes, differently coloured sleeves, sleeves edged with cloth of other colours, fringes, embroideries and the like, were all forbidden. But, as Priuli noted a few years later, it proved impossible to stamp out the 'blasphemy'

of French fashions; and Venetians did admire a showy woman.
As Marino Sanuto, the diarist, once remarked, women were
'really exquisitely lovely . . . adorned with jewels and finery.'
Sanuto, however, was principally interested in making a career
in politics. A man of utter probity, a conservative who looked
upon himself as a latter-day Cato, he was also something of a
pompous ass. It was characteristic that he should have chosen to
address the Great Council on the Turkish menace just a few weeks
after a satisfactory peace had been concluded, and it was even
more typical of the man that he should be so pleased with his
performance. 'Everybody praised and blessed me . . . the Doge
praised me too. Moreover the attention during my speech was
so great that no one spat.'

From that triumphant moment Sanuto spoke regularly and
though he was not always allowed to finish a bad reception did
nothing to reduce his self-esteem. 'Anyone who does not want
me in the Senate,' he wrote once, 'would make an enemy of God
and the Republic.' But though he was elected Senator for a term,
it was his diary that earned him posthumous fame, for Marino
noted both the great and little things of life at a time of shattering
crises, unusual splendour and intellectual ferment – the age of
Gentile Bellini, Carpaccio, Veronese and the flowering of Renaissance scholarship in Venice.

This was an age of great riches, abject poverty, and that notorious Venetian pride – pride which was shortly to lead the Republic
to yet another brink of ruin. Other states had long resented
Venice's expansion and envied her her mainland empire. In 1503,
when Venice occupied areas of the Faenza and Rimini, a furious
Pope reportedly told Machiavelli that unless Venice trimmed her
sails he would 'join with France, with the Emperor – with anyone,' to bring about her downfall, and even Priuli remarked
that it was perhaps unwise for Venice 'to snatch at every passing
fly.' Not that Popes themselves were noted for their lack of greed
– Alexander VI was said to have poisoned a Venetian Cardinal in
1503, and the Venetian ambassador arrived on the scene to find
'all the doors shut, and his Holiness occupied in counting gold.'

But resentment of Venice was not confined to Rome. Florence

also bore her a grudge, the Republic's wealth was widely envied, her pride amost universally detested, and the peace she had concluded with the Turks provided a blanket excuse for other powers to gang up against her. The Venetians were 'traders in human blood,' the French ambassador told the Emperor, 'traitors to the Christian faith,' who had shared out the Mediterranean with the infidel and now wanted to hold all Europe in subjugation. In short, it was France, the Pope and the Emperor who had their eyes on Venetian territory.

In February 1508 the Emperor Maximilian, the French governor of Milan, the Spanish ambassador and the Papal legate concluded a draft agreement to recover territories which Venice had allegedly 'usurped.' A Venetian diplomatist managed to get a transcript made and sent it on to Venice. Perhaps because of this, Louis of France dragged his feet, but that spring Maximilian attacked. His forces were repelled with the aid of French troops from Milan, and then Venice advanced into Friuli, captured Trieste and Fiume and occupied Gorizia. By June, Maximilian was forced to make a humiliating peace – but Venice's partner, King Louis, now took offence, and stepped firmly into the opposing camp.

In December 1508, at Cambrai in France, an alliance was signed for 'war against the Infidel.' It was a convenient euphemism. The League of Cambrai was in reality a pact for an assault on Venice. Spain, the Papacy, the Dukes of Savoy, Ferrara and Mantua all joined the plot as well and decisions were exactly made on how the Venetian territories would be carved up when they were captured. In April 1509 the French invaded and the Pope excommunicated Venice. Venice immediately forbade publication of the Bull, called in experts on canon law to challenge its legality, mounted a propaganda campaign against the Pope, and hastily mustered her military defences.

Professional mercenaries were engaged, and local militias levied throughout the *terraferma*. Young provincial noblemen abandoned thoughts of horse-racing for the season and looked forward to tasting the excitements of a battle. In Venice itself, however, the 'Royals', the 'Valorous,' the 'Triumphants,' the 'Immortals' and other groups of the Compagnia della Calza continued to hold feasts and comedies and dances; young men still baited bulls in the piazzas and broke into convents to flirt with young nuns. While they cavorted and got drunk, the army that protected them marched towards a confrontation with the enemy at Agnadello and a shattering defeat.

When news of this disaster arrived in Venice in May 1509 senior Venetians lost all their poise and gravity. Normally dignified Senators reeled and staggered through the streets wailing that everything was lost. Interest payments on the Monte Nuovo were suspended; there was another run on the banks; Priuli denounced the Doge for panicking; Sanuto wrote that if he had been a Senator he would have proposed alliance with the Turks.

With the enemy barely a hundred miles away and the army lost, no effort was made to save the provinces – indeed the Signoria immediately absolved its subjects there from their oaths of allegiance. When the storm blows the reed bends, and in this way, as a young nobleman of Vicenza, Luigi da Porta, realized, Venetians stood a chance of retaining their private property in the *terraferma* while losing their public authority. Nevertheless, as Luigi suggested, many Venetians must now have regretted 'abandoning the sea for the attractions of the mainland.'

The French duly occupied Verona, and German troops under a local renegade, Leonardo Trissino, took Vicenza and sent the winged lion of St. Mark there, which Luigi da Porto thought 'as beautiful as . . . the most famous sculptures of the ancients,' tumbling from its column. Nicolò Barbarigo's sons lost their estate in the Veronese; Caterina Cornaro, ex-Queen of Cyprus, was driven from her idyllic home at Asolo.

Trissino marched on to take Padua, where the local peasantry rose up to occupy their masters' lands, and so, within a month of Agnadello, the enemy occupied all the mainland towns except Treviso.

In Venice everything was in turmoil. The city was packed with refugees; supplies of water were running low. In contrite tones the government begged for peace. Yet, realizing that

Trissino's force was very small, the Signoria did gather enough strength to reoccupy Padua. Crowds gathered on the Piazzetta to jeer as Trissino, his Paduan collaborators and three hundred German prisoners (who, Sanuto noted, were 'barefoot, and smelt horribly') were brought in, and meanwhile a crowd of young Venetian toughs rushed off to Padua where they engaged in an orgy of vandalism, loot and rape.

The recapture of Padua, however, was hardly enough to dispel the trauma of heavy defeat. As Marino Sanuto made his way to the Senate after dinner one day 'the palace and houses suddenly shook, and there were two great explosions.' Sanuto joined the crowds running towards the Arsenal.

A scene of chaos and devastation met his eyes. Stones fell like rain, walls collapsed; the Tana storehouses were utterly destroyed, so were many houses near the Arsenal. 'I saw many corpses drawn from the ruins,' wrote Sanuto, 'some without heads and some in pieces.' Everybody thought the cause was sabotage. Foreigners were hauled in off the streets, even the Archbishop of Crete was arrested – and members of the Ten sat up all night interrogating them. But the true cause turned out to be a spark from a hammer igniting gunpowder.

Meanwhile Venice's own citizens were growing restive, at which their leaders were summoned into the Hall of the Great Council and told that they, not the nobles, were the privileged class. They had life tenure as civil servants, which nobles rarely had in government posts. They had freedom to concentrate on business while the nobles' mercantile activities were interrupted by terms of dangerous and expensive service. 'You eat the roast meat while we content ourselves with the smell of it,' ran the argument; 'we have the titles but you take the prizes; we have the leaves, and you the fruit.' Life, it seemed, had never been so good, and the citizens do seem to have left in a more tractable frame on mind.

But this was only one crisis surmounted. In the same terrible year catastrophic news arrived that the Portuguese had smashed the forces of Egypt and Calicut. The spice trade seemed to be lost for good now; all galley voyages were suspended, and many a wise Venetian reckoned that 'this marked the beginning of the ruin of the Venetian state.'

Slowly, however, things began to improve. The Pope had regained the Romagna and was prepared to lift his interdict – on condition that the Republic conceded its right to appoint bishops and drop its previous insistence on taxing clergy and trying clerics for secular crimes. Regretfully the Signoria consented – and in 1510 the Pope not only raised the interdict but joined with Venice against Ferrara and the King of France. The Republic was no longer isolated.

In the years that followed the Republic exploited every rift between her enemies, and switched her alliances about as opportunity offered and at a most hectic rate. By 1513 she was in league with France and Spanish guns were speaking out across the lagoon from Mestre – but the risks proved justified. By the end of the war, in 1517 – thanks to her consummate diplomatic manoeuvrings and not least to the rebelliousness of the peasants in the occupied territories, notably in Padua and Friuli who now realized that the Republic had offered them much better protection against their local lords than, say, the Emperor – Venice had recovered not only Padua but Verona, Brescia and Bergamo as well. And Venice was also to recover from the economic dislocation caused by the Portuguese exploitation of the sea routes to the Indies.

One road to recovery lay in the textile industry, which attracted considerable investment and was soon expanding at a phenomenal rate – from an output of 1,306 cloths in 1516 to 4,701 in 1521 and 26,539 by 1569. Silk, leather and metal production also grew; soap and glass products became important exports, and the earnings of Venetian printers rose as well – Aldo Manuzio's son-in-law and partner was to accumulate a fortune of 80,000 ducats by the time he died.

Another road to recovery lay in the agricultural exploitation of the recovered mainland territories. The rich had long been buying estates there as capital gains investments, paying twice as much for properties as was justified by their yield of three or four per cent. But the years between 1510 and 1580 were to see a fourfold increase in the incomes from such holdings—and money was still to be made in trade.

In 1513 the Turks renewed Venetian trading privileges at Constantinople, and occasionally, particularly from the 1520s, there were quite considerable quantities of spices to be shipped from the Levant. This turnabout was due less to the stories Venetians circulated to the effect that spices lost their aroma on the long sea voyage to Lisbon, however, than to political conditions in the Orient which caused the bulk of the crop to come by the old Arabian route from time to time. Moreover, there were still pilgrims to be shipped to Palestine; Venetian merchantmen were still busy carriers of salt, oil from Bari and salt from Istria, Trapani and Cyprus; and Venice's financial expertise and the quality of her market intelligence still ensured her position as a major centre for exchange.

Alvise Pisani and his brothers had dealings with many countries; and the cloth, tin, salt, wool, bow-wood, spice and grain stored in the basement of their family home (now the Gritti Palace) reflected the diversity of their trading operations. Particularly active as suppliers to the textiles and dyeing industries, they also bid for merchant galleys, farmed the wine tax, and owned considerable private property.

Alvise himself had an estate near Rovigo and mills near Treviso, and he also ran a bank. Reopened in 1504, the bank survived the 1509 crisis and built its deposits up to a quarter of a million ducats — a success due in part at least to that vital ingredient, information. In 1518, for example, Alvise learned that Lorenzo di Tani's bank in Rome had failed before di Tani's own brother in Venice knew it, and so was able to cash his claim before the brother fled. Alvise became one of the ten richest Venetians of his time, able to spend 40,000 ducats on dowering his daughters, buy a cardinal's hat for his son, and spare time to hold several governmental posts. After his death in 1528 his funeral Mass was celebrated on an appropriately triumphant note at the Rialto church to the sound of fifes and trumpets.

Great ceremony had also marked the opening of Girolamo di Priuli the diarist's bank in 1507. Mass was sung at the Rialto, then Priuli, accompanied by his scarlet-robed associates and by a band, marched to the booth where 69,000 gold ducats had been stacked. There Girolamo declared his bank open 'in the name of God,' and the public crier proclaimed this important information through the city.

Trust was the foundation of Venetian banking. It was encouraged by the fact that the people involved were few and knew each other personally. But their trust was not invariably justified. Pisani's bank paid up in full after his death; Priuli's failure in 1513 was genuine enough; but when Matteo Agostini's bank failed in 1508 he himself was found to owe sixty per cent of the assets and to have transferred them to Mantua, outside Venetian jurisdiction, just a month before the crash.

Nevertheless Venice's basic financial resilience pulled her through the crisis years. Though she was never to regain her former leadership, her trade was reviving, food was cheap again, and the city's very wealth continued to attract a stream of immigrants to swell the numbers of the city's poor. Attempts were made to distinguish between Venetians and foreigners, 'rogues' and genuinely 'low and wretched people' among the beggars. But since many of them, claiming to be impoverished Venetians of excellent family, usually covered their faces to hide their shame it was often impossible to distinguish the bogus from the really needy. So the government forbade beggars to hide their faces unless they were licensed to do so.

The city's charitable institutions, the almshouses, hospitals and orphanages maintained by the craft associations, by those devotional confraternities the Scuole, by the Church and by the State were still unable to cope with the demand, and in 1501, when Nicolò Morosini set out to build thirty almshouses for impoverished fellow-noblemen – each consisting of two rooms, a kitchen and an area at canal level to store a gondola, unseasonal furniture, wood and wine – the competition for them was probably intense. It certainly was for salaried government posts. There were about 800 such jobs, most of them tenable from one to three years, but since some of them could be held in plurality, less than a fifth of all the 2,500 nobles qualified to hold them actually held office at any given time. Hence the numbers of poor members who turned up at Great Council sessions every Sunday ready to sell their votes and vie for minor office.

Major offices, by contrast, tended to go exclusively to rich nobles. This return to the unashamed plutocracy of former times was a direct consequence of the government's need for money in the crisis years. Not only were state 'benefactors,' that is contributors, made Senators, and young nobles prepared to pay for the privilege of admission to the Great Council at eighteen instead of twenty-five, but prestigious offices were going to the highest bidders. In 1516, for instance, Alvise Loredano bought his procuratorship of St. Mark with a loan of 14,000 ducats and a gift of 12,000 to the State which he actually laid before the Council in twelve bags.

Three months before this Marino Sanuto had gone to the Great Council expecting to be nominated, if not elected, Avvogador di Commun – but found that the only candidates considered were those who brought in bags of money. He himself had to 'scrape together 500 ducats, God knows how,' in order to be elected Senator for a term, but, thereafter, being a man of modest means, he met with no success and in 1520 sat down in disgust, wondering why he, a patriot of a famous family who had done some service to the state and wished to render more, was always rejected. The answer, he concluded, was that 'every office is filled for money.'

Nevertheless there were Venetians, even noble Venetians, who turned away from wealth and disdained politics. Two such noblemen, Tomasso Giustiniani and Vicenzo Querini, withdrew from the world altogether for a time, joining the Camaldoli hermits – and were to achieve some prominence in the reformist Catholic revival. On the other hand their pious friend Gasparo Contarini, who was ultimately to become a Cardinal, reckoned that though 'the contemplative life may be nobler than the active' the latter was 'more meritorious,' affording opportunities 'to help one's neighbour in his spiritual life.'

Although a pietist, Contarini was a man of his class, a staunch defender of the Venetian system, and a despiser of the new rich.

'It happeneth often,' he wrote in his celebrated treatise on *The Commonwealth and Government of Venice* (translated into English by Lewes Lewkenor in 1599), 'that those of the basest sort, yea of the very skum of the people, do scrape together great wealth' by applying themselves to 'filthy artes and illiberal occupations.' Such people's industry, their 'intollerable sauing' and rejection of life's comforts in the cause of fortune-gathering was anything but admirable in Contarini's view, and their rise was accompanied by the fall of honest citizens 'liberally brought up' who 'often times fall to pouertie,' through adverse fortune or neglect of their wealth through an addiction 'to noble and liberall studies.' So it was, he concluded, that 'filthy and ill manerd men savouring of nothing but gaine, utterly ignorant of good artes' gradually 'come to gouerne the commonwealth,' while men of 'honest and of liberall condition' lost their power. In this phenomenon Sanuto might have explained his own failure, but Contarini saw it as a cause of rebellion and civil strife.

Contarini was conservative, yet he was intrigued by a question few conservatives are imaginative enough to ask: how is it that the lower orders accepted a governmental system from which they are excluded? The fact that ordinary Venetians supported government by the nobility seemed 'scarcely credible' to Contarini. The answer, he thought, was that 'the people hath not been wholly rejected.' The 'better sort' could acquire positions of power in the civil service and even aspire to the office of Chancellor, 'the Prince of the Common people'; plebeians and gentlemen participated equally in the mass, justice was at least in theory administered equally to all; and the State saw to it that food was cheap and plentiful, provided free housing for many of the aged, and sustained disabled Arsenal workers and poor mariners.

Contarini's picture of Venice as a welfare state was exaggeratedly rosy, but though its welfare did not measure up to ideal standards of our own day, compared to other states of the time it was advanced indeed. Centuries of experience had branded an awareness of the need to forestall social discontent into the minds of Venice's rulers, and it was this sensitivity which lay at the root

of political stability for which Venice was to become so justly
famed.

Venetians were already famous for the delicacy of her entertainments. The Venetian circuses were certainly far less crude
than those of ancient Rome – apart from bull-baiting, which was
stopped as 'unseemly' in 1520. But they were at least as complex.
A procession to mark one of the great feast days of the Church
in 1515 included various tableaux described by Sanuto. There
was 'a great wooden San Rocco dressed in gold, with a live
boy as an angel showing him the plague, the twelve tribes and
Moses kneeling before Aaron's staff,' and 'Christ going into
limbo to release the holy fathers, with the limbo complete with
devils.'

Processions celebrating alliances, which in the early 1500s had
changed with astonishing rapidity, were no less vividly presented.
One held in 1513 had been led by twenty-seven small boys dressed
as angels carrying the arms of the signatories of the new league;
the Scuola di San Rocco staged a tableau of Venice and St. Mark,
actors represented Venice's new allies (the Pope, the King of
England and of Spain) and a somewhat discomfited King of
France, her enemy, while St. Theodosia's hand, St. Martin's foot,
the body of San Rocco and the red hats of Venetian cardinals
were among the relics on display.

More private entertainments also exhibited the Venetian flare
for the spectacular. In 1516 the 'Innocenti' club of the Compagnia
della Calza staged a comedy by Plautus in the courtyard of Ca'
Pesaro, enlivening it with representations of Hell's flames, fiends
and goats, and a 'necromancer' who towed a chariot bearing
'Adonis' onto the scene attended by a crowd of dancing 'nymphs.'
Even the laying of tables and the presentation of food became
subjects for high art. Scented water was sprinkled about at banquets; napkins were folded to resemble mitres, boats or pyramids;
and the oysters, bread and sugared joints of roast meat served up
on specially rich occasions were carefully gilded.

The poor who leave posterity little record of their lives may
well have slept in slum tenements several to a bed and covered
themselves with the rags they wore in daytime, but the affluent

certainly slept in richly furnished palaces on lace-decorated sheets and took the air in gardens 'delicate and rare.' Some pleasures – watching the execution of malefactors, or visiting other islands in the lagoon – were enjoyed by rich and poor alike. On the other hand there were inevitable divisions in taste between generations as well as between classes. By 1512 Venice's 'depraved youth,' as Girolamo Priuli called them, were enjoying 'lascivious and damnable French dances.' But then for sober seniors like Priuli the pleasures of the stomach were preferable to the dance. At their Secretary's dinner the Council of Ten ate pheasants, partridges, fried oysters and marzipan – though the state was already clamping down on extravagant eating habits.

In May 1512 it issued a decree regulating the number and nature of dishes to be served at banquets, and ordering cooks and waiters to report any such affairs for which their services had been engaged so that the *provveditore* sopra le Pompe could send out inspectors to check on the proceedings. Such inspectors were not always treated with respect, however, and on at least one occasion surreptitious diners caught at an illegal feast bombarded them with bread and oranges to make them go away.

Security was much more rigorously enforced than laws relating to economy. State papers less than two or three years old could not be seen even by reliable noblemen writing histories, and the Ten insisted on censoring such books before allowing publication. Along with security went propaganda. In 1515 the Ten appointed an official historian to improve the State's reputation at this 'time of turbulence.' They did not like the results, however, much preferring Sanuto's history produced in 1520 in which he claimed that since Venice was founded by nobles and not shepherds it must be superior even to ancient Rome. The propagation of such myths, Contarini's account of the constitution, and other similar literature, was ultimately to succeed in raising Venice's prestige abroad, but meanwhile Venetian ambassadors were subjected to all sorts of taunts.

In March 1516 the ambassador to the Court of Henry VIII of England heard jibes about the Republic's 'bad faith' and about

Venetians being 'only fishermen.' He did not let them pass.
Fishermen, he pointed out, had founded the Christian faith, 'and
we have been those faithful fishermen who defended it against
the forces of the Infidel, our fishing boats being galleys . . . our
hooks the treasure of St. Mark, and our bait the life-blood of
our citizens who died.'

Even nobles, like Bartolommeo Moro who attacked corruption
in the government, expressed pride in the Venetian state. 'The
Greek republics did not last more than 450 years,' said Moro,
'the Roman 700, while this one has already lasted more than a
1,000.' The cause, he added, was 'concord: and so it will be until
the end of time.'

In statements such as these one senses a certain lack of confidence mingled with the pride. The shocks of the war years had
engendered something of a siege mentality and Venetians were
already fearful of the threat that the great emergent powers like
France, and particularly Spain, posed to their Republic's integrity.
That Venice kept her independence was due in no small measure
to the abiding practicality, realism and caution of her rulers. Such
qualities were also displayed by lesser Venetians in the way they
conserved their family fortunes over the years.

The Barbarigos, for example, who had recovered their mainland estates lost in the 1509 war, contrived to maintain their
assets and a decent standard of living by obtaining paid government office. Of Nicolò's sons, Andrea was elected a Lord of the
Arsenal in 1512 – a job worth 130 ducats a year as well as a free
house – Francesco served a term as Captain of Vicenza, Vittore
was Count of Zara, while the fourth brother, Giovanni Alvise,
held several offices. This generation preserved their capital. In
the next, however, there were two daughters to be dowried and
the family's remaining land in Crete had to be sold. But the
terraferma estates were retained and even extended by the acquisition of further property through marriage.

The Barbarigos were primarily landlords. But though estates
such as theirs tended to be adorned nowadays with comfortable
villas, Andrea Mocenigo exaggerated when in 1525 he accused
the nobility of being 'seduced' from trade by the 'luxury' of

country life. Men like the Barbarigos were deeply concerned about the profits to be gained from their estates. Even Alvise Cornaro, theatre builder, art patron, health fanatic and exponent of theories about good building design, was at least as much concerned with agricultural theory and land reclamation with a view to obtaining a better return on his investments.

The continuing passion of the Venetian nobility for making money was also exemplified in another mushrooming of banks. No fewer than four were founded in the 1520s, although only one, Antonio Priuli's, survived the decade. One reason for this phenomenon was the lack of good Venetian coin. Now that so much less German silver came to Venice, thanks to the diversion of the pepper trade, there was an increased demand for 'bank' money – transferrable credits on a banker's books. But for precisely the same reason banks were loath to pay out cash. The state tried to stabilize the situation and maintain confidence by requiring each bank to lodge 25,000 ducats in securities, forbidding them to make deductions for payments made in cash rather than by transfer, and banning the purchase of cash with credits from a bank. Bankers were also ordered to keep stocks of money on their counters, to count it out to creditors demanding cash in full public glare, and not to give creditors orders on other banks, pretend there was a mistake in the accounts, or use any other subterfuge to fob off a customer demanding payment in scarce coin. Finally, in 1526, when two of the new bankers went into liquidation (one of them, Andrea Arimonte, promptly dying, according to Sanuto, of 'a melancholy of the bank') the government decided to install its own supervisors to force payment on demand in gold, though it did order the acceptance of bank credits unless a contract expressly provided otherwise.

Others besides noblemen provided banking services. One of the more active of these smaller bankers was Anselmo the Jew, who, like others of his faith, was now forced to wear a yellow hat and live in a separate quarter called the ghetto. Moneylending became a major occupation of Venetian Jews, largely because of restrictions imposed by the guilds whose members feared underemployment. However, contrary to the impression Shakespeare

gave, Jews tended to lend at half the interest Christians did, and
in a city where everyone grasped what he could were more sinned
against than sinning, hounded by friars who blamed every natural
calamity on them and often blackmailed by the government into
paying heavily to remain in Venice and pursue their occupations.
In October 1525, for example, the government rejected a proposal by the Chiefs of the Ten that Daniele Bomberg be allowed
to continue printing in Hebrew for a fee of 100 ducats, and
maintained its refusal until the offer was raised to 500.

The Republic's possessions overseas were also squeezed for
money, though not quite as intensively as during the war. A
German who visited Cyprus in 1508 reckoned that 'the poor
common people' who gave a third of their crops and two days'
labour service a week to the state were 'so flayed and pillaged
that they hardly have the wherewithal to keep soul and body
together.' Even allowing for some exaggeration on this visitor's
part, the claim made by the Cypriot nobility in a petition of
1520 that Venetian rule had brought the fruits of a 'most happy
peace, to the great satisfaction of the entire people' was patently
untrue. Handsome buildings had been constructed and large
areas of waste land reclaimed for the plough, but while relations
between Venetians and the local nobles seem to have been good
the common people still carried a considerable burden – supplying manpower and money for the island's defences, supporting
their lords, and furnishing a profit for the Venetian mother city.
Moreover, they always paid more than they should have done,
for corrupt officials of the Cyprus treasury pocketed a large part
of the taxes they collected.

Yet when Bartolommeo Contarini reported this in 1519 the
Council 'became tired of listening to him' and forced him to
stop, and though in 1521 a 'Grand Chancellor' was appointed
to sort out Cyprus's public accounts, and ten years later another
Chancellor with a bigger staff, the administration remained
corrupt. Moreover, though serfs able to afford fifty ducats could
buy their freedom, many villages in the state domain were leased
to private lords. By 1529 many peasants were serving their
masters three days a week, and even when the rate of labour-

service decreased quit-rents rose to a common level of forty per cent of a peasant's crops.

In 1522 Soleiman the Magnificent conquered near-by Rhodes, home of the Crusading orders, which transferred themselves to Malta. Venice, however, held on to her territories in the east, though at some cost to her pride. The Signoria congratulated the Sultan on his conquest in almost cringing terms, and though it regained a privileged position at Constantinople that year, henceforth Venetian ships had to salute any Turkish ship they passed at sea.

By 1525 the Arsenal which maintained Venetian warships had recovered from the great explosion of 1509. The site now covered about sixty acres, boasted a dozen covered docks, absorbed 200,000 ducats a year, and employed up to 2,000 workers. Yet the workers were not entirely content. Employment soon slumped to half that number, wages rates were subject to reductions and the discipline which so large an enterprise demanded was not always accepted meekly; there was occasional sabotage, constant pilfering, and constant arguments.

Rivalry between ship designers was fierce, so fierce indeed that it sometimes led to fighting. Matteo Bressan, however, contrived to maintain his lead over his rivals. In 1522 he was commissioned to build twelve out of the twenty-one galleys being laid down, whereas no other master got more than two. Yet competition was not confined to professional shipwrights.

In the 1520s Vettor Fausto, public lecturer in Greek, decided on a new career in naval architecture. Equipped with a knowledge of mathematics and of ship design in Roman times, he set out to design a quinquireme. The idea seemed intensely revolutionary, but in 1525 he was allotted a yard in which to build his ship. The government also commissioned round ships of new design, including a great galleon designed by Bressan. The Signoria was well pleased with its first great galleon, but satisfaction with Matteo's ship could not match the excitement generated at the launching of Fausto's quinquireme in 1529.

Fausto had been boasting that the fifth oar on his ship would pull more effectively than the third oar on any ordinary galley;

others forecast it would be an utter failure. The issue was tested on an April evening when Fausto's ship was raced against a conventional light galley. The Doge, foreign ambassadors, half Venice, turned out to watch this clash between a product of an ancient craft tradition and the brain-child of a fashionable humanist.

The signal was given and the two ships started off. The galley took the lead at once; but then, at the turning point where all the dignitaries sat, Fausto's vessel overtook it and forged ahead to win. The fruits of classical learning had been vindicated, and the celebrations continued until nightfall.

In service, however, Fausto's ship proved a disappointment. It was expensive to run, and many sailors were to die from exposure on its crowded, unprotected decks. Still, shipbuilding was booming again; the Turks seemed a little less menacing; the Republic had weathered the crisis of the Cambrai League; and Venetians were beginning to adjust successfully to the loss of their monopoly of the spice trade. Venice had recovered from a whole series of catastrophes. But the slow tide of history continued to run against her.

Chapter IX

Retrenchment

With Italy once again in turmoil as imperial troops plundered their way southwards towards the sack of Rome, the spring of 1527 brought a flood of refugees pouring into Venice. The city was accustomed to influxes of 'beggars, rogues and vagabonds,' after the autumn harvest especially, when the harvest had been bad; but the size of this latest influx, its unusual timing, and the commercial dislocation the war had brought in train posed particular difficulties. And the problem was compounded when rivers of the hinterland broke their banks that May, flooding vast tracts of land and ruining the crops. By the end of June trade had ground almost to a standstill, while food prices had risen fast, thanks, as Sanuto wrote, to 'the great crowd of foreigners in this city.'

The government expelled as many immigrants as it could, giving them eight soldi each before throwing them out of town. It also imported extra corn from Cyprus. When grain prices continued to rise, more corn was ordered from Cyprus, but Cyprus itself was running short. Foodstuffs were unobtainable from Austria and the mainland of Italy because of the war, though some were imported from Egypt; and despite the state's offer of bounties to shipowners bringing in corn, its ban on grain exports, and its despatch of commissars to scavenge the countryside, the situation continued to deteriorate.

In the autumn the government spent 3,000 ducats on subsidies, but the cost of the cheap flour it distributed rose nevertheless.

Between April and December the official price for wheat sold at the public granaries rose thirty per cent, and the rise was not offset by any rise in incomes. The result was a hunger which did not abate even when the government began to make a weekly distribution of free rye bread to the poor.

That winter Sanuto was beset by children crying 'Bread, bread, I'm dying of hunger and cold,' as he walked about the city. The many festivals and masquerades the authorities staged presented a sorry contrast, he thought, to the misery in the streets when a great horde of poor peasants scratched about for scraps of food. 'You cannot hear Mass,' wrote Sanuto, 'without ten paupers coming to ask for charity, or open your purse to buy something without the poor asking for a farthing' – and outsiders from near-by Burano, from the famine-ridden hinterland and from the war-ravaged countryside beyond continued to stream in.

Sanuto was wrong in alleging that 'no public measures are taken' to relieve the overwhelming mass of poor. The government continued to subsidize flour and provide certain quantities of free bread; only the more bread doled out, the more alms given, the more free soup provided by the German merchants residing in the city, the more penniless and starving souls rushed in.

It was at least as bad in other cities. 'Give alms to two hundred,' wrote Luigi da Porta of Vicenza, author of the romance on which Shakespeare was to base the plot of *Romeo and Juliet*, 'and two hundred more appear. You cannot walk down the street without crowds surrounding you begging for charity, hunger written on their faces, their eyes like gemless rings.'

Nor was the great hunger the only scourge. There was a series of terrible epidemics too. A plague outbreak encompassed several parishes round the Frari in 1527, and in the spring of 1528 it struck with even greater virulence. Then a new disease reached Venice – typhus. Boatmen were forbidden to bring outsiders into the city; plague victims were confined to their homes; 'contagious' clothes and bedding were burned by order of the government. But the toll of dead mounted steadily – from typhus mainly in spring and early summer, then from plague (the worst outbreak for half a century), and thereafter from malnutrition.

With the city already clogged with sick and dying, the government had at last taken steps to co-ordinate relief. In March a Ducal Councillor and the *provveditori* alla Sanità had proposed to the Senate that 'two, three or more' temporary refuges should be erected and furnished with straw, to lodge the indigent. Others proposed reserving the refuges for sick and helpless Venetians to the exclusion of the immigrants, while some wanted a ban on begging, and a new poor relief rate to be collected by priests and parish deputies and distributed by the Office of Health.

As it eventually emerged, the new law set out to watch the welfare of the poor, the health of the sick and the feeding of the hungry, while ridding Venice of 'knavery and mendicancy.' 'Foreign' beggars were to be repatriated, able-bodied Venetian beggars, other than those 'unfitted' by their birth to manual work, were to be drafted into the navy on half pay, while the care of the disabled and of women and children fell mainly to the parishes or in the case of the homeless to the administrators of the four new 'hospitals' and other charitable institutions.

Each parish was to take care of its share of the needy. In addition, each master, artisan and tradesman was ordered to employ up to four beggar-boys as apprentices; nunneries were to take as many suitable girls as possible, while other beggar-children were set to work in the hospitals to earn their keep. Finally the situation was stabilized by forbidding paupers to move outside their parishes without a certificate from their parish priests, and the whole complex system of relief was now co-ordinated by the Office of Health in conjunction with the local Patriarch.

For the first time welfare had been placed upon a systematic footing. But it was a scheme for Venice only. No attempt was made to integrate it with the haphazard relief efforts staged by Venetian cities in the hinterland, though this proved necessary enough.

The 1528 harvest turned out as badly as the last one. The drought that year was long and terrible and when rain eventually fell in August Sanuto likened it to 'so much gold fallen from heaven for the good of the poor.' But the famine was yet to reach its peak. From autumn onwards the public granaries were constantly surrounded by expectant crowds, and by June 1529 they were almost empty – whereupon a wag scrawled 'House to Let' on the doors of the San Marco storehouses. By November the government was selling beans instead of grain or flour.

The rains came in good time in the spring of 1529, and though Sanuto doubted if the peasants, 'most of whom' were 'subsisting on grass,' had strength enough to cut and thresh the corn, the harvest proved excellent. That summer corn prices in Venice dropped to a more tolerable level at last. The great famine was over.

With the end of the famine came an end to the war which had devastated half of Italy and contributed so much to Venice's travails. By the settlement the Republic lost the war gains she had made in the Romagna, Lombardy and along the Adriatic, and henceforth it abandoned further attempts to extend its rule any further into the Italian mainland. Nevertheless Venice's holdings in the *terraferma* remained substantial, and the recent scarcity of foodstuffs encouraged her to exploit them with more rigour.

In 1529 a third of all the peasants' communal lands in the backward Treviso and Friuli regions were taken into the state domain, and meat having become especially scarce the Signoria ordered the importation of 15,000 beef-cattle a year from the provinces. This produced an outcry from the *terraferma* towns about the lack of feed, the enclosure of plough-lands and the shortage of meat and milk products that the order would entail. Why should a rich city like Venice feed on beef at the expense of subject territories when the rest of Italy was content with pork?

The Signoria felt it wiser to halve its demands. After all, it could still feed its guests adequately enough. In 1532 Grimani entertained Prince Farnese to a banquet that consisted of ninety courses, and there were still many Venetians with the means to live on almost as lavishly as before. When a fire broke out in the Cornaro Palace that year, and three people died while gouty old Zuane Cornaro was carried out to safety, his silver was salvaged by the basketful, together with three coffers full of coin, vast quantities of cotton and sugar, and 400 bushels of wheat. Yet poverty was more in evidence than wealth despite the end of famine.

Beggary persisted despite all attempts to stamp it out and a list of beggars sentenced to the galleys in August 1539 shows them to have come from as far afield as Arezzo, Milan, Pisa, Sicily and even France. There were still plenty of Venetian beggars, too, including professionals. Some who begged proved to have had several hundred ducats in investments; others faked disabilities of all sorts, from the loss of a leg to Parkinson's disease, and one particularly notorious beggar, Francesco of Brescia, posed as a crippled woman to gain the sympathy and cash of passers-by.

The Scuole dei Zotto and degli Orbi cared for many of the genuinely lame and blind; the many other charitable institutions included the Scuola di San Fantin, which consoled criminals on their way to execution, and the Casa della Zitelle, which saved young girls from sin, while in 1531 charity merged with patronage when the Ten decided to award poor Marino Sanuto a pension of 150 ducats for continuing to write the history of his times. Like many an author he grumbled that 'this money is as nothing by comparison to the time and labour' expended on the task, but he accepted it, persevering, as he put it, out of love 'for fatherland and letters,' and when he died in 1533 he left all his books to the state.

Sexual morals being no less relaxed in Venice than in the rest of Italy, Sanuto also left two illegitimate daughters. Indeed the appetites of inhabitants and visitors alike were amply catered for by a plentitude of prostitutes, whose praises and perils were sung in a volume of contemporary verse – the fine eyes of the fifteen-year-old Stellina, the beauty of the well-born Lucia dagli Alberi, the venereal disease of Angela Zaffetta (whom Cardinal Hippolito de Medici was said to have patronized) and many more. From 1539 the Magistrato alla Sanità was responsible for controlling prostitutes, but for reasons of health rather than of morals, because Venice did not frown on fornication as it did on homosexuality. Even noble rank would not necessarily save a sodomite from execution.

Heterosexual relationships were encouraged by mixed dancing, which had become very popular among all classes; so too had dialect comedies, satire generally, and scurrilous verse in particular – such literature being sold in the bookshops at Rialto, the Frezzeria and San Moisé. The Merceria, on the other hand, resembled the Lycean academy,' according to a contemporary, because of the number of shops there marketing literature of somewhat higher quality. Best-sellers, however, were much as they are today – cheap tales of languishing maidens and ladies saved; manuals on arts and crafts, especially domestic ones, like Nicolò d'Aristotele's book on needlework published in 1537. The state encouraged the printing industry by granting patents for inventions as well as copyrights and by laying down standards; insisting, for example, that books be printed on paper that did not blot. This protection was justified, for in no other trade was pride in workmanship higher. Samples of Aldo Manuzio's work were buried with him when he died, and at the author Rangone's funeral copies of his books opened on favourite pages were carried in procession after his corpse, along with ornaments from his house and a model of his parish church.

Quick to recognize the danger printing posed in the dissemination of false doctrine in this age of the Reformation, the church had already banned the works of Martin Luther, and from the later 1540s religious censorship was introduced. But for the moment the Venetian presses ran on unhindered and their products were prized throughout the literate world. Venetian lace-makers and dyers were almost as renowned, textile production was still expanding at a considerable rate, but shipbuilding remained the single biggest employer in the city, and the state took good care to protect it too.

In 1531 the government forbade the purchase of ships built abroad and it also acted to increase the number of shipyard craftsmen, hastening the transformation of apprentices into masters. Between 1530 and 1560 the number of master carpenters and caulkers doubled, and most of them found their way to the

Arsenal, to jobs less well paid but rather more secure than those offered in the private yards.

The *arsenalotti* had become a multi-functional caste within the Venetian social-political system. They acted as city firemen and as palace guards, carried torches at a Doge's funeral and bore his successor through the Piazza on their shoulders. They enjoyed career opportunities as bowmen, ships' carpenters and sailing masters too, but their major business was always building ships.

Although trade was gradually expanding again, and for a brief period from 1530 Venice was once more the chief purveyor of spices to western Europe, galleys were no longer used for merchant voyages to Flanders and Southampton, and much more rarely on the Beirut and Alexandria runs, the goods being carried by merchantmen of larger tonnage. As a result galleys were used almost exclusively for military purposes, but the design of such warships often differed from those of former times, and many experiments were made to achieve better manœuvrability and fire-power.

In 1532 that latter-day Archimedes, Vettor Fausto, builder of the celebrated quinquireme, offered to adapt five 'galee bastarde' to a new design – an offer which was accepted with the sensible condition that he restore them to their original form at his own expense if the experiment turned out a failure. He subsequently worked on finding a way to build traditional galleys using less timber and to make them more manœuvrable by changing the number of oars per bench and galley-men per oar. But many other types were produced at the Arsenal. One of the twelve construction chiefs employed there in 1544 listed *fuste bregantine*, twenty-oared frigates and even high-pooped galleons among the ships he built.

The stockyards of the Arsenal gradually filled up, but the problem of finding mariners remained acute. 'The people is so comfortable and well-to-do,' wrote the celebrated admiral Cristoforo da Canale in 1539, 'that nothing less than overwhelming need would induce them to embark in a galley.' With the number of volunteers continuing to decline the state demanded that every guild within the city, every *terraferma* town and every colony provide its quota of recruits to serve as oarsmen with the fleet (which they generally found from the ranks of able-bodied paupers) and drafted ever more convicts into service. Not surprisingly, this trend encouraged poorer seamanship and a tendency for conditions aboard ship to deteriorate.

The galley captains who strutted about in expensive armour, silk cloaks, ermine, and even cloth of gold, were an arrogant crowd – more concerned about the gilding on their galleys than the weary oarsmen who propelled them. This, after all, was the age of Benvenuto Cellini, and no young Venetian aristocrat was to be outdone in swashbuckling or ostentation by any other men in Italy. Another spate of sumptuary legislation passed in 1535 was aimed incidentally at limiting the luxury of naval captains. But whether or not this had any effect, nothing was done to curb ill-treatment of the sailor.

The condemned men with their shaven heads were the worst treated, supervised by a 'gaoler,' shackled to their oars except in time of battle, never allowed to quit ship until their sentence had been served. When not actually rowing they were forced to sew sails and mend the crews' clothes, and they were fed almost exclusively on biscuit. No wonder, then, that a two years' sentence to the galleys was reckoned the equivalent of five years' imprisonment. The 'slaves' – men literally bought for the service or prisoners-of-war – were little better treated. Usually distinguished by a tuft of hair that grew up in Tatar fashion from their otherwise completely shaven heads, they fetched wood and water and helped the ships' carpenters, in addition to rowing, and only the diminishing proportion of volunteers got full seamen's rations and pay, though for the sake of morale and the captain's satisfaction each man was now issued with shirts, breeches and stockings, a red cap and a uniform coat and cloak.

Harsh discipline was considered necessary now that so many seamen were pressed men and chained convicts, but it did not prevent the Venetian navy showing sturdy resistance to the warships of Suleiman the Magnificent when they attacked in 1537. The Turks were repulsed from Corfu, Nauplia and Crete; the notorious corsair Dragut was dealt with by Venetian galleys and on one notable occasion Venetian round ships fought off a much superior Turkish force. But the enemy nevertheless won this latest round of the protracted struggle to master the eastern Mediterranean, and in 1540 the Republic was forced to cede not only Aegina, Mykonos and the northern Sporades, but Nauplia and Malvasia as well – her last foothold in Morea.

Despite this dwindling of the Empire overseas, in Venice itself state, Church, corporations and individuals continued to pour money into buildings. Jacopo Sansovino from Tuscany was only one architect to prosper on such patronage. He rebuilt the Cornaro Palace after the fire of 1532, completed the Libreria Vecchia and designed the Loggetto, a convenient place for noble-men to take the air and discuss affairs without mixing with the lower orders, while in his capacity as superintendent of public works he also worked on the Ducal Palace designing the magnificent Scala d'Oro. Sansovino also built on his own account, redeveloping the site of a house he owned in the Merceria in such a way as to convert a property worth twenty ducats a year into one producing 170. Michele Sanmichele also ran a booming architectural practice, though most of his commissions came from the hinterland. The painter Titian, by contrast, made his way largely as official painter to the Serenissima, holding this appointment from 1516.

But state patronage was only a fraction of the total available. Individuals spent ducats by their thousands, adorning their splendid palaces and villas. The Church spent conspicuously as well, despite a revival of earlier laws limiting its acquisition of real estate in the city, while between 1516 and 1564 the Scuola di San Rocco spent no less than 55,000 ducats on building a great hall and engaging Tintoretto to decorate many of its walls and ceilings.

Spending on this scale by a Scuola attracted criticism. 'Building cuts into the revenues of the poor,' wrote Alessandro Caravia in 1541. Nor did he think the Scuole were motivated by piety in mounting such splendid floats for processions always 'with some new contraption . . . spending their money on crazy things.' In 1543 the Council of Ten itself condemned 'superfluous expenditure' by Scuole 'on elaborate devices and banquets,' since it dissipated 'money . . . which ought to go . . . to the poor.' Nevertheless, in the 1550s the Scuola di San Rocco spent about 450 ducats a year on processions as against 650 on alms, and by the mid 1570s virtually the same amount on both, though it also spent sizeable amounts on dowries, hospitals and medicine. The hospital of SS. Giovanni and Paolo, for example, increased its beds from 130 to 450 between 1556 and 1565, although this was partly a response to governmental pressures applied to all large charitable institutions to maintain veteran galley-men and soldiers.

The proportion of the city's poor had increased again, thanks to those periodic harvest failures in the hinterland. As Caravia noted in 1541, there were 'innumerable poor in Venice, hungry and barefoot people well acquainted with hardship.' The Church did much to alleviate this poverty, not only through direct alms-giving but through the influence of certain movements it embraced.

In 1550, for example, the followers of Ignatius Loyola, founder of the Jesuits, who had himself visited Venice in 1536, established a community to succour the poor in the hospitals of the Incurabili and SS. Giovanni and Paolo, as well as to reclaim prostitutes for God. The Capuchin Order also made a contribution. But whilst religious orders and parochial authorities mobilized the charitable instincts of Venetians, the co-ordination of relief remained in governmental hands.

The state controlled the disbursement of charitable bequests through the Procurators of St. Mark, but it was most obviously effective in maintaining food supplies and controlling the price of basic foods. Even in famine years it contrived to keep the price of the loaf stable – albeit by lowering the regulation weight from time to time. It maintained granaries at Rialto and San Marco, took in two-thirds of all imported wheat for distribution both to individuals and to the city bakers, and like ancient Egypt in the time of Joseph, it stockpiled coarse wheat and even millet for use in lean years.

Like some Egyptian Pharaohs, too, the state continued to discriminate against immigrants, dumping paupers over the border

H

or sending them to the galleys. During one spasmodic burst of immigration it got rid of 3,600 beggars in this way. But thanks to growing unemployment there was a growing number of indigenous paupers too.

Ever since the latest Turkish war there had been insufficient work available at the Arsenal to allow many of the caulkers especially to earn living family wages. The problem was partly alleviated by a renewal of the practice of rotation hiring, but mainly by the processing of a new shipbuilding programme.

From 1545 the State aimed to construct a hundred light galleys and twelve great ones – twice as many as before – even though there were already 131 light galleys and numerous other vessels in service. The motive here was not the welfare of the shipbuilders but the maintenance of a work-force in preparation for another war with the Turks. This contingency was postponed for as long as possible, however, by Venetian agents in Constantinople who plied Turkish ministers with bribes so fat that one agent spent over 12,000 ducats in two years on such 'salaries' and 'courtesies.'

In private yards the tendency was to build fewer merchant ships of much larger size. By 1559 there were as many as forty square-riggers, displacing about 450 tons apiece, carrying cargoes as far afield as Constantinople and England, though the two most frequented sailing points beyond the Adriatic were Syria and Cyprus.

Such ships proved much easier to defend than the old armed merchant galleys, particularly against pirates – especially the sea-predators called the Uskoks who had begun to infest the Adriatic from their bases at Senj and Fiume and to rustle cattle from off-shore Venetian islands. But for all offensive purposes the well-tried galley with its crucial speed still held the day.

The state showed its concern about preserving its security not only by keeping a strong navy but through its counter-espionage methods supervised by three special inquisitors and by attempting to weld the population together by an enforced religious and ideological conformity – qualities for which their potential enemies, the Turks, were so much envied.

The 1540s saw a new court established to try cases of heresy and the banning of all heretical works, while in 1551 the Inquisition was admitted to Venice. Religious censorship may not have been enforced quite so rigorously as elsewhere but Venetians were subjected to harassment, searches and seizures, and punishment for broadcasting their opinions and views. Between 1550 and 1600 the flames of intolerance were fanned up high against Lutherans, Jews and disseminators of all 'false doctrine.'

In 1550 all Marranos, the crypto-Jews expelled from Spain, were ordered to leave the city. The so-called 'German' Jews, though suffered to remain, were locked in their ghetto every night once the curfew trumpet sounded, and in October 1553, anxious to placate the Pope, the Ten ordered all copies of the Talmud and other works of Jewish learning to be publicly burned.

The formation of a guild of printers and booksellers in 1549 made state censorship easier to exercise, and control of the presses was tightened further in 1567 by a statute which deputed the Inquisitor, the Public Reader, and the Ducal Secretaty to ensure that books not only contained nothing 'contrary to religion, hostile to princes or against morals,' but that they were positively 'worthy to see the light.'

The same year the printers guild dedicated themselves again to the service of God and the honour of the Republic in a new statute establishing themselves as a 'college.' This statute provided for the performance of Masses, the election of officers, payment of subscriptions, and rules for meetings, including provisions for fining members who dared interrupt the prior. But the statutes had also been vetted by the Ten, which used the association to control printers as a whole.

The results of the clampdown was first a blossoming of underground presses, and when stringent security measures smashed these, the slow decline of Venice as a printing centre. Freedom of the presses was soon only a remembrance. The arteries of higher learning gradually hardened, and while retaining closer cultural links with Reformist scholars in northern Europe than any other city in Italy Venice began to decline as a centre for free-ranging intellects.

The reason for censorship, apart from the pressure of the Church, was the eternal one – to procure an ideological solidarity and a high level of patriotism in the face of outside threats – in this case from the Turks – and the bolstering of the Republic's reputation as a well-regulated state also contributed to this purpose.

The myth of the Republic disseminated by the early chroniclers, then with more sophistication by Contarini and a succession of official propagandists, was taken up by foreigners, and men of affairs throughout Europe were soon well versed in the details of the Venetian system – the limits placed on the Doge's powers, the gold and silver ballot balls used in the elections, the overlapping roles of the Senate, the Collegio and all the other governmental bodies which checked each others' activities. The Republic and its constitution were presented as uniquely perfect. Yet power, prestige and influence depended more on wealth than ever it had done. Even the democracy of the nobility – a group of about 2,500 men controlling a total population of about two millions – was restricted by the old ethos that the rich among them were the best.

In theory all of them were qualified to sit on committees and fill the most powerful posts, but in practice these offices went to members of the inner group. Even the ideal training system by which young nobles gained experience in a succession of posts graded in responsibliity, which served to sift out the most able for top office, applied to few now apart from the wealthy *élite*.

The nobility as a whole was declining in numbers, yet the proportion of the poor among them was increasing. Their poverty induced corruption – the sale of votes, the venal exploitation of minor offices – and a tendency on the part of honest men to avoid posts involving more expense than income. More nobles, too, were holding out their hands for charity. Between 1536 and 1556 no fewer than 300 joined the Scuola di San Rocco, many of them, no doubt, paying their subscriptions in anticipation of future need of the Scuola's help.

Noble families with some wealth fought hard to keep it, sending daughters into nunneries to save on dowries – often to the detriment of the convent's moral atmosphere – leaving fortunes to a single heir and preventing the alienation of estates by their descendants. Sons who did not inherit were nevertheless looked after. 'All my [five] sons,' ran the testament of Stefano Tiepolo in 1550, 'should live together at equal expense,' without dividing their goods until the last of them should reach the age of thirty. But the concomitant of such arrangements was a tendency for only one brother to marry, whereupon the others would move upstairs leaving *piano nobile* to the matrimonial pair.

This communal family household was an extension of a common education – usually private education commonly comprising Latin and Italian grammar, basic mathematics and tuition in writing 'every sort of letter quickly.' The sense of family community often extended to partnership in business and was often so close as to lead one contemporary to suggest that when one brother took a wife all the others shared her favours.

Family partnerships in household and business were good, wrote one noble, because sons would live 'with more love, more honour, greater profit and less expense.' They certainly helped to preserve family capital, but since as many as half of all noblemen remained bachelors, and their proportion was growing, this pattern of existence presaged the disappearance of the Venetian nobility.

The root cause was the lack of suitable opportunities to revive declining fortunes. The road of commerce, which Andrea Barbarigo had trodden so successfully a century and more before, held attraction for few noblemen these days. Daniele Barbaro, the humanist and architectural patron, had made his fortune in overseas trade in the first half of the sixteenth century, and Guiseppe Dolfin, who traded as a coral specialist at Alexandria and then in timber back at Venice, where he became a member of the Ten before his death in 1585, was quite exceptional as a successful merchant-noble. More typical was Francesco da Molin. He began his career just as Barbarigo had done as a 'bowman of the quarterdeck' (though by that time the 'bowmen' were armed with arquebuses) and as a holder of minor legal offices, and then went out to Crete 'to see if I could not increase my savings in an honest, honourable way.' But presumably he failed, for he made no further mention of business in his diary, and on returning to Venice he concentrated, with no spectacular success, on obtaining salaried office.

Nevertheless some noblemen contrived to live in a style at least as magnificent as any of their ancestors. Most of the grandest Venetian palaces we recognize today were built in the 1500s; so were many of the delightful villas that grace old Venetian estates in the hinterland, many of them built by that most famous architect, Palladio.

Andrea di Pietro della Gondola had been born in 1508, served an apprenticeship as a stonecarver at Padua, and then moved to Vicenza where he was eventually taken up by Count Trissino for whom he built a villa in classical style, which earned him his nickname 'Palladio.' Trissino took him to Rome in 1541, and on his return to Vicenza, his sketch-books filled with studies of Roman antiquities, Palladio designed a whole series of town palaces and country villas. But his eyes were soon fixed on Venice, forty miles away, where he found a patron and friend in Giacomo Contarini. Palladio repeatedly entered competitions to design public structures there without success, and had to content himself for the most part with commissions to build villas for rich Venetians in the *terraferma*.

He built one for Daniele and Marcantonio Barbaro at Maser – probably the richest sixteenth-century villa in all north Italy. Basically a farm house, it had a *piano nobile* (which Veronese was to decorate with mythical subjects and scenes of aristocratic country life), and though the fountains made the gardens a particular delight they also supplied water for the kitchen, so that all in all it presented a triumphant combination of the practical and the ideal – a residence totally appropriate to a humanist like Daniele, who was an Aristotelean scholar and farmer, mathematician, engineer, and editor of Vitruvius.

Palladio's designs displayed an intellectual passion for proportion, and though, mathematics and humanist scholasticism apart, Venetian intellects were less adventurously engaged than they had been fifty years before, Venetian eyes had more than ever to excite them now – carved and gilded ceilings, delicious friezes, terrazzo floors and water gardens. The affluent covered their walls with leather, gilt and costly tapestries, and decorated fireplaces with the forms of cherubs and of sirens. Tables were heaped with silverware and china, libraries adorned with velvet-bound books. Lutes and daggers, tables, chests, and carpets – every artefact about the house and person of a Venetian gentleman of means and of refinement was in itself a work of art.

For clothes the discerning would go to the Bontempellis' shop at San Salvatore, where the finest cloths were sold, and have it made up for their wives at Giovanni's dressmaking establishment at San Lio. Women of fashion carried handkerchiefs laced with gold and gloves of painted leather, and spent hours beautifying themselves – bleaching their hair, painting their breasts, staving off the ravages of age by applications of raw veal or even dung to their faces. And in time such fashions, as fashions do, crept on down the social scale.

Although the Inquisition was operating and non-conformity was stifled, the mood of Venice was no stricter morally. Prostitution was still rampant, innkeepers commonly kept teenage girls to sleep with patrons, 'adulterous dances' were still danced, and for his latest painting in the chamber of the Ten Veronese chose to depict an opulent Juno, rather than a chaste St. Mark, showering riches on a female Venice.

For all her joys and new magnificence Venice herself was ageing now, becoming ever less adventurous. Her centuries-long leadership in commerce had been whittled away, and though her accumulated wealth made her one of the very richest cities in all Europe, and investment in industry compensated for her losses, other states were catching up with her prosperity. The port was busy still and the early 1560s saw a late re-flowering of trade with the Levant, but the English herring fleets and the galleons of Spain crammed with bullion from the Americas were tapping new sources of wealth beyond Venetian reach; and Seville and Antwerp were overtaking her as centres for world trade. Venetians were still shrewd observers of the world, but years of success and comfort had blunted the courage if not the avidity of the nobility.

They were reluctant to undertake great risks in the pursuit of profit, less fiery in their willingness to engage competitors across the seas. Their eyes turned inward more to concentrate upon the mainland instead of foreign markets and to preserve existing fortunes instead of making new ones.

Chapter XII

The Final Years of Glory

In 1570 the population of the Venetian empire in the *terraferma* numbered about 1,500,000. Little more than ten per cent of them lived in towns of any size. Primarily agricultural, the *terraferma* was a very mixed area economically. Subsistence peasant farming was still characteristic of Friuli and the Belluno, Treviso and Rovigo regions, while the agriculture of the fruit-growing area round the rich corn-growing plains of Verona and the Vicenza region with its mulberry trees was highly market-orientated. Moreover, Brescia and Bergamo boasted important metallurgical enterprises, producing pots and pans, agricultural implements, tools and armaments, Verona was a centre for linen manufacture, and Vicenza of a silk industry.

Compared to the leech-like policies of other Italian city states, Venice treated the *terraferma* leniently. The economy of these disparate regions was allowed to integrate around the regional towns without being rigorously tied to the needs of Venice. Venetian officials supervised defence works, including those great forbidding walls still to be seen around the upper town of Bergamo, and they collected taxes, which produced a surplus for Venice of rather less than a ducat a year per head of population. The Republic also maintained a firm grip on Church patronage – but otherwise its grip was lax. No effort was made to impose Venetian socio-political structures. Feudalism and even *droit de seigneur* were allowed to persist in some areas, but, while many provincial officials were corrupt, political wisdom bred of long experience led Venetian governors to play the role of mediators, balancing the interests of lords and peasants – indeed often siding with the latter and even sending off a number of recalcitrant non-noble landlords to Venice to a quiet death by drowning.

Lions of St. Mark stood imperiously upon their pillars in every major town; governors had their names inscribed on the walls of public buildings; but Venice preferred not to govern by decree, and Venetian influence was felt most keenly in those areas where Venetians had set up as landlords. As capital had been withdrawn from commerce more Venetian fortunes had been invested in land, and Venetian owners were often highly energetic in improving their estates.

About the middle of the century as much as a third of the land in western Venetia was uncultivated waste. By 1580 many of these acres had been reclaimed for cultivation. Enterprising individuals like the Priulis and Barbaros, for whom Palladio built the Villa Maser, were responsible for much of this increase, being at least as concerned with good estate management as with the breeding of their horses or the luxury of their villas. But sometimes landowners clubbed together in consortia to reclaim wasteland, and the development also owed something to the government which subsidized and co-ordinated reclamation projects through a special Board set up in 1556.

The state was motivated to take this action by the pressure the rapid population increase was placing on Venice's own food supply. 'Whereas 30,000 bushels of wheat a month used to suffice,' remarked Alvise Cornaro in 1556, '45,000 are now too little.' Grain prices and shipping costs had soared while grain production in the *terraferma* had declined, sometimes to half its former level, because of over-cultivation.

Yet Venice's population continued to grow despite a plague outbreak in 1555–6. The bounties offered to Venetian shipowners bringing in grain, the orders issued to Venetian landowners to send in their crops, and the offer of local tax and customs exemptions to non-Venetians sending grain to Venice were only short-term measures; and though, in the long term, the new policy did alleviate the problem, Venetians who had invested in land expecting only modest returns found themselves reaping handsome profits – for grain prices continued their inexorable rise. As they did so, more maize, a high-yield crop, first introduced in about 1550, was planted. Maize, source of that ubiquitous dish of the Veneto, *polenta*, was a novelty ill-received by Venetians used to good white wheaten loaves. Supplies of decent bread were often to run short – but there was still no lack of Venetian circuses.

These processionals and displays were staged deliberately to distract the people and enhance the state's prestige. According to one state document such 'triumphs' were 'admired by all those who flock to this city, and are subsequently reported in . . . various kingdoms . . . throughout the world.' One such 'triumph' celebrated the coronation of Doge Lorenzo Priuli's wife, Zilia Dandolo, in 1557. Sixty senators, over 200 young noblewomen, the Dukes of Savoy and Urbino, and the entire diplomatic corps went on parade. There was a triumphal arch erected by the city's butchers, and when the Dogaressa, wearing cloth of gold, high chopines, and horn-shaped cap with a white veil hanging from it, arrived at the Molo upon the *Bucintoro* she was welcomed by a guard of honour, a fanfare of silver trumpets, a salute of guns, the fluttering of banners, and the cheers and screaming of the crowd.

She took the oath, presented purses of gilt thread to the Chancellor and Councillors, attended a *Te Deum* and a procession of guildsmen, and when night fell took her place upon the throne in the Great Council Hall, where, to the sound of trumpets, drums and a band of fifty fifes, she received 360 selected guildsmen who entered carrying silver trays of sweetmeats and presents. There was a three-hour display of fireworks, a dance and banquet which lasted until dawn, then three more days of processionals, regattas, and a bullfight in the palace courtyard.

Two years later the Dogaressa was allotted fifty ducats a month to help her maintain eight ladies-in-waiting clad in silk, two boats adorned with tapestries, and a wardrobe appropriate for state occasions – for the greater glory of the Republic. She was also exempt from the sumptuary law of 1562 which forbade women wearing pearls after ten years of marriage and limited dishes served at banquets. Under this law meat and fish were not to be offered at a single meal; the consumption of trout, sturgeon, lake fish, pastry and confectionery was restricted; oysters were not to be eaten at dinners given for more than twenty guests – and even a maximum serving of marzipan was prescribed. Restrictions were also placed on the decoration of gondolas and the colours they could be painted. But no restriction was placed on the building of country villas, and with *villegiatura* now so popular and agricultural estates so much more profitable a building boom was already in progress in the hinterland – providing numerous commissions for the architect Palladio.

It was he who designed the Villa Rotonda, that perfect creation standing four-square upon its verdant hill outside Vicenza, and planned the Villa Malcontenta for the Foscari brothers – a genteel farmstead near Venice on the Brenta, graced with Tintoretto frescoes. But Palladio received other commissions too – to build a new convent, and theatres and stage sets. He designed the wooden theatre at the Carità, built in 1565, and the celebrated Teatro Olympico at Vicenza, though this was completed after his death by his follower, Scamozzi.

The Teatro Olympico was commissioned by a club of local humanist nobles, and Venice had similar clubs, their activities ranging from theatricals, banquets and the singing of madrigals to intellectual debates. But it could be dangerous to propagate unorthodox ideas, even in the comparative privacy of a club. In 1561 the 'Accademia della Fama' founded by Frederigo Badoer in the later 1550s was actually suppressed and its leaders punished.

Nevertheless, compared with most states, Venice was still tolerant. Discrimination against Jews did not prevent the Doge rewarding a Jewish doctor who had risked his life trying to contain the plague epidemic of 1567. Banned books could still be bought in Venice, and displays of pornographic material remained a feature, even of the Merceria on Sundays, though a law of 1565 did ban booksellers from showing any but devotional publications on holy days. Scandals were frequent. During the 1560s a Dolfin and a Cornaro both abducted nuns from convents;

Bianca Capello eloped with a Florentine, and subsequently had an affair with Francesco de Medici and became Duchess of Tuscany, while in 1560 a priest, Giovan Pietro Leon was executed for having cohabitated with nuns, procured abortions, committed infanticide, misappropriated money from charitable bequests and earned more money selling the nuns' embroidery than a pimp did from a popular whore.

On the other hand, after a typhus outbreak the debtors' prisons were fumigated and the streets and canals of the city were cleaned up regularly now that each precinct had to keep garbage collectors permanently employed. Unskilled labourers such as these earned about nine soldi a day, three and a half more than a woman sailmaker, but considerably less than the average wage, and far less than a master mason, who grossed upwards of thirty-two soldi a day. But a master shipwright, a foreman caulker, or a gunfounder – the aristocrats of the labouring classes – could earn as much as 110 ducats a year plus free housing.

The Arsenal which employed a high proportion of these top wage-earners could accommodate over 100 galleys now in addition to small craft. Its storehouses were crammed with benches, oars and footboards; spare masts, rudders, spars and vast quantities of ropes, arms, pitch, sails and ironwork. But the private yards were booming, encouraged by government subsidies for ships of over 360 tons and by a revival of the spice trade.

Venetian agents stationed at Alexandria and Aleppo near the Baghdad-Basra route from India suffered competition from the French these days, but the quantity of spices coming through Turkish controlled territory often exceeded the amount the Portuguese brought in by the long sea route. In 1560 Venice actually obtained the lion's share of the crop, and between 1560 and 1564 Venetian round ships brought in about 550 tons of pepper every year from Alexandria – as much as they had done before Portugal had snatched the trade.

This unexpected turnabout was due to the poorly-paid Portuguese guarding India and the approaches to the Red Sea accepting bribes to allow large consignments of spices to pass along the old routes. When they realized what was happening, moneyed Venetians took fresh heart and hastened to profit from the change of fortune.

One young nobleman as eager to respond to it as any of his merchant forebears would have been was Alessandro Magno. Taking 2,000 ducats and some silk, he rushed off to Alexandria in April 1561, arriving four weeks later. Moving on to Cairo, he bought some pepper and settled down to wait for another caravan whose arrival was believed imminent. He waited a month, passing the time seeing sights and visiting the pyramids, but still the caravan had not appeared, and with pepper prices rising and his ship about to leave, Alessandro bought cloves and ginger instead, and arrived back in Venice that October to sell his spices at a 266 ducat profit.

Others did far better. The risk-all adventurism of earlier Venetians might have disappeared, but not their open-hearted avidity. They maintained no hypocritical silence about their ruthless pursuit of money – they proclaimed it. 'The desire to grow rich,' wrote a contemporary, 'is as natural in us as the desire to live.' 'Riches,' he continued, 'rule families and cities . . . increase good fortune, insulate us against the shocks of ill-fortune, and . . . contribute . . . a marvellous dignity to every activity.' Venetians might foster a myth about the perfection of their Republic; they did not deceive themselves about their priority in life.

Money was still being made and spent in plenty. Less now in overseas trade than once had been the case perhaps, despite the upsurge in the spice trade – although the first news-sheet produced in the city in 1566 devoted most of its space to mercantile news – and a considerable proportion of the trade in wool, silk, spice and sugar was now left to the Jews. But more was being made in industry and agriculture. Despite their traditional disdain for 'mechanical' occupations, many nobles and 'original citizens' not only invested in industry they engaged actively in its management. One branch of the Vendramins ran a soap factory, others were involved in textile enterprises – an industry which reached a peak of production in 1569 turning out close on 27,000 cloths – and there were large-scale operators, too, in sugar-refining, tanning, shipbuilding, insurance and banking.

It was the bankers who were blamed for the widening gap in value between the gold ducat and the ducat of account. They were hardly responsible for the marked inflation of the sixties, however. The root cause was the lack of gold available to finance the volume of trade. Nevertheless, the bankers' solvency was questionable, and in 1569 when the five private banks, all owned by noblemen, were ordered into liquidation only one proved able to pay out in full. The Jewish pawnbroking businesses provided another Venetian banking service – a service tantamount to usury, in which Christians still invested, however, though from 1566 this was forbidden and the lending rate limited to ten per cent.

The later sixties were bad years for Italian Jews. They were expelled from Genoa and Florence in 1567, and two years later the Pope sent most of his Jews packing too. The Jews were experiencing one of their perennial crises. So was Venice. With the Turkish menace looming larger, an expensive defence programme was ordered involving the fortification of colonies and exposed *terraferma* districts in Friuli – and this coincided with another famine, and an outbreak of the plague which took almost three times its usual toll of victims.

In September 1569 fire broke out in the Arsenal. One nobleman, Francesco da Molin, who was in bed with fever at the time, woke up to see 'windows breaking, walls opening, beams burning and so much fire everywhere' that he thought the Day of Judgement had arrived. But the mood of the *arsenalotti* themselves was more dangerous still.

Determined to improve the Arsenal's efficiency, the government had introduced a new law in 1569. 'The masters of our Arsenal,' ran the preamble, 'work in great confusion,' some of them in any dock which pleased them, while others wandered about 'without doing any work' at all. Among other measures, it was decided not to pay them for Saturday afternoons, which they spent entirely queuing for their pay. This proved the last straw for many *arsenalotti*, and at noon the following Saturday 300 of them rushed into the Piazza armed with axes and mallets, menaced the chiefs of the Ten, and burst into the College chamber. The Doge managed to persuade them to disperse – whereupon the Ten arrested the ringleaders and threw them into gaol, and the Arsenal Commissioners proceeded to interview each master individually and cajole or threaten him into towing the line.

The famine, however, was not to be solved so simply. By the autumn of 1569 the public granaries had run out of flour. 'People mad with hunger,' wrote da Molin, 'wandered through the city' looking for shops with bread for sale, but they were lucky to find any at a price they could afford. The government doled out ship's biscuit instead, then loaves made from millet – at which there was an angry outcry, as well there might be, for the shortage was exacerbated by the activities of Venetian profiteers.

True to the money-grasping ethic, a number of noblemen had been buying up grain at controlled prices 'under cover of the poor,' and selling it as bread on the free market at well over twice the price. As a result, in April 1570 the public granaries had to shut their doors and the government decided to distribute flour to bakers who were ordered to make bread for the poor. The bakers, however, sold off the flour for what they could get, and only when parish chiefs were sent to supervise the bakeries did the poor get their bread on production of certificates proving need.

The Turks, meanwhile, were demanding that Venice cede them Cyprus, which they claimed Christian pirates were using as a base against them. But Cyprus, which was taxed much more heavily than the *terraferma*, produced a net income of over 300,000 ducats a year for the Republic. It was far too valuable to give up lightly.

Relations between Venice and Turkey deteriorated; trade between them ground to a standstill; and when an ambassador arrived to state the Sultan's latest terms Venetians waited with bated breath to see what banners would be carried at the next official procession – white ones indicating peace, red for war, or blue for truce.

It was the red banner of war. Reckoning on the support of the

The Final Years of Glory

The Final Years of Glory 227

Pope and Spain, the Signoria had stood firm. A vast Turkish armada was soon sailing towards Cyprus, and in August 1570 Girolamo Zane, looking every inch a warrior with his Spanish-type armour, grizzled hair, shrewd eyes and pointed beard, was entrusted with the banner of St. Mark. He set sail with over 100 galleys to join a dozen papal ships and forty-nine Spanish galleys under the Genoese admiral Doria off Crete. But the campaign never got under way.

Many of Zane's ships were undermanned and his crews lacked training. He lost men from fever and then lost time recruiting replacements in the Archipelago and arguing out a strategy with Doria. Eventually Zane returned to Venice having accomplished nothing and was immediately put on trial.

Meanwhile the Turkish general Mustafa had attacked Nicosia. Confident that help was on its way, its defenders refused to surrender, but the bastions of cotton bales they had thrown up proved vulnerable to the 'artificial fire' the enemy shot at them, and the sheer weight of the Turkish onslaughts and sickness in the ranks eventually broke their discipline. Some Nicosians mounted a rebellion, the banner of St. Mark was lowered, the Turkish flag hauled up. Nicosia had been lost.

The Turks aimed next at Famagusta, which was garrisoned by about 8,000 Italian and Greek troops. Their commander, Marcantonio Bragadin, sustained their morale through assault after assault. Hopes of eventual relief stood high in Famagusta, and the government in Venice was determined to effect a rescue.

The efforts to mount a campaign in 1571 verged on the heroic in view of the difficulties faced at home. Venice had been struck by typhus in 1560, plague had visited Brescia and Padua with unremembered force, a sudden trade recession had thrown many Venetians out of work, and by the autumn the Ten, anxious to fend off public riots, was desperately ordering the Procurators of St. Mark and the Scuole to divert all charitable funds at their disposal to the 'miserable poor.'

The new 'Holy League' with the Papacy and Spain was celebrated by a great procession in the Piazza. A tableau depicted the Grand Turk as a huge dragon with a crescent on its head, a float featured three youths representing Faith, Hope and Charity, while other dumbshows interpreted the significance of the occasion to the crowd. Mummers represented Pope Pius V, King Philip II, and the Doge; a naked Moor decked out with wings and horns represented Charon rowing the enemy to Hades; there were floats depicting the reed huts of the original Venetians and the coining of ducats, and religious paintings specially commissioned for the occasion were also paraded.

Meanwhile about ninety ships were being fitted out for battle. The names of the captains appointed to command them – Contarini, Zeno, Gradenigo, Pisani, Barbarigo, Querini, and the ringing name of Dandolo – evoked many a past glory. At last the fleet sailed out to join allied armadas led by Doria and Don John of Austria, and together they moved east towards the isles of Greece.

In September 1571 the Venetian Senate was still debating the vexed question of getting supplies through to beleaguered Famagusta, but though help was now on the way the city had already been starved into surrender. Twelve days afterwards its commander Bragadin had been flayed alive, his skin stuffed and paraded before the Turkish army set astride a cow. Bragadin's fate was not entirely undeserved. His zeal had led him to refuse a hostage for the safe return of Turkish ships made available to repatriate the garrison, and he had slaughtered his Turkish prisoners on the eve of the surrender. Nevertheless, his death was soon to be avenged. The allied ships were shortly bearing in towards Lepanto, and a confrontation with the Turkish fleet.

Augustino Barbarigo, the Provveditor-General, flying a yellow pennant, commanded the port wing with fifty-three galleys; Doria, flying a green flag, had as many on the starboard bow, while Don John led the central group of sixty-one, a blue pennant fluttering at his masthead. There were Venetian ships in every division. The *Fortune*, the *Sea Horse*, the *Double Dolphin*, the *Christ Raised*, the *Great Christ Raised* and the *Great Christ Risen Again* all followed Barbarigo; others sailed with Doria, while *Our Lady*, the *Pyramis*, the *Palm*, *St. Theodora*, *St. Jerome* and

St. John were among those following the flagship of Don John.

Battle was joined on October 7th and ended in a famous allied victory – which Cieco d'Adria in Venice promptly claimed he had forecast from his study of the Kabbalah. The struggle had ended with defenceless Turks pelting the Christians with oranges and lemons, at which the allies retaliated in kind, provoking 'considerable laughter' on both sides. But the carnage had been horrible. Thousands had died, including Provveditor-General Barbarigo and other Venetian noblemen. Moreover, Lepanto did not regain Cyprus for the Republic. Nor did it stop the Turkish advance westward, though it may well have helped change the route of the advance.

Venice nevertheless experienced a great moment of release. Thanksgiving services were held in St. Mark's; Calio Magno composed a special oratorio entitled 'The Triumph of Christ, for the victory over the Turks'; public orations honouring the dead were delivered at a state banquet; the Germans decorated their Fondaco with tapestries, illuminated it with torches, and let off fireworks there on three successive nights – and another carnival pageant wound its way round the Piazza.

While 189 musicians played music by Gabrieli, 'Hope' and 'Charity' marched again and 'Faith' rode her chariot, trampling a 'Turkish serpent.' Turkish prisoners walked in chains between the floats that followed – the four cardinal virtues, personifications of Rome and Spain, 'a prospect of the straits of Gibraltar and the Pyrenees,' 'Venice' attended by a stucco lion, and a woman dressed in red velvet and palm and laurel wreaths representing 'Victory.'

Another seven tableaux followed, symbolizing the Venetian year – the first signifying New Year's Day, from which sweets were scattered into the crowd, the fat figure of Carnival time; an old, bent, black-clad woman representing Lent; 'Easter' portrayed by cows and dairymaids; jewel-decked women surrounded by children sounding glass trumpets and merchants showing off their wares to symbolize Ascension Day; 'Bacchus' represented the first of August; there were singers and drinkers for 'St. Martin's Day'; and finally a winged, white-bearded

'Father Time' and a wintry demonstration of 'the Triumph of Death.'

Each city precinct also staged its show. The sleazy market district to the north of the Rialto bridge was transformed into a fairyland with tapestries, bunting, candles and canopies. Happy crowds thronged the streets, paintings by the Bellinis, the Bassanos Titian, Raphael and other masters were brandished about, and the general mood was so relaxed that, as contemporaries asserted, even pickpockets took a holiday.

Then in December 1571, in 'gratitude to Jesus Christ our beloved defender and protector' and to emphasize Venice's fervent crusading spirit, Jews were expelled from the Republic's territories. Those on Corfu, however, do not seem to have been affected, and less than two years later Jews were allowed to resume their banking operations in Venice – on condition they pledged 50,000 ducats to provide small loans to the poor at the charitable interest rate of five per cent.

This concession coincided with the peace with Turkey in which Solomon Ashkenezi, a Jew born in Venetian Udine, who had subsequently emigrated to Poland and then Turkey, represented the Sultan. By the agreement Venice ceded Cyprus, and promised to pay a war indemnity of 300,000 ducats and an annual tribute of 1,500 for the isle of Zante. The war had been lost despite Lepanto; indeed the Turks had already replaced the great fleet the allies had destroyed.

Pope Gregory XVIII was furious at the settlement, which had been negotiated secretly without reference to him. Excommunication was even mooted, but some judicious concessions, notably over the question of religious censorship soothed the ruffled feelings of the Pope (that year the Holy Office summoned Paolo Veronese for incorporating secular figures in his painting of the Last Supper, at which he coolly changed its title to 'Supper in the House of Levi').

Venice had sufficient reason, after all, to make peace at almost any price. Turkish raids during the war had inflicted serious damage on the Ionian islands; the thinly populated Venetian colonies along the Dalmatian coast were highly vulnerable to the Turkish-controlled interior; and in Crete the wild, long-haired goat-herds of the mountains and the oppressed peasantry of the plains seemed near rebellion again. There were fears of revolt in Venice too, for the war had occasioned another critical food shortage – compounded, according to a contemporary, by 'the avarice of the ministers in buying and distributing bad food,' which 'occasioned much sickness, many deaths and great disorders.'

A host of crippled war veterans and others demanding care placed an impossible burden on the city's charities – moreover, the plague of 1571 had aggravated the slump, which served to increase misery and discontent within the city even further.

The recovery was slow. Private shipbuilding had declined along with commerce as the spice trade slipped out of Venetian hands again. Large quantities of cotton continued to be shipped, but Venetian markets for this and other oriental goods were soon restricted to Italy and Germany, as the English and Dutch began trading in the Mediterranean on their own account. Wool and silk manufacture had passed their production peaks, the city's sugar refineries suffered from the loss of Cyprus, and employment remained static while the population continued to increase.

The threat of a popular rising slowly receded, however. Indeed, when fire broke out in the Doge's Palace in May 1574 the *arsenalotti* not only rushed to put it out but refused a reward of 500 ducats offered them – a performance they repeated at the end of 1577. It was only a small symptom but it reflected the skill with which Venice was ruled. The government might be run by a knot of rich old men, but they were highly sensitive to the city's mood and knew what was required to keep it stable. A contemporary praised them, not entirely unjustly, as 'the best and wisest of men, and he also analysed that special brand of patriotism which motivated the Venetian ruling class and held the Republic together. It was a community, he explained, dedicated to the preservation of all they cherished most – their goods, their children, family and friends, and that 'most exalted good' of all, 'virtue.'

Virtue and excellence were the standard to be aimed at, and in 1574 when Henry III of France arrived the sumptuary laws were suspended for ten days so that the nobility could turn themselves out with a magnificence many of them could ill afford to impress their visitors with just those qualities. The King was lodged in the Foscari Palace, which was appropriately furnished with hangings emblazoned with gold lilies. He was shown round the Arsenal, where a galley was assembled, launched and armed within an hour in order to impress him; taken through a triumphal arch designed by Palladio and decorated by Veronese and Tintoretto; honoured with a banquet for 3,000 people at which 1,200 dishes were served; serenaded on the Grand Canal by Latin songs sung in his praise; and shown a water pageant in which 'sea monsters' belched out smoke. It was a display of Venetian accomplishments in which common people also played their parts – yet an experience of quite another kind served ultimately to solidify a patriotism among all classes such as mere pageantry and even the Turkish war had failed to do.

In 1575 typhus flared up in the *terraferma* once again. Quarantine regulations were immediately imposed – at which traffic between Venetian towns ground to a halt and industry seized up for lack of raw materials. Verona lost more people from hunger consequent upon unemployment than it did from the disease. 'These wretches,' ran a petition, 'cannot hope for any relief for they are imprisoned in a city which is forbidden to trade with its neighbours.' But worse was yet to follow. In March the plague struck Venice.

An inscription in the Scuola di San Rocco recalls its terrible impact: 'In 1576, when Alvise Mocenigo was Doge, a contagious pestilence flared up. None ever lasted longer; none was ever more destructive. It was a just punishment for our sins.' The city was strewn with corpses, there were sobs and wailing in every street, and a stampede developed as terrified people rushed out to the countryside. Shops, factories and schools shut their doors; attendance at the Great Council meetings dropped from 1,500 to 250.

'Someone who had spoken in College in the morning,' wrote the contemporary Morosini, 'had gone by the evening.' At least 300 nobles died of the disease. But the plague hit even harder at the poor, who could not escape so easily and whose squalid tenements found particular favour with the black rats and their fatal fleas.

The plague raged with full force all that summer. By the time it eventually died down, as many as 50,000 Venetians had perished, Padua had lost a third of its population and the inhabitants of the *terraferma* as a whole had been reduced by between a quarter and a third. Yet, terrible as it was, the great scourge had some salutary effects. The city's population had been expanding much faster than its economy, and the plague had acted as a purgative in getting rid of excess mouths to feed. Though the quarantine measures had disrupted the economy, steps were taken to get industry quickly on its feet again. Foreign craftsmen were allowed into Venice, amnesties were granted to banished sailors, glass-makers, shipbuilders and textile-workers, and the wages of master craftsmen saw a considerable leap forward.

Moreover, it is to the great plague of the 1570s that Venice owes one of her greater glories – the Capuchin church designed by Palladio and called the Redentore. The government had vowed to build it as a peace-offering to God when the plague was at its height. Indeed, many believed that the pestilence had subsided on the very day that solemn pledge was taken, and so effective were Venetian prayers believed to be that in 1579 the plague-afflicted Genoese begged the Doge to hold a special service and processional to rid them of the affliction.

The Redentore rose up only very gradually – exceeding the original estimates by almost 700 per cent – but every July thereafter the Doge and Senators kept their vow to attend a commemorative mass there, crossing to the Giudecca by pontoon bridge in solemn cortège and in full panoply. And the new *festa* continued to unite Venetians of all classes in a fervour of thanksgiving until the terror of the plague at last receded into distant memory.

Venice, the city of three hundred churches, was approaching its millennium. She still possessed an empire, a reputation for stability, and a talent for spectacle unmatched in all the world.

And yet her powers were fading fast. The geographic position which had made her the richest city in Europe now disadvantaged her as trade routes changed, and other powers were soon plucking away her laurels as mistress of the seas. The luck which had so long attended her was deserting her by stages, and as it did so she began to sink into decline.

Chapter XIII

Piracy and the Economic Crisis

For a moment in the 1580s it seemed that everything was going well. The Republic, wrote Nicolò Contarini, was on good terms with all countries; trade was flowing into the city in greater spate than ever before, and Venice abounded 'in all things which the fertility of land, the industry of man and a suitable location customarily bestow on a well-regulated commonwealth.' But foreign ships were carrying an increasing proportion of her commerce, and Venice's good foreign relations reflected a need to adopt a more passive role than she had done in the great days. The powers of Spain and Turkey over-shadowed her; the Dutch and English, whose skilful and aggressive seamanship had made them powerful from the Baltic to the Atlantic were soon prowling the Mediterranean hungry for commercial pickings. This, after all, was the hey-day of the piratical Sir Francis Drake and buccaneers sailing under many flags were about to deliver a death blow to Venice's sea power.

Venetian merchantmen still called at Spanish ports and sailed to the Levant, but they tended to hug the coastline more and more, constantly afraid that some predator would pounce on them. The pirates themselves were of various allegiances. There were Muslim corsairs from the coast of Barbary, and the knights of St. Stephen and St. John who plundered in the name of Christ; there were the Uskoks of the Fiume coast who hunted on their own account; Spanish galleons based at Naples, and, finally, the English and the Dutch.

Venetians also turned to freebooting from time to time, and in 1584 Gabriele Emo was beheaded for plundering a Turkish galley – but Venetians were much more sinned against than sinning. When Spain fought England, or the Christian powers engaged the Turks, both sides ignored Venetian neutrality – though sometimes their scruples did lead them to torture the mariners they captured into signing false confessions to the effect that their ships had been carrying Jewish or Turkish goods – and the Republic was none too successful in dealing with such pirates.

A Venetian flotilla under Filippo Pasqualigo did succeed in chasing the Knights of St. Stephen and of St. John out of Cretan waters in the early 1580s, but Venice's losses continued to mount steadily, partly because of a misplaced trust in the Christian powers; partly because of poor intelligence. In 1584 *provveditore* Nicolò Surian had urged the Senate to pay less attention to the Turks and be more vigilant against westerners in eastern waters. Florentine, Maltese and Sicilian privateers calling at Venetian ports, he warned, 'obtain as much reliable intelligence as they want about the ships of Your Serenity,' he reported, yet when Venetian warships arrived they could get no information or, even worse, false information concerning the whereabouts of pirates. A few more galleys were sent out in an attempt to cope, but the Venetian fleet was no longer large enough to provide adequate protection.

No new galleys had been built for years and the number in service had steadily declined. In 1581 there had been 146 galleys available, by 1586 there were only ninety-five. With work at the Arsenal confined to maintenance and repairs, many craftsmen had turned elsewhere for work, some of them emigrating to other ports, and employment falling off, wage rates were low – and that meant trouble.

In November 1581 a crowd of caulkers had stormed government offices demanding better pay. When it was refused, they had ransacked a public granary. Moreover, even when a modest construction programme did get under way, employment at the Arsenal did not rise. In 1592 only 431 carpenters, 786 caulkers and 161 oarmakers were employed there – barely half the number of the early 1570s in the aftermath of the hollow victory of Lepanto. The state still offered subsidies and even finance for shipbuilding in private yards, but the industry as a whole was never to make a complete recovery from the recession, and ship-builders found their living standard depressed still further because of another amazing increase in the cost of food.

In the late seventies and early eighties the price of wheat rose by about twenty per cent; between 1585 and 1590 by another twenty-five per cent, and between 1590 and 1595 by no less than seventy-five per cent, thanks to a famine affecting the entire Mediterranean. Until the late 1580s the earnings of other workers seems to have kept pace with inflation, but then real wages fell quite alarmingly – because of a population explosion from under 135,000 in 1581 to almost 156,000 by 1593. With immigrants pouring into the city seeking work, unskilled labourers such as porters, who were obliged to work at the Arsenal eighteen weeks a year for a miserable pittance or else pay to be exempted, could hardly have been able to make ends meet. But Venice's sailors were even worse off.

As *provveditor* Surian commented in 1583, no one volunteered for the fleet unless he was a criminal, a simpleton, a debtor, or a drunk. A man 'might die of hunger' on his rations; the crews were harshly treated and the captains often pocketed the men's pay and prize money, so that convicted bankrupts sent to the galleys to repay their debts sometimes lost all hope of ever being released. Others were commonly kept long beyond their proper term – yet if a man broke ship the other oarsmen on his bench would have a hand cut off.

In winter, when the pirates were most active, the single blanket shared between three men could not keep the cold and rain out, so that many lost a limb from frost-bite and an enor-mous number of the convict oarsmen died. 'It costs Your Serenity good money to feed, clothe and treat . . . these poor wretches,' reported Nicolò Donà in 1599, yet they 'are ill-clad . . . scantily fed . . . and never looked after when they fall sick.'

Such was the condition of the men who crewed Venice's navy – the five galleys guarding the Istrian coast against the

Uskoks, the Governor of the Condemned's four ships which patrolled the northern Adriatic, the seven under the Captain of the Gulf in the southern Adriatic, the twelve galleys commanded by the *provveditor* dell'Armata defending the approaches to the Ionian islands, and the four triremes guarding Crete. Yet the captains had their own complaints about inadequate pay – which helps to explain both their ill-treatment of the crews and the increasing scarcity of noblemen prepared to serve.

Pasqualigo himself protested vehemently that 'salaries which were adequate three hundred years ago cannot possibly support the present cost of living' – and other office-holders felt the same. In 1594 Tommaso Contarini, ambassador to Ratisbon, complained that his pay 'barely suffices for food, stabling, bread and wine' and that he had to subsidize his mission out of his own pocket, there having been hardly any increase in expense allowances since 1561. It was a wonder, indeed, that Venetian commanders and administrators were as effective as they were. But there were noblemen in Venice in financial difficulties too: the once wealthy Zeno family of San Pantaleone, beggared by the cost of providing three ships for the Turkish war and by the flooding of estates in which they had invested very heavily, were trying desperately to maintain a household of twenty-four people on the rents of a few dilapidated houses.

As Procurator Contarini had remarked ten years before, the nobility, rich and poor alike, were over-burdened. The successive blows of war, plague and famine had left daughters without dowries, widows without subsistence and children without nutriment, and though some families still had incomes in excess of 20,000 ducats, and a fair number made between 4,000 and 8,000 a year, an increasing number relied on charity.

Between 1587 and 1589 twenty-five noblemen and women, including the bearers of such proud names as Zorzi, Canale, Dolfin and Balbi had plumbed the sorry depths of penury sufficiently to get doles from one charitable trust alone; and between 1590 and 1620 as many as fifty nobles petitioned the Senate for tax relief or other financial favours. Fewer and fewer of them married, and then ever later in life so as to sire fewer children, so that the nobility continued to decline more sharply.

Outside the noble class some men were still able to afford the rich living so many noblemen still indulged in far beyond their means – but they were vastly outnumbered by the poor, and while the Scuole Grandi were still rich enough to provide for their own needy members and some outsiders too they could make little impression on the growing ocean of need. The Scuole still spent large sums on processions, though this was excusable in that the government demanded that they contribute to state pageantry and the ceremonial display of a Scuola's relics was in itself a means of raising money. Moreover, the San Rocco foundation increased its charity from an average of 2,500 ducats of account a year in the 1570s to almost 4,850 in the 1590s. But because of inflation even increases of this order could not keep pace with need. Nor could the cheap loan services provided by the Jews, nor all the provisions made by the city's four main hospitals which between them supported about 3,000 children and provided dowries for 300 girls a year.

Stinking, starving immigrants continued to flood the city from famine-stricken areas begging for soldi, even interrupting worshippers in church. In 1595 the government at last ordered the conversion of the old leper colony of St. Lazzaro into a refuge for the 'unfortunates,' so that they would 'not have to die in the streets . . . without the sacraments of the holy church, as has often occurred' – though the Great Council motion prompting this action also called for the city to be 'purged' of the 'many enormous scandals and sins' perpetrated by the 'turbulent crowds of beggars.' In 1600 the Governors of the Mendecanti petitioned for a site on which to build a hospice to help 'keep the city and the churches . . . free of poor beggars, who have made the streets tiresome, molesting everyone,' and to save at least some 'wretched spirits . . . from . . . the devil who has ensnared them with every kind of excess and brutal vice.' For the rest the government could only reinforce the poor laws and expel 'foreign' beggars from the city.

Such was the dangerously unstable situation with which a group of nobles called the *giovani*, or young men, aimed to cope. Intellectuals who aimed at a popular revival of Venetian letters, the *giovani* were also ardent reformers. They wanted to change Venetian politics, revive Venice's economy and reintroduce 'frugality, modesty, goodness and other honest customs' into Venetian life. Since their movement's leader, Leonardo Donà, had been ambassador to Spain and to the Emperor, and others of them, including Nicolò Contarini and Paolo Paruta, had also had wide experience in governmental posts, they were not without influence. Nor did they lack support.

Their first and most dangerous achievement came in 1582 when they successfully challenged the Council of Ten – a *coup* they brought off through the power base of the usually subservient Quarantia al Criminal. The Ten were stripped of many of the powers they had accumulated. Fiscal policy was handed over to the Senate, the Ten's junta of Senators was abolished, and the whole tight plutocratic system, by which a handful of powerful nobles had manipulated everything, was opened up by ensuring that many more poor nobles gained admission to the Senate.

In foreign policy Donà, who had lost a brother at Lepanto, was anti-Turk, but other *giovani* were much more afraid of the looming threat of Spain. Their economic ideas, however, were of more immediate importance. These involved enlarging the mercantile marine by buying ships from abroad, encouraging Venetian industry, albeit at the expense of industry in the *terraferma,* reforming the money system, and reducing the national debt.

Repayments of the vast 5.7 million ducat debt incurred during the Turkish war had already begun, and it was finally paid off in 1584, saving the exchequer 500,000 a year in interest payments. By 1600 the state had also begun to liquidate its old consolidated loan fund, but the currency problems proved intractable. Imperial thalers and Spanish reals and pieces of eight had become the dominant European currencies, and the American silver minted in Spain in such vast quantities continued to create problems for the ducat and to force prices even further upwards. On the other hand, the government did eventually solve that perennial problem, the unreliability of the Venetian banking system.

Of the 103 banks ever founded in Venice all but seven had failed, and in 1584 the bankers Pisani and Tiepolo went bankrupt too, causing great confusion in the business world, which was now deprived of an efficient credit system. An attempt to establish a state bank in 1584-5 was abandoned in the face of vociferous opposition, but at last, in 1587, one was established – the Banco della Piazza di Rialto.

Since the new bank could not lend or speculate (although overdrafts were in fact granted despite this ban), it immediately inspired confidence; and since it was allowed to transfer payments on its ledgers the wheels of Venetian commerce began to move more easily. Six years later, when bills of exchange were ordered to be settled by the bank, Venetian bank money became a foreign exchange currency too; and although a private bank was allowed to open up a few years later, to supplement these commercial services, it was made subject to stringent regulations.

The government also reacted energetically to the Uskok pirates. It tracked down Uskok spies in Venetian ports, equipped four strong 'bastard galleys,' and ordered all freight brought through the Adriatic from Turkish ports to be shipped on them, charging double the usual freight rate for this safe service. As a result of these and other measures the port of Venice reached a high level of activity again in the last years of the century. Some of the spice trade was regained; the city's closely supervised textile industry maintained output; export demand was high. Moreover, by 1600 the *terraferma* was producing enough food to feed the cities again, and sometimes a surplus for export too. Despite the continuing inflation Venice seemed to be hauling herself towards prosperity once more.

The recovery might be short-lived, but the Republic had cause to thank God for it. Most Venetians were probably no less pious than they used to be, even in this age when faith was being shaken by immense doctrinal rifts – though there were men who dared blaspheme outside the house of the papal nuncio – but their piety was less intense. Flagellant processions were still held, but the participants were specially hired for the occasion, and the cult of St. Rocco no longer drew the crowds. Moreover, though one foreign observer considered that 'there was no other place where churches are more frequented, sermons more attended, divines more respected [nor] divine worship celebrated with more magnificence,' the crowded convents were a reflection of the large numbers of dowerless spinsters; the oaths of chastity so many noblemen took reflected the need to preserve inheritances; and the popularity among noblemen of the church as a career owed as much to prospects of obtaining rich bishoprics as to the purity of their vocations.

The piety of the *giovani* was genuine enough, but their theology was highly patriotic. Their attitude towards Rome was largely dictated by Venetian interests, and in particular by the interests of the Venetian nobility. They wanted good relations with the papacy – for when relations with the papacy were good, bishoprics and abbeys tended to be distributed in accordance with Venice's wishes – but not at any price. They viewed the Jesuits with great suspicion, especially when they established a school in Padua to compete with the local University; they refused to surrender the Greek Bishop of Cythera to Rome, though they did confiscate copies of the offending book which he had written; they gave the ostracized Galileo a safe refuge at Padua; and protested strongly against a papal decree of 1592 demanding that all Italian bishops go to Rome to be examined and confirmed.

Relations were soon strained further still. The Pope declared Ancona a free port in an attempt to divert commerce from Venice, occupied Ferrara and tried to grasp a share of the traffic along the River Po. On the other hand, Venice offered asylum to outlawed papal subjects, persisted in maintaining her old methods of appointing parish priests, and reduced the anti-Lutheran campaign it had maintained for more than forty years. When Clement VIII's Index was issued in 1593 the Venetian government took great offence, for in extending censorship to books on secular subjects it threatened to take censorship out of state control. Paolo Paruta, a leading *giovane* and Venice's envoy to Rome, told the Pope: 'You can't change the world and make everyone perfect,' and added that time not spent on 'bad' books could be spent on actions that were worse.

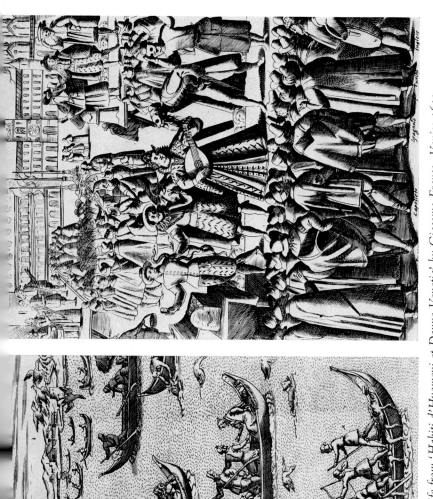

Scenes from Venetian life from 'Habiti d'Huomeni et Donne Venetia' by Giacomo Franco, Venice 1609

But though the papacy conceded the Republic's right to share censorship with the ecclesiastical authorities, in 1596 the Index was published in Venice. As a result, the number of presses in the city fell from 125 to forty, and by 1601 the government had become so alarmed at the decline that it forbade printers to leave the city. It did not relax its grip on the press, however. Indeed, in 1604 it was to empower the printers' guild, which it used as an immediate agency of control, to put any printer who refused to join it out of business.

At the time relations with the papacy turned for the worse, in the 1590s, the city was attaining a new state of visual perfection – the Fondamenta Nuova had recently been built along the northern bank of the city, the Piazza had been repaved, the stone bridge at the Rialto had been completed. And this was the moment that a young Englishman, Fynes Moryson, and his brother arrived in Venice *en route* for the Holy Land.

From the book Fynes wrote we know that the Morysons arrived from Padua by the daily barge that ran along the River Brenta. Their fellow passengers included the usual motley crowd – monks, students, courtesans, gentlemen – and it was from travellers such as these that Fynes picked up so many of his stories. The perennial anecdote he retold – about the Venetian who, mounting a horse and failing to make it start, extracted a handkerchief from his pocket and remarked, 'No wonder it won't move, it's facing into the wind,' was apocryphal – but Moryson's account presents a true if often salacious picture of Venice at the end of the sixteenth century.

'Chanels of water passe through this city,' he wrote, 'as the bloud passeth through the veines of a mans body,' though the tides rose up to seven feet when the Sirocco blew. The Morysons saw all the sights – the crowded Rialto, St. Mark's, the Arsenal, the ghetto, the ferry points where gondolas plied for hire day and night, the many gardens abounding with 'rare herbs, plants and fruits,' the public libraries and the markets where it was the men who generally did the household shopping. Mutton and veal were sold there 'in little portions and by weight,' Fynes noted with surprise. And there were also 'plenty of fish, hennes, egges,'

I

on display; 'great abundance of red . . . and pickled herrings, sardelle, anchove and like pickled fishes'; as well as Parma cheeses, mushrooms, snails and 'the hinder part of frogs.' Such dainties, however, were only for the rich. The 'common sorte' eat 'little or no flesh, or fish . . . but only hearbes, pulse, snailes and shell-fishes,' while ordinary labourers subsisted on 'pure white bread,' vegetables, oil and wine.

Moryson found the noblemen insupportably proud, but the plump ladies in their high chopines and low-cut gowns fascinated him. 'They shew their naked necks and breasts, and likewise their dugges,' which they padded with linen and whitened with cosmetics. 'Their haire is commonly yellow, made so by the sunne,' and was worn piled up upon their heads and decorated with silk flowers and artificial pearls.

During Carnival time women commonly went about in masks like the men and 'wearing Men's breeches,' having them 'all open before, and part behind.' As for the courtesans, to whom Fynes devoted a great proportion of his attention, they kept the front of their dresses open all the time – to 'auoide wrinckling,' as he explained.

In due course Moryson and his brother left these fleshpots for the Holy Land. Like true prudent Englishmen they set out well prepared, taking their own supplies of dried fruit, 'cooling syrups,' and 'laxative medicines.' They visited Constantinople, Jaffa, Lydda and Jerusalem, but Moryson's brother died in the Levant, and Fynes returned alone to Venice.

Moryson's comments on Mediterranean shipping throw light on one reason for Venice's sorry decline as a maritime power. English ships, he wrote, voyaged to Syria in half the time of a Venetian – partly because their ships handled more easily, but also because their captains were encouraged to be more daring, for Venetians, like other Italian sailors, were paid by the day, which led them to put into harbour at the least sign of bad weather, while the English were paid by the voyage, and so 'beate out stormes at sea.'

By Moryson's time the Uskoks were becoming more active again. In 1592 they had pounced on the *Vidala*, which had put in at a cove to shelter from a storm and ran off with 130,000 ducats' worth of merchandise, and they became increasingly destructive, the more so since they enjoyed widespread sympathy from so many inhabitants of the Dalmatian coast. Like their contemporaries the Zaporozhian Cossacks, the Uskoks found it convenient to present themselves as Crusaders. They would go to church on their bare knees to give thanks to God for a profitable expedition, and give a tithe of their plunder to the clergy too – on which account, perhaps, the Franciscans and Dominicans based at Senj and their local parish priests not only encouraged them but were said to participate in the raids.

In 1598 a Venetian force attacked one Uskok position killing a hundred of them, and in 1600 the Hapsburgs intervened to keep them quiet, though only for a time. In 1607 Uskoks sacked a Venetian ship carrying Turkish goods for Scutari, took a frigate carrying despatches from the Signoria to its ambassador at Constantinople and various other vessels, gathering in booty valued at 150,000 crowns. Once they even took a Venetian galley. And the Uskoks were not the only threat to Venice's commerce.

From 1596 a buccaneering Spanish Viceroy had begun to detain more and more Venetian ships calling in at Naples, and to seize Venetian ships as far distant as Corfu, on the pretext that the goods they carried belonged to Jews. The Barbary pirates, the Turks and the Maltese also took their toll, and so, increasingly did Dutch and English freebooters.

Venetian galleys did capture a few privateers in the very early 1600s, but with their comparatively poor manœuvrability, poor seaworthiness and openness to the elements in winter, they were not really adequate to cope with the tall-ships from the north. In 1603 alone Venice lost twelve large merchantmen to them, and thereafter their losses mounted alarmingly.

Venetians were particularly indignant about the English, since the two states were on good terms diplomatically. Yet having virtually shut the English market to them with high duties and become 'most expert and powerful on the seas,' as Contarini put it, they had now entered Venetian waters 'in the guise of brigands, although they brought merchandise too,' and were treating 'every ship they met as an enemy without distinguishing whether it belonged to friend or foe.' The star freebooter, however, John Ward, had in fact been banished from England. He operated from Tunis, and his first real success came in April 1607 when he took that magnificent armed merchantman the *Reniera e Soderina* as it sailed in majesty between Syria and Cyprus. Ward added sixty bronze guns to its armament and, using it as his flag-ship, proceeded to gather in 400,000 crowns' worth of booty from Venetian ships in that year alone.

The Venetian merchant marine which had already shrunk considerably in the last decades of the sixteenth century – partly because of changing trade routes and piracy, but mainly because of competition from foreign ships – was now pulverized by the pirates. By 1606 there were only thirteen home-built ships of any considerable size, and even when fourteen foreign-built ships were added, their combined tonnage was twenty-five per cent less than the merchant marine of 1559. Moreover, there was a lack of good seamen trained to fight. Young Venetian nobles still drew stipends as bowmen of the quarterdeck but they never actually went to sea, and the crews that did were 'poor, worthless and unscrupulous creatures,' according to Nicolò Lion writing in 1605. Not only were they reluctant to fight but they often helped the enemy and joined in the plunder. The galley commanders based at Corfu reported much the same: 'Cabin-boys and ships-apprentices parading in old leather jerkins hired from a second-hand shop' had been enrolled as fighting men. 'They had never seen, still less, handled, firearms before and . . . are the first to lay down their arms when they encounter enemy ships, and plunder the cargo of their own vessels.'

As shipping losses mounted so did insurance premiums. By 1607 armed ships bound from Alexandria had to pay premiums of up to fourteen per cent, charges of sixty per cent were not unknown, and no one was willing to insure an unarmed ship at all.

The consequence for the shipyards was serious. 'Whereas in former times ships and boats were constantly being built,' ran an account written in August 1607, 'the yards are now abandoned and the few vessels which were still in use are being dismantled by thrifty persons' who perferred to use their timber and iron rather than expose them and their other capital 'to manifest danger' at sea. A report written in 1609 attributed the decline of the Venetian marine to the hiring of faster English and Dutch tall-ships, complete with foreign officers and crews who were 'more skilled than the Venetians' to ship Venetian goods, as a result of which 'there are no ships built in this city and . . . the seaman's craft is dying out.'

It was hardly surprising in view of shipping losses. In 1606 Francesco Morosini claimed to have lost 'four good ships and a galleon, some of them wrecked the others captured by pirates.' 'Thanks to the heavy losses . . . suffered at the hands of English . . . and other pirate ships, and to the obvious and imminent danger of similar or even greater misfortunes,' merchant leaders had complained the year before, 'trade with the Levant, on which this market chiefly subsists is now reduced to such a wretched state that unless the government . . . takes effective steps it will collapse completely. . . . There are ships in this city now ready to sail for the Levant but unable to leave, because the merchants . . . will not expose their capital and wealth to the certainty of loss.'

Venetian trade was declining along with its shipping. After 1595, when the Dutch reopened the Cape route, Venice's remaining share of the spice trade gradually declined. Between 1597 and 1599 her turnover at Aleppo shrank by a quarter, and Venetian merchants based there reckoned they would soon be forced out of business altogether, 'because of the many Dutch vessels that have gone to India.'

Their pessimism proved justified. Thanks partly to instability within the Turkish Empire, by 1611 Venetians were importing only a third of what they used to from Aleppo; by 1612 there were only three Venetian merchants at Constantinople where once there had been twenty; and Venetian cotton imports from Cyprus had declined to a quarter of what they had been in 1599. The old proverb, 'The white and the black' – pepper and cotton – 'make Venice rich' no longer held true.

The depression reached its depth between 1602 and 1612.

Customs receipts plummeted; production fell off; some of the largest Venetian enterprises went bankrupt. The free ports of Leghorn and Marseilles were attracting foreign shippers away from Venice, damaging Venice's hold on the wool trade, and by 1609, when Galileo climbed the Campanile of St. Mark's to demonstrate the wonders of the telescope to members of the Signoria, they might well have wondered, as they surveyed the city and the lagoon through this extraordinary new instrument, how much busier a sight the dockyards, wharves and anchorages had presented not so very long before.

Not that the government had been inactive in trying to reverse the trend. The adoption in 1608 of galleasses – 'moving fortresses,' as Nicolò Contarini called them – each carrying a hundred or more trained soldiers and armed with thirty guns, together with the reintroduction of compulsory convoys, was leading to more privateers being sunk or taken, and there is evidence to suggest that by 1611 shipping business was picking up and insurance premiums falling. But the new galleasses were horribly expensive, inefficiently maintained, and the recovery itself did not amount to much.

In 1610 the Commissioners of Trade reported miserably that 'our Western trade is quite dead, our eastern trade reduced to a few ships, and even the dribble of merchandise that does reach us does not find a ready purchaser, because foreign merchants have removed their houses elsewhere.' Fewer and fewer convoys sailed to Egypt, Syria or Constantinople, and by 1611 most of them ventured no farther east than Crete. Venetian merchants still crossed the Alps to trade in Germany, and operated in Cracow and at Prague, but the markets of France, England and the Low Countries had been lost; Dutch and English merchants were making ever greater inroads into the markets of central Europe; the great Thirty Years' War which broke out in Germany in 1618 was to lose Venice her last remaining major customers in Europe; and the final humiliation came in 1625 when the government was forced to classify spices the Dutch had begun to bring into Venice as western goods.

Agriculture, the growing sector of her economy, helped most

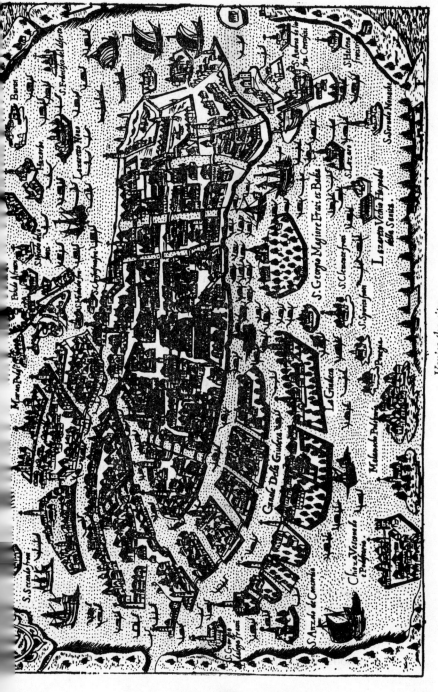

Venice the city

to pull her through the crisis. More and more marginal land was being brought into cultivation, and Venetian land-ownership was growing too – which cheapened the price of food and enriched some few members of the noble class. The elaborate surveys of the provinces of Bergamo and of Brescia carried out in 1596 and 1610 reflected the increased importance the government attached to the mainland. Rice had been introduced as a profitable crop in the Veronese and Polesine, and at Zante raisins were also to prove a major export crop. Venice was still an important market for Apulian and Cretan olive oil, Dalmatian produce and sulphur from the Marche, but though port activity was maintained, as customs receipts show, most ships docking there were foreigners, and industry was again suffering from slump.

Though as many as 20,000 cloths were being produced, the export of textiles suffered from the shrinkage in the Levantine trade and an upsurge of competition from the Milanese. Moreover, the sugar-refining and luxury industries, such as glass, ceramics, silk, brocade and jewellery manufacture, for which Venice was still famous, could not take up the slack.

The depression kept wages low and led to a perceptible reduction in the incomes of all classes. In June 1601 an oarmaker, Antonio de Zuane, led a strike at the Arsenal over wages, threw all his money into the *provveditore's* face and cursed him and all blacklegs who continued to work there. The strike was crushed, and de Zuane executed. In 1602 there was more serious rioting when bakers refused to accept the debased coins the people offered them for bread, and several months later workers in the woollen industry appealed to the government for higher wages, a demand their employers considered 'most unjust' in view of the falling price of bread.

The Scuole Grande, who were forced to contribute almost twenty per cent of the cost of the reserve fleet and buy oarsmen for the navy, were hard put to it to maintain their charitable services, while more and more nobles, and even agents of the Signoria itself, began to visit the Jewish second-hand dealers to hire hangings, tapestries and other finery for ceremonial occasions, being unable to afford to buy such things outright.

Nevertheless, 'triumphs,' shows and spectacles continued to be staged with undiminished brilliance, and according to Fynes Moryson even a funeral was 'not counted honourable . . . that costs not some 400 Ducates.' Every Scuola maintained its choir; Giovanni Gabrieli now had charge of the splendid musical resources of St. Mark's; torchlight processions were held, consuming vast quantities of the whitest wax; and Dogaressas were still inducted with unparalleled magnificence. In 1597, when Doge Giovanni's fat and smiling wife had made her formal entry to the palace, she was surrounded by a host of retainers, a pair of dwarfs, and hundreds of gentlewomen dressed in silver and white silk, while the *Bucintoro* was followed by a whole fleet of expensively decorated vessels incorporating fantastic and ingenious machines. The cotton-spinners' boat resembled a chariot with great rolling wheels drawn by a pair of 'sea-horses' with moving legs, while the forty organizers of the fête travelled in an elegant water-borne temple which Scamozzi had designed.

The great square and the Piazzetta were veritable anthills of spectators, 'every corner . . . crowded . . . every column, beam and cornice . . . occupied.' People had knocked nails into the walls to support themselves on some high perch, 'while others clung to the battlements and . . . chimney-tops.' They were all rewarded with a splendid spectacle.

A long procession led by artillery men wound its way round the white-carpeted Piazza: 900 companions of the Arti walked two by two twirling silken banners, tossing them into the air and catching them as they returned to earth. Then came ten captains dressed in scarlet, drummers and trumpeters wearing crimson silk and gold, the Doge's pipers, the master shipbuilders, forty-two ladies carrying white fans, some city magistrates, the Lord High Chancellor, the Doge's daughters, more ladies dressed in black, more magistrates dressed in violet silk, girls in green damask and yellow satin, and finally the Dogaressa attended by two senators.

After the service in St. Mark's she inspected the guildsmen in their splendid booths – barbers, silversmiths, tailors and hosiers; the mercers, with their image of the Virgin, the armourers,

silk-weavers and engravers, the furriers with their fine display
of sable, leopard and tiger-skins, the carpenters, blacksmiths,
masons and the rest.

The ball that night lasted until two the following morning,
there were the usual games and regattas; poets sang the Dogaressa's praises, the public flattered her in prose, and on the third
day she was presented with a Golden Rose blessed by the
Pope.

The celebrations had been far more expensive than those for any
previous Dogaressa; but the expense was no longer easily afforded.
What went for the city applied even more to individual Venetians.
'The Gentlemen of Venice,' as Fynes Moryson remarked, were
'trayned upp in pleasure,' and their taste for luxury died hard.
Certainly many of them were spending far beyond their means.

By 1597 Dardi Bembo and his brother were in debt to the
tune of 31,000, and he continued to support his large family,
it seems, only thanks to the generosity of his brother-in-law,
a bishop. In 1608 Domenico Loredano claimed to have an income
of only 408 ducats – less than enough to maintain six nuns – on
which to keep his mother, wife, son and six daughters; yet he
clung on to a residence in town, a villa in the country and kept ten
servants. And these were by no means isolated cases.

The salaried government jobs which circulated among the
poorer nobles, the minor sinecures, pensions and annual dole
of flour some of them received could not support luxurious
living on this scale, and though the sons of poor nobles might
receive a free education and daughters a dowry from some
charity, the better-placed tended to support themselves by
exploiting family connections for patronage, by marrying for
money, probably outside their class and to an increasing extent
by entering the church. Five sons of Dionisio Contarini, who
went bankrupt in 1601, went into state service of one sort or
another, but two entered the church, hoping for preferment – and
preferment came quickly if one was in favour with the government.

The Republic still nominated the incumbents of every major
see and abbey in the empire. It used its huge patronage to help

its favourites and those families who had become impoverished by the service to the state. But it also took care to ensure that positions of clerical authority were held by Venetian patriots – a policy which paid handsome dividends when in 1606 a most dangerous clash broke out between the Republic and Rome.

Chapter XIV

The Age of Adjustment

Relations with the papacy had long been strained – not because the Republic favoured the Reformation (although, much to Rome's annoyance, it did maintain mutual diplomatic ties with the heretical English), but because it felt its secular authority to be threatened by the Counter-Reformation. This fear was embedded in the Venetian tradition, and the issues now involved had led to strife before. In 1603–5 the government revived old legislation licensing church building and restricting the church's acquisition of landed property. But Camillo Borghese, who mounted the papal throne in 1605, objected strongly to being Pope, as he put it, 'everywhere except in Venice,' and when the Republic brought two clergymen to trial before its own courts the thunder clouds soon broke.

The Pope insisted that the two clerics be handed over to the ecclesiastical authorities for judgement, that the Republic accept the authority of the Inquisition over laymen, and repeal the two offending acts. The Signoria refused to do anything of the sort, and in December 1605 the Pope threatened to place the Republic under interdict.

The government was now confronted with a grave dilemma. Capitulation would involve abdicating its powers over the church; resistance could bring excommunication, involving the risk of civil discord, serious financial loss, and even war. But in February 1606, when the Papal Nuncio again demanded the surrender of the arrested clergy, the new Doge, that prominent *giovane*

Leonardo Donà, refused, and in the spring of 1606 the interdict came into force.

Informed by the experience of the two previous excommunications, the government was well prepared to meet the situation. Clerics had been instructed not to accept any papal bulls, to stay in their posts, continue with their duties, and to inform on their superiors if they ordered otherwise. Reliable nobles were detailed to keep an eye on monasteries, and theological experts were engaged to fortify the government's case.

The principal consultant engaged for this purpose, the fifty-two-year-old Fra Paolo Sarpi, had been a member of the club frequented by many *giovani*, and was a personal friend of the new Doge. A polymath, whose interests ranged from optics and physiology to political science, Sarpi was absolutely committed to the Republic's line, and no mean propagandist. Gibbon was to call him one of the four supreme 'historians of modern languages,' and historians of the liberal-intellectual tradition have since canonized him as their hero. But though Sarpi had friendly dealings with Protestants and Jews his opinions of Cretans and Jesuits were far from liberal. (Cretans, he believed, should be treated like 'wild animals' – while Jesuits were 'sworn enemies to goodness and truth.') And though his theological arguments were sometimes effective, they served to justify rather than inspire the actions of his employers.

The government's campaign was more effective in its security than in its theological aspect; the few reluctant bishops who tried to resign were persuaded to toe the line, and persistent opponents were arrested or boarded up in their convents. But apart from the clergy of Bergamo who were governed by the Archbishop of Milan there was comparatively little opposition – a Carmelite prior of Verona, some monks and nuns on Murano, a few canons of Padua, some Theatines and Capuchins, and, of course, the Jesuits, who were expelled. The Benedictines, on the other hand, refused to open any letter at all in order to be able to plead ignorance of the Pope's commands, and most other clergy took their line from Francesco Vendramin, the new Patriarch, who gave firm support to his fellow-nobles in the government and pretended never to have heard of any interdict.

Pageantry rather than theological tracts served to explain the situation to the people. On Corpus Christi Day 1606 the government staged what the English Ambassador, Sir Henry Wotton, described as 'the most sumptuous procession that ever had been seen here.' The Scuole Grande provided floats illustrating the righteousness of the Venetian cause: Christ and two Pharisees, for example, with the motto 'Render to Caesar that is which is Caesar's' – and the Friars staged a tableau showing Saints Francis and Dominic helping the Doge to support a collapsing church. All of which served to bolster the people's confidence and show the Pope that Venice enjoyed the service of sufficient clergy despite his ban.

But while Venetian patriots argued the Signoria's case abroad, a considerable amount of anti-Venetian literature was published there, and although Venice received offers of support from Protestants in France, England and Holland, the bankers of Genoa offered a large war loan to the Pope. Moreover, even though some powerful Venetians verged on Jansenism in their views, most of them did not want to be driven into the camp of 'the reformed religion,' and in June 1606 Senator Angelo Badoer actually proposed that the government climb down. The majority was against him and the resistance was continued. Troops were raised in the *terraferma* and Albania, and recruiting agents rode as far afield as Germany, Switzerland and Lorraine. The Republic's fleet was prepared and its forts were strengthened. The government even began buying up specie on credit so as to deny the enemy cash with which to pay its troops. But when the mounting costs of it all threatened the social equilibrium the government began to soften.

By then Rome was also prepared to compromise, and early in 1607 a compromise was reached. That April the two offending clerics were handed over to the French Ambassador who passed them on to Cardinal Joyeuse. The Cardinal then announced that the censures were removed. Matters had returned to normal, but though Venice claimed that the handover did not prejudice her authority to try ecclesiastics, in effect she had climbed down.

Nevertheless, Rome had not won all its points and still felt vengeful. That October three hirelings attacked Sarpi in the street, stabbing him about the head and neck. Sarpi survived to write his celebrated history of the Council of Trent, and to lament the increase of pro-papal sentiment in Venice – but henceforth he wore chain-mail under this cassock and took a bodyguard of well-armed friars with him when venturing out into the city. Venice continued to protest that she was more Catholic than Rome; Rome continued to suspect Venice of Protestantism, and there the matter ended.

When Sarpi died in 1623 he was something of a local hero; but there had been hostile demonstrations at the funeral of Doge Donà in 1612. The high hopes placed in the *giovani* of which he had been a leading member had not been realized. The Senate now dictated policy rather than the Ten, but the problems posed by the great economic crises had not been solved, and in the end the *giovani* themselves were swept into the mainstream of Venetian conservatism. Whenever some change or innovation was proposed, commented Sarpi once, there would always be a majority against it, and so it continued. The Republic was suffering from a certain hardening of the arteries.

The mood of the government was nervous and defensive, and understandably so, for Venice was now the only independent, self-supporting state in Italy, and the Spanish particularly seemed very threatening. As a result, the pall of secrecy surrounding government business grew ever thicker and the fear of conspiracy became almost pathological. A thousand primed and loaded muskets were kept in the Ten's room at the Palace; the secret denunciations boxes were regularly emptied for evidence of traitorous behaviour; in 1607 Angelo Badoer was imprisoned merely for talking to representatives of foreign powers; when Alvise da Riva of the Quarantia al Criminal protested against the cost of the war with Austria of 1615–17 and accused members of the government of profiteering he was arrested too, and within the next three years at least two more nobles were accused of treason. But the worst example of siege nerves was displayed in the so-called 'Spanish conspiracy' of 1618.

Venetians going to work one May morning that year observed the bodies of two men dangling upside-down from a gibbet in the Piazza. A few days later a third corpse, with bad torture marks upon it, appeared. These sights provoked considerable speculation. The dead were agents of the Spanish Ambassador, the Marquis Bedmar, it was said; Bedmar had hatched a nefarious plot to seize Venice on Ascension Day; pro-Spanish Venetian nobles were involved; the Ten had murdered some 500 suspects; the Republic had thwarted its equivalent of England's Gunpowder Plot.

Yet the 'Bedmar plot' seems never to have existed – or if it did the Ten kept evidence of it secret. And, like any security service, the Ten made its mistakes – they hanged Antonia Foscarini for treason in 1622 and subsequently proclaimed him innocent.

Alvise da Riva had been right in insisting that the war of 1615 (in which, ironically enough, Venice received help from Holland whose privateers had done so much to destroy her mercantile power) had stretched the Republic's resources to breaking point. It had certainly compounded another money crisis. Spanish reals and Imperial thalers were the primary currencies which funded Venetian east-bound trade, and Spanish silver in particular was vital to Venice's own money supply – so much so that the government customarily insisted that merchants exporting silver reals deliver twenty or twenty-five per cent of them to the mint to be converted into Venetian soldi; and when war loomed it banned the circulation of all foreign silver currencies except the scudi of Genoa, Florence and Milan.

But the silver shortage persisted long after the war. In 1637 the government had to buy bullion and reals from the financier Giovanni Venramin in order to mint enough new coins, paying him in cash, gold and partly by a sizeable loan from the state bank – an amalgamation of the old Banco di Rialto and the Banco Giro founded in 1619. In effect the operation was funded by a deficit underwritten by the state. But the silver shortage led both to deficit finance and to a progressive devaluation. The Venetian lira fell by over a fifth in terms of fine silver between 1570 and 1630 and by two-fifths in terms of fine gold.

And this devaluation reinforced a period of marked inflation.

Between 1563 and 1635 expenditure at the Arsenal rose by 350 per cent. Yet despite inflation wage rates had remained virtually static until well into the 1620s, and real wages in certain trades may even have fallen – because of the plentiful labour supply. Inflation and increased war expenditure also had a marked effect on welfare. The 48,000 ducats the Scuola di San Rocco spent on charity between 1601 and 1610 fell to 42,000 in the subsequent decade, thanks largely to its having to find nearly 26,000 ducats for the navy between 1614 and 1621, 15,000 of it in a single year, 1617–18. Other Scuole were similarly affected, forced to borrow heavily and allow their almsgiving to slump in money as well as in real terms.

State revenues, however, seem to have kept pace with inflation. Between 1590 and the early 1600s they rose twenty-five per cent to two and a half million ducats a year, and by 1610 to almost four millions, of which almost half came from the city, 1.3 millions from the *terraferma* and more than 840,000 from overseas. But though state expenditure increased and a large proportion of it was still devoted to the navy, the Arsenal did not see much benefit, for the government was buying so many more foreign-built tall-ships. By 1618 there were eight English and twelve Dutch warships in service, and before long there were fifty such ships – as many as there were galleys.

Industries other than shipbuilding suffered too, although for different reasons. Shoddy goods manufactured in Ragusa were being shipped to Turkey masquerading as Venetian. Inferior soap, some of it made by Venetian *émigrés* and stamped with the half-moon, the dove and other Venetian trade marks, was also finding its way into foreign markets, earning the Republic's manufactures, which were subject to careful quality control by the government, an undeservedly bad name. Yet while some industries were hampered by unfair competition Venice remained a major centre for stamped leather work and lace, and if Venetian shipbuilders lagged behind those of other countries in technology there was one Venetian industry which benefited from technological pioneering.

In 1606 Girolamo Magagnati had found a way to colour crystal without spoiling its transparency; he also pioneered the manufacture of plate-glass window-panes. Before long Venice was supplying all Europe with mirrors, fake jewellery, and drinking glasses of all kinds – yard-long flutes for the Dutch, thick crystal tankards for the English, and flat drinking dishes for the Italians. Venetian crystal-makers and Venetian glass-blowers were held in such high esteem that in 1618 an Englishman, James Howell, came to Venice especially to learn their expertise.

Howell was by no means the only English visitor, for the city was also acquiring a considerable tourist industry. Thomas Coryat, Richard Lassels, pioneer of the educative Grand Tour for homesick English schoolboys, John Evelyn and Philip Skippon were only a few of the many foreigners who came – and from the accounts they left it is easy to see what attracted them. The curious situation and glittering beauty of the city were factors of course, but so were the fascinations of its political system, and the manners of its nobility.

Coryat thought that the Venetian noblemen, with their beards, their long black gowns, and habit of bowing low with hand on heart as they passed each other in the streets, presented models of dignity – a view shared by Lassels, who considered them 'the most sightly, the most proper and grave men that ever I saw.' Nevertheless, Coryat also relished the sex and violence of the place, and described the blood that flowed in street-fights, the sight of felons receiving the strappado, and the *bravi* armed with gauntlets and stilettos who lurked 'like hungry lyons' along the waterfronts at night, waiting to claw their prey, rob them and toss their corpses into the canal. But, above all, Coryat rejoiced in the local courtesans. Many of them were 'so loose,' he informs us, they opened 'their quiuers to every arrow.' He, however, only patronized the best – those who decked themselves out like goddesses of love, who charmed their clients with elegant discourse and serenaded them with lutes before introducing them to their play-rooms and their perfumed beds.

Coryat pictured Venice itself, however, as a 'mayden citie' –

maiden because it had never been conquered. He admired its 'many faire gardens,' was intrigued by the custom of dressing the dead in Franciscan habits (which he attributed to the Venetians' belief that burial in a friar's cowl would 'procure them remission of a third part of our sinnes'), and, like all other visitors, was impressed by the polygot crowds in the market-places – Italians, Poles, Slavs, Turks, Armenians and Persians; the Greek priests in bushy beards, the red-hatted western Jews, and the oriental Jews in yellow turbans; 'all conspiring in this one thing,' as Lassels wrote, 'to sell dear and buy cheap.'

Then there were the attractions of the charlatans and mountebanks who peddled their cure-alls in the Piazza and staged puppet plays; the dangers of those 'licentious varlets' the gondoliers, who were so anxious to carry Coryat out of his way to be rooked for charity at some house of religion; the sight of the *Bucintoro*, of course, a vessel 'so exceeding glorious' as to have no peer – except perhaps for 'the *Prince Royall*, which was launched at Wollige about Michaelmas last.' Not least there were the Sunday games of volleyball, which attracted crowds of up to 1,500 to the Piazza San Stefano, and the music of St. Mark's, where Claudio Monteverdi was now Chapel Master (having been seduced there from Mantua in 1613 by a salary of 300 ducats), and of the Scuola di San Rocco, whose choir and orchestra of sackbuts, cornets, viols and oboes were 'so delectable . . . so super-excellent,' wrote Coryat, 'that it did euer rauish and stupifie.' The Venetian theatre he found less impressive, though he did see women act, 'a thing that I neuer saw before.'

But if Coryat was primarily interested in the earthier aspects of Venetian life, James Howell, though he also relished a sexual metaphor, was fascinated above all by Venetian government and institutions. For him Rome was the prostitute, Venice the virgin city and the heroic defender of Christendom against Islam. 'The Eastern Emperours have divers times set upon her skirts,' he wrote, and 'the Gran Turk hath bin often at Her, but he could never have his will of Her.' Howell attributed the longevity of the Republic to its conservatism and wealth, the temperament and patriotism of the people, the exclusion of clerics from government the security system and the limitations placed upon the Doge's power.

Howell provided his English readers with a full account not only of the Venetian constitution but of the government's involvement in industry, building and dredging, food and water supplies, wages and health and welfare, as well as law, order and defence. His account can be seen as the blossoming of the Venetian myth planted in England by Lewkenor's translation of Contarini's book, and this myth was to stimulate constitutional debate in Cromwell's England, influence the Founding Fathers, and ultimately the constitutions of Pennsylvania and other American states.

But if Howell noticed no 'symptom of decay' in the Venetian system the new British Ambassador, Dudley Carleton, shrewdly perceived a critical change which had overtaken the ruling class. The nobility, he reported in 1612, had 'growne factious, vindictive loose and unthriftie.' Having abandoned trade and bought up land and houses, they were now enlarging their stables and generally giving themselves a good time, aiming at ever more 'show and gallantrie.' The frugal merchant noble had become a spendthrift country squire.

It was a cultural change which had political implications, for those who failed to switch their investments from trade to land were losing not only their substance but their political power. Moreover, as land became perceptibly more profitable, resources were switched increasingly from industry as well from shipping and overseas trade. By 1636 Venetian nobles had acquired forty per cent of all the arable land in the Padovano, over a quarter in the Polesine, and nearly a fifth in the Trevigiano and Dogano – a total of 11.7 per cent of all cultivated land in the _terraferma_. By 1682 this proportion had increased to 14.7 per cent. Moreover, the state itself was taking over an increasing acreage of communal lands despite violent protests from the peasants in some areas.

Investment in land was accompanied by speculation in the produce of that land. By 1620, according to one account, Venetian nobles were not only trading 'in grain of every kind, wines, silk, wool, iron, wood and even charcoal' but using their money and 'the authority they possess,' to 'get their hands on goods and necessities for a small price, which they sell again at a greedy profit and with excessive distress to the poor.' Nevertheless, Carleton was right in suggesting that spending often tended to outpace income. Vast sums were being spent on country palaces with as many as a hundred rooms and incorporating private chapels, concert salons and even private theatres.

Theatrical performances were lavishly staged in town palaces as well. Monteverdi's *The Rape of Proserpine* received its première at the Mocenigo Palace on the occasion of Giustiniana Mocenigo's marriage to Lorenzo Giustininian, and in 1624 the same composer's *Il Combattimento di Tancredo e Glorinda* was also performed there. Many poorer nobles who tried to ape such luxury were reduced to poverty more speedily, and noblemen began to go cap-in-hand to foreigners, begging for charity in order to keep up their houses and gondolas, while competition for the paying jobs in government became more intense than ever.

In September 1620 just such a group of poor noblemen were discovered equipping themselves with extra voting pellets in order to vote themselves, their friends, or anyone else ready to bribe them, into office. On the other hand, there were many unprofitable posts for which no candidates could be found at all. Some of these simply remained vacant; others had to be assigned to noblemen regardless of their wishes. The impoverishment of all but a minority of the ruling class, and their declining numbers threatened to destroy the whole governmental system.

More immediately the situation was leading to open political warfare between rich and poor in the Great Council. In 1626 Ranier Zeno launched a bitter attack against the wealthy, powerful nobles in general and Doge Giovanni Cornaro in particular, accusing them of sharing out all the plums of office exclusively among themselves. His outspokenness earned him a beating-up from the *bravi* of the Doge's son Giorgio, yet Zeno, who had considerable support in the Great Council, continued to attack the Signoria. He rated them for failing to keep rich bishoprics vacant and using their incomes to provide pensions for poorer nobles. He even attacked the secretaries of the Ten for encouraging that Council to exceed its powers. The Council of Ten was reformed in 1628, but Zeno's brave oratory could not reverse the decline of the nobility. If only half of them could afford to marry in the 1500s only forty per cent did so now, and since most noblemen could only afford to dower one daughter at the most, by 1629 there were over 2,000 noble nuns in Venice.

The crisis of the nobility was subsumed into a greater one in 1630, however, when bubonic plague struck again. The population of Venice and Venetia was reduced by as much as forty per cent. Verona lost half of its inhabitants, and though Venice suffered less, between twenty and thirty per cent of her population died. By December 1631 there were only 1,666 nobles left over the age of twenty-five, one sixth fewer than in 1620. It was to prove a critical blow to the Republic's governing class, even if death was somewhat slow to come; and the plague also dealt a heavy blow to the economy, producing another terrible slump in both agriculture and industry.

With the labour shortage driving wages up again, the government tried to control them, thus triggering off serious riots. Inflation continued, and a general withdrawal of capital in Venetia as a whole intensified an already severe depression. The plague and its concomitant disasters coincided with a general European crisis occasioned by the Thirty Years' War and with increased competition from English manufacturers – all of which combined to cause Venetian textile output to fall from 23,000 cloths in 1620 to some 14,000 in 1635.

And the ill-luck which had dogged Venice for so long was not to desert her even now, for in 1635 the Turks attacked again and the ensuing war was to last for twenty-five long years.

Turkey encompassed all Venice's remaining possessions overseas. For decades past the Republic had made peace with Turkey a priority, but the Turks were no longer disposed to reciprocate, and Venice was in poor condition for a fight. Though operations at the Arsenal were expanded, after six years of war there were only 1,208 masters employed there, and as late as 1644 the navy could boast no more than eighty-five galleys.

In 1645 the Turks mounted a major assault upon Crete, their primary objective. They took Canea, and in 1646 Rethymnon too, aided by Cretans who rose up eagerly against their hated masters. Venetians hated Cretans almost as much, believing, as Howell wrote, that their 'Women's teeth' were so poisonous that 'if a woman bite a man any thing deep he will never recover.' But they valued the Cretan land even more – for its fruit, its honey and its muscatel – and they pulled out every stop to keep it.

Taxation rose again; offices and state lands were auctioned; new forced loans were exacted; priests urged their parishioners to give more; and Giacomo Marcello proposed the sale of noble status to rich non-nobles – all to raise money for the war effort. Marcello had two main grounds for his proposal – fear of a popular revolt if taxation rose any higher and the need to inject new blood into the nobility for the sake of better government. How could one select 'the best man' for office, he asked, if there were so few candidates from which to choose? But the idea that ability meant less than a birthright cut across a tradition hallowed since 1381. 'No one can ever become Noble by force of gold,' declared Angelo Michiel inaccurately. Nobility, in his view, could only stem from 'good blood,' or else be earned by 'fine brave deeds.' Nevertheless, the Great Council voted for Marcello's proposal. In return for contributions of 60,000 ducats each, five families were at once entered in the Golden Book, and by 1669 eighty families had been ennobled at a payment of up to 100,000 ducats each. Venice's ruling caste was no longer quite exclusive.

Thanks largely to the contributions of the new nobles, Venice maintained her war effort. In 1648 and again in 1650 her forces in Candia, her chief stronghold in Crete, withstood Turkish sieges. Fighting was fierce on other fronts as well. But, Crete apart, the population of her extensive eastern frontiers proved loyal, her navy vigilant, her artillery effective and her fortifications strong. Nevertheless the strain was severe. Yet to read John Evelyn's account of his six months' stay in Venice in 1645 one would hardly imagine that the Republic was at war.

Evelyn lodged at the 'Black Eagle' near the Rialto, indulged in the pleasure of 'the eastern baths,' an experience which cost him 'one of the greatest Colds and rheums that I had in my whole life,' watched the Ascension Day festivities and the great Ascension Fair, when everybody seemed at 'liberty, and jollie.' He was there, too, for the Carnival, a time of 'universal madnesse' when people of all classes disguised themselves in fancy dress, pelted each other with eggs 'fill'd with sweete waters, & sometimes not over sweete.' Evelyn condemned the 'barbarous custome of hunting bulls about the Streetes & Piazzas, which is very dangerous,' observed that Venetian ladies still washed their hair in urine, that the wearing of high pattens was reserved for noblewomen, and that women of the citizen class stole glances at passing men from beneath their veils of taffeta.

There was music everywhere – from the caged nightingales the shopkeepers along the Merceria kept outside their premises (which made Evelyn think it 'the most delicious Streete in the Worlde'), from the serenaders on the Grand Canal ('their Hide-park, where the Noblesse go to take the air'), and from the beggar-sanctuary of the Mendicanti and the other three chief Hospitals, whose musical performances made a considerable difference to their collection plates.

There was also the opera – a feature of the city's life rather than a privilege for the nobility since the San Cassiano theatre had opened in 1637. Evelyn attended a performance of *Hercules in Lydia*, where he was as impressed by the thirteen scene changes as he was by the singing, though he subsequently invited the soprano to a fish dinner where she sang for him again.

He also watched gaming at San Felice, visited the Arsenal and the glass works on Murano, watched the dissection of a corpse in the University of Padua, saw a wedding and a circumcision in the ghetto, and marvelled at the treasure of St. Mark's – the golden, gem-encrusted breast plates, the dozen golden crowns, the two 'unicornses hornes,' the various 'heads of saints,' as also the 'great morcell of the real Crosse, one of the nailes, a Thorne, a fragment of the column to which our Lord was bound, when scourged. . . . The . . . Ensigne of Victorious *Constantine*, a piece of St. *Lukes* arm, a rib of St. *Stephen*, a finger of

Mary Magdalene & a world of Reliques I could not remember.'

Venice, he concluded mistakenly, must be one of the 'considerablest states' in all the world, and apart from encountering some riotous soldiery in Padua only one experience he described indicates that Venice was at war at all – the ship he had planned to take to Jerusalem was commandeered to take supplies to the beleaguered garrison in Candia.

Despite the relaxed atmosphere the city affected, the Republic was using every weapon it could lay its hands on to save Crete. It even considered germ warfare, accepting an offer made by a Jewish doctor at Zara in 1649 to administer a 'quintessence of plague' into the Turkish camps through the medium of cloth goods which the Turks customarily bought. But though the doctor was ultimately sent out to Crete nothing more is known of the venture. In 1651 Venetian and Turkish fleets clashed off Paros and subsequently in areas as far apart as Dalmatia and the Dardanelles. Towns and islands changed hands, brilliant victories were won and grievous losses suffered. Venice acquired a new hero and martyr in Admiral Lazzaro Mocenigo, killed in a moment of victory at the Dardanelles; the French sent help to Candia; the peace party in the Council was repeatedly shouted down; Doges came and Doges went and still the struggle continued.

Meanwhile work was proceeding on Palladio's design for the monastery of San Giorgio Maggiore which stands serenely across the waters from the Doge's Palace; Cosimo II of Tuscany had come to Venice, and Thomas Killigrew, ambassador of the exiled Charles II of England, had been thrown out of town. Abbot Vettor Grimani and his brother Pietro had murdered the wealthy Francesco Quirini-Stampalia and were outlawed; the Arsenal built its first modern ship of the line, using an English ship as a model; a great fraud was discovered in the Banco Giro; French periwigs were banned; and Cavalli's *Il Calisto* received its first performance.

The new baroque vogue was making stage sets as well as buildings ever more ornate. Scene changes became more frequent, and more use was made of elaborate machines. Young Philip Skippon, who stayed in Venice during the middle 1660s, described an opera staged at Grimani's theatre: 'Before the curtain was drawn up,' he wrote, 'a trumpet sounded, and a violin answered it very well. . . . In the prologue some of the actors hung in the air, and then flew cross the stage.' One representing a Fury 'flew downwards . . . and then he flew up again . . . clouds seemed to move, and the walls of a castle to be blown up.' But another production at Grimani's was even more spectacular. The curtain rose to reveal 'an amphitheatre filled with spectators,' and there followed scenes in which ships were burnt at sea and a Sybil vanished into the ground in flames. Even the smaller theatre of San Salvatore could stage a scene of a mock earthquake. But Venetian comedies were somewhat rougher affairs than the operas.

'Before the play began,' wrote Skippon, 'the gentlemen and company were impatient, and . . . stamp'd and whistl'd, and call'd to one another. Those that sate in the boxes did frequently spit upon the company in the pit, so that all appeared very rude.' The play itself 'was very immodest and obscene,' and anything in it that failed to reach this standard was hissed. Nor were such performances patronized by the lower classes only. The gentry also came, 'some with their wives or whores,' although disguised by masks. Some noblemen, indeed, 'stood near the stage,' and would 'often interrupt the actors, and discourse with them.' Skippon also left a full account of a comparatively recent Venetian institution, the gaming-house at San Salvatore, where Venetian nobles took the bank and large sums would change hands at games of basset and of hazard.

The illusionary flamboyance of Venetian stage sets, the beggar noblemen accosting foreign tourists, the gambling for high stakes at San Salvatore were more than straws in the wind: they were symptoms of a certain decadence. The men who governed the Republic were hardly less shrewd than their predecessors; Venetian entrepreneurs were no less keen to turn an honest or dishonest penny, and Venice could still produce intrepid men of war. But there was a feeling of power ebbing away, and a concomitant emphasis on enjoying life while opportunity afforded.

In sum, it was an escapist mood, and the harsh reality of the situation was only driven home in the autumn of 1669 when

Francesco Morosini, commander-in-chief in Crete, formally surrendered to the Sultan's army. Apart from three outposts at Grabusa, Suda and Spinalunga, the great island, which Venice had held for four centuries and more had been wrenched from her grasp – despite the loss of more than 30,000 men and an expenditure of four and a quarter million ducats. The war had strained the Venetian economy, rocked her institutions, exhausted her nobility, and seen half her overseas empire snatched away. Venice had been broken as a leading Mediterranean power.

Chapter XV

Luxurious Decline

The last Turkish war had skimmed the fat off the Venetian economy. Public and private institutions had been forced into debt, a number of rich families had been ruined; Venetians long resident in Crete had returned to Venice in desperate poverty.

Once again a partial recovery set in. Turkish merchants returned to trade at the Rialto, commerce with Germany increased, and between 1670 and 1702 the number of ships docking at Venice rose by seventy per cent. The recovery was not uniform, however. Between 1675 and 1677 the Republic's consulates at Aleppo and Alexandria closed down 'because of lack of business,' and though Venetians remained at Smyrna they experienced keen competition from the English and the Dutch.

The decline of the shipbuilding and textiles industries also continued. Of the Republic's forty-four large sailing ships in 1693 only nine had been built in Venice, the Arsenal employed a thousand fewer workers than it had done in 1645, and the output of woollen cloths fell from 10,000 in 1665 to 2,800 in 1701. This was only partly offset by the growth of sugar, glass and paper production and the considerable expansion of the silk industry. Between 1670 and 1750 Venetian production of top quality organzine doubled to over 160 tons a year – but the silk was manufactured on the *terraferma*, and much of the raw wool, alum and other raw materials imported through the port of Venice were also destined for the hinterland rather than for Venetian industries.

The state-sanctioned power of the city's guilds to stop wages falling even when the price of food fell and to enforce a closed shop and exploit the consequent labour shortage had much to do with this. Manufacturers had 'little say in the making of the cloth,' ran a complaint of 1673. Their workers decided. Venetian workers cared 'little about doing a good job,' ran another in 1689, since they were 'sure, by government ordinances, of [obtaining] a certain wage.' But the closed shop stayed and more textile manufacturers moved out of Venice in order to escape the guilds.

While skilled workers left the city, unskilled labourers still poured in, mainly from the Grisons, hoping for work, and though the government was eventually to increase its protection of industry Venice became even more obviously a city of porters, watermen and artisan-shopkeepers, with very few large or even medium-sized industrial enterprises apart from the Arsenal.

Venice was still a centre for the fine arts, and musicians like Corelli and Tartini prospered. Patronage still flowed from clubs and confraternities, and particularly from free-spending noblemen who had invested in land rather than in industry.

In 1722 Venetians possessed sixteen per cent of the arable land in the *terraferma*; by 1740 they owned twenty per cent – nearly a million acres. This increase owed much to the compulsory selling up of common lands to pay off tax debts accumulated by peasant communes. Yet though noblemen had title to seventy per cent of these Venetian holdings only ten per cent of the Venetian nobility owned estates of any size at all, and some of these spent far beyond their incomes.

Entire fortunes were squandered on high living. Almorò Pisani, who died in 1682 had forbidden his heirs to sell the family estates, but his descendants nevertheless squandered what they could, spending their wives' dowries and selling up the family jewels too. Almorò's grandson used every asset he could lay his hands on in order to enlarge the family palace and build a fabulous new villa at Stra, and his son, Alvise, who served as ambassador in Madrid and Paris, entertained and bought horses on such a lavish scale that he was forced to sell the remaining family jewels and to borrow heavily on the security of the estates he could not sell. The same went for many more families far less affluent than the Pisanis, reinforcing the long-term trend of the nobility's decline.

The trend was only partly arrested by noblemen forming gaming syndicates to earn money. In 1676 large-scale gambling became a feature of San Moisé. Sixty to eighty tables were laid out there, each presided over by a nobleman who served as croupier. According to the Frenchman St. Didier, who went there in 1680, it seemed rather a grim place, despite the glittering chandeliers and the disguises the noblesse among the clientele was obliged to wear. The silence was greater than in any church, and 'the calmness and phlegm with which vast sums are won and lost is so extraordinary, that one might consider it a school . . . to teach deportment . . . rather than a place of amusement.' Venetians were pioneers of the poker face and the stiff upper lip. And stiff upper lips were needed when in 1684 another war began with Turkey which was to last for fifteen years.

Plans were co-ordinated with Venice's allies, Austria and Poland; the sixty-six-year-old Francesco Morosini was called out of retirement to assume supreme command; Hanoverian and other German troops were hired at 200 francs a head, and the ranks of the nobility were opened up again to anyone prepared to contribute 100,000 ducats towards the war effort. Of the forty new families entered in the Golden Book over the next twenty years most had made their piles as bankers, wholesalers, contractors, industrialists and tradesmen, though a fair number were lawyers and civil servants of the 'original citizen' class, and some were nobles from the *terraferma*. The new nobles helped to fill more empty governmental posts, but their numbers were too few to mitigate the increasingly corrupt, incestual aspects of the government. Their main contribution was their money – and this helped the Republic to put up a very brave show in the war.

Venice aimed not only to cling on to her remaining overseas possessions – Tenos, the six Ionian islands, her Dalmatian outposts and her three remaining Forts in Crete – but to occupy the seventh Ionian island, Santa Maura, and clear the sea-roads to mainland

Greece. The ageing Captain-General Morosini succeeded admirably. He took Santa Maura, and in 1685 led his motley force of 8,500 Venetian, Hanoverian, Maltese, Slav, Florentine and Papal troops to capture the old Venetian colony of Korone and destroy the castle at Kalamata. Next year, while other Venetian forces were advancing in Dalmatia, he occupied the strategic ports of Navarino, Methone and Nauplia – and for good measure blew up the temple of Minerva at the top of the Akropolis.

Trophies were soon arriving back in Venice – a headless marble lioness from Athens, and the great lion of Piraeus which still stands guard outside the Arsenal today. But the victories were more glamorous than decisive, for the main Turkish effort was directed against Vienna. Even so, Morosini's great advance did not continue long. Athens was abandoned in 1688; an attack on Negroponte failed; and then, leaving Girolamo Cornaro to besiege Monemvasia, Morosini returned to Venice – for Doge Giustiniano had died that March and he had been elected to succeed him.

The tide then turned the Republic's way again. Monemvasia, then all of Morea fell into Venetian hands once more, and the Republic promptly set about exploiting it in its time-honoured way. The Greeks soon came to hate the Christian Venetians more even than the Muslim Turks. The people of Methone complained of Venetian officers 'debauching our wives and daughters' and of Venetian priests 'speaking against our religion and constantly urging us to embrace theirs, which the Turks never did.' They prayed for the Turks to return, but had to suffer the Venetian rule for a little longer yet.

In 1691 Venice lost Grabusa, one of her last footholds in Crete; an attempt to take Canea failed, and old Doge Morosini went out to take command in person. He died at Nauplia early in 1694.

Thanks largely to the efforts of her allies, Venice did well out of the peace concluded at Karlowitz five years later. She retained Morea, Santa Maura, Aegina, and many of her Dalmatian conquests and ceased to pay tribute to the Turks for Zante. Her overseas empire had suddenly expanded; fortune was smiling on the Republic once again.

Yet her basic economic problems had not been solved. Early in the 1700s the government was forced to devalue the lira by a quarter – a step which dealt a grievous blow to those who had invested in fixed interest bonds. Moreover, with so many family fortunes being eroded and industrial investment still at a low ebb, in 1696–7 the government tried to divert the considerable sums still spent on luxuries to more productive use by reviving the sumptuary laws. Lavish expenditure on parties, dress and jewellery was condemned; periwigs costing more than twelve ducats were banned and so were expensive fans and muffs except in masquerade. Such measures only nibbled at the problem, however – and hit at the industries producing 'useless' luxuries at a time when they were contributing increasingly to Venice's wealth – for the city was fast becoming the pleasure capital of Europe.

Visitors were no longer limited principally to pilgrims and young gentlemen on an educative grand tour. The very cream of European society was also beginning to favour Venice, and they were heavy spenders. The Queen of Poland came twice, in 1699 and 1705, and King Frederick IV of Denmark and Norway stayed for three months in 1709, enjoying the sophistication of its comforts and its increasing range of excellent entertainments. There was the 'downright madness' of the Carnival, as the Earl of Perth had called it, when the powerful could relax incognito, enjoy the shimmering displays of fireworks, watch youngsters chasing bulls through the streets, and boys firing pistols as they flew up and down on rope-borne chariots between the Campanile and the Doge's palace. There were also the entertainments afforded by convivial gatherings of academics, by gambling and the *villegiatura* season, and the charms of the nearby countryside – and in addition to all this the husky tones and honeyed sweetness of the Venetian accent and the city's excellent music.

The works of Monteverdi, Cimarosa and Albinoni were much performed; sung Mass at St. Mark's could last as long as five hours, and the public came in droves to musical services at the hospitals. Vivaldi, the 'coughing priest,' became *maestro di violino* at the Pietà in 1701; Pietro dal Oglio, later to achieve

Scene in the grounds of a Venetian palace

fame at the imperial Court of Russia, was choirmaster there in 1713–14, while Baldassare Galuppi, master of comic opera, religious composition and the keyboard, became Director of Music at the Incurabili. This was the great age of Venetian music. The audiences were huge, and the affluent took care to send their daughters to one of the four musical *conservatoires* run by the hospitals in order to improve their chances in the marriage market by giving them the best possible musical tuition.

The institution of marriage itself, however, was undergoing something of a transformation, thanks to the emergence of that curious institution, the *cavalliere servente*. Derived from the idealized knightly loves of medieval times, these cavaliers were virtually personal gigolos, accompanying their ladies almost everywhere. As such they allowed noble women to attend social occasions outside their own houses, to which they had previously been virtually confined when their husbands were preoccupied with affairs. But the institution seems also to have provided the growing number of bachelor nobles with some female companionship – an alternative to the wife-sharing which was allegedly practised in those noble households where only one brother married, and a supplement, if not necessarily an alternative, to maintaining a share in a mistress.

The effeminate, dandified *cavalliere servente*, like those powdered, scented abbés who had more interest in music than the church, also reflected the new emphasis on life's pleasures, as did the increasingly sophisticated and pseudo-simple vogue for the country life. The *villegiatura* seasons lasted seven weeks in summer and another seven in late autumn. During these periods members of high society would indulge in picnics, dance 'peasant' dances in 'peasant' dress, change their costumes up to four times in a day, spend as much as 300 crowns a month on sugar, coffee and chocolate, and generally attempt to recreate an idyllic 'country life' of nymphs and shepherdesses. In short, this was the last great holiday of the nobility before the age of revolution. But though the relaxed and pleasurable life drew in the foreigner it conflicted sharply with the needs of realistic government.

From 1714 to 1718 Venice fought yet another war with Turkey,

K

and this one was disastrous. Suda and Spinalunga, her last and lonely Cretan forts, were lost; so was Tenos, which the Republic ruled since 1390. Corinth, Nauplia and Methone all fell; the rebellious inhabitants of Monemvasia capitulated to the enemy; and when peace came all Venice held by way of an empire overseas was a handful of Dalmatian bases and the Ionian islands. The government planned a new and modern army of 22,000 men, including artillery and engineers corps and costing five millions a year, but henceforth it steered well clear of adventures.

Neutrality at all costs was the keynote now, and the solemn reburial of the sainted bones of Doge Pietro Orseolo II, conqueror of Dalmatia seven centuries before, was only a pious act of pride in history. The Republic had resigned all pretensions to being a great power, and its governing class showed an ever decreasing interest in the task of government. *Villegiatura* kept leading ministers away from their desks for weeks on end. Few noblemen cared to stand for office, and most could not afford to – including numbers of the new nobility who had spent most of their substance simply by buying themselves in. Instead, those in funds spent their days as elegantly as possible; those with long lineages looked down on their jumped-up colleagues; and all of them showed disdain for the 140,000 ordinary Venetians.

They 'look upon themselves as so many princes,' wrote an English visitor, Edward Wright, at the beginning of the 1720s. They expected to be addressed as 'Excellency' and to be bowed and scraped to – but the respect was rarely earned. Noblemen were not only unpopular, many of them were conscious 'of how ill they deserve of the people' but they took good care to guard against any tendency for public resentment to spill over into public disorder. Venice was not governed by even the passive consent of the people so much as by the police, and the Venetian constables, the *sbirri*, were 'so odious to the people' that it was regarded as 'scandalous' to be seen speaking to them.

Resentment was mitigated to some extent by emigration. There was a strong and increasing trend among Venetians to find work abroad, particularly in Austria; even Canaletto and Piranesi left to further their careers in England and in Rome. Some painters and sculptors still made comfortable livings in Venice, and even enjoyed a certain rise in status – the painters now had a 'college' rather than a guild, and sculptors demarcated themselves very carefully from ordinary stone-masons – but the great vibrant age of the visual arts was in decline now, like the ruling class itself.

The decline extended to the guilds as well. Once quite rich, few of them could now afford the best painters to decorate their halls, since most of the industries in which they worked no longer prospered. Attempts were made to do away with restrictive guild practices, but even when successful this did not seem to help. Venice still exported glassware, arms, soap, wax and textiles; it still sent woollen caps to Barbary and drugs to the Levant; but soon there were only four leather-embossing shops where once there had been seventy-one, the number of printing presses shrank from seventy-seven in 1752 to fifty in 1765, and the wool trade continued its decline.

Financial troubles had accompanied industrial decline. The Banco Giro had to suspend payments in specie altogether in 1717 and did not return to the standard until 1739. Nevertheless, the city was rich enough to repave the Piazza in 1722, raising the level against the force of floods, to develop the entrance to the lagoon; at Malamocco in 1725–6 so as to let in larger ships, to launch another *Bucintoro* in 1728, and from 1732 to install public street-lighting.

The coffee-house provided another new feature of the Venetian scene, and at least one nobleman sensed its promise as an investment. Ludovico Cornaro paid a considerable lump sum and a further 25,000 a year for his concession – and he provided facilities for gambling as well as coffee-drinking at his establishment. The Grimani, on the other hand, invested in the theatre, owning no fewer than three, including the largest in the city. As many as seven of Venice's theatres were entirely devoted to performances of opera – more than any other town in Italy. But Venetian comedy was also flourishing.

Its most famous exponent, Goldoni, came from the middle class and started out as a lawyer. He wrote libretti for Galuppi's *opera buffe*, dramatized Richardson's *Pamela* with considerable success, and turned his hand to tragedy as well. But of all his 250 or so plays it is for his dialect comedies that he is remembered. Goldoni poked fun at ordinary folk, and especially at merchants and lawyers (whose style of advocacy tended in any case to be theatrically exaggerated), though the nobles received rather less attention – direct satire aimed at the ruling class being forbidden. But popular as his plays were in his own lifetime, Goldoni had a rival, Carlo Gozzi.

Born in 1720, the son of a penurious noble who never entered the Great Council, Gozzi wrote comedies for Sacchi's company and then produced plays in his own right as a means of maintaining the decrepit family house in Venice and the no less decrepit family villa in the country.

The Gozzi-Goldoni rivalry extended beyond the stage to rival literary clubs, and each set had its gallery mob to applaud their own man's play and disrupt performances of the other's – until at last Goldoni left for Paris, and, like Piranesi, Tiepolo and Vivaldi before him, died in exile.

Crowds of porters and gondoliers were always to be seen hanging about outside the theatres whiling away time playing knucklebone and cards until their masters should reappear or a client turn up. These eternal Venetian watermen had a hard time of it now. Work was difficult to find; even the smuggling was not what it had been, and legitimate traffic at the port itself was certainly drying up.

Competition from Ancona became especially acute after 1732 when it was declared a free port, and Trieste and Fiume also provided competition uncomfortably close to home. In 1736 the Republic at last declared Venice to be a free port too, but the measure could not reverse the long-term trend. In 1737–8, 274 ships anchored at Venice; in 1738–9, 193 ships did so, and in the following year only 164 – and the number of foreign-owned ships that called declined more sharply still. Moreover, even in the 1750s, by which time the port was clearing as much tonnage as it had done in its hey-day three centuries before, this was far less than most major European ports handled, and the cargoes were almost exclusively confined to goods destined for the hinterland and to the export surpluses of the Ionian islands and of the Venetian possessions of the Dalmatian colonies.

Nevertheless, Venice continued to increase in popularity as a resort. At one moment in 1737 the city contained no fewer than five dispossessed crowned heads, including the Young Pretender – a quirk of fate which Voltaire relished in *Candide*. But incumbent sovereigns also came – the Elector of Saxony and the Prince of Wolfenbüttel, the Dukes of Bavaria, Würtemburg and York, and in 1769 the Emperor Joseph II, who arrived incognito and soon returned bringing his three brothers with him.

If crowned heads and princes were the pacemakers, many others followed. These included adventurers like John Law, Baron Poellnitz and Guiseppe Babano (alias Count Cagliostro, alias the Marquis Pellegrini), who arrived in 1788 and sold a number of his 'elixirs of youth' before fleeing from the police; while among the more respectable visitors were two formidable English ladies, Mrs. Piozzi – Dr. Johnson's Mrs. Thrale – and Lady Mary Wortley Montagu.

For the fifty-year old Lady Mary the widespread use of masks was not the least of Venice's attractions. It was conductive to 'a universal liberty that is certainly one of the greatest *agremens* in life.' It allowed everybody who was anybody to live his own way without fear of being censured by society. Moreover, Venice, with its great number of unoccupied palaces, was cheap enough for her to live in 'very genteelly' on the allowance her deserted husband sent her. Lady Mary lodged on the Grand Canal and was introduced into Society by Pietro Grimani, sometime Ambassador to Britain and currently Procurator of St. Mark's. The Doge himself showed her round his private gallery, the Papal Nuncio offered her his box at the opera, the nineteen-year-old Francesco Algarotti, budding literary dilettante, was always in attendance, while for English company there were Lord Mansel and Sir Henry Englefield.

Though Lady Mary did not entirely share the vogue, the prevalent fashion among Venetian ladies in Venice was for high sentiment. This was the age of boudoirs, pet dogs, langours, sufferings, toilettes taking hours, and frequent attacks of the vapours. Yet while fluttering their fans and stressing their supposed frailties, ladies also used their wiles to further their husbands' careers, to discuss politics, and even engage in business. One such, a Pisani-Grimani, owned and managed the San Benedetto theatre; another, Caterina Sagredo Barbarigo, kept a *casino* on the Giudecca which the Inquisition, no longer the feared and active institution it once had been, nevertheless decided to close down in 1747; Marina Pisani kept another, and though this was also closed down in 1756 both ladies promptly opened up again at new addresses.

Gentlemen still dressed in uniform black, but they wore curled periwigs, smothered themselves in perfumed oils and lotions, displayed exquisite snuff-boxes and exquisite manners. Some of them seemed almost as sensitive as the ladies – in 1753 one nobleman, Giovanni Cornaro, actually petitioned for a separation from his wife on the grounds that 'her feet stank.' But the most effete gentlemen on the Venetian scene were the *cavallieri serventi*, who attended their chosen ladies at their boxes at the theatre, stood by them as they received callers, rowed to and fro along the Giudecca with them, taking the air, and even accompanied them to Mass. Many noblemen seem to have seen little of their own wives, although many of them played the cavalier to others.

The Venetian cavalier, with his exaggerated charm and careful preening, was a far cry from the Venetian nobleman of earlier ages, with his cropped hair and stern manner. Even more pitiful, however, was the sight of the budding young gentlewomen in the convent schools who aped ladies of fashion, bared a maximum of neck and shoulder at Mass in order to attract the attentions of some man – in the knowledge that the odds against their ever marrying were high.

Those who did find husbands, however, often celebrated their release from seclusion and their narrow upbringing by leading a life of sheer abandon. The word jealousy became almost obsolete among the Venetian upper class, and it is hardly surprising that Giacomo Casanova should have boasted of so many easy conquests.

The state did try to improve the moral tone in a rather effete and ineffectual way. In 1774 it abolished the public gambling halls – only to leave the field open to the private gambling institutions. It also condemned 'loose behaviour' in noblewomen and in 1774 forbade ladies entering a theatre unmasked or wearing 'immodest' garments. It was less concerned with the morals of the poor, however, and almost smiled on prostitution.

All this was symptomatic of the European social scene in general. So was the blend of conformity with disbelief in matters of religion. A Venetian senator might find the doctrine of transubstantiation ridiculous, but he still knelt down in church. And Venetian society was typical, too, in presenting a sharp contrast between richness and poverty. Mrs. Piozzi was appalled by the odoriferous crowds around St. Mark's and the beggars and cripples 'unfit to be surveyed by any eyes except those of a surgeon.' Samuel Sharp, however, who came to Venice in the 1760s, betrayed an unmistakably capitalist spirit in his attitude to the Venetian poor. The common people lived 'very well,' he thought, though the comparison he obviously had in mind was London's Gin Lane, for he ascribed their relative prosperity primarily to 'their ignorance of gin and brandy.' Moreover, he attributed most of the unmistakable poverty he did see to the Venetians' love of gambling – though even he was puzzled by 'the swarms of beggars' which, in view of the abundance of charitable foundations in Venice, he thought 'surprisingly great.'

Venice's air was clean, and there were neither 'dirty barges, nor dirty men,' as there were in London. But to the extent that Venetians seemed comparatively well off, this was due, as Sharp realized, to the government's policy of favouring the capital at the expense of the subject territories. 'Every other town in the territory of the Republick,' he wrote, 'appears poor in comparison of the mother-city,' for the government discouraged 'every invention, or manufacture' that clashed with the immediate benefit of Venice herself.

These measures failed to produce enough employment, however, and the government proceeded to expel the immigrants, who had flocked in from the Grisons earlier in the century and to attract new craft skills to Venice. Venetians went to Dresden to learn how to make fine china; and Hewelke of Dresden and Geminiano Cozzi of Modena (who was subsidized by the state to the tune of 360 ducats a year for twenty years) were among those who set up factories and earned Venice her reputation for transparent porcelain exquisitely decorated with wreaths, roses and ribbons, gods and shepherdesses.

The protectionism in which the government indulged to maintain the city's industries was practised with even greater fervour by the guilds. In 1767 the printers went as far as to forbid their own sons from entering the trade within their fathers' lifetimes in order to reduce the competition. And if this was one small symptom of economic decline another declared itself in 1777, when the Mendicanti, the Incurabili and the Ospedaletto, institutions which had sustained a major part of Venice's social security burden for centuries past, went bankrupt and had to be taken over by the state.

The sources of Venetian wealth had each dried up in turn – first trade, then industry, and now agriculture too. The population of Venetia rose by about a third during the 1700s, yet agricultural output saw little growth and the burden of the failure can be attributed in large measure to the lack of interest in more efficient farming techniques on the part of Venetian owners. As in France, population pressure encouraged the leasing of land in small plots rather than land improvement and better farming methods. The favour which the state showed owner-farmers by charging them two per cent less tax than leasers was insufficient to reverse the trend. The attentions of most landlords were restricted to their rents and country residences. Opportunities for reclaiming marginal land and putting commonlands to the plough had been virtually exhausted, and such innovations as were introduced, usually by large-scale tenant farmers, mostly involved the substitution of maize for other cereal crops. Moreover, since maize, though its yield was high, impoverished the soil and there was insufficient manure to reinvigorate it, thanks to the ploughing up of pasture land, the problem was compounded to the point of crisis.

The result was a mass of discontented peasants hardly able to make ends meet in the countryside and yet unable to find work in the *terraferma* towns whose industries were starved for the benefit of Venice. Moreover, though there were a few agrarian entrepreneurs – notably the Zenobios, who invested very profitably in grain for export to America in the 1780s and 1790s – the crisis ultimately affected many of the land-owning nobility too, and at a time when the decline of the class as a whole was hastening into a rush towards extinction.

Barely half as many noblemen survived to marriageable age in the eighteenth century as had done in the seventeenth, and only a third of these were marrying. Many a nobleman merged himself into the population at large out of shame at his poverty, and by 1797 the entire class formed only 0.8 per cent of the population – half the proportion of 1645. Nor was the introduction of new members enough to save it. In 1775, when it was decided to admit another forty outsiders to the Great Council, there were only ten applicants, and the gypsy astrologer, Domenico Bernardi, knew his market when in 1760 he advertised a secret method of 'ensuring' the provision of heirs to 'families of importance, which are threatened with lack of offspring.' In 1740 the last Grimani-Calergi died without issue; a rich branch of the Valieri suffered the same fate, and many others were well on the way to disappearing too.

Pensions paid to poor nobles rose from 39,532 in 1736 to 102,692 in 1775, and to 130,179 in 1790. On the other hand the wealth that most of the rich families left tended to gravitate to other wealthy families with whom they were connected. So did the plum government jobs – the embassies to Rome, Vienna and Madrid, for example, which paid anything up to 12,000 – and much the same seems to have happened to the Church. The fifth Venetian Pope, Clement XIII, elected in 1758, was a Rezzonico, a family which kept one of the very richest palaces in Venice, and it had long been customary for a nobleman, often a close relation of a Doge, to become Patriarch of Venice.

The ruling caste was perched upon a dangerously shrinking base of power and, apart from its constant concern to muzzle opposition, its administration of affairs was languid. The Signoria was only slightly more positive in its response to the changing political climate than the *ancien régime* in France, and it was soon to pay a similar price.

There had been hints of revolution for some time, not least within the ranks of the nobility itself. As early as 1741 Lorenzo Tiepolo had been placed under house arrest for urging that the powers of the Inquisition and the Ten be curbed. Francesco Foscari was similarly penalized in 1756, and some five years later Angelo Quirini, a new champion of the poorer nobility, was imprisoned for yet another attack on the Republic's all-powerful agencies of security and censorship. He was released two years later after some hectic debates in the Senate over the advisability of reform. And opposition within the ruling caste did not end there.

Quirini left for France in 1777, there to consort with the arch-critic of contemporary societies, Voltaire; but others took his place. In 1779 Carlo Contarini, spokesman for the poorer nobles, complained that 'everything' was 'in a mess. . . . Our commerce is languishing, as the number of bankruptcies continually prove; food is exorbitantly expensive; and what used to suffice to maintain our families and left a margin to help the state, is now insufficient to keep us alive.'

When he was arrested, Giorgio Pisani fulminated against 'the disproportions in wealth . . . unwarranted exactions' and government waste, demanded increased pay for poorer magistrates, promotion by seniority, better dowries for noble girls, and even threatened to overthrow the ruling clique and redistribute wealth in favour of the poor.

Pisani had the cap of liberty printed on his visiting cards, but though his stand (for which he and his friends were imprisoned in 1780) was made in the name of equality and fraternity, it was meant only to benefit the poor among the noble class. In this Venice was conforming roughly to the pattern in contemporary France, where the Revolution was to be precipitated by a revolt of the nobility. As in France, too, there were diffuse rumblings among non-noble industrialists and widespread discontent among the largely inarticulate peasantry. The ordinary Venetian knew no more of Rousseau and the *philosophes* than did the *sans-culottes* in Paris – and he had rather less cause to rebel, since although bread prices rose, they did not approach the rate of increase that they did in Paris in 1789. Nevertheless, the Venetian government was in a very nervous mood.

Its nervousness was reflected in its enthusiastic response to reactionary trends within the church. In 1772 restrictions on the number of priests were removed and the Jesuits were read-mitted. True the rich Benedictine monastries were among others dissolved between 1770 and 1793 (bringing another 35,000 acres into secular hands, a third of it into the ownership of the nobility), but the Republic's dire need of a lightning conductor to divert growing discontent led it to oppress the Jews again. When Pope Pius VI revived the worst features of the ghetto system in 1775 Venice followed suit almost immediately. From 1777 Jews were forbidden to employ Christians, barred from manufacturing, brokering and property ownership, and forced to wear the long-abandoned scarlet hat. In the 1780s their conditions were eased a little, but life remained unpleasant for them, and with their wealth long since milked into the state exchequer they sank further into poverty. By such means did the Republic stand up to the challenge of the Enlightenment. It was a stance based on nervousness rather than conviction, and it was doomed to fail.

Venetian society was too literate not to be subject to a high rate of cultural osmosis. Even the anti-semitic Andrea Tron read Voltaire and became the lover, and ultimately the husband, of Caterina Delfin, Venice's answer to Mme. Geoffrin, the celebrated and 'enlightened' Parisian hostess. The *Encyclopaedia*, that Bible of sceptical rationalism, was published at Padua; freemasons formed secret lodges, and the Spaderia and the Ancilotto cafés became notorious as meeting-places for people of advanced political ideas.

But flirtations with ideas alone do not make revolutions. Discontent among the inarticulate mass of the population is usually required to overturn a governmental system, and one barometer of such discontent is crime. No fewer than 73,000 people had been executed or given a life sentence with the galleys between 1741 and 1762, and the tightening of the Venetian policing system suggests a continuing undercurrent of unrest. The local *sbirri* were supplemented now by quasi-military gendarmes; and the Ten's special agent, Cristoforo Cristolfi, was said to be worth a battalion of grenadiers since crowds tended to melt away spontaneously whenever he appeared.

The army, on the other hand, though it cost considerable sums, was in a very sorry state. Its officers were corrupt, the troops were dressed in rags, and musketry practice was actually forbidden in order to save powder. These were the years in which the government built the great sea walls which still serve as her main barriers against the sea – yet Venice was otherwise incapable of defending herself. As Doge Paolo Renier himself admitted, 'we live by luck. . . . We depend entirely on the idea of Venetian prudence which other people have about us.'

Yet Renier himself personified the corruption of the system. According to one senior minister, he owed this election in 1779 to buying 300 votes at fifteen ducats apiece. He also sold state offices and even licences to beg. More attractively, he is said to have married a former rope-dancer from Constantinople called Margaret Dalmaz. Yet for all the gossip Doge Renier was no greedier than many of his predecessors. He was a fine orator, a shrewd politician, and the talk that he engendered reflected less on him personally than on the sorry state of the Republic as a whole.

The once-great city state exuded decadence out of every pore. Living off gambling, charity and tourism, and kept in order by the Ten, the system was as decrepit as some of the elderly ladies the young William Beckford described puffing French horns and bassoons in the orchestra of the Pietà. Drains overflowed; the streets were mucky when it rained; but the city was still beguiling. Lights glimmered at night from every window and from every gondola; musicians travelling on illuminated barges filled the evening air with serenades. But like an old whore, the city seemed more attractive after sunset than by daylight, and like the penurious old courtesan she was, she offered her embraces to almost any passing stranger.

In 1782 she welcomed the ugly and awkward Grand Duke Paul of Russia, posing ineffectually as the 'Count of the North.' Venice applied all her cosmetics for the occasion. There were rich illuminations, presentations, vast feasts, gala operas, balls and presentations. The client and his entourage, however, paid only half their bill for lodgings, left no tips at the Arsenal banquet, and gave nothing for the orphanage girls as was the custom. Paul did deliver a compliment: Venice, he was overheard to remark, 'showed the effect of good government,' and the Venetian people formed 'but a single family.' No doubt this was a diplomatic courtesy of the sort state visitors are primed to make by their advisers; it was nevertheless a foolish statement from a foolish prince.

Only ten per cent of the 1,200 surviving nobles were men of substance; only 300 gondoliers were in permanent employment, whereas once there were 3,000. The number of jobs was declining, although the population had not diminished; yet in 1787 the number of public holidays was reduced on the grounds that they encouraged 'idleness.' The jollifications during the harsh winter of 1788, when bonfires were lit and games were played on the frozen lagoon, served to distract attention from the high mortality from cold and exposure; and by 1789 almost a sixth of the city's population lived on charity.

The hinterland was rife with disaffection. The towns were poor, and though the armament shops of Bergamo still found customers, the textile looms had ground virtually to a standstill. Employment in the silk industry slumped from 12,000 in 1750 to a mere thousand by 1792, and the great peasant majority was worse off than it had been for years. Overseas the administration was corrupt – peasants were bled by taxation, and virtually none of the revenue was spent on local needs. The rich island of Corfu had two million olive trees thanks to earlier government subsidies, but so much of the corn it produced was reserved for export that its people often starved.

Only a police régime and the absence of any effective focus to unite the disparate groups of malcontents preserved the Republic. Noblemen dared not even discuss politics in the privacy of the salons now, and the exaggerated suspicion with which Goethe was met by stupid officials when he arrived at the Venetian outpost of Malcesine on Lake Garda in 1786 hoping for spiritual renewal, symbolized the trembling fear with which Venice regarded her neighbours. Venice was no longer 'this beaver-republic,' as Goethe described her, and seeing the aged Doge in golden gown and ermine cape, surrounded by a host of cheerful-looking noblemen in bright blond wigs, he could not suspect the fear that these men felt.

When Doge Paolo Renier died in February 1789 the announcement of his death was delayed lest the news disturb the Carnival. On March 9th, Ludovico Manin, a noble of very recent lineage, was elected to succeed. Eight weeks later the States General met at Versailles. The Revolution was already under way in France – and it would soon touch Venice.

The Venetian government increased its vigilance but otherwise did not react. The city's shops still opened up at dawn; Venetians in employment still worked until the sun went down; and Senators showed no greater interest in state affairs.

According to Giovanni Pindemonte, its sessions consisted of a succession of decrees read at breakneck speed to which members paid hardly any attention. They would stroll about the room chattering among themselves, and in winter tended to leave the chamber altogether and huddle round the fire in an adjoining room. When the decrees had been read they would be voted on *in toto*, whereupon the sessions would be immediately adjourned. The success of a meeting was gauged solely by the time taken to transact this business. If it went quickly the shout 'a short Senate' would go up and the Senators would rush off happily like prover-bial boys out of school; if it took longer they would fret and fidget, impatient to return to their pleasures. 'Perfumed tables, gilded carriages, splendid equipages, music, dancing, gardens, gambling, theatres and debauchery,' wrote another contemporary 'were the only objects which excited any interest' at all.

A state visit by the Emperor Leopold II in 1791 showed relations with Austria to be cordial. Yet, despite the urging of diplomatists and others, the Republic steered well clear of an alliance. Even when France moved towards extremism and ultimately to the idea of exporting revolution the Republic maintained its cautious neutrality. There was some logic in this policy. The Republic might not be democratic, but neither was it a monarchy or absolutist as the principal states in Europe were. Furthermore, Venice was afraid that her powerful neighbour Austria might ultimately decide to swallow her up as it had helped to swallow up Poland. Absolute neutrality seemed to be the only answer. The Venetian empire constituted a power vacuum, but her government threatened no one – and hoped no one would threaten her.

So alliance with Austria was repeatedly declined; no offence was taken when the Venetian embassy in Paris was attacked; and though Venice gave asylum to France's future King Louis XVIII for a time, she also exchanged envoys with the French revolutionary government. In February 1795, when the Venetian Resident in Basel warned that the French intended to invade Italy, the Signoria gave no credence to him. France and Austria would fight it out on the Rhineland. There seemed no prospect of the war extending to Venetian territory.

On Ascension Day 1796, Doge Manin and his attendant cohorts of grinning noblemen were rowed out to the Lido as usual upon the *Bucintoro* to act out the ancient ceremony of the 'Marriage with the Sea.' On its return the crew was treated to a splendid dinner. It began with Spanish bread, puff pastry, cream, oranges, and salted tongue; continued with tripe, liver, boiled calves feet, pigeons, roast veal and turkey and concluded with custards, cream cheese, apples, asparagus, fennel, artichokes, prunes, dried chestnuts, cakes and comfits. There was a bottle of muscatel beside each place, and as much wine as any man could drink. It reads like a banquet to end all banquets, and appropriately so, for, though no one present knew it, the *Bucintoro* had taken its last voyage.

In the summer of 1796 French troops under General Buonaparte suddenly overran Piedmont and Lombardy and beat the Austrian armies (which had crossed Venetian territory to engage him) at Marengo. The French then proceeded to bivouac in the western provinces of the Venetian *terraferma*, and the Venetian government was forced reluctantly to act. Orders went out to improve the defences of the lagoon; the fleet was called in; troops were recruited in Dalmatia, Istria, Albania and the Ionian Islands, and levies assembled in the *terraferma*. A new forced loan was raised, new taxes were imposed on servants, gondolas, landlords and tenants, a tithe was demanded from the church, and offices were sold to raise more money. But alliances were still avoided. Austria, Naples, Rome and Savoy were welcome to oppose the French intruders; the Republic would not align with them. Part of the *terraferma* might be lost, but the experience of the League of Cambrai war almost three centuries before had shown that the Republic would probably regain them.

An offer of alliance with the French was similarly refused, for fear that it would bring an Austrian attack, but though Venice rejected a French protest about her military preparations she did eventually agree to countenance the presence of French troops in her territory for a six months' period – and in return for a million francs.

The very presence of the revolutionary army in the *terraferma* acted like a catalyst, however. Some journalists dared to write in praise of liberty, and there was some heady talk among the young of revolution and of that meteoric hero Buonaparte. In the countryside the requisitions of the invading troops caused some resentment, but many peasants were even more resentful of landlords and came to see the French as saviours.

Early in 1797 there was a popular rising in the countryside of Bergamo. With French help, the insurgents disarmed the local police, plundered the provincial treasury and proclaimed a state of freedom. A similar movement soon overtook Brescia. Its Governor fled and the insurgents, led by a citizen called Fantucci, declared that they had 'recovered their natural rights.' Crowds of rebels advanced on village after village, demolishing customs houses, erecting trees of liberty, revolutionizing the people. Crema rejected the Republic's rule that March; so did the town of Salo on Lake Garda.

Counter-revolutionary 'patriotic' movements were also organized, always with the support of the local clergy, who were solid in their opposition to the 'godless' revolution. But the scattered clashes between partisans and rival villages often had more to do with rights to land and personal grudges than high-flown ideas of patriotism and freedom. Moreover, the French not only actively encouraged the anti-aristocratic cause, they actually helped local rebels occupy particular Venetian strong-points, including Peschiera.

Venice protested to Buonaparte in vain; and when the French demanded that the Dalmatian Slavs in the garrison of Verona be withdrawn, since on April 17th they had attacked French troops outside the citadel, the Venetian government complied. With only a few Italian troops left to defend it, Verona soon fell into revolutionary hands – and the French now took to the offensive openly.

'Friends and citizens,' ran their proclamation to the people of Vicenza, 'the perfidious nobles of Venice have . . . forced you to take up arms against the phalanxes of Buonaparte. . . . But the Signoria had already decided to withdraw its troops from Vicenza – and from Padua and Treviso too – to concentrate on the defence of the lagoon.

The calamitous rush of events had produced a predictable run on the Banco Giro. But the bank remained solvent, and it seemed, too, that the city itself might be successfully defended. A plan of defence had been drawn up; troops were pouring in from the *terraferma*; and citizens were being mobilized. Stocks of food were adequate, and the fact that an Alberghetti still supervised the the casting of artillery at the Arsenal, as his forefathers had done ever since 1487, strengthened the feeling that the city which had never yet been conquered would not be taken now.

On 29th April 1797 the Senate, fortified in its determination by a rumour that the French and Austrians had agreed to carve up the Venetian empire between them, urged the adoption of further defence measures. Propaganda was prepared calling Buonaparte 'an Attila' and the French invaders Huns, and when a French ship the *Liberator of Italy* tried to enter the lagoon the comman-dant of Fort San Andrea opened fire and killed its captain.

L

This act of defiance was to prove a solitary one, however. On April 30th the Doge, the six counsellors, the three heads of the Quarantia al Criminale, the six *Savii Grandi,* the Chiefs of the Ten, and the *Savii* responsible for the abandoned *terraferma* met to consider a French ultimatum, which demanded the release of all political prisoners, the expulsion of the British envoy and the introduction of a democratic form of government. They decided to agree to the release of the prisoners and to negotiate the form the new government should take with the French. In effect they had decided to capitulate, yet their judgement was as shrewd in its way as old Doge Dandolo's when he had diverted the fourth Crusade to take Constantinople almost six centuries before.

It had become clear that the population of the city was divided and that a popular rising might command the support of as many as 15,000 people. A rebellion and a French attack could not be coped with simultaneously; resistance would damage the precious fabric of the city and put property at risk. But a complaisant attitude might yet allow something to be salvaged from the wreck of fortune, and when the Doge put the cabinet's collective recommendation to the Great Council it was clear that the government had judged the mood of the nobility correctly too. There were 598 votes in favour of the motion: only seven against. But by the time the two Venetian negotiators reached French headquarters at Marghera, Buonaparte had received news of the resistance offered to the French ship. He now demanded the arrest of the fort commandant responsible and the three Inquisitors of State before he would negotiate.

The path had been chosen and had to be followed to the end. Josafa Priuli, Filippo Calbo and a Querini, all of whom wanted to resist, were shouted down and on May 4th the Great Council duly agreed to Buonaparte's demands. The Republic, however, was not to be allowed to die in peace. Rumours of the proceedings had leaked out to the public. Tommaso Zorzi, a Venetian grocer and leader of the city's democrats, was already demanding a place in the government, and while ministers tried to persuade him to be patient for a day or two the Republic's Slavic soldiers were in uproar. Angry about their pay arrears – and probably stirred up by members of the pro-war faction – they had begun distributing handbills accusing the Signoria of betraying the people, annoying the French Minister, and burning down Zorzi's house. Rumours abounded and grew fantastic in the telling. People were fearful, angry and confused.

Concerned above all now to stave off anarchy, the Signoria paid off the Slavs and arranged to ship them home. Then on the morning of the 9th May 1797, having failed to bribe the French into offering better terms, the Doge's conference decided by a majority of ten to seven to accept the latest French demands. Three days later the matter came before the Great Council.

The atmosphere was tense as Doge Manin made his final speech to the barely half-full chamber. He proposed that they accept his abdication, proclaim a provisional government, pay a sizeable war indemnity, surrender the Empire and the best part of the fleet, and, finally, abolish their own status as noblemen. As he spoke the sound of shots was heard. The Slavs were making a riotous departure. The session was rushed to an undignified end: 512 in favour, twenty against – and the ex-nobles rushed home to secure their property.

Mobs were already on the streets shouting 'Viva San Marco,' looting, fighting. The gold was torn off the *Bucintoro*, the statues of 'Strength' and 'Prudence' which flanked the Doge's throne were smashed. Cannon were fired, but even so the police could not keep order, and chaos ruled for four days until Venetian ships at last brought in French troops. Only then was the Great Council's last decision publicly announced.

There were some shouts of anger; some cheers of hope. Venice, the 'eldest Child of Liberty,' had lost independence; the Republic which had survived a thousand years was dead.

Epilogue

The French ransacked the Arsenal, carried off the four bronze horses which Dandolo had taken from Byzantium, toppled the marble lion from its column in the Piazzetta and erected a Tree of Liberty in the Square. The gates of the ghetto were ceremoniously torn down; a new calendar was introduced with a new 'revolutionary' name for every month, and the Golden Book of the nobility was burned.

Venice was now a democratic 'provisional municipality,' and a regatta was held to celebrate the fact. But Venetians still bowed, as if by reflex, to the occasional ex-nobleman who passed them in the streets; a Committee of Public Safety took the place of the Council of Ten, and those who had benefited from the new régime did not rejoice for long. In January 1798 the French handed Venice over to the Austrians.

At once the order of things was overturned again. Slogans proclaiming 'the Rights of Man' were painted out, the local government was disbanded, and the Jews, so recently enfranchised, lost their civic rights. When Russian troops under their brilliant and eccentric leader Suvorov poured through the Veneto in 1799 to help throw the French out of the rest of Italy, Venetians might well have wondered whom they would belong to next – but in 1805 they were signed over to the French.

Venice was proclaimed part of the new Kingdom of Italy and Eugene de Beauharnais 'Prince of Venice.' Jews regained their civil rights; the remains of the *Bucintoro* were converted into a gun-ship called the *Hydra*; the Banco Giro was wound up and the Monte Napoleone floated; the monasteries were dissolved, public parks laid out, and the Scuola di Santa Maria della Carità converted into the Accademia art gallery. Venice was made a free port again and her ships allowed to trade with any country except England – though the activity of the English Navy in the Mediterranean inhibited a trade revival, and adjustment generally was very difficult.

Some men of prominence, including Giovanni Pindemonte, made their peace with the new régime and even took a part in government, but many others took deep steps down in the world. The proud Pisanis sold Napoleon their splendid villa at Stra, and although some ex-nobles retained considerable fortunes and estates the incessant process by which the new rich supersede the old progressed with greater speed than hitherto.

The Jews, so recently noted for their poverty, were soon to be counted among the more prosperous of the commercial class, but the class itself was neither as numerous nor as wealthy as formerly. Napoleonic Europe provided no stability for markets, especially those for the luxury goods in which Venice specialized. The Cozzi porcelain factory had to close down in 1812, and Venetian industry as a whole suffered seriously from the Napoleonic wars, particularly from a blockade which continued throughout the winter of 1813–14.

After the war, Venice became an Austrian province once again, but though the restoration of the imperial régime, exercised by a Viceroy who resided in Venice and in Milan in turn, brought stability it brought considerable disadvantages as well. Taxation was heavy. Lombardy and Venetia contributed a quarter of the entire tax income of the Empire, although they only accounted for an eighth of its population, and though the intellectual climate benefited from increased contacts with a wider academic world, university professors were appointed from Vienna and imperial propaganda was disseminated in Venetian schools. The press was censored more stringently than ever – even Dante was subject to correction – and the power of the Church was now unchallengeable. But it was the pervasive infiltration of German culture which aroused the greatest resentment.

Police spies and informers had been features of the Venetian scene for centuries, but the security services were now run by men of an alien culture; the *Bucintoro* was now used as a prison ship and Venetians found it distasteful to account in German zwanzigers and florins. Few Venetians wanted the old Republic restored, but people, particularly of the middle class, hankered increasingly after independence and revolutionary ideas sown by the revolution and fed by xenophobia were ultimately to blossom into a new form of civic patriotism.

The grounds for resentment were cultural, for Austrian rule brought considerable economic benefits despite taxation. The money system was stable; Venice was still the entrepôt for the Austrian-dominated *terraferma*, and enjoyed the additional benefit of being part of the greater Austrian market, while the port's free trading privileges encouraged a steady flow of traffic. The number of arrivals and departures at the port of Venice rose by fifteen per cent between 1817 and 1850, and though an increasing proportion of these ships left empty, production of the city's industries nevertheless increased, albeit slowly, and employment was rising after the calamitous slump which had followed the fall of the Republic.

The manufacture of mirrors, beads and artificial pearls provided jobs for as many as 4,500 hands, even though a high proportion of those employed were women and children. Other traditional crafts like the manufacture of gold and silver, brocade, lace, velvet, leather goods, soap, pottery, candles, and sugar also saw increases. Venice, even after its decline, remained the chief printing centre in Italy; the Arsenal ticked over, albeit at a low rate, as did the private shipyards of the lagoon, and if many members of the lagoon population were still dependent on fishing and seafaring the railway soon came to boost employment.

A thousand men were taken on to build the first bridge linking Venice with the hinterland, and the opening in 1846 of the Venice–Vicenza railway which ran over it provided an important stimulus to the economy.

Nevertheless, contemporary visitors were impressed above

all by the sad decay and fading glamour of the city. Byron had savoured its dying glory, and most of the Romantics who followed him noticed both an almost ghost-like quality in the place and a certain passivity among its people. Turner, Sickert, Boudin, and Manet were all to find inspiration in the city which once had been such a splendid nursery for great artists; but the latter-day standard-bearers of the great tradition – Canaletto, G. B. Tiepolo, Guardi – had long since passed into oblivion. So had Cimarosa, and the musical performances at St. Mark's, once so splendid, were, in the opinion of at least one English observer, nothing short of disastrous these days.

The descendants of the old nobility lived on the past, dutifully recording the genealogies of their ancestors, treasuring their remaining heirlooms and recounting the former glories of their Republic. Lesser Venetians manned an increasing number of hotels, pensions, shops and cafés to serve the visitors who flocked in. By 1847 the Royal Danaeli Hotel, housed in what was once the Nani-Mocenigo Palace, was recognized as the best in Venice. Florian's was already famous among the cafés, but though Florian's provided French newspapers and fork breakfasts and suppers, it was expensive and would not permit smoking, so the officers of the Austrian garrison and most visiting Germans addicted to the pipe favoured the Café Quadri, while such Venetians of quality as the city still contained tended to segregate themselves at the Café Suttil.

Operas and ballet still drew large audiences to the Fenice theatre; the old San Benedetto theatre still functioned; dramas were performed at the Teatro Apollo, comic opera at the Teatro San Samuele and circus acts at the Teatro Malibran.

Yet a powerful undercurrent of discontent was swelling up beneath the regular leisurely pace of life in the Venice of the 1840s. Alien rule was no longer a novelty and the Venetian working-man was probably as well off as he had ever been. The Austrians were no more popular for that, but it was the more affluent, literate classes rather than the workers who were restless. Their ideal was liberal, democratic, nationalist, and it is ironic that their first major protest should have taken the form of opposition to the one truly progressive act of the government – the plan to extend Venice's railway to link up with Milan.

This protest evokes a picture of outraged conservatives fighting for the *status quo* – yet the signatories to it included Daniele Manin and other heroes of the 'bourgeois-liberal' movement. Manin, a lawyer, was a member of the 'middle class,' yet the 'liberation movement' which he was to lead harked backward to an idealized pride in the old Republic, and was triggered into action by developments outside Venice.

Early in 1848 there was a rising in Sicily and constitutions were granted to four Italian states. This news provoked disturbances in Padua and then in Venice – at which the Austrians arrested Manin and his fellow agitators and proclaimed martial law. But on the evening on 17th March 1848 news arrived of a revolution in Vienna itself.

A crowd rushed to the prison to demand the release of Manin and his colleagues, and the Austrian governor, rattled by the news from Vienna of events in his own capital, complied. He even allowed the formation of Civil Guards – yet it was not until Milan rebelled that Manin was pressurized by his following into taking action. On 22nd March 1848 the Venetian revolutionaries, including the new Civil Guard, marched. They seized the Arsenal and persuaded the Austrians, who lacked sufficient troops to suppress them, to leave without a fight. Amid scenes of great rejoicing Venice was proclaimed an independent republic again – the Republic of St. Mark.

Manin was declared its President, and all Venetians to be equal. But the Venetian revolution had been part of a movement affecting the whole of Italy, and Italian nationalism competed with local patriotism for the allegiance both of the people and their leaders, and Pan-Italian nationalist sentiment seems to have gained ground as the Austrians set out to re-establish their authority. A motley array of Piedmontese soldiers and north Italian citizens in arms prepared to throw the Austrians out of northern Italy. Imperial troops were repulsed from Vicenza and then the Piedmontese defeated Marshal Radetzky and took Peschiera. But from then on the Austrians had it all their own way.

Vicenza fell, then Treviso, Padua and Rovigo, and, realizing that their Republic could not stand alone and preferring an Italian King to an Austrian Emperor, the Venetian government reluctantly followed Milan, Piacenza, Modena and Parma in declaring for union with Piedmont. Manin withdrew into private life. But on the very day, 6th August 1848, that the Piedmontese Commissioners arrived in Venice the Austrians reoccupied Milan. Five days later Austria and Piedmont concluded an armistice, and at this the Venetian democrats decided to take their city's fate into their own hands once again. The Piedmontese Commissioners were expelled, Manin was acclaimed dictator, and while the revolution collapsed in the rest of Italy, Venice prepared herself for battle.

Venetians were encouraged when early in 1849 Garibaldi and Mazzini captured Rome and declared it a Republic. The Hungarian rising still distracted the Austrians; volunteers drifted in from all parts of Italy to help Manin's régime, and appeals for aid went out to the liberal governments of England and of France. But though hopes stood high the odds were stacked against the new Republic.

One by one the forts surrounding the lagoon fell into Austrian hands, the city came under street blockade and from 30th June 1849 under artillery bombardment. The Roman Republic collapsed that summer; the Hungarian revolt was quelled; the support from England and France which Manin counted on did not materialize, and the enemy was prepared to offer only the harshest of surrender terms.

Venice had held out for almost eight weeks, as cannon balls whistled in to rip through Tintoretto's paintings in the Scuola di San Rocco and damage almost every important building in the city. Yet Venice was to reach starvation point and be racked by cholera before, on 24th August 1849, Manin finally resigned and sailed away to exile.

Venice surrendered; and the black and yellow flags of Austria flew once more above St. Mark's. But resentment against the Austrians did not diminish – indeed a plot was hatched to kidnap the Emperor Franz Josef when he came to Venice in 1852. Yet although feeling undoubtedly ran high, the shrewd Ruskin, who lived among the Venetians through two winters in the 1850s, conducting his curious autopsy upon the body of Venetian architecture, observed no repression, and 'never once was able to ascertain, from any liberal Italian, that he had a single definite ground of complaint against the Government. There was much general grumbling and vague discontent; but I never was able . . . to discover what it was that they wanted, or in what way they felt themselves injured.'

Austria was bending over backwards, in fact, to placate local opinion. By 1857, when Franz Josef and the Empress paid Venice a state visit, all the harsher aspects of the régime had been relaxed and then the amiable Archduke Maximilian was installed as Governor. Yet the liberals had all the inertia of self-styled men of principle. 'We don't want Austria to mend her ways,' wrote Manin from his Paris exile, 'we want her to go.' And at last, in its ponderous way, the Austrian government did come round to the idea of going.

In 1866 they actually offered to hand Venetia over to the King of Piedmont (under whom the rest of Italy had been united after the war of 1859) in return for his neutrality in any Austrian war with Prussia. But the King was already allied to Prussia, so it took the Prussian victory at Königgräz to wrench Venice out of Austria's lax grip.

Venetia was ceded to France, which was to conduct a plebiscite on the question of union with Italy – much to the annoyance of Garibaldi, who had planned to invade Venetia himself and was outraged by the Venetians' failure to liberate themselves. But the conclusion was no less satisfactory for the lack of blood. The plebiscite produced the anticipated majority and Venice achieved her quietus at last – as capital of an Italian *préfecture*.

The Foscari Palace was emptied of Imperial troops – and gradually, and sadly, the city was also emptied of the last descendants of the Doges. In 1864 the last male Mocenigo and the last Grimani died – by which time their handsome family palaces had become respectively a hotel and a post office. The last of the Sagredo line, which traced its lineage back a thousand years, was buried in 1871; and the last surviving Contarini, a clan which had produced eight Doges, eked out the remainder of his days in an obscure lodging-house.

Venetian palaces meanwhile became fashionable for strangers to die in. Richard Wagner, who had composed *Tristan* in one such palace, died in another in 1883; and in 1889 Robert Browning expired in the great Ca' Rezzonico, which he had bought some years before – by which time the first steam launch had made its appearance on the Grand Canal, and the city, so long stranded in the economic doldrums, was beginning to share in an economic renaissance.

The railway which the Austrians had introduced was followed by steam power and electricity. The Arsenal was enlarged and soon employed as many men as it had done in its prime, while, thanks to the opening of the Suez Canal in 1869, considerable sums were invested in port improvements and Venice was soon handling tonnages of a magnitude formerly undreamt of. Industrial production grew in proportion, placing such pressure on the available communications that by 1906 a new causeway was planned capable of carrying electric trains and motors cars.

Improved communications brought in more tourists and still more wealth, and the ordinary Venetian's standard of living rose quite sharply. Between 1882 and 1907 prices rose by about thirty per cent; but wages outpaced them. Fewer children went about barefoot; the worst slum properties disappeared. Yet complaints were already being voiced about smoke from factory chimneys and the visitations of ever larger ships.

Since then the Campanile has collapsed and been rebuilt, Venice has survived two great wars – and still the blessings and curses of the industrial age are debated, more particularly since November 1966, when a sudden storm breached the sea-wall and the flood tide rose a full six feet in the Piazza.

The fear of Venice sinking beneath the sea is as old as the city itself, and the level of the Piazza has been raised repeatedly throughout the ages. High waters were recorded as early as the ninth century; the island of Malamocco was actually swallowed up in 1102, and in 1339, so the chroniclers reported, 'the city was in exceeding danger of drowning.' Nevertheless, if the flood-line was rising at a rate of nine centimetres per century in 1900 it is rising at ten times that rate today.

The possible reasons for this – the shrinkage of the polar ice-cap, the movement of the Alps and Apennines, the effect of artesian wells in reducing the highly pressurized water level on which the entire area rests, the gradual reduction of the lagoon basin (a point which the observant Goethe noticed two centuries ago) – have all been hotly contested. But in the main the accusa-tions have been levelled against industry – at the deep channels dredged to serve the industrial complex of Mestre-Marghera, at the great ships which plough their way through the lagoon, and at pollution.

The problems are being tackled. The Italian government's new law for Venice may (or may not) procure sufficient funds to allow the installation of special floodgates at the entrances to the lagoon, the repair of the sea walls, and the building of aqueducts as alternatives to artesian wells. There are plans to improve Venice's housing, to modernize factories and fight pollution, while UNESCO has mounted an international appeal to restore the rotting fabric of many of the city's buildings. The attempt to save Venice may be successful, although nothing less than a new canal by which ships could reach the industrial zones without entering the lagoon at all (as recommended in the as yet neglected Tosi plan) seems likely to provide a long-term solution in view of the projected increases in the size of ships. But even if Venice is to be saved physically the danger remains of its being preserved as an exhibit under glass, divorced from the ordinary Venetians who give the city life.

The age of industry has already humbled her as Popes and Emperors, never could. The population declines year by year as people abandon apartments liable to flood and move out to the industrial suburbs. Meanwhile the original city is fast being taken over by the property speculator, the rich outsider, and in summer by the invading hordes of tourists – many of whom show greater delight at the pigeons in the Piazza than at the mosaics of St. Mark's.

But on November 21st each year the exiles return home and, together with Venetians still residing in the city, swarm in vast numbers to the great church of Santa Maria della Salute. It is the only great *andate* of the old Venetian calendar still celebrated with fervour. Then and only then does Venice belong to herself. For the rest, as if ashamed of her abased role in the world as tourist trap, dormitory suburb, and fun fair for the jet set, she settles slowly into the waters, clutching her vast treasure to her bosom.

Bibliographical Note

A comprehensive bibliography of Venetian history is obviously far beyond the scope of these few pages. Instead, I have set out to indicate some of the principal printed sources, to list a selection of other books which I found particularly useful, and to suggest titles, both scholarly and popular, for further reading, placing special emphasis on works in English. Books have been roughly categorized as 'general,' 'economic,' 'constitutional,' 'social,' etc., but the inclusion of a title under one heading is not to suggest that it may not also be relevant in other contexts. There is simply no room for repetition.

Although this book has been based on printed and, for the most part, secondary sources, the basic collections of documents in the Archivio di Stato in Venice and the manuscript collections of the Marciana Library and the Museo Correr must be mentioned. So far as primary printed sources are concerned, the Deputazione veneto di storia patria (later the Deputazione di storia patria per le Venezia) has published many statutes, chronicles, memoirs and miscellanea, and others continue to appear in the Archivio di Stato's *Fonti per la Storia di Venezia*. Particular collections include Roberto Cessi's *Documenti relativi alla storica di Venetia anteriori al mille* (2 vols., Padua, 1942), on the very early period, and on Great Council decisions his *Deliberazioni del Maggior Consiglio* (Acts of the Italian Constitutional Assemblies, 1950). Reports of Venetian ambassadors abroad are contained in E. Albèri's *Relazione degli ambasciatori veneti al Serato* (Florence, 1839–63), and the course of Anglo-Venetian relations from 1202 to 1675 is described by the *Calendar of State Papers Venetian* (38 vols., 1864-1940), while the most convenient collection of foreign ambassadors' reports from Venice is the microfilm collection of the Giorgio Cini Foundation in Venice. Chronicles and memoirs especially worth mentioning include those of Martino da Canal (*Cronaca veneziana in lingua francese dalle origini al 1275*, Florence, 1972) and Domenico Malipiero (*Annali veneti dell'anno 1457 al 1500* Archivio Storico Italiano, series 1, VII, Florence, 1843), the diaries of Girolamo Priuli (*Rerum Italicarum Scriptores* Città di Castello, 1911, and Bologna, 1933-8) and of Marino Sanuto (58 vols., Deputazione veneto di storia patria, Venice, 1879-1903).

The basic journals of Venetian historical studies are the successive series of the *Archivio Veneto, Nuovo Archivio Veneto* and *Archivio Veneto-Tridentino*, while the *Bollettino dell'Istituto di Storia della Società e dello Stato Veneziano* and *Studi Veneziani* record much modern scholarship, as do the *Civiltà veneziana: Studi* series of the Cini Foundation's historical section, their *Civiltà europea e civiltà veneziana: Aspetti e problemi* series and their invaluable series of symposia (all published in Florence) dealing with various aspects of Venetian civilization from the beginnings to the nineteenth century, viz. – *Le Origini di Venezia* (1964), *La Venezia del mille* (1965), *Venezia dalla prima crociata alla conquista de Constantinopoli del 1204* (1966), *La Civiltà veneziana del secolo di Marco Polo* (1955), *La Civiltà veneziana del Trecento* (1956), *La Civiltà veneziana del Quattrocento* (1957), *La Civiltà veneziana del Rinascimento* (1958), *La Civiltà veneziana nell'Età barocca* (1959), *La Civiltà veneziana del Settecento* (1960), *La civiltà veneziana dell'Età romantica* (1961), and *Venezia nell'Unità d'Italia* (1962).

Samuele Romanin's *Storia documentata della repubblica di Venezia* (10 vols., 1853-61; new ed., Venice, 1912-21) is the basic general history and also contains much primary source material. Its French counterpart is Pierre Daru's *Histoire de la République de Venise* (9 vols., Paris, 1853). General histories in English include Horatio Brown's *Venice: an historical sketch of the Republic* (London, 1893), Alathea Wiel's *Venice* (London, 1894) and W. Carew

Hazlitt's rather dry *The Venetian Republic* (2 vols., London, 1900). W. R. Thayer's racy *A Short History of Venice* (New York, 1905), the last straightforward survey I have found in English, appeared almost seventy years ago, but in German there is H. Kretschmayr's solid *Geschichte von Venedig* (3 vols., Gotha-Stuttgart, 1905-34), while the most important recent general work is Cessi's *Storia della repubblica di Venezia* (2 vols., Milan-Messina, 1944-6).

Studies of particular periods include Cessi's contribution to the *New Cambridge Medieval History* (Vol. IV, Cambridge, 1966, including an excellent bibliography on pp. 868-80). Horatio Brown's chapters in the *Cambridge Medieval History* and the *Cambridge Modern History*, though old-fashioned and concerned primarily with political developments, are not to be despised; nor are the conscientious and often tedious histories by Francis Hodgson (*The Early History of Venice*, London, 1901, and *Venice in the 13th and 14th Centuries*, London, 1910). David Chambers's *The Imperial Age of Venice 1380-1580* (London, 1970) is admirably bright, concise and up-to-date; the symposium on *Renaissance Venice* edited by J. R. Hale (London, 1973) contains some high-powered scholarly essays (though it appeared too late for me to take account of it in writing this book) and Fernand Braudel's monumental *The Mediterranean and the Mediterranean World in the Age of Philip II*, (2 vols., London, 1972-3) is rich in references to Venice. W. J. Bouwsma's *Venice and the Defence of Republican Liberty* (Berkeley, 1968) is thorough in its treatment of ideas and politics of those most popular periods among contemporary historians of Venice, the Renaissance and Reformation, while G. Benzoni has recently produced a useful synthesis on *Venezia nell'Éta della Controreforma* (Milan, 1973). Maurice Rowdon's amusing *The Fall of Venice* (London, 1970) is one of the few popular books in English dealing with the neglected final period of the Republic.

More serious studies dealing with particular personalities, crises and episodes include V. Lazzarini's *Marino Faliero* (Florence, 1963), Gaetano Cozzi's *Doge Nicolo Contarini: Ricerche sul patriziato agli inizi del seicento* (Venice, 1958), Frederico Seneca's *Il Doge Leonardo Donà* (Padua, 1959), *La politica veneziana dopo l'interdetto* (Padua, 1957), and his *Venezia e Papa Giulio II* (Padua, 1962); D. Weinstein's excellent little study *Ambassador from Venice* (Minneapolis, 1960) deals with Pietro Pasqualigo's embassy to Lisbon in 1501 and incidentally with the background of Portugal's discovery of the Cape route to India and Venice's reactions.

In economic history the best general work is still that by Gino Luzzatto, contained in his *Studi di storia economica veneziana* (Padua, 1954) and his *Storia economica di Venezia dall' XI al XVI secolo* (Venice, 1961), while his *Economic History of Italy from the Fall of the Roman Empire to the Beginning of the 16th century* (trans. Philip Jones, London, 1961) provides much material on Venice within a broader context. Reference should also be made to the essay on Luzzatto's contribution to Venetian history by the doyen of Venice's historians Frederick C. Lane in *Nuova Rivista Storica* (Vol. XLIX, 1965). *The Cambridge Economic History* contains some relevant material, notably by R. de Roover; the essays in *Politica e economia di Venezia nel Trecento* (Rome, 1952), Lane's review article 'Recent studies on the Economic History of Venice' (*Journal of Economic History*, XXIII, 1963), his own important contributions contained in *Venice and History* (Baltimore, 1960) and his classic studies of *Andrea Barbarigo: Merchant of Venice 1418-1449* (Baltimore, 1944) and *Venetian Ships and Shipbuilders* (Baltimore, 1934) are all worth reading, and, while on the subject of Venice and the sea, Wiel's *The Navy of Venice* (London, 1910) contains some entertaining incidental material.

Brian S. Pullan has edited an invaluable collection of articles on *Crisis and Change in the Venetian Economy in the 16th and 17th centuries* (London, 1968) and Domenico Sella has examined Venetian commerce in the seventeenth century (*Commercio e industrie a Venezia nel secolo XVIII*, Venice, 1961). Other more specialized economic studies include H. Simonsfeld's *Der Fondaco dei Tedeschi in Venedig und die deutsch-venetianischen Handelsbeziehungen* (2 vols., Stuttgart, 1887) on German-Venetian trade relations, and Alberto Tenenti's analysis of piracy and its impact on Venetian trade and shipping in *Naufrages, Corsairs et assurances maritimes à Venise 1592-1609* (Paris, 1959), and *Venezia e i corsari*

1580–1615 (Bari, 1961) translated by T. B. Allan as *Piracy and the Decline of Venice 1580–1615* (London, 1966). F. C. Spooner has examined Venice's monetary problems in relation to her Levantine trade between 1610 and 1614 in *Studi in onore di Amintore Fanfani* (Milan, 1962); on banking C. F. Dunbar's 'The Bank of Venice' (*Quarterly Journal of Economics*, No. 6, 1892) is still useful. I benefited from Lane's contribution on investment and usury to *Explorations in Entrepreneurial History* (Vol. II, ser. 2., pp. 3–15), but was unable to trace a copy of Guiseppe Stefani's *Insurance in Venice from the Origins to the End of the Serenissima* (2 vols., Venice and Trieste, 1956).

On population the standard works are by K. L. Beloch (*Bevölkerungsgeschichte Italiens*, Vol. III, Berlin, 1961) and Daniele Beltrami (*Storia della populazione di Venezia dalla fine del secolo xvi alla caduta della Repubblica*, Padua, 1954), while E. Rodenwaldt has dealt with the particular aspect of the impact of the plague at a critical period in *Pest in Venedig 1515–77* (1952). On agrarian history and the *terraferma* see Beltrami's *Saggio di storia dell'agricultura nella Repubblica Venezia durante l'Eta moderna* (Florence, 1956) and his *La penetrazione economica dei veneziani in terraferma* (Venice-Rome, 1961) which deals with labour and landownership in the seventeenth and eighteenth centuries.

On Venetian colonialism and the empire overseas reference should be made to S. Borsari, *Studi sulle colonie Veneziane in Romania nel XIII secolo* (Naples, 1963), B. Dudan, *Il dominio veneziano di Levante* (Bologna, 1938), A. Pertusi (Ed.), *Venezia e il Levante fino al secolo XV* (Proceedings of the first international convention on the history of Venetian civilization, 1968, Florence, 1972/3). On the exploration and development of Venetian colonies from the twelfth to the fifteenth century see Freddy Thiriet's *La Romanie vénetienne au moyen age* (Paris, 1959); on Cyprus, G. F. Hill's *A History of Cyprus* (4 vols., Cambridge, 1940–52); on Crete, A. Blanc *Il dominii veneziane a Creta nel trecento* (Naples, 1968) and William Miller's *Essays on the Latin Orient* (Cambridge, 1921); also the latter's history of Frankish Greece from 1204 to 1566 (*The Latins in the Levant*, London, 1908).

On Venetian venturers of various kinds see J. Barbaro and A.

Contarino, *Travels to Tana and Persia* (Hakluyt Society, 1873), and R. S. Lopez in the *JEH*, Vol. III, 1943, pp. 174–80. On Marco Polo there is Sir Henry Yule's version (*The Book of Ser Marco Polo*, 2 vols., London, 1871, 3rd. ed., 1903), that of Moulle and Pelliot (*The Description of the World*, 2 vols., London, 1938) and the recent English translation by R. Latham (*The Travels of Marco Polo*, Harmondsworth, 1958). The best critical introduction is by Leonardo Olschki (*Marco Polo's Asia*, trans. J. A. Scott, Berkeley and Los Angeles, 1960).

On the constitutional aspects see Guiseppe Maranini's *La Costituzione de Venezia* (2 vols., Venice, 1927–31). For Gasparo Contarini's celebrated work see Lewes Lewkenor's Elizabethan translation, *The Commonwealth and Government of Venice* (London, 1599).

Works illustrating aspects of Venetian social history include G. Gracco's *Società e stato nel medioevo veneziano* (Florence 1967), which deals with the twelfth, thirteenth and fourteenth centuries, A. Ventura's *Nobilità e popolo nella societa veneta del '400 e del '500* (Bari, 1964), J. C. Davis's *The Decline of the Venetian Nobility as a Ruling Class* (Baltimore, 1962), Brian Pullan's formidable *Rich and Poor in Renaissance Venice* (Oxford, 1971), and also Marino Berengo's *La società veneta al fine del settecento* (Florence, 1956) and O. Logan's *Culture and Society in Venice 1470-1790* (London, 1972), which though more concerned with high culture than with society is useful on the Church affairs and contributes something on the relatively neglected later period.

On life and manners the basic work is still P. G. Molmenti's *La storia di Venezia nella vita privata* (3 parts, Bergamo, 1905–8), translated by Horatio Brown *Venice: Its Individual Growth from the Earliest Beginnings to the Fall of the Republic* (6 vols., London, 1906–8). However, Margaret Newett's essay on 'The Sumptuary Laws of Venice in the 14th and 15th Centuries' (*Historical Essays by Members of the Owens College Manchester*, ed. Tout and Tait, London, 1902) is a rich source on its subject, and much interesting material is to be found in T. Okey's delightful *The Old Venetian Palaces and the Old Venetian Folk* (London, 1907), Molmenti's *La Dogaressa di Venezia*, (Turin, 1887; translated by C. Brune as

The Dogaressa, London, 1887), various other Molmenti studies, Andrea da Mosto's, *I Dogi di Venezia nella vita pubblica e privata* (Milan, 1960), and Guido A. Quarti's *Quattro secoli di vita veneziana nella storia, nell'arte e nella poesie* (2 vols., 1941). On popular songs about Lepanto see Quarti's *La Battaglia di Lepanto dei canti popolari dell'epoco* (Milan, 1930); on civic display E. H. Gombrich's 'Celebrations in Venice of the Holy League and the Victory of Lepanto' in *Studies in Renaissance and Baroque Art* (ed. M. Kitson and J. Shearman, London and New York, 1967), and also Bianca T. Mazzarotto's *La feste veneziane* (Florence, 1961). On Venetian music see *Studi di musica veneta* (Venice, 1968) and on the conservatories of the late seventeenth and eighteenth centuries in particular, Denis Arnold's article in *Proceedings of the Royal Musical Association* (1962,3, pp. 31–47). On printing, printers and censorship there is S. Castellani's *La Stampa in Venezia* (Venice, 1889) and Horatio Brown's *The Venetian Printing Press* (London, 1891), while Cecil Roth's *The Jews of Venice* (Philadelphia, 1930) is a useful study of the various Jewish communities through the ages.

Contemporary accounts and assessments of Venice by foreigners which I have drawn on include *Canon Pietro Casola's Pilgrimage to Jerusalem in the Year 1494* (Manchester, 1907), (Thomas) *Coryats Crudities* (London, 1611), Fynes Moryson, *An Itinerary* (3 parts, London, 1617). James Howell's *SPQV: A Survey of the Signorie of Venice* (London, 1651), Richard Lassels, *The Voyage of Italy* (Paris, 1670), John Evelyn's *Diary* (London, 1959), E. Wright, *Some Observations* (2 vols., 2nd edition), Philip Skippon's 'Account of a Journey' (in Vol. VI of Churchill, *A Collection of Voiages*, 1732), Samuel Sharp's *Letters from Italy* (London, 1766), and Goethe's *Italian Journey* (trans. Auden and Mayer, London, 1962). For the impressions of a more recent literary visitor see Mary McCarthy's *Venice Observed* (Lausanne, 1956, and Harmondsworth, 1972).

For a contentious, partisan account of the fall of the Republic which conveys a strong period flavour see J. Hinckley's translation, *An Accurate Account of the Fall of the Republic of Venice* (1804). Successive editions of Murray and Baedeker guidebooks give the 'feel' of Venice in the nineteenth and early twentieth centuries, while Ruskin's voluminous *The Stones of Venice*, however eccentric on architectural matters, contains some shrewd observations about the Venetians of his own times. The basic document on the present Venetian crisis is the UNESCO *Rapporto su Venezia* (Paris-Milan, 1969), and for proposed solutions and in particular the contribution of Renato Tosi see the Reports of the *Commissione di studio dei provvedimenti per la conservazione e difesa della laguna e della città di Venezia* published by the *Istituto Veneto di Scienze, Lettere ed Arte*.

Index

Abu Said, 96
Accademia art gallery, 295
'Accademia della Fama', 222
Acre, 43, 48, 68, 76, 78, 79, 86, 140,
  143; loss and recapture, 54; fall, 80
Aden, 180
administration, 44–5, 77, 92; overseas,
  121; mainland empire, 100, 136, 210,
  220; nobility's grounding in, 125–7
Adria, Cieco d', 229
Adrianople, 60
Adriatic, 2, 60, 64, 68, 75, 238, 241
Aegean islands, 61–2, 74
Aegina, 210, 73
Agnadello; battle, 188
Agostini, Matteo, banker, 177, 192
agriculture, 190, 219, 264, 308; not
  self supporting, 133; excessive
  demands, 205; expansion, 248, 250;
  produce speculation, 262–3; decline,
  282
Ajas, 79, 80, 82
Albania, 160, 256, 290
Albèri, E., 304
Aleppo, 26, 223, 247, 270
Alexander III, Pope, 51–2
Alexander V, Pope, 128
Alexander VI, Pope, 186
Alexandria, 19, 48, 49, 76, 86, 113,
  166–7, 183, 223, 246, 270
Alexius I, Emperor, 37
Alexius IV, Emperor, 57, 58, 59
Algarotti, Francesco, 279
Allan, T. B., 308
Allessio, 153
almshouses, 103, 174, 192
Alonso of Calabria, 168
Alps: caravans over, 27, 32, 66, 95
Altinum, 6
alum, 49, 68, 82
Amalfi, 22, 32, 33, 34, 37, 95
America, 181, 217
amusements, 70–1, 79–80
Anafestus, Paulicius, Dux, 10
Ancilotto café, 285

Ancona, 22, 67, 76, 117; competition,
  242, 278
Andronicus, Emperor, 82, 116
Anselmo the Jew, banker, 198
Antioch, 42, 43
Antwerp, 87, 217
Apulia, 32, 76, 139
Aquileia, 1, 18, 27, 110, 117;
  Metropolitan of, 8; Patriarch of, 45,
  146
Arab conquest, 5
Aragon, 107
archery, 89
architecture, 145, 155
arengo (assembly), 3, 35
Argos, 121, 157, 160
Armenia, 81, 86, 96, 113, 127
arms manufacture and trade, 47, 75, 83,
  98, 167, 277, 287
army: decline, 286
Arnold, D., 310
Arpad, Hungarian leader, 26
Arsenal, 42, 73, 86, 93, 120, 167, 172,
  176, 194, 208, 212, 243, 291, 294, 296,
  298, 301; expansion, 152, 160, 200,
  223, 259, 264, 267; decline, 185,
  236–7, 270; explosion at, 189; fire,
  225; reforms, 225–6; strike, 250
arti, 73–4, 92; see also guilds art:
  patronage, 210–11; decline, 277
artists, 88, 123, 297
Ashkenezi, Solomon, 230
Askelon, sea battle, 43
Asolo, 110, 170
assessment office, 98
Athens, 121, 273
Augsburg, 129
Austria, 117, 202, 257, 272, 288, 289,
  290; rules Venice, 294–300
Avignon, 86, 98, 113

Badoer: conspirator, 90, 91; Angelo,
  256, 257; Frederigo, 222
Balbi, Francesco, merchant, 140–1, 147,
  149, 157

Baldwin, King of Jerusalem, 43
Baldwin of Flanders, Count, 55, 58, 59; becomes Eastern Emperor, 59–60
Baldwin II, Emperor, 67
Baldwin III, Emperor, 74
Banco della Piazza di Rialto, 241
Banco di Rialto, 258
Banco Giro, 258, 267, 277, 291, 294–5
banks, banking, 99, 122, 176–7, 188, 191–2, 198–9, 225, 240–1, 258, 308
Barattiari, Niccolò, 50
Barbarigo: family, 197–8; Doge Agostino, 169, 175, 179, 181; Andrea, 130–48 *passim*, 215, 307; Augustino, 227; Caterina Sagredo, 280; Josafa, 162–3; Doge Marco, 169; Nicolò, 130; Nicolò (Son of Andrea), 156–7, 167, 188
Barbaro: family, 220; Daniele, 215, 216; Ermolao, 171; J., *308*; Josafa, 144; Marco, 109
Barbaromani family, 11
Barbary: Coast, 122, 235, 277; pirates, 245
Barbolani family, 22, 23
Bardi, Girolamo, 2
Bari, 23, 191
Barozzi family, 22
baroque vogue, 267–8
Basil II, Emperor, 32
Bassano, 100
'battle of the pinewoods', 11
Baty, Great Khan, 78
Baxon, Theodore, 120
Beatus, 13
Beauharnais, Eugene de, 294
Beckford, William, 286
Bedmar, Marquis, Spanish Ambassador, 258
beef production, 205
beggars, 192, 204, 206, 212, 239, 281
Beirut, 122
Bellini: Gentile, 145, 176, 186; Giovanni, 145; Jacopo, 145
Bellinzona, battle, 134
Belluno, 99, 115, 124, 219
Beloch, K. L., *308*
Beltrami, D., *308*
Bembo: Dardi (14 C), 87, 96; Dardi (15 C), 252; Piero, 166; Pietro, 170–1
Benedictines, 285
Benzoni, G., *306*
Berengo, Marino, *309*
Bergamo, 100, 133, 134, 135, 146, 190, 219, 250, 255, 287, 290
Bernado, Domenici, astrologer, 283
'Bianchi' movement, 124
Black Sea trade, 34, 75, 80, 83, 98, 116; convoys, 64, 96, 122; agreement with Turks, 153
Blanc, A., *308*
Bocconio, Marino, 84–5
Bohemund, Count, 37, 38
Bologna, 76
Bomberg, Daniele, printer, 199
Bon, Gabriele, 174, 175
Boniface, Marquis of Montferrat, 55, 57, 59

Bono, Giovanni (John the Good), 2
book-keeping, 177
bookshops, 207, 222
Borghese, Camillo, 255
Borsari, S., *308*
Boston, Lincs, 8, 7, 96
Bouwsma, W. J., *306*
Brabant, 87
Bragadin: Giorgio, 129; Marcantonio, 227, 228
Braudel, F., *306*
Brenta, river, 27, 44
Brescia, 100, 133, 134, 135, 136, 146, 147, 190, 219, 227, 250, 290
Bressan: Leonardo, 171–2; Matteo, 200
Brides, Feast of, 33, 45–6
Brondolo, 13, 26
Brown, H., *305*, *306*, *309*, *310*
Browning, Robert, 301
Bruges, 86, 87, 139, 140, 142, 143, 162
Bucintoro, 149, 221, 251–2, 261, 277, 289, 293, 295, 297
bull-baiting, 188, 195, 266
Buonaparte, General, 289–90
Buono of Malamocco, 19
bureaucracy, 126
Burgundy, 162
Bussone, Count Francesco (Carmagnola), 134–6, 141–2
Byron, Lord, 297
Byzantine Empire, 31, 102, 107, 152, 153; loss of Italy, 5–6, 7–8, 10; Venice a satellite of, 13–15, 17, 21; aid from Venice, 22, 32, 37–8; trade with, 23–4, 26–7, 32–3, 37, 43; break with Venice, 48–9; payment to Venice, 38, 44; *see also* Constantinople

Ca d'Oro, palace, 132, 145
Cabot, Sebastian, 180
Cabral, Pedro Alvarez, 180, 181
cafés, 298
Cagliostro, Count, 279
Calbo, Filippo, 292
Calicut, 180, 182, 184; defeat by Portugal, 189–90
Caloprini family, 31
Cambrai, League of, 187, 201
Campanile, 123, 274, 301
Canal, Martino da, 69, 71–2, 75, 76, 77, 305
Canale: Antonio, 159; Cristoforo da, 208
Canaletto, Antonio, 276, 297
canals, 17, 34
Candia, 62, 74, 102, 112, 265, 267
Candiano: family, 31; Doge Pietro I, 24; Doge Pietro II, 28; Doge Pietro III, 29, 32; Doge Pietro IV, 29–30; Vitale, 30, 31
Canea, 152, 155, 265, 273
cannon, 115, 117
Cáorle, 21, 29, 117
Cape Malea, sea battle, 44
Capello: family, 67; Bianca, 223
capitano, 100
Capo d'Istria, 106–7, 118
Cappello brothers, 139, 140, 142, 143, 144

Capuano, Cardinal Pietro, 56
Capuchins, 211
Caravia, Alessandro, 210, 211
careers, 66–7, 130–1
Carleton, Dudley, British Ambassador, 262
Carmagnola *see* Bussone
Carpaccio, Vettor, 155
Carrara: Francesco da, 115, 124, 125; Jacopo da, 99; Marsilio da, 99, 100, 110, 115
Casa delle Zitelle, 206
Casanova, Giacomo, 280
Casola, Pietro, 173, 310
Cassiodorus: description of early Venice, 3, 5
Castellani, S., *310*
Castello district, 12, 46, 93
Caterina, Queen, 164–5, 170–1, 188
caulkers, 105, 155
cavalliere servente, 275, 280
Celsi, Doge Lorenzo, 111
Ceneda, 124, 125; Bishop of, 110
censorship, 196, 213, 295, 310; religious, 207, 213, 230, 242–3; pornography, 222
Centranigi family, 35
Cephalonia, 38, 168, 179, 182, 184
Cervia, 157
Cessi, R., *304, 306*
Chalkis, 61
Chambers, D., *306*
charity, 103–4, 119, 127, 154, 174, 192, 202, 203, 210–11, 231, 238, 259, 282, 287; *see also* Scuole
chess, 69
Chief of Soldiers, 11
children: charities, 239; employment controlled, 151
China, 78, 79, 81, 111, 184
china industry, 282
Chioggia, 9, 13, 26, 41, 51, 117, 118, 131
church, churches, 3, 6, 15, 17, 123, 145, 233; as a career, 242; cultural hub, 28–9; patronage, 219; Persia, 98; politically suspect, 128; proposal to merge Eastern and Western, 57; and state, 252–3, 254–5, 284–5; schism, 128; *see also* Papacy
citizenship, 88–9, 189
civil defence, 117
Civil Guard, 298
Clement VIII, Pope, 242–3
Clement XIII, Pope, 283
clockmakers, 105
cloth trade, 15, 16, 26, 50, 69, 87, 101
clothes, 145, 217
coffee-houses, 277
coins, 167; debasement, 250; minting, 56, 79; shortage, 198
colleganza contracts, 76
colonies, *see* Venetian Empire
Columbus, Christopher, 168
Comacchio, 11, 12, 13, 16, 20, 24, 95
commoners: opportunities, 126–7; political weakness, 156, 194
Commynnes, Philippe de, 175
Compagnia della Calza, 188, 195
consortia, 76

Constantinople, 3, 5, 7, 40, 44, 82, 96, 107, 116, 152–3, 212, 248; trade, 140, 160, 191, 200, 247; Latin kingdom, 57–60, 61, 74; *see also* Byzantine Empire
constitution, 262, 309
Contarini: family, 77, 301; Ambrogio, 163–4; Andrea, 174; Bartolommeo, 199; Carlo, 284; Domenico, 36; Enrico, 40; Gasparo, 193–4, 214, 245, 262, 309; Giacomo, 216; Lucrezia, 149; Ludovico, 127; Marin, 132; Doge Nicolo, 235, 238, 240, 306; Tommaso, 238
convoy system, 64, 87, 95–6, 101, 139, 248
Corfu, 37, 38, 57, 61, 63, 120, 148, 166, 184, 209, 287
corn: supply, 44; tax, 75; trade, 9, 11, 15, 27, 76, 122; *see also* grain, maize, wheat
Cornaro family, 170; Alvise, 198, 220; Angelo (Pope Gregory XII), 128; Caterina *see* Caterina, Queen; Frederigo, 114–15, 119; Doge Giovanni, 263, 280; Ludovico, 277; Doge Marco, 109, 110, 113, 114; Zuane, 205–6
Cornaro Palace, 210
'correctors', 64
corruption, 151, 169, 175, 197, 214, 272, 286
Coryat, Thomas, 260–1, 310
costume, 124, 280
cotton: production, 170; trade, 76, 101, 114, 122, 139, 140, 143, 231, 237
Council of Sages, 45
Council of Ten, 91, 92, 104, 108, 109, 126, 129, 141, 151, 155, 179, 183, 196, 213, 257, 264, 284, 294; powers reduced, 240
counter-espionage, 212
Counter-Reformation, 254
Cozzi: Gaetano, *306*; Geminiano, 282
Cracow, 248
crafts, craftsmen, 16–17, 28, 47, 69, 154, 155, 167; attraction, 281–2; emigration, 271; living standards, 88
Crema, 134, 149, 150, 290
Cremona, 16, 134, 141, 179
Crete, Cretans, 37, 57, 60, 61, 74, 76, 138, 140, 148, 153, 157, 178, 179, 209, 227, 231, 236, 238, 248, 255 265, 270, 272, 308; settlement, 62–3; ,revolts, 80, 102–3, 111–12; lost to Turks, 265–9
crime, 104–5, 285–6; penalties, 46–7
Crimea, 78, 102
Cristolfi, Cristoforo, 286
Croatia, 110
Crusades, 102; first, 40–1; third, 54–5; fourth, 55–60; of 1461, 157
culture, 123–4, 145, 171; and censorship, 213–14; German, 295
currant production, 184
currency crises, 177–8, 225, 240, 258
Curzola, sea battle, 83
customs dues, 28, 37, 76, 88, 102, 248
Cyclades, 62

Cyprus, Cypriots, 37, 82, 83, 86, 96,
  113, 114, 116, 119, 120, 131, 164–5,
  178, 184, 191, 202, 212, 227, 247, 308;
  administration, 164–5, 170, 199–200;
  annexation, 169–70; loss to Turks,
  226–30

daily life, 22, 28, 34–5, 41–2, 45–8,
  50–1, 100–1, 123–4, 172–3, 191–7
Dalmatia, 14, 15, 21, 27, 28, 33, 34, 37,
  42, 54, 107, 111, 160, 230, 245, 267,
  272, 273, 290; loss, 110, 118
dancing, 207
Dandolo: Andrea, 83; Doge Andrea,
  106, 107; Doge Enrico, 54, 56–60;
  Giberto, 75; Doge Giovanni, 80;
  Giovanni, 109; Dogaressa Zilia, 221
Dante, Alighieri, 86
Dardanelles, 183, 267
Daru, P., *305*
Davis, J. C., *309*
defence works, 219
Delfin, Caterina, 285
devaluation, 258–9, 273
diet, 53, 87–8, 196, 221–2, 243–4
diplomacy, 96, 160, 172, 171, 190, 212
dockyards *see* Arsenal
Dogado, 44
Dogano, 262
Doge, Dogeship, 20–1; election, 35, 54,
  76–7, 128; powers, 18, 45, 64–5, 92,
  127, 155, 214; titles, 9–10, 64
Doge's barge, *see Bucintoro*
Doge's palace, 17, 34–5, 46, 50, 69, 71,
  128, 132, 145, 274; fires, 42, 231
Dolceto, Alberto, 140, 143
Dolfin, Guiseppe, 215
Domenchini, Giovanni, 124
'Dominium', 156
Doria: Doge Leonardo, 240, 255, 257,
  306; Nicolo, 237
Doria: admiral (*c.* 1354), 107; admiral
  (*c.* 1571), 227, 228; Paganino, 116;
  Pietro, 117
drugs, 16, 277
Ducal Counsellor, 126
Ducas, Alexius (Murtzuphlus), 57–8
Dudan, B., *308*
Dunbar, C. F., *308*
Durazzo, 37, 38
Dux, 12
dyeing industry, 28, 47, 132, 191, 207

earthquake: of 1223, 64; of 1284, 79;
  of 1348, 106, 108
'eastern baths', 266
Eastern Orthodox Church, 8
economy, 27–8, 34, 85–6, 132, 159, 169,
  205–6, 224–5, 259, 264, 273, 296, 307
Egypt, 5, 49, 80, 139, 202; trade, 17,
  26, 34, 74, 80, 83, 87, 98, 113, 131,
  182, 183, 248; war with Portugal,
  184, 189–90
emigration, 276
Emo, Gabriele, 236
employment, 154, 287
England, 87, 111, 181, 196, 212, 217,
  231, 245–6, 247, 248, 262, 295, 305

Epirus, 37, 38, 60
Episkopi estate 114, 119
estates: primogeniture, 215
Este, 68; Marquis of, 24; Nicolo d',
  125
Euboea, 60, 61 *see also* Negroponte
Eugenius IV, Pope, 145
Evelyn, John, 260, 265–7, *310*
Exarchate, 3, 7–8
excommunication, 87, 89, 91, 168, 187,
  190, 254–6

Fabri, Fra Felix, 165
fairs, 27, 54
Faliero: Francesco, 174; Doge Marino,
  108–10, 127, 306; Pietro, 104
Famagusta, 82, 116, 164, 227
family household, 215
famines, 202–5, 226
Fano, 44
fashion, 124, 145, 185–6, 217
Fausto, Vettor, 200–1, 208
Feltre, 115, 124, 125
Ferdinand, King, 176
Ferrara, 16, 29, 44, 89, 139, 187, 190,
  242; capture of 68; loss, 91;
  Marchioness of, 149
festivals *see* public festivals
feudalism, 219
Filargi, Pietro (Pope Alexander V),
  128
financial system, 47, 67, 98–9, 121, 191,
  241, 277; *see also* currency crises
fishing, 1, 11, 12, 27
Fiume, 187, 212, 235, 278
Flabianco, Doge Domenico, 35
flagellants, 71, 72, 174, 241
Flanders, 87, 96, 122, 139, 144, 167,
  183
floods, 202
Florence, 99, 131, 132, 134, 154, 175,
  187
Florian's, 298
Fondaco dei Tedeschi, 123
food: prices, 49, 105, 202, 203, 211,
  237; shortages, 231; supply, 95, 220–1
forced loans, 54, 75, 98, 107–8, 118–19,
  126, 148, 168, 290
foreigners, 88, 103
Fortunatus, Patriarch of Grado, 13
Foscari: Doge Francesco, 133–4, 155–6;
  Francesco, 284; Jacopo, 149, 151–2,
  155
Foscari Palace, 300
Foscarini: Antonia, 258; Ludovico, 151
France, 96, 122, 162, 176, 178, 181,
  187, 190, 197, 284, 288, 289; Venetia
  ceded to, 300
Francesco of Brescia, beggar, 206
Franks, 12
Franz Joseph, Emperor, 299, 300
Frari, church, 145, 203
Frederick Barbarossa, Emperor, 51–2,
  68
Frederick IV, King of Denmark and
  Norway, 274
freemasonry, 285
friars, 71–2

Friuli, 24, 29, 146, 160, 179, 187, 190, 219, 225; conquest of, 128–9
fur trade, 27

Gabrieli, Giovanni, 229, 251
Galata, 81
Galbaio: Giovanni, 11–12; Maurizio, 12–13
Galileo, Galilei, 242, 248
galleys, 81, 87, 101, 120, 132, 165, 172, 200, 208–10, 264; conditions on, 209, 237–8; construction, 152, 212, 236; patrols, 238
Gallipoli, 60, 61; sea battle, 129
Galuppi, Baldasare, 275
Gama, Vasco da, 180
gambling, 79, 185, 268, 272, 277, 280, 281
games, 261
Garda, lake, 146
Garibaldi, Giuseppe, 299, 300
Garzoni, Andrea, 176
gastaldo (trade association officers), 73
Genoa, 34, 37, 40, 41, 42, 43, 44, 57, 62, 67, 68, 74, 79, 80, 94, 95, 98, 110, 115, 118, 134, 233; wars with, 75, 81, 107, 116ff.
Georgia, 81, 144, 163
germ warfare, 267
Germany: Germans, 103, 122, 123, 127, 163, 167; trade, 27, 129, 137, 142, 182, 231, 270
Gianotti, Donato, 84
Gibbon, Edmund, 147, 155
Giorgio the Greek, 152
giovani, 239–40, 242, 257
Giovanni, Doge, 251
glass industry, 47, 73, 190, 260, 270, 277
Goa, 182, 184
Goethe, Johann Wolfgang, 288, 302, 310
gold: shortage, 225
Golden Book of the Nobility, 84, 99, 265, 272
Golden Horn, 66, 82
goldsmiths, 85
Goldoni, Carlo, 277–8
Gombrich, E. H., 310
Gondola, Andrea di Pietro della (Palladio), 216–17
gondoliers, 261, 278, 287
government posts competition, 192–3
Gozzi, Carlo, 278
Grabusa, 269, 273
Gracco, G., 309
Gradenigo: family, 67, 93; Doge Giovanni, 110; Doge Pietro, 80, 83, 87, 89–91
Grado, 9, 23, 33, 117; Patriarchate, 8, 13, 18
grain: price, 202–3, 226; supply, 211, 220–1; trade, 86, 96, 283; see also corn, maize, wheat
Grand Canal, 26, 41, 46, 147, 279
Grand Chancellor, 126
Great Council, 45, 65, 89, 91, 111, 151, 174, 175, 292; membership, 80, 83–4, 193, 283

Greece, Greeks, 44, 75, 86, 159, 160, 273; bases, 102, 152; see also Byzantine Empire
Greek Orthodox Church, 63–4, 112
Gregory VIII, Pope, 36–7, 54
Gregory XII, Pope, 128
Gregory XVIII, Pope, 230
Grimaldi, Napoleone, 118
Grimani: family, 277, 300; Antonio, 178; Marco, 104; Pietro (c. 1649), 267; Pietro (c. 1780), 279; Vettor, 267
Grimani-Calergi family, 283
Gritti palace, 145, 191
Gualdrada, Dogaressa, 29, 30
guilds (artc), 127–8, 154, 213; powers, 154, 271, 282; decline, 277
Guiscard, Robert, King, 37–8
Guistiani family, 22
Guistiniani: Leonardo, 150; Tomasso, 193
Guistiniano, Doge, 273
gunners, 176

Haifa, 40
Hale, J. R., 306
Hassan Beg, Emperor of Persia, 162, 163
Hazlitt, W. C., 305
Health, Board of, 169, 204, 206
hemp, 131, 154–5
Henry V, Emperor, 44
Henry III, King of France, 232
Henry V, King of England, 128, 130
Henry VIII, King of England, 196
Heraclea, 9, 11, 12, 14, 33
heresy, 213
Hewelke of Dresden, 282
Hill, G. F., 308
Hinckley, J., 310
Hodgson, Francis, 306
Holy League: against France, 176; against Turkey, 227–8
Holy Roman Empire, 14, 21; trade, 32, 52
homosexuality, 206–7
Hospitallers (Knights of St. John), 80, 102, 200
hospitals, 71, 72, 103, 192, 204, 211, 239, 266
housing stock, 132
Howell, James, 260, 261–2, 310
Hun invasion, 2
Hungary, Hungarians, 24, 26, 48, 67, 117, 179, 299

immigration: immigrants, 88, 103, 192, 202, 203, 211–12, 233, 239, 271, 281–2
Incurabili, 282
India, 81, 82, 102, 111, 223, 247; sea route, 180
industry, 69, 85–6, 154, 190, 224–5, 259, 264, 281–2, 295, 296; see also crafts
inflation, 225, 237, 241, 258–9, 264
Inquisition, 213, 217, 284
insurance industry, 225, 246
investment, 98, 122; in land, 144–5, 156–7, 167, 220, 262–3, 271
Ionian Islands, 168, 178, 230, 238, 272, 290

iron trade, 23, 98
Isaac, Emperor of Byzantium, 57, 58, 59
Isaac, Exarch of Ravenna, 9
Isabella, Queen, 176
Iscoli family, 22
Istria, 5, 12, 14, 28–9, 131, 160, 191, 237, 290
Italy: Lombard invasions, 7–8; Norman invasion, 37; French invasion, 289; independence, 300; *see also* Venetian Empire
Ithaka, 184

Jaffa, 40, 121
James I, King of Cyprus, 119
James II Lusignan, King of Cyprus, 164
Jensen, Nicholas, 154, 167
Jerusalem, 40, 43, 54, 79
Jesalo, 11, 12, 14, 50
Jesuits, 242, 255, 285
Jews, 104, 184, 198–9, 224, 239, 294, 295, 310; discrimination against, 122, 148–9, 160, 213, 222, 225, 230, 266, 285
Johann of Speyer, printer, 154
John of Austria, 228
John the Baptist, St., 60
John the Deacon, 6, 8–9, 19, 32, 33
John the Good, 2
Jones, P., 307
Joseph II, Emperor, 279
Joyeuse, Cardinal, 256
justice, 52, 126; corruption, 151, 175
Justinian, Emperor, 3

Kallerges, Alexios, 74
Karlowitz, peace of, 273
Keffa, 81, 83, 163
Königgraz, battle, 300
Korone, 61, 74, 102, 178, 179, 273
Kretschmayr, H., 306
Kubla Khan, 78, 81, 82

lacemaking, 207
lagoon area, 9–10, 11, 12–13
land, 262; investment, 144–5, 156–7, 167, 220, 262–3, 271; reclamation, 220, 250
Lane, F. C., 87, 307, 308
Lassels, Richard, 260, 310
Latham, R., 309
law, 23, 65, 131; as career, 126, 154; enforcement, 69; *see also* justice, maritime code, sumptuary legislation
Lazzarini, V., 306
League of Cambrai, 187, 201
learning, 95, 105–6, 150–1
leather trade, 50, 190, 277
Leghorn, 248
Lemnos, 61, 157
Leon, Giovan Pietro, 223
Leopold II, Emperor, 288
Leopold, Duke of Austria, 114–15
Lepanto, 121, 153, 157, 178; sea battle, 227–8, 237, 310
Lesina, 128

Levant, 15, 34, 87, 139, 140, 144, 167, 247, 308; *see also* Egypt, Palestine, Syria, Turkey
Lewkenor, Lewes, 309
Libreria Vecchia, 210
Lido, 117, 118
Limburg, 87
linen manufacture, 219
Lion, Nicolò, 246
Lippomani, Girolamo, banker, 177
Lisbon, 47, 180, 181, 182, 191
literacy, 106, 123–4, 207
Liutprand, King of Lombardy, 11
living standards, 87–8, 105, 123, 281, 301
loan stock, 168
loans, 47, 49; Office, 49; *see also* forced loans
Lodi, 150
Logan, O., 309
Loggetto, 210
Lombard League, 51
Lombardy, Lombards, 5–6, 8, 9, 10, 12, 27, 34, 289, 295
London, 122, 140, 143
Lopez, R. S., 309
Loredano: Alvise, 193; Domenico, 252; Giovanni, 102; Doge Leonardo, 181; Paolo (c. 1338), 102; Paolo (c. 1367), 112; Pietro, 129, 147
Lorenzo, friar, 71
Lorraine, 87
Louis IX, King of France, 67
Louis XII, King of France, 187–8
Louis XVIII, King of France, 289
Louis, King of Hungary, 109, 110
Louis of Blois, Count, 55
Loyola, Ignatius, 211
Lucca, 88, 99, 154
Luther, Martin, 207
Lutherans, 213, 242
Luzzato, G., 307

McCarthy, Mary, 310
Machiavelli, Niccolò, 186
Maclodio, battle, 135
Magagnati, Girolamo, 260
Magno: Alessandro, 224; Calio, 229
mainland, bridge link, 296
'maiores', 7
maize, 221, 282
Malamocco, 6, 11, 13, 14, 117, 277, 301
Malatesta, Carlo, 135, 157
Malipiero: Domenico, 167, 305; Doge Pasquale, 156
Malmsey, 157
Malvasia, 210
Manfredonia, battle, 118
Manin: Daniele, 298, 299, 300; Doge Ludovico, 288, 289, 293
Mantua, 6, 18, 187
Manuel, Emperor, 49
Manuel, King of Portugal, 182
Manuzio, Aldo, 171, 190, 207
Manziket, battle, 37
Maranini, G., 309
Marcello: Bartolomeo, 153; Giacomo, 265
Marengo, battle, 289

Margate, 96
maritime code, 65–6, 153
Marranos, 213
marriage: among nobility, 215, 238–9, 264, 275, 280; 'With the Sea', 33, 53–4, 289
Marseilles, 34, 67, 248
Martin V, Pope, 128
Maser, villa at, 216, 220
Maura, Fra, geographer, 180
Mauro, Romano, 47–50
Maximilian, Emperor, 187
Maximilian, King of the Romans, 176
Maximilian, Archduke, 300
Mazzarotto, B. T., *310*
Mazzini, Giuseppe, 299
Mazzorbo, 6, 117
Medici, Francesco de, 223
medicine, 69, 73, 103, 104; as a career, 105, 126, 154
'mediocres', 7
Mediterranean; piracy, 135; trading network, 34
Melos, 62
Memmo, Doge Tribuno, 31
memory training, 138
Mendicanti, 282
mercenaries, 99–100, 272, 293
Merceria, main street, 49, 108, 207, 222, 266
Mestre-Marghera, 302
metal trade, 50, 122, 190
Methone, 61, 74, 82, 102, 107, 157, 179, 273, 276; sea battle, 107, 108
Michele, Doge Dominico, 43
Michiel: Angelo, 265; Francesco, 162; Doge Vitale I, 40
Michiel, Doge Vitale, 47
Milan, 179, 298, 299; wars with, 132–7; 139, 140–1, 146, 149–50, 152, 153
Miller, W., *308*
mint, 147; illegal, 177–8
mirrors, 296
Misericordia, Scuola, 92, 103
Mocenigo: family, 300; Doge Alvise, 232; Andrea, 197–8; Guistiniana, 263; Lazzaro, admiral, 267; Doge Pietro, 164; Doge Tomasso, 128, 132, 133; Tommasso, 117
Mohammed II, Sultan, 159
Molin, Francesco da, 215–16, 225, 226
Molmenti, P. G., *309, 310*
monasteries, 285, 295
Monemvasia, 157, 178, 182, 273
money market, 67, 99, 258, 308; *see also* banking, currency crises
Mongolia Mongols, 78, 102
Monk of St. Gall, 16
Montagagna, 154
Montagu, Lady Mary Wortley, 279–80
Monte Napoleone, 295
Monte Nuovo, 177, 182, 188
'Monte Vecchio' 75, 160, 168, 177, 240; *see also* public debt
Montebelluno, 148
Monteverdi, Claudio, 261, 263, 274
moral standards, 173–4, 185, 206–7, 217, 222–3, 281

Morea, 60, 61, 148, 157, 159, 273
Moro, Bartolommeo, 197
Morosini: family, 31, 77, 119, 232; Bernardo, 105; Domenico, 31; Doge Francesco, 269, 272–3; Francesco, 247; Marco, 90; Nicolo, 192; Rogiero, 82; Tomasso, Patriarch, 63–4
Moryson, Fynes, 243–4, 252, *310*
Mosto: Alvise da, 147; Andrea da, 147; Andrea da (scholar), *310*
Moulle, scholar, *309*
Mudazzo, Michellotto, 129–30, 136
Murano, 6, 88, 117
music, 266, 274–5, 297, 310
Mykonos, 121, 178, 210

Naples, 117, 120, 179, 235, 245, 290
Napoleon, Emperor, 289–90
Narni, Francesco de (Gattemalata), 146
Nasser Muhammed, Sultan of Egypt, 83
national debt, *see* Monte Vecchio, public debt
Nauplia, 121, 182, 184, 209, 210, 273, 276
Navarino, 178, 179, 273
Naxos, 62, 169, 178
needlework, book on, 207
Negroponte, 61, 74, 102, 120, 160, 273; sea battle, 107; loss, 159
Netherlands, 231, 247, 248
Newett, M., *309*
Nicosia, 164, 227
nobility, 108, 214–18, 264, 271–2, 283, 297, 309; entry, 84, 265, 272; land ownership, 156–7, 262–3, 271; poverty, 174–5, 238, 252, 263, 283, 287; training in administration, 125–7
Norman invasion, 37–9
North Africa, 15, 34, 41
nuns, nunneries, 214–15, 264; scandals, 185, 222–3
Nuremberg, 129, 163

oath of office (*promissione*), 54, 64
Obelerii family, 11
Obelerius, Doge, 13, 14
occupational distribution, tenth century, 27–8
Oderzo, 6, 9
offices, buying, 192–3
Oglio, Pietro dal, 274
Okey, T., *309*
oligarchy, 84; emergence, 77
olive oil trade, 11, 15, 27, 191, 250
Olivolo, 9, 12–13, 14, 26
Olschki, L., *309*
opera, 266, 268, 277, 297
orchestras, 261
orphanages, 192
Orbi, Scuola degli, 206
Orseolo: family, 31, 35; Domenico, 32; Giovanni, 32, 34; Doge Ottone, 32, 34, 35; Doge Pietro I, 30–1; Doge Pietro II, 32, 33, 276
Orso, Bishop of Olivolo, 16
Orso, *Dux*, 10
Ospedaletto, 282

Otto I, Emperor, 29
Otto II, Emperor, 30, 31
Otto III, Emperor, 32

Paciolo, Luca, 177
Padovano, 262
Padua, 1, 6, 29, 44, 69, 90, 91, 99, 117,
  125, 190, 227, 233, 242, 291, 299;
  capture, 100, 189; loss, 110, 188;
  Venetian estates, 145, 262
painting, painters, 74, 145, 155, 276-7
palaces, 173, 216
Paleologus, Emperor Manuel, 133-4;
  Emperor John, 146-7; Emperor
  Michael, 74
Palestine, 43, 49, 54, 74, 139, 148-9,
  183
Palladio, Andrea, 216-17, 222, 232, 233
Paolino, Fra, 85
Papacy, 113, 146, 187, 190, 227-8,
  242-3, 254-7; see also
  excommunication
paper industry, 270
Parma, 99, 299
Paros, sea battle, 267
Partecipazio: Doge Agnello, 14, 17;
  Doge Giovanni II, 24; Doge
  Giustiniano, 16; will, 16; Doge Orso
  I, 23-4; Doge Orso II, 28
Paruta, Paolo, 240, 242
Pasqualigo, Pietro, 307
patronage, the arts, 271
Paul II, Pope, 150
Paul, Grand Duke of Russia, 287
Paulino, Leone, 72
Pavia, 16, 26, 27
Pellestrina, 26, 118
Pellio, scholar, *309*
Pepin, King, 13-14
pepper, trade, 11, 49, 50, 76, 81, 139,
  166-7, 247; see also spice trade
Pera, sea battle, 107
perfumes, 16
Persia, 81, 96, 98, 111, 162, 309
Pertusi, A., *308*
Pescatore, Enrico, Count of Malta, 62
Peschiera, 290, 298
Peter I, King of Cyprus, 114
Peter II, King of Cyprus, 116
Petrarch, Francesco, 95, 99, 106, 110;
  embassy, 107; settles in Venice, 111;
  retirement to Padua, 113
Philip II, King of Spain, 227, 228
Piacenza, 11, 16, 150, 299
Piave, river, 27
Piazza, 50, 71, 123, 243, 261, 277
Piazzetta, 128, 294
Piedmont, 289, 299
Pietro, Fra, 103, 106
pig breeding, 178
pilgrims, 123; transport, 40, 41, 66-7,
  83, 87, 121, 165, 191
Pindemonte, Giovanni, 288, 295
'pinewoods, battle of the', 11
Piozzi, Mrs., 279, 281
piracy, 17, 33, 64, 102, 246, 307; see
  also convoy system

Pisa, 34, 37, 40, 41, 42-3, 79, 80, 95
Pisanello, painter, 113
Pisani: family, 295; Almorò, 271;
  Alvise (c. 1500), 177, 191, 192; Alvise
  (c. 1700), 271-2; Giorgio, 284;
  Marina, 280; Nicolo, 107; Vettor, 117,
  118
Pius II, Pope, 157-8
Pius V, Pope, 227, 228
Pius VI, Pope, 285
Placoni, Giovanni, 86
plague, 349; of 1348, 106-7; of
  1359-61, 110; of 1438, 147; of 1477,
  160; of 1498, 176; of 1502, 185; of
  1528, 203-4; of 1567, 222; of 1560,
  227; of 1576, 232-3; of 1630, 264
Po, river, 5, 11, 16, 20, 21, 24, 27
podesta, 100
poisoning, 129-30
Pola, 118; sea battle, 117
Poland, 144, 272, 289
Polani family, 22
Polesine, 125, 169, 250
police force, 276, 286, 287-8, 296
political system, 92, 127, 285-6; defects,
  151, 214-15; see also Doge, Council of
  Ten, Grand Council, nobility
Polo: Andrea, 78; Marco, 79-83, 93-4,
  309; Matteo, 78-80; Nicolo, 78-80
poor relief, 204, 211, 239
population, 220, 237, 308
porcelain industry, 282, 295
pornography, 222
Porta, Luigi da, 188, 203
Portugal, 181-3; and spice trade, 180,
  181, 184-5, 189-90, 223-4
Poznan, 163
Prague, 248
printing industry, 154, 167, 190, 199,
  207, 277, 282, 296, 310; and
  censorship, 213-14, 243
prisons, 223
Priuli: family, 220; Antonio, 198;
  Girolamo, 169, 178, 180, 181, 185,
  186, 188, 191-2, 196, 305; Josafa,
  292; Doge Lorenzo, 221
Priuli palace, 145
Procurators of St. Mark, 103-4, 126, 211
professions, incomes, 154
promissione (oath of office), 54, 64
propaganda, 196
prostitution, 110, 145, 206, 211, 217,
  256, 260, 281
Provveditori alla Sanità *see* Health,
  Board of
public debt, 107, 122, 132; see also
  Monte Vecchio
public festivals, spectacles, 53-4, 71-2,
  105, 123-4, 128, 155, 164, 195-6,
  203, 221, 227-8, 229-30, 232, 250-2,
  256, 266, 274, 287, 310
public hangings, 155
public hygiene, 123, 145, 169, 223, 286
public offices, 238, 252, 276, 283
public order, 69, 175
Puegnano, 130
Pullan, B. S., *307*
puppet plays, 261

Quarantia Criminal, chief court, 126, 240
quarantine regulations, 175, 232
Quarti, G. A., *310*
Querini: family, 89, 93; Marco, 90, 91; Nicolo, 91; Pietro, 90; Vicenzo, 193
Quirini: Angelo, 284; Matteo, 52

Ragusa, 110, 259
railway, 296, 297–8, 301
Ramuso, Hieronimo, 171
Rangone, author, 207
Ravano, Prince of Euboeia, 63
Ravenna, 1, 3, 10, 11, 12, 67
Red Sea, blockade, 182, 223–4
Redentore, church, 233
refugees *see* immigration
relics, 18, 40, 41, 60, 67, 153, 195, 266–7
religion, 23, 53, 145–6, 185, 241–2, 281; disputes, 8, 10; *see also* Scuole
Renier, Doge Paolo, 286, 288
Rethymno, 265
Rezzonico family, 283
Rhodes, 40, 43, 86, 114, 200
Rialto, 9, 14, 17–18, 34, 41, 110, 123, 172, 191, 243
rice trade, 50, 250
Rimini, 186
Riva, Alvise da, 257, 258
Rodenwaldt, E., *308*
Roger, King of Sicily, 44
Romagna, 190
Roman Catholic Church, 8
Roman Empire, 1, 2
Roman Republic, 299
Romanin, Samuele, *305*
Rome, 290; sack, 202
rope making, 86, 131, 154
Roth, C., *310*
Rovigo, 169, 191, 219, 299
Rowdon, M., *306*
Ruskin, John, 300, *310*
Russia, 27, 144, 163
Rustico of Torcello, 19
Rustichello of Pisa, 83

Sagredo family, 300
sailors, 101, 208–9, 246; insurance, 73; living standards, 87–8, 237–8; wages, 66, 88, 177
St. John, Knights of *see* Hospitallers
St. Mark: chapel, 30–1; church, 35, 36, 38–9, 42, 50, 52, 71, 72, 113, 172, 243, 248, 274, 299, 303; hospital, 72
St. Stephen and St. John: knights of, piracy, 235, 236
St. Theodore, Church of, 17
Saladin, 54
Salo, 290
Salonika, 48, 57
salt: industry, 1, 5, 119; tax, 54, 154; trade, 9, 11, 15, 16, 20, 27, 86, 96, 99, 114, 131, 191
Samarkand, 162
San Giacomo di Rialto, piazza, 121
San Giorgio Maggiore, monastery, 267

San Giovanni, church, 145
San Giovanni Evangelista, Scuola of, 72, 92, 103
San Lazzaro, island of, 72, 239; a refuge for paupers, 239
San Marco, Scuola di, 72
San Niccolò, convent, 117
San Nicolo, port, 107
San Paolo, church, 145
San Pietro di Castello, church, 31, 36
San Rocco, Scuola di, 195, 210, 214, 239, 259, 261, 299
San Stefano, church, 145
San Zaccaria, church, 23, 50
Sandwich, 96
Santa Elena, 93
Santa Maria Formosa (Zobenigo), church, 26, 29, 46
Santa Maria Gloriosa, church *see* Frari
Santa Maria della Carità, Scuola di, 53, 72, 295
Santa Maria della Salute, church of, 303
Santa Maura, 272, 273
Sanmichele, Michele, 210
Sansego, sea battle, 22
Sansovino, Jacopo, 210
SS. Giovanni e Paolo, hospital, 211
Sanudo: dynasty, 121; Andrea, 166; Benedetto, 166; Marco, 62; Marino (Torsello), 86
Sanuto, Marino, 173, 176, 184, 186, 188, 189, 193, 195, 202, 203, 204, 205, 206; history, 196
Saracens, 22, 23, 32, 41, 43; trade embargoes, 30, 80
Sardinia, 86, 107, 176
Sarpi, Fra Paolo, 255, 257
Savii, (Sages) 45, 92
savii ai Ordini, 96, 126
Savoy, 187, 290; Count of, 114
sbirri (police), 276, 286
Scala d'Oro, 210
Scala: Antonio della, 125; Can Grande della 99; Mastino della, 99–100
Schio, 140
scholarship, 95, 105–6, 150–1
sculptors, 276–7
Scuole (religious brotherhoods), 72–3, 92–3, 103, 104, 119, 127, 154, 155, 168, 174, 192, 206, 227, 250; charity, 239, 250, 259; patronage, 210–11; public spectacles, 251, 256
Scutari, 153, 160
sea power, 22, 33, 42, 75
sea walls, 286, 301
Sebenico, 128
'secret denunciation', 151
security, 91, 151, 196, 212; *see also* Council of Ten
Sella, D., *307*
Selvo: family, 22; Doge Domenico, 36–9; Dogaressa Theodora, 36
Senate, 65, 92, 134, 135, 141, 257, 288, 291
Seneca, F., *306*
Senj, 212, 245
Serravalle, 110
sestiere, 69

Seville, 217
sexual morality, 206–7
Sforza, Count, 150
Sharp, Samuel, 281, *310*
shipbuilding, 17, 22, 28, 73, 86–7, 100,
    120, 154–5, 171–2, 207–8, 212, 223,
    225, 231; slumps, 160, 167, 236–7,
    247, 259, 270; revivals, 223–4, 248;
    see also Arsenal
ships, shipping, 96, 184, 246, 247;
    design, 200–1; maritime code, 66,
    113; types, 86–7
Sicily, 17, 26, 75, 83, 86, 176, 298
Sigismund, Emperor, 129–30, 136
Signori di Notti, 69, 90, 126, 175
'Signoria', 156
silk: industry, 88, 102, 154, 190, 219,
    231, 270, 287; trade, 37, 224
silver, 240, 258
Simonsfeld, H., *307*
Skiathos, 153
Skippon, Philip, 260, 267–8, *310*
Skopelos, 153
Skyros, 61, 153
slave trade, 15, 16, 21, 23–4, 28, 37,
    66, 83, 98, 101, 122, 144, 173
Slavs, 20, 21, 22, 23, 24, 28, 33;
    mercenaries, 291, 292–3
Smyrna, 48, 82, 270
soap industry, 132, 190, 224, 260
social structure, 5, 7, 29, 73–4, 77,
    150–1; *see also* commoners, nobility,
    poor
social welfare, 127, 154, 194, 204, 231
Soleiman the Magnificent, 200, 209–10
Solomon, Master, 122
Soranzo: *provveditore*, 165; Doge
    Giovanni, 91–2
Southampton, 87
Spaderia café, 285
Spain, Spanish, 135, 144, 176, 179,
    187, 190, 197, 217, 227, 228–9, 240,
    245, 257–8
Spalato, 110
Spalatro, 128
spice trade, 15, 16, 26, 49, 50, 81, 98,
    101, 121–2, 139, 162, 189–90, 191,
    201, 208, 223–4, 231, 247; and sea
    route, 180–3
Spinalunga, 9, 269, 276
Spinola, Nicolino, 68
Spooner, F. C., *308*
Sporades group, 153, 210
stage sets, baroque vogue, 267–8
Stefani, G., *308*
Steno: Doge Michele, 108, 109, 123,
    127; Paolo, 104
Suda, 269, 276
Suez Canal, 301; proposal for, 183
sugar: industry, 114, 132, 170, 231,
    250, 270; trade, 50, 87, 101, 224, 225
sulphur, 250
sumptuary legislation, 85, 104, 110,
    124, 173, 185–6, 209, 221, 273, 309
Surian, Nicolò, 236, 237
syphilis, 185
Syria, 5, 17, 26, 34, 42, 49, 74, 80, 87,
    122, 139, 140, 162, 183, 212, 248

Tana, 98, 144, 309
Tani, Lorenzo di, 191
Taranto, sea battle, 22, 23
Tartini, Giuseppe, 271
taxation, 49, 75, 88, 107, 108, 109,
    121, 136, 148, 153–4, 159, 168, 191,
    219, 265, 271, 290, 295
Teatro Apollo, 297
Teatro Malibran, 297
Teatro Olympico, 222
Teatro San Samuele, 297
Tegallianus Marcellus, Dux, 10
telescope, 248
Templars, 80
Tenedos, 116, 118
Tenenti, A., *307*
Tenos, 121, 178, 272, 276
Tertiary order, 71
textile industry, 69, 190, 207, 224, 241,
    250, 264, 270, 271, 277, 287
Thayer, W. R., *306*
theatres, 222, 261, 263, 266–8, 277–8,
    280, 297
Theodoric the Goth, 3
Thessalonika, 134
Thessaly, 48
Thibaud, Count of Champagne, 55
Thiriet, F., *308*
Thirty Years War, 248, 264
Tiepolo: family, 77, 89; Baiamonte,
    90, 91; G.B., 297; Doge Jacopo, 62,
    64, 65; Jacopo, 80; Doge Lorenzo,
    70, 77; Lorenzo, 284; Stefano, 215
timber trade, 15, 23, 27, 34, 50, 83, 86,
    98, 101
Timofeo of Lucca, Fra, 175
Tintoretto (Jacopo Robusti), 210, 222,
    232
Titian (Tiziano Vercelli), 210
Torcello, 6, 12, 117
Tosi, R., *310*
Toulouse, 34
tourism, 260, 274, 302
trade, 50, 66–7, 100–2, 108, 121–2,
    131–2, 217; declines, 181–4, 247–8,
    277, 278–9; embargoes, 17, 23, 30,
    80; expansions, 15–16, 26–8, 32–3,
    37, 47–8, 60, 76, 191, 270, 296, 301;
    and piracy, 235–6; regulation, 73–4,
    113, 183–4; routes, 34, 86, 97; *see
    also* convoy system, shipbuilding
trade associations *see arti*, guilds
Tradonico, Doge, Pietro, 21–3
Traù, 110, 128
Trebizond, 82
Trevigiano, 125, 262
Treviglio, 150
Trevisan, Zaccaria, 125
Treviso, 13, 29, 51, 69, 70, 91, 99, 100,
    115, 118, 124, 125, 188, 191, 219,
    291, 299
tribunes, 24
Tribuno, Doge Pietro, 24, 26, 28
Trieste, 115, 118, 187, 278
Tripoli, 122
Trissino, Leonardo, 188, 189
Tron, Andrea, 285
troop transport, 67

Tunis, 68, 122
Turkestan, 27, 81
Turkey, Turks, 102, 129, 135, 148–9,
    152, 153, 159, 160, 168, 176, 191;
    war of 1461, 157; war of 1499,
    178–82; war of 1537, 209–10; war of
    1570, 226–30; war of 1635, 264–9;
    war of 1684, 272–3
typhus, 203, 223, 227, 232
Tyre, 43

Ulm, 129, 142
UNESCO, 302
Urban II, Pope, 40
Uskoks, 212, 235, 241, 244–5
Usnagi, Francesco de, 177
usury, 69, 98, 108, 122, 225
Uzbek Khan, 98

Valverde della Misericordia, Scuola di,
    72
vendettas, 28, 31
Vendramin: citizen, 118; Doge Andrea,
    138, 157; Francesco, 255–6; Luca,
    138
Venetia, 7, 220, 264, 282, 300
Venetian Empire, 219, 276;
    administration, 63, 100, 136, 144–5,
    175, 210, 220; mainland, 43–4, 100,
    118, 124–5, 136, 154, 187–90, 205,
    219, 241, 262, 289, 290, 308; overseas,
    60–2, 74, 93, 183–4, 199, 210, 273;
    see also Crete, Cyprus, Dalmatia
Venice: banner, 39; loss of
    independence, 293, 294–5; origins,
    1–2, 6, 14; sieges, 14, 26, 117–18,
    299; threat from the sea, 301–2
Venramin, Giovanni, 258
Ventura, A., 309
Verde, Bartolommeo, 103
Verme, Luchino dal, 112
Verona, 68, 99, 125, 139, 145, 151, 188,
    190, 219, 232, 290
Veronese, Paolo, 186, 217, 230, 232, 250
vicecomes, 43
Vicenza, 29, 68, 99, 125, 188, 219, 222,
    291, 296, 298, 299
Villa Malcontenta, 222

Villa Rotonda, 222
villegiatura seasons, 275, 276
Visconti: family, 100, 107; Filippo
    Maria, 134–6, 149; Giangalezzo, Duke
    of Milan, 125
Vivaldi, Antonio, 274
Voltaire, François, 279, 284

wage levels, 88, 105, 154, 223, 236, 237,
    250, 259, 271
Wagner, Richard, 301
Ward, John, 246
Weinstein, D., 307
wheat production, 99, 102
'white' Venetians, 63
Wiel, A., 305
Winchester, Bishop of, 130
Windelin of Speyer, printer, 154
women: in business, 280; fashions,
    85–6, 244; and Scuole, 92;
    sumptuary laws, 104; wage rates,
    223; trade, 87, 224, 227
Wool industry, 154, 231, 250
Wright, Edward, 276, 310

Young Pretender, 279
Ypres, 76
Yule, Sir Henry, 309

Zacharias, Pope, 15
Zaffetta, Angela, 206
Zane, Girolamo, 227
Zante, 184, 230, 250, 273
Zara, 33, 56, 67, 86, 91, 110, 179;
    rebellions, 42, 54, 68, 102
Zeno: family, 77, 238; Carlo, 117, 118;
    Caterino, 162–3; Maria, 60; Doge
    Rainiero, 70, 71, 72, 74, 75, 76;
    Ranier, 263–4
Zenobio family, 283
Ziani: Doge Pietro, 49, 61; Doge
    Sebastiano, 49, 50, 52
Zorzi: Bertuccio, 144; Tommaso, 292
Zotto, Scuola dei, 206
Zuane, Anronio de, 250